Thatcher's Fortunes

By Mark Hollingsworth

The Press and Political Dissent: A Question of Censorship

Blacklist: The Inside Story of Political Vetting
– with Richard Norton-Taylor

The Economic League: The Silent McCarthyism
– with Charles Tremayne

MPs for Hire: The Secret World of Political Lobbying

A Bit on the Side: Politicians – Who Pays Them? An Insider's Guide
– with Paul Halloran

The Ultimate Spin Doctor: The Life and Fast Times of Tim Bell

Defending the Realm: Inside MI5 and the War on International Terrorism
– with Nick Fielding

Saudi Babylon: Torture, Corruption and Cover-Up Inside the House of Saud

By Paul Halloran

A Bit On the Side – Politicians – Who Pays Them? An Insider's Guide
– with Mark Hollingsworth

THATCHER'S FORTUNES

The Life and Times of Mark Thatcher

Mark Hollingsworth
and Paul Halloran

MAINSTREAM
PUBLISHING
EDINBURGH AND LONDON

First published in Great Britain in 2005 by
MAINSTREAM PUBLISHING COMPANY
(EDINBURGH) LTD
7 Albany Street
Edinburgh EH1 3UG

ISBN 1 84018 972 X

A catalogue record for this book is available
from the British Library

Typeset in Baskerville Book

Printed in Great Britain by
Clays Ltd, St Ives

Contents

'Greed is all right. I want you to know that. I think greed is healthy. You can be greedy and still feel good about yourself.'
– Ivan Boesky, speaking before a campus audience at the University of Berkeley, 12 September 1985

Preface

On Wednesday, 25 August 2004, the day that Mark Thatcher was arrested for helping to finance an attempted coup d'état in the oil-rich state of Equatorial Guinea, the Internet search engine Google registered 18,500 hits from people looking for information about the event. Suddenly, the controversial multimillionaire son of the former prime minister was catapulted back onto the front page of every national newspaper and to the forefront of people's minds. While a distraught Lady Thatcher was flying back to London from her holiday in Richmond, Virginia, after receiving news of his detainment, everyone wanted to know: had her beloved son really conspired with mercenaries in an illegal putsch intended to overthrow a foreign head of state? It was like a plot from a *Boys' Own* thriller. Indeed, this tale of conspiracy, violence, arms dealing and international realpolitik bore an uncanny similarity to *The Dogs of War*, the bestselling novel by Frederick Forsyth, Mark Thatcher's favourite author.

For the past decade, Mark Thatcher has kept a relatively low profile, living in South Africa. He was still consorting with nefarious characters and colourful rogues but, apart from a typically ill-judged involvement in a loan-sharking scheme, he was below the radar screen of controversy. Now Lady Thatcher's son was back in the spotlight and his alleged involvement in the attempted coup encapsulated his life and times – scandal, political skulduggery, comic ineptitude, extraordinary characters, financial chicanery and family embarrassment.

The dramatic search of his house and arrest in South Africa also revived questions about Mark Thatcher's other notorious escapades and the mystery of how he accumulated a fortune during his mother's eleven-and-a-half-year tenure at 10 Downing Street. For although he is the son of the longest-serving prime minister of the twentieth century, his business activities have not come under any official scrutiny. In the United States, the commercial affairs of the president's relatives are closely monitored, particularly when they relate to government or international contracts. In stark contrast, Mark Thatcher has been allowed to keep the source of his vast wealth secret. He has not been a director of any companies since 1984, apart from Emergency Networks Inc., and hides his money through an intricate series of offshore bank accounts and companies, and by the skilful use of intermediaries and nominees.

This book is about how Mark Thatcher amassed that fortune while his mother was prime minister, his exploits in South Africa after she left Number 10 and his bizarre involvement in the stranger-than-fiction coup plot to seize power in Equatorial Guinea. It is an attempt to untangle some of the confusion surrounding his commercial deals and the myths that have grown up around them. But it is not just the story of how a young man with no prospects became fabulously rich comparatively quickly and without visible financial means of support. It is also an account of how the son of the most controversial and politically successful premier of the twentieth century used his access to the very highest echelons of government and state. And, most significantly, of how Lady Thatcher herself had knowledge of and in some cases actively assisted in and promoted contracts from which Mark benefited financially.

This book's origins lie in 1981 when Paul Halloran was working for *Private Eye*. One day he was visited in his office in Greek Street, Soho, by a retired naval commander and pilot. His name was E.K. Somerville-Jones and he had a story to tell. Somerville-Jones had retired from the navy and wanted to continue to work. He was first employed by International Military Services, the government-owned arms-export agency, selling guided missiles. He was not very successful, so ended up as a pilot for one of Britain's major defence contractors. But Somerville-Jones was unhappy. He had been flying on the company's private jet to Holland, Switzerland and the USA, delivering what he called 'bribe money' on behalf of his employer. Paying off 'foreigners' was one thing, he said, but what he objected to was that some of the bribe cash was being kicked back to his own senior executives, with suitcases full of the money being ferried by him from Switzerland to London. The former naval commander always maintained that a good proportion of it was on its way to Whitehall. But when he complained to the chairman's office, he was told 'to stop noseying around and causing trouble'.

Encouraged by Somerville-Jones, Halloran began investigating this aspect of the arms trade. However, it was only after Margaret Thatcher left 10 Downing Street in November 1990 that key sources began to talk. From 1991 onwards, people who had held the Thatchers in awe or owed something to them were prepared to open up. In general, these people were exasperated with Mark's rudeness and arrogance. In their view, he had shamelessly exploited his mother's name to promote his own business interests or to ingratiate himself with them through her.

In 1992, Paul Halloran linked up with Mark Hollingsworth, then working on similar investigations for Granada TV's *World In Action*, and ever since we have – with periodic long sabbaticals – been unravelling the mystery. How did a young man who in 1979 was a failed accountant and a part-time jewellery salesman become a multimillionaire? What did the former prime minister's son actually do and how did he accumulate his fortune? He declared no profession, apart from the meaningless 'consultant'. He rarely had offices, apart from small anonymous rooms with uninstructive nameplates. His 'firm', Grantham, was not registered as a corporation. Everything was shrouded in remarkable secrecy. Business deals were conducted through middlemen and shareholdings were held by nominees. Virtually no part of his commercial affairs was accountable to the public or the regulatory authorities and so there was no paper trail.

Piecing together the puzzle of how Thatcher acquired his millions has been a challenging and often frustrating experience. Lines of enquiry have led to blind alleys, trails have run cold and information from several potential sources proved unreliable. There is a Mark Thatcher industry in the British media, which has produced as many legends and hoaxes as genuine disclosures. Consequently, this biography could not have been written without the cooperation of a small but key group of sources. They know who they are but nobody else will. The people who helped us the most are the ones we cannot thank publicly. To borrow Tennessee Williams's phrase from *A Streetcar Named Desire*, we have been dependent on the kindness of strangers.

In the UK, we are particularly grateful to Wolfgang Michel for his generous support and insights into the opaque world of the international defence industry. Michel is a remarkable and laconic man. He merits a book on his own. For their invaluable research into Mark Thatcher's time at Harrow, we are grateful to Jon Lewis and Mary Kalmus. Many thanks to Chris Wake for his excellent profile of Simon Mann and to Jessica O'Keefe for her highly efficient and diligent research on Equatorial Guinea. We are also indebted to April Tod, who introduced us to her amazing network of contacts in the world of Formula One. She seems to know everyone. And very special thanks are due to Brigitte Chandless, who compiled the photographs with skill and energy.

The following deserve our appreciation either for their help in supplying information or for agreeing to be interviewed: the delightful Misbah Baki, Simon Berthon, Emmett Borcik, Steve Brownson, Michael Cockerell, Charlie Crichton-Stuart, Alan Curtis, Sir Edward du Cann, Thomas Friedrich, Ed Harriman, Nigel Hart, Chris Hutchins, Gerald James, Peter Jansen, the television producer and director Don Jordan, Paul Lashmar, David Leigh, Jason Lewis of the *Mail on Sunday*, Ivor Lucas, the former British ambassador in Oman, the former *Daily Express* journalist Norman Luck, Patrick Masters, James Montagu, Nigel Morgan, Barrie Penrose, the defence consultant John Reed, the late Tiny Rowland, Kate Roy, Olga Sheppard, the late Tony Shepherd, Simon Sloane, the international oil trader Gary Smith, Andy Stewart, Paul Vickers and Dorothy Wyndham-Lewis.

Our search for Thatcher's fortune has taken us to many countries. In the United States, we would like to thank Al and Jane Ross (for their hospitality in New York City), Nathan Adams, Juval Aviv of Interfor Inc., Frank Greve of the *Philadelphia Inquirer*, Margaret Hall in Washington, DC, Christopher Ogden of *Time* magazine and author of *Maggie*, Maureen Orth of *Vanity Fair* and the investigative writer Gerald Posner. At the National Security Archive, we are particularly grateful to Will Ferroggiaro for his diligent and selfless research on our behalf. In Texas, Gary Howard, his family and many influential friends have been a constant source of friendship and support, and we were fortunate to engage the services of Jack H. Taylor, an excellent investigator based in Dallas. We also appreciate the cooperation of Jay Laughlin, former president of Ameristar Fuels Inc.

Further south, in South Africa, we acknowledge the reporting of David Jones, who has been a resourceful and incisive correspondent for *Today* and the *Daily Mail*. In Latin America, we received assistance from Maria Laura Avignolo, Patrick Buckley and Leonardis Walger. In Hong Kong, we owe a huge debt to Amanda and George Rosenberg for their generous hospitality, to Neville De Silva of the *Hong Kong Standard* and Nancy Ng and Raymonde Sacklynne of *Target* magazine for their help in introducing us to sources of information.

Our publisher Mainstream is blessed with the best and hardest-working staff in the business and this book was no exception. Our editor, Ailsa Bathgate, was excellent and we appreciate her commitment to this biography. A bonus was the contribution of Mary Ann Nicholas, especially her invaluable advice on the cover design.

Lord Bell of Belgravia, Mark Thatcher's loyal and long-suffering public relations adviser, has been entertaining visitors with declarations that all the allegations about his heroine's son are untrue and abusive, and nothing substantial will ever be published. Fortunately, many of his visitors immediately telephoned and regaled us with his latest opinions. His cheerful indiscretions sustained us and provided a source of amusement. Equally, Thatcher's lawyers, Peter Carter-Ruck and Partners, kept a watching brief on the media but it is curious that despite 21 years of allegations about his conduct, not once have they threatened to sue anyone for libel on behalf of their client.[1]

As for Mark Thatcher, he has always refused to be interviewed by us. His only direct communication was an impatient letter sent by fax to Mark Hollingsworth while working at *World In Action* in 1992. He wrote: 'Dear Mr Hollingsworth. As you have previously been informed, I do not wish to speak to you nor do I have anything to say to you. Goodbye. Mark Thatcher.'

Mark Hollingsworth
and Paul Halloran
London, July 2005

ONE

A Very British Coup

If MT's [Mark Thatcher] involvement is known, the rest of us and the project is likely to be screwed – as a side-issue to people screwing him. It would particularly add to a campaign, post-event, to remove us. Ensure doesn't happen.

– Simon Mann[1]

Thank God my father isn't here to see this.

– Mark Thatcher[2]

On this particular occasion, Margaret Thatcher insists on greeting and meeting all the guests at Number 10. But it is not a grand reception for a foreign head of state at Downing Street. It is her son Mark's lavish Christmas drinks party at his sprawling 15,000-square-foot mansion at 10 Dawn Avenue in the exclusive Cape Town suburb of Constantia. Despite being recently widowed and increasingly frail, the 78-year-old former prime minister is irrepressibly cheerful and bullish as more than 70 guests enter the vast house with its bullet-proof curtains and state-of-the-art security equipment in every room.

It is the early evening of Monday, 22 December 2003, and Mark Thatcher is in his element. He greets his friends warmly with his catchphrase 'Hello, darling' and his usual impatience and nervous tension are noticeably absent. The guests gather around the sun-drenched kidney-shaped swimming pool to enjoy a sumptuous array of canapés and expensive South African wine. It is a classic Mark Thatcher cast-list: gun-runners, second-hand car dealers, mercenaries, oil traders, diamond merchants, estate agents. Many of them wear light but dull suits with sober ties and assemble on the upper deck of the house, known as the 'Safari Lounge', where they hold whispered conversations in hushed tones. 'It was a typical Mark crowd,' said a friend. 'The Cape Town socialites mixing with the neo-criminal classes.'

But Baroness Thatcher might not have been so genial if she had known she was socialising with the key conspirator who was at that very moment secretly plotting to overthrow the president of an oil-rich African state. For standing nearby was Simon Mann, a mysterious charismatic 51-year-old former SAS officer and Old Etonian who lived nearby on Dulchet Avenue, Constantia. He had made millions from providing private soldiers to protect vulnerable diamond mines and oil refineries and train state armies in war-torn Africa. Surveying the scene was Mann's political adviser Greg Wales, the carefully spoken, well-connected former partner at Arthur Andersen, the now-defunct accountancy firm, who had flown in from London mainly for the party. And lurking by the pool was Crause Steyl, the ambitious South African pilot who had just been hired by Mann for the operation.

The former prime minister had known the professional adventurer for at least four years. In 1999, she was having breakfast with her son by the pool of his house when Mann arrived. He was wearing a grubby T-shirt and running shoes, and Margaret Thatcher, obsessed by appearances and clothes, made no attempt to hide her distaste. But then a friend whispered in her ear, 'Simon Mann. Ex-Troop Commander. 22 SAS.' Her whole attitude changed. 'Oh, well that's fine, then,' she whispered back and greeted him warmly. Margaret Thatcher has always had a soft spot for the military and was the only premier to inspect an SAS troop privately. Despite his scruffy appearance, she became very fond of Mann.

Mark Thatcher was equally enamoured. 'Simon is my best friend,' he once said. The former SAS officer lived nearby at Villa Musica, a palatial mansion where he hosted extravagant drinks parties around one of the two swimming pools. Guests were served champagne by a butler and could not miss evidence of his fortune – the sculptures, the tennis court, the paddocks and the garages for five cars. Secretive, softly spoken and genteel, Mann is a throwback to the nineteenth-century colonial buccaneer. 'He is a humane man but an adventurer. He is very English, a romantic and tremendously good company,' said Paul Greengrass, who directed the former SAS officer in his film

Bloody Sunday. Mann played the part of Colonel Derek Wilford, commanding officer of the First Battalion of the Parachute Regiment, the unit that went into the Bogside on that fateful day.[3]

Mann is the archetypal establishment insider. Born in 1952, his father, George Mann, was a highly decorated officer in the Scots Guards during the Second World War, then captain of the English cricket team and chairman of Watneys, the British brewing giant.[4] His mother was South African, the daughter of the chairman of the main railway company and a director of De Beers. Young Simon Mann followed the family path to wealth and influence: Eton, Sandhurst, the Scots Guards and a member of White's, the St James's private club patronised by the Prince of Wales. In 1972, he passed the gruelling selection procedure and became a troop leader in G Squadron 22 SAS. After serving in Cyprus, Germany, Central America and Northern Ireland, Mann left the army in 1979 and joined KAS, a private military company run by Colonel David Stirling, founder of the SAS. But it was not a success. KAS Enterprises was linked to scandals involving the misuse of World Wildlife Fund money and industrial espionage during major takeover bids.

After the demise of KAS in 1991, Mann rejoined the army. During the Gulf War, he served as an intelligence officer for General de la Billière, commander of the British forces during the Gulf War, based in Riyadh, Saudi Arabia. But hostilities lasted barely a year. Now aged 40, Mann was interested in making money and in 1993 joined Executive Outcomes (EO), a private military company which was hired by African governments to combat insurgency and sabotage. It was founded by Tony Buckingham, a former oil-rig diver and runner for Ranger Oil, and Eben Barlow, a former member of the South African Defence Force and the 'Buffalo Battalion', an outfit responsible for implementing the government's strategy of regional destabilisation on its borders during the apartheid era. In Angola, EO landed a $40 million contract when it was hired by the MPLA government to rebuff the rebel UNITA forces and recapture the oil refinery in Soyo in the northern tip of the country. Using mostly former South African Special Forces officers (some still serving), Mann and Barlow commanded the 800-strong unit and successfully defeated the insurgents.

Instead of paying the bill in cash, the Angolan government gave EO lucrative diamond concessions and the company's commercial network was born: Heritage Oil and Gas, Branch Energy, Diamond

Works and Branch Minerals. Managed by Buckingham, new minerals and oil wells were found and exploited. Suddenly, the mercenaries were multimillionaires. Mann continued to run the military operation but EO was attracting political hostility from the new ANC government in South Africa, who viewed its operatives as being too close to the old apartheid regime. The president of Angola, José Eduardo dos Santos, told Mann that he was also under pressure from the Americans and so EO's Angolan operation was disbanded.

In response, Mann set up Sandline International, which was marketed as a more 'politically respectable' version of EO. In 1996, he recruited Colonel Tim Spicer, an old friend since they served together in the Scots Guards, and Sandline was hired by the regimes in Papua New Guinea ($36 million) and Sierra Leone ($6 million) to crush rebel forces. But Mann and co. could not avoid controversy. When Sandline infamously shipped arms to Sierra Leone in contravention of a UN embargo, it caused an international outcry.

By the late 1990s, Mann was a wealthy man. With the spoils of his African adventures, he invested in Diamond Works and Branch Energy, and when they were floated on the Toronto stock exchange, he collected an estimated $10 million. In 1997, the military entrepreneur bought Inchmery, a Palladian mansion on a 20-acre estate perched on the banks of the Beaulieu river in Hampshire, for £4 million. The house once belonged to the Rothschilds and during the Second World War its land was used as a training ground for Polish paratroopers preparing for D-Day. When an old pine tree blew over in a storm a few years ago, it was found to be riddled with bullet holes. For a man in perennial search of intrigue and skulduggery, the property was irresistible and, typically, Mann purchased it using an offshore company, Myers Developments, registered in Guernsey.

But Africa was still alluring and in 1999 Mann and his wife Amanda moved to Cape Town after seeing an advertisement headlined: 'Is this the most beautiful beach house in the country?' For a mere £200,000, Mann bought Villa Musica in the secluded and elite suburb of Constantia. He set up a new private military company Logo Logistics, bought a plane – an Aerostar 600 – parked his Bentley and enjoyed the benefits of his African escapades. He went fishing, bought sculptures, entertained royally and, in August 2002, secured South African citizenship. With more time on his hands, it was inevitable that he would meet his near neighbour Mark Thatcher.

Simon Mann is exactly the type of character that appeals to the former prime minister's son: wealthy from exotic diamond deals, a past dominated by risky operations in obscure countries, a fast and colourful personal life and yet very much a member of the upper-class British establishment. Like his mother, Mark Thatcher is fascinated by the secret world of Special Forces and intelligence officers. He would spend hours listening to accounts of Mann's daredevil exploits and nefarious adventures in Sierra Leone and Angola. 'I knew Mark quite well,' recalled Johann Smith, a former member of South African military intelligence. 'He always surrounded himself with former soldiers and the special-forces clique. I got the impression that he would have loved to have been part of that scene.'[5]

Like Mann, Thatcher was a risk taker and they dabbled in some joint commercial ventures. 'Simon and Mark discussed a number of business deals together – in mining, aircraft and fuel brokerage,' said Greg Wales, a friend of both men.[6]

They also socialised frequently with their wives and would lunch at The Meeting Place, overlooking Simonstown Bay, or at the Table Bay Hotel near Cape Town. Without their spouses, Thatcher, Mann and friends would drive down to Camps Bay after lunch for what they called 'sundowners'. With everybody crammed into his silver 5-series BMW, Thatcher drove like a maniac down the coast and they would drink at the Harbour House or Vilamoura until sundown. It was here that the son of the former premier would display his legendary charm.

'Oi you, rocket scientist,' he shouted at one hapless waiter. 'Come over here, sunshine, so I can get my hands round your scrawny neck.' When the maître d' came over to the table and asked, 'Is there a problem, sir?' Thatcher replied, 'Yes, your job is to serve me, not for me to serve you.'

By the Christmas of 2003, Mann was an honoured guest at the Thatchers' home but only a select few at that party knew about his secret plan. Less than three months later, the former SAS officer would lead a gang of South African and Armenian soldiers of fortune in an audacious attempt to oust President Teodoro Obiang, the murderous dictator of Equatorial Guinea (EG). But they were not motivated by the desire to remove a cruel perpetrator of human-rights abuses. It was claimed that they had struck a secret deal with Severo Moto, the exiled opposition leader, whereby they would receive a lucrative share of the oil revenues and security contracts in exchange for installing him in power. Moto strongly denies that there was any agreement.

The genesis of the plot can be traced back to early July 2003, when Crause Steyl, a South African pilot with a taste for high jinks and adventure, met up with his friend Simon Mann, the former SAS officer now based in Cape Town, at the Sandton Sun and Towers Hotel in Johannesburg. The two could not have been more different: Steyl, the tough, resourceful Afrikaans-speaking pilot who relished the thrills of flying into African danger zones, and Mann, the sophisticated, softly spoken Old Etonian, member of White's and former Scots Guards officer who was now a wealthy man and looking for new ventures. But they had worked closely together for ten years, notably in Namibia. Steyl was the South African director of Ibis Air International, which was EO's private air force. By the mid-1990s, Ibis Air included a fleet of Boeing 727s, at least two Mi-17 helicopters, two 'Hind' Mi-24 gunships, several small fixed-wing aircraft (one of which had surveillance capabilities) and at least two jet fighters. It was a formidable operation and for two years Ibis Air was instrumental in transporting EO mercenaries into African war zones. Steyl was an integral part of EO and worked closely with Mann. He was sufficiently an insider that in 1994 he joined Mann as a director of Branch International Ltd, a holding company for a string of subsidiaries and associated firms engaged in the hunt for oil, gold and diamonds. Steyl and the former SAS officer kept in touch and by the time of their meeting the pilot was looking after Mann's private plane – a US-registered Aerostar 600 six-seater with a fast-piston engine valued at $350,000.

Mindful of loose talk, Mann chose his words carefully. 'I've been asked by the boys to assist in a conflict in an African country that is very rich in oil but this time we are not supporting the government of the day,' he said mysteriously. The clear implication was that the pilot would be assisting the rebels of the country with helicopters and aircraft. Steyl viewed it as just another mission, if slightly more dangerous than usual. 'The plan is not final but it is very risky,' said Mann, adding that Tony Buckingham, his former business partner, did not know about the operation. Steyl later learned that 'the boys' was a euphemism for a small group of businessmen Mann claimed were backing the coup.

Later that month, Mann allegedly met Severo Moto, the chief political opponent to President Obiang, at his Madrid villa to discuss the bounty his merry band of mercenaries would receive for toppling the regime in Equatorial Guinea. According to documents obtained by the authors, it was agreed that Mann, known as 'Captain F', would be paid £10 million and his four lieutenants would receive £1 million each within two months of seizing power. The mercenaries would be paid $3,000 each and, after the coup, they would receive a $30,000 bonus and guaranteed jobs in the presidential guard. Mann was promised an EG diplomatic passport and his troops would become full citizens and be incorporated into the armed forces. The agreements, dated 22 July 2003 and signed by Simon Mann, also stated that the new EG government would buy back the weapons purchased by the operatives.

After overthrowing the regime, Mann and his cohorts were promised a series of lucrative contracts as well as a share of the oil royalties. A company would be set up with Mann as the CEO, and he would retain a 33 per cent stake. The firm's first task would be to recover 'all the national capital that has fled due to the illegal activities' of President Obiang and they would receive 30 per cent of any assets recovered on a 'no cure no pay' basis plus their costs. It would also be in charge of the intelligence agencies and armed forces, and oversee the outsourcing of security contracts for the police, customs, tax and environmental control. And the company would recruit the 100-strong private guard to the new head of state (Severo Moto) for a fee of £4,000 per man plus all costs and expenses.

Mann viewed Moto as someone who could be manipulated. 'We'll have a problem with him but once we've put him in power, we'll change things,' he told a friend.

It was an attractive and seductive package, and easily affordable given EG's newly discovered wealth. A tiny country of 500,000 people on the west coast of Africa, EG's appearance on the map is almost exactly square, clearly the product of imperial interference. Most of the population live on the island of Bioko, just off the Cameroonian coast, but the largest area is the mosquito-infested, jungle-covered province of Mbini on the mainland. Until recently, the country's capital, Malabo, had the atmosphere of an overgrown village in the jungle, with one hotel, a telephone directory with just two pages, little or no electricity and hardly any running water. Stray dogs wandered in and out of the airport terminal, which resembled a shack with a corrugated tin roof.

That all changed in 1991 when Mobil discovered the Zaffiro oilfield off the EG coast. A year later, production began and US oil giants Marathon and Amerada Hess followed suit after another discovery in the Gulf of Guinea. Suddenly, EG was flooded with what the locals called '*keza*' – rich Westerners determined to cash in on the latest oasis of black gold. A new airport terminal was opened and flights increased from Europe – notably there is now a direct flight from Zurich to Malabo – and Texas. Malabo now boasts two swish hotels, where rooms cost at least $150 a night and prostitutes linger outside the gates hoping to service visiting businessmen. Local residents are stunned to see BMWs and Mercedes racing down newly constructed roads and stopping at functioning traffic lights. 'The oil has been for us like the manna that the Jews ate in the desert,' said President Obiang.[7]

Based on production that is expected to top a staggering 500,000 barrels a day by the end of 2005, EG has the fastest-growing GDP in the world. But sadly and predictably, the wealth has been siphoned off by its rulers and the people remain poor, illiterate and sick. In July 2004, a US Senate investigation concluded that at least $35 million has been misappropriated by President Obiang, his family and government officials into secret offshore companies. In 1998, according to the IMF, the EG government received $130 million in oil revenues and Obiang simply pocketed $96 million of it. He moved $16 million into a Bahamas bank account. Between 2000 and 2002, $13 million in cash was deposited into accounts controlled by Obiang at the Washington DC branch of Riggs Bank, occasionally in suitcases filled with millions of dollars in 'unopened plastic-wrapped bundles', according to a bank employee. The actual amount siphoned off for personal use is unclear. 'Money unaccounted for in EG: perhaps as much as $500 million,' stated a Global Witness report. But Obiang remains unashamed and defiant. In November 2003, he twice declared on television that he is in sole control of the oil revenues and details of earnings would remain 'a state secret'.

Ironically, the EG government claim that it has been ripped off by the oil companies from the moment that the black gold was found. The Ministry of Justice claimed that the contract left EG with only 15 per cent of the revenues. An IMF report in 1999 bore this out when it stated the first contracts guaranteed an inordinately high 30 per cent rate of return for the oil operators, and the government royalty was much lower than that received by other oil-rich African states.

But Obiang's protests ring hollow given that he has moved much of the proceeds abroad for his personal aggrandisement. He bought a large house in Potomac, Maryland, for $2.6 million (paid in cash) and another mansion in the US for his wife, Constancia, for $1.15 million. A property source says he also owns two houses in Cape Town – in Clifton and in Bishops Court – valued at $4.5 million. The president owns shares in energy, hotels, construction, cocoa and pharmaceutical companies. In 2004, he bought his sixth aircraft – a Boeing 737 private jet – for $55 million. Decked out with a bedroom and an area for video games, it is too big to land at · many international airports. Millions have been squandered in Hollywood, where the president's son, Teodorin, cruises around in his Lamborghini Murcielago with a briefcase full of cash and a bevy of female starlets and rappers. During one weekend shopping spree in South Africa, he spent nearly £1 million on three luxury cars, notably a black Bentley Arnage and a cream Bentley Mulliner, and has bought a house in Constantia. His latest ventures include a studio, a rap label and an elite hotel in Los Angeles.[8]

By any standards, Obiang is a bloodthirsty, corrupt, repressive dictator. Born on 5 June 1942, he was a soldier for most of his career and rose to be head of the armed forces. On 3 August 1979, Obiang deposed his uncle, Francisco Nguema, in a coup d'état and during the show trial the former president was hung from the ceiling of the courtroom in a steel cage like an animal. He was executed by firing squad soon afterwards. The new ruler declared that the country would be liberated from the suppression of the previous regime but Obiang soon turned EG into a one-party paranoid police state with no free press, and elections were so rigged that the opposition did not bother to participate. Political show trials are a permanent feature of the courts. Any foreign visitor is likely to be followed by intelligence informers and arrested by the police, who will strip the film from their cameras.

Torture and violence are commonplace. 'If you've ever seen a person limp on both legs, you know you're in EG,' said John Bennett, former US ambassador to EG.[9] Obiang has also been accused of being a cannibal. His political *bête noire* Severo Moto claimed that the president was told by local soothsayers and sorcerers (known as '*marabou*') to execute his advisers in order to retain his grip on power. 'He has devoured a police commissioner [buried without his testicles or brain],' Moto claimed in an interview with a Spanish radio station in 2004. 'We are in the hands of an authentic cannibal who systematically eats his political rivals . . . Obiang wants me to go back to Equatorial Guinea so he can eat my testicles. That's clear.'[10]

As the oil wealth floods in, President Obiang has adopted a messianic status and a penchant for megalomania. In July 2003, the state-operated radio declared that the president could 'kill without anyone calling him to account and without going to hell because it is

God himself, with whom he [Obiang] is in permanent contact, who gives him this strength'.

Obiang's rival, Moto, is a former student priest who lives in exile in Madrid with his family. He has been plotting insurrection for the past ten years. In 1997, he was arrested by the Angolan authorities, who found him on board a boat carrying a consignment of arms reportedly for use in a coup attempt. 'Of course Moto was behind the latest coup,' said Adolfo Marugan, an EG political activist, in 2004. 'He does nothing else. He makes another attempt every six months.'[11] Moto's strategy is to secure international support by attacking Obiang's human-rights record and corruption. His British advisers have promoted him as a 'Nelson Mandela-type' figure and lobbied the US government to encourage international pressure and sanctions against Obiang. The payback for Washington DC would be that Moto, once in power, would not renegotiate the oil contracts with US firms and would encourage foreign investment. But in the months leading up to the 2004 coup, Moto received more support from Spain and his political campaign was backed by the then prime minister José María Aznar.

Back in the summer of 2003, Mann was spending most of his time in London raising money for the coup, usually in informal settings. 'It was a casual conversation at a drinks party around a swimming pool in January [2004],' recalled a businessman who was approached. 'He said it was about "a security project" at an African mine. It was all very casual and vague but the hook was the quick profit. If you showed interest, then you were invited to another meeting and given more details. Once Equatorial Guinea was mentioned, I declined and heard no more about it.'[12] Those who were intrigued were asked for £100,000 and told their return would be £1 million 'within a few weeks' plus access to oil concessions.

In September 2003, Mann summoned Steyl to his rented house in Cape Town. 'The fund for the operation is almost ready,' said the former SAS officer. 'The code for confirming that the funds are in place will be "The Pictures Have Arrived". Mann added that his accomplice, Nick Du Toit, a former commanding officer of the South African elite 32 battalion who had worked for him at Executive Outcomes, was already in EG setting up front companies in sea fisheries and air ambulance services to disguise their true intentions. Du Toit was also recruiting from a rich seam of unemployed restless South African former soldiers and Special Forces operatives. 'You had all these guys who had fought for apartheid suddenly without work when apartheid ended,' said Johann Smith, a former South African military intelligence officer and now a political risk analyst. 'It took just four phone calls to get a battalion assembled. Still does.'[13]

The fund was based in a Royal Bank of Scotland account in Guernsey. It was set up by Simon Mann under the name of his offshore company Logo Ltd and covered operating costs for the coup. The chief fund-raiser, according to the EG government in a High Court writ, was the controversial middleman Ely Calil.

Born in 1945 in Kano, Nigeria, Calil inherited a modest fortune in 1970 when his father bequeathed him half of Nigerian Oil Mills. But it was not until General Ibrahim Babangida assumed power in a coup in 1985 that his wealth multiplied. A quintessential Lebanese trader, Calil, who had known the General since Babangida had been quartermaster-general of the Nigerian army, exploited his friend's 'Thatcherite' open-market economic reforms. He manufactured batteries, sold Berliet trucks and traded in Nigerian oil. He also set up front companies for the General and managed his private financial interests. When Babangida was succeeded by General Sani Abacha, another notoriously corrupt president, Calil continued to thrive. 'He has that swarthy Levantine look but he's not a flamboyant character like Adnan Khashoggi,' said Nigel Morgan, a political risk analyst who has observed him for many years. 'He's very sophisticated and quietly spoken.' But Calil has no evident sense of humour. 'His friends never called him Smelly [Calil's nickname] to his face,' added Morgan.[14]

By the mid-1990s, Calil was using his wealth to cultivate contacts within the British establishment. He bought a vast mansion on Old Church Street, Chelsea, now valued at £12 million, and owns a smaller house behind the Science Museum in South Kensington that he uses for confidential meetings. His properties are decorated lavishly with eighteenth-century French furniture and jewelled ivory statues, and Calil likes to entertain extravagantly; but he has an understated charisma and is not a wild extrovert, despite being married three times. Like most Lebanese middlemen, trading on his political contacts is integral to his estimated $80 million fortune. He has been a friend to Jeffrey Archer since the early 1970s and once attended a charity fundraising dinner at 10 Downing Street while John Major was prime minister.[15] Calil is also close to Peter Mandelson and in 1997 arranged for him to rent one of his flats in Holland Park. The beleaguered cabinet minister had been forced to sell his Notting Hill house after failing to declare a £373,000 loan from fellow minister Geoffrey Robinson.

Financial controversy has dogged much of Calil's career and in 2002 he was arrested in connection with illegal commission fees paid by a subsidiary of the French oil company Elf-Aquitaine to the late Sani Abacha while he was dictator of Nigeria. It was a humiliating experience. On 21 June 2002, Calil was questioned by French police in a Paris hotel room over claims that he received a $40 million kickback from Elf for fixing an oil contract with Abacha. He then spent the weekend in jail and was released without charge. He has strongly denied all the allegations but the payments relating to the Elf-Aquitaine case are still being investigated by the French examining magistrate.

Despite the Elf case, Calil remains an influential powerbroker in West Africa. He is a sworn enemy of President Obiang in Equatorial Guinea and told *Africa Confidential* that 'he was a friend of opposition leader Severo Moto, the supposed beneficiary of the plot, and had given "modest" financial support in recent years'.[16] In the summer of 2003, Calil hosted several meetings in London with businessmen trying to raise funds for Moto. His alleged role in the putsch was disclosed in an intelligence report compiled by Nigel Morgan, the political-risk analyst who knew and spoke to many of those implicated within days of the failed coup. The report states that Calil promised $750,000, and others who pledged funds included Gary Hersham, a UK property developer ($500,000); Karim Fallaha, a Lebanese business associate of Calil ($500,000); Simon Mann ($500,000); and two British businessmen, Greg Wales and David Tremain ($500,000 each). After the coup attempt, it was also reported that Lord Archer had paid $134,000 into Simon Mann's company bank account that funded the operation. All of those named strongly deny involvement in any conspiracy.

By mid-October 2003, Mann believed that the funds were in place and was almost ready to roll. He called Crause Steyl and they met again at the five-star Sandton Sun and Towers Hotel, Johannesburg, which became virtually the HQ for the coup. Mann outlined the logistics of the operation and this time there was more urgency in his voice. 'I need someone to fly eight people from the Canary Islands to a country near the Equator without Customs knowing,' he said. The plan was to move Moto from Spain without being noticed and then fly from the Canary Islands to EG – a four-and-a-half-hour flight.

Steyl agreed and Mann immediately paid him $15,000. Steyl hired a Beechcraft King Air 200 – perfect for flying long distance without refuelling – and on 20 October flew to Madrid and the Canary Islands to investigate the feasibility of the plan.

On his return, Steyl reported back to Mann and on 13 December 2003 they met with Nick Du Toit to discuss details. The location was indicative of the comic cloak-and-dagger nature of the operation. Intent on secrecy, they met at a holiday caravan park just east of Pretoria and held an impromptu barbecue. The plotters sat around on folding chairs, drinking beer and gnawing at over-cooked T-bone steaks while discussing the logistics. The word 'coup' was rarely, if ever, mentioned during the meeting. Instead, 'the Project' was the codeword used.

Mann tried to run the coup like a military operation. 'Secrecy is paramount,' he told Steyl. But some of his schemes were extraordinary, inviting comparisons with episodes in *Tom Brown's Schooldays*. During the barbecue summit, the former SAS officer said that a Russian cargo plane, an Ilyushin 76, would fly into Malabo carrying several 4x4 luxury vehicles. These would be offered to President Obiang as a gift to lure him to the airfield. Twenty minutes later, a second plane, containing Moto and a hidden troop of mercenaries armed with guns, mortars and rocket launchers would land. The mercenaries would burst out, capture or shoot Obiang and his aides and execute the coup. After the expected bloody firefight, Moto would be escorted to the presidential palace and installed as the new ruler. 'It might sound crazy,' recalled Steyl, 'but Simon Mann is a very persuasive guy.'

Sitting in the caravan park, Mann told Steyl that he needed a military helicopter as 'a gunship' for when they landed in EG for the fast movement of supplies and military missions. The coup leader promised $150,000 up front but said more was needed. 'I want you to meet someone who will invest in the helicopter,' he said, without naming the individual. A few days later, Steyl claims that he was taken to meet the investor in Lanseria airport, much used by businessmen because of its low landing charges and proximity to central Johannesburg. The man who was waiting was none other than Mark Thatcher.

'He was crazy, man, as mad as a cow,' recalled Steyl. 'He was jittery, very nervous, not polite or friendly, very abrupt.' He noticed Thatcher's nervous tic, whereby one of his eyes looks one way and the other stares in the opposite direction – very unnerving to someone meeting him for the first time. The pilot, unaware at first of Thatcher's identity, extended his hand and introduced himself, saying, 'I'm Crause Steyl, who are you?'

Thatcher looked startled and replied, 'Who *am* I?' before refusing to identify himself. But later in their conversation it dawned on Steyl that he was speaking to the son of the former British prime minister. At first, he felt reassured to be dealing with someone at the heart of the British establishment, thinking that this would ensure protection for such a risky venture. But that feeling subsequently dissipated when Thatcher demonstrated his incompetence as a businessman and his bizarre mannerisms. His habit of barking orders imperiously and aggressively at his driver also revealed his personal insecurities. 'If this is the kind of guy who is involved, then what have I got myself into?' Steyl reflected. But as Thatcher was only an investor and not part of the operation, he was relatively unconcerned. Two days later, on 22 December 2003, the pilot flew down to Cape Town and attended Thatcher's pre-Christmas drinks party.

Mann introduced the former premier's son to Steyl to demonstrate that it was a serious enterprise and not just a wild stunt. Thatcher agreed to finance the helicopter and, according to the pilot, knew it was being used in EG, although they never referred directly to the coup.

In addition to his interest in fast cars, Thatcher has always been fascinated by aviation. He has been a keen helicopter flyer since 1982 and qualified as a pilot after being instructed at Blackbushe airport, Surrey. He also bought a B206 Bell jet ranger helicopter in 1992 for £185,500, using an Isle of Man company, and spent another £70,000 on its interior. In Cape Town, Thatcher piloted a military-style Huey helicopter, which was used extensively by US forces during the Vietnam War. And so he was familiar with such flying machines.

Back in Cape Town in early January 2004, Thatcher chose two 1960s Allouette II helicopters, which he leased on a short-term basis, and was a passenger during the test flight. But the specialist pilot during the flight said they were too old and inadequate for the journey to EG. It was like choosing a Morris Minor for a Rolls Royce operation. 'It won't work for what they want to do,' Steyl told Thatcher.

Unperturbed, Thatcher met Steyl at Lanseria airport and agreed to rent instead a lighter and more modern Allouette III, which was more suitable. Steyl e-mailed a budget of costs for January, February and March to Thatcher and Mann, and it was instantly approved. But then the nerves set in. A few days later, the coup leader called Steyl in an anxious mood. 'I've spoken to Mark and I've told him to have a less hands-on role in the Project,' he said. 'If the British press finds out, they will have a field day.' This is corroborated by a long memo written by Mann on 12 January 2004, which detailed possible threats to the success of the plot. Under the sub-heading 'MT', he wrote: 'If his involvement is known, the rest of us and project is likely to be screwed – as a side-issue to people screwing him. It would particularly add to a campaign, post-event, to remove us. Ensure doesn't happen.'

The paranoia about the involvement of Baroness Thatcher's son did not stop the money flow. Four days later, on 16 January 2004, Mark signed a subcontractor's agreement with a Steyl company called Triple A Aviation Ltd, which committed him to a $500,000 investment in an air-ambulance company. Thatcher insisted on a contract in his own name, claims the pilot.

Mark Thatcher acknowledges that he has been a close friend of Simon Mann for many years. In court documents, he admits that he met the coup leader in November 2003 while in London and discussed 'a transport venture in West Africa' and 'a mining transaction in the Guinea basin'. In fact, they had several meetings, often over lunch at Noura, a restaurant on Hobart Place around the corner from Margaret Thatcher's house on Chester Square. Thatcher accepts that he agreed to finance the chartering of a helicopter for one of those enterprises. But he denies knowing about the coup. He claims that it was not until early January that he 'began to doubt Mann's true intentions and suspected that he might be planning to become involved in mercenary activity in the West African region', leading him to question whether the helicopter might be used 'in such mercenary activity'.

There is no doubt in Steyl's mind that Thatcher knew what the helicopter was being used for from the beginning. 'Are you going to fly it up to EG yourself?' asked the former premier's son. 'He [Mark] knew what was going on,' recalled the pilot. 'I only knew him in the context of the EG business. I didn't know him before and I haven't met him since. Also, he never once asked me about the budget or how the profits would be made to secure a return on his investment. He just sent me the money.' On 8 January 2004, $20,000 was transferred from Thatcher's personal bank account in New York City to Triple A Aviation's account in Bethlehem, Orange Free State. A week later, another $255,000 arrived from Thatcher's HSBC account. But there was a problem: the budget for the helicopter was

$500,000 and the remaining $225,000 was not forthcoming.

It appeared that Thatcher was dithering, perhaps nervous or hoping someone else would pay the outstanding amount. But Steyl was reassured by Mann that the rest of the money would follow and, in any case, Thatcher did not ask for his money back. Assuming that his nervous new investor would pay up, Steyl hired a pilot to fly the Allouette III to Walvis Bay, Namibia, where it stayed for the next three weeks. Steyl then asked Du Toit, a key lieutenant of Mann, to secure permission from the EG government to fly into their airspace. 'Don't worry,' he replied. 'We don't need it now.' The helicopter remained parked in Walvis Bay.

By this point – mid-February 2004 – Mann was beset by funding problems. He called Steyl and asked if there was money left from his up-front payment and Thatcher's 'investment'. Steyl had spent much of it on staff, pilots and expenses in test flights to the Canary Islands but he was able to transfer $100,000 into Mann's company account in Guernsey, some of which was from Thatcher's coffers. Steyl does not know how the coup leader spent the funds, although some of it contributed to the purchase of a Boeing jet. And so that was how Thatcher's $275,000 was used for the attempted coup, although he did not know it at the time.

Despite this transfer of funds, there was still a cash crisis. Mann needed $5 million but barely had $2.75 million and so was forced to use his own resources. But these were rapidly diminishing. As Mann's reserves dwindled, the pressure to act was increasing and time was running out. 'The pictures have not arrived,' the coup leader told Steyl in a coded telephone conversation.

Recklessly, Mann decided to proceed with the coup regardless. On 17 February 2004, he flew from Johannesburg to Harare, Zimbabwe. That same day, Steyl flew to the Canary Islands, the former Spanish colony, and linked up with Moto, who had been meeting Prime Minister Aznar of Spain. There, at the Steigenberger hotel, they waited for the signal to fly to EG and unseat Obiang.

Two days later, two DC3 aircraft left Wonderbroom airport near Pretoria, each with 30 mercenaries, mostly former members of the South African 32 Battalion. They were bound for Kolwezi, a two-kilometre airstrip in the Democratic Republic of Congo (DRC), where – under an arrangement with a local rebel leader – they would refuel an aircaft arriving from Harare commanded by Mann. But neither the guerrilla leader nor the fuel turned up and so the two aircraft flew to Zambia and the mission was abandoned. Moto, still in the Canary Islands, was informed and he returned to Madrid.

The operation failed mainly because of the technical difficulties but also because Obiang and his security forces were tipped off and on a high state of alert. But this did not deter Mann and co. from trying again. Mann had already secretly travelled to Manyame Airbase, Harare, and bought an armoury of weapons. They included 10 Browning pistols, 61 AK rifles, 20 PKM light machine guns, 100 RPG7 anti-tank launchers, 80 x 60 motor bombs, 150 offensive hand grenades and 75,000 rounds of ammunition. The coup leader handed over $90,000 in cash and agreed to pay the remaining $90,000 on delivery but he was not given end-user or firearms certificates.

With the weapons ready for collection and bolstered by a new donation of $134,000 by a certain 'JH Archer', Mann authorised a second coup d'état. On Saturday, 6 March 2004, he flew on a Hawker Siddeley private aircraft from Kinshasa in the DRC to Zimbabwe using a South African passport. There he waited for his fellow conspirators. According to Steyl's testimony, very early the next morning Steyl, Moto and two of his aides, Karim Fallaha, and British businessmen Greg Wales and David Tremaine, boarded a King Air 200 twin turbo prop aircraft at Aero Club, a small airport at Las Palmas in the Canary Islands.

Steyl was due to depart for Mali at 6 a.m. on Sunday, 7 March. But there was a motorbike competition on the airstrip which took the whole day and so they did not take off until 5 p.m. They flew very low to avoid air traffic control and the mood was relaxed and friendly. The Africans did not speak English, so it was a low-key atmosphere on the plane, with many passengers sleeping. Wales spent most of the flight exchanging texts with Mann, while Moto, a calm, patient man, was quiet and reserved. Incredibly, before the flight, Steyl claims that in order to keep the nature of the mission a secret, Calil and Wales had told Moto that he was being flown to Gabon to see President Bongo. Calil and Wales deny that any such conversation took place.

By the time they arrived at the remote desert city of Bamako, the capital of Mali, for refuelling at midnight, they believed that the coup had already occurred. But the parallel flight by Mann's mercenaries had been far more eventful. At 6.10 p.m., a white US-registered Boeing 727-100 with a blue stripe along the side of its fuselage, containing 64 soldiers, principally South African former Special Forces operatives, took off from Pietersberg. The aircraft landed an hour later at Harare International airport, where it was due to collect the arms and ammunition bought by Mann. Like Moto, they did not know their real mission. But one operative was entrusted with two large packages stuffed with dollar bills – one contained $30,000 for expenses like fuel and landing fees, and the other contained $98,000, which Mann intended to use as bribes during the coup. Also on board were copies of security contracts with an EG aviation firm and a DRC mining company which would be used as a cover story in case they were captured.

The mercenaries were due to meet Mann at the airport, refuel, load the weapons and fly to EG. Half an hour after arriving in Mali, Steyl received a text from his brother Neil, the pilot on the Boeing 727-100 in Harare, stating: 'Simon [Mann] is missing. I don't know what is happening.' Four hours later, there was another SMS message: 'Now they are arresting us.'

Steyl switched off the radio and told Karim, Wales and Tremaine that Mann and his operatives had been captured. They were dumbfounded and shocked. It was only then that Karim, who spoke limited Spanish, told Moto about the real purpose of their flight: an attempted putsch.

Mann had been arrested at Harare airport as he waited for his private soldiers to collect the arms. When the Boeing 727-100 taxied across to the military area, the pallets of ammunition were there waiting with the coup leader. Then the Zimbabwe chief intelligence officer turned up and inspected the crates. Mann offered him $10,000 'to look the other way'. But he refused, the aircraft was compounded and they were captured. Meanwhile, Nick Du Toit, another thirteen mercenaries (six South African, seven Armenians) and four locals who were already in Malabo were also arrested and accused of plotting a coup. He claimed that they were merely involved in setting up a fishing-and-hunting business in partnership with Obiang's cousin.

Mann also denied the coup allegations. 'There was no plot or understanding or conspiracy in which I was involved,' he said in a statement to the police in Chikurubi prison in Zimbabwe. 'It is a matter of great regret to me that some of my friends and acquaintances such as Sir Mark Thatcher and Ely Calil have been accused of conspiring with me . . . I wanted to purchase the weapons to be used in DRC for guarding a diamond mine where our company had been contracted to provide security services. The negotiations to purchase the weapons were made openly . . . It was the obligation of the Zimbabwe Defence Industries to advise us about the legal requirements.'

Back in Mali, Moto and his advisers decided to fly back to the Canary Islands, where they were all arrested, taken into custody and interrogated by immigration officials. Everything changed when the Spanish government was consulted. At 6.40 a.m., Moto spoke to a Spanish intelligence officer and 20 minutes later the official returned and announced, 'You can all disappear. You are free to go.'

Steyl, shocked by the decision, replied, 'But I don't have a passport.'

'It does not matter,' said the intelligence official. 'You can return to your hotel. I'll get you a taxi.'

An exhausted Steyl and others returned to their hotel, the Steigenberger, and read the news on the Internet of how the coup plotters had been arrested in Harare. Later that afternoon, 10 March, Steyl sent a text to his older brother Piet, who lives in Johannesburg: 'Have the newspapers said anything about grass roof [his code for Mark Thatcher]?'

'Who is grass roof?' replied Piet.

'Mark Thatcher.'

'No.'

'Thatcher still owes me $225,000.'

Stranded and penniless, Steyl and Tremaine flew to London and asked Tony Buckingham, Mann's former business partner, for advice. 'Calil won't help you,' he replied. 'You're wasting your time.' When he returned to South Africa later that week, Steyl was convinced that Thatcher would have left the country and so there would be no proof of his financial connection to the coup. He was therefore shocked to discover that Thatcher was still living in Cape Town.

Reflecting on the debacle, Steyl said, 'None of us thought we would get stopped on the way and we didn't think overthrowing Obiang would be a problem. There has never been a war in EG and we were confident that our guys, who were highly trained with decent weapons, could do the job. The problem was keeping the new government in power.' There were fears that Nigeria might launch a counter-coup but when Steyl raised this with Mann, he replied, 'Don't worry, we'll just bribe the Nigerians in the normal way.' The priority of persuading the indigenous EG people to support the new regime was the reason behind the choice of former members of the 32 Battalion, many of whom were black Portuguese.

The spectacular failure of the coup was mainly due to Mann impetuously and recklessly proceeding because of financial

31

pressures. He lived an extravagant life with his second wife Amanda, known as 'the Duchess', and had six children to support. He had spent a lot of other people's money – an estimated $2.5 million – and mismanaged the funds. Also, Moto was allegedly insisting that they act before the Spanish elections on 15 March, because he hoped to gain Prime Minister Aznar's official approval before Aznar retired.

In front of his crew and mercenaries, Mann was loftily confident about money. 'Don't worry, we'll sort it out later,' he said. 'There's $10 million in cash in Obiang's palace alone. The oil companies are paying $400 million in royalties and we'll have a share of that loot. EG is the Kuwait of Africa.' But in private with his advisers he was looking visibly stressed and emotionally drained. He revealed his fears in a confidential memo on 12 January: 'This is potentially a very lucrative game. We should expect bad behaviour: disloyalty, rampant individual greed, irrational behaviour (kids in the toy-shop type), back-stabbing, bum-fucking and similar ungentlemanly activities.' And yet a month later, facing a $1 million budget shortfall and under increasing pressure, Mann threw caution to the wind.

Even before they boarded the aircrafts, the operation had been compromised. As early as December 2003, a report by Johann Smith, the former military intelligence officer and political analyst, linked Du Toit's recruitment of ex-32 Battalion soldiers in South Africa to a possible coup attempt in EG. The previous month, Smith had been tipped off by Antonio Neto and Laurenzo Sive, former 32 Battalion members. Such soldiers were not retained in the South African army because they had fought for the apartheid regime. Many of them were, therefore, unemployed and ripe for private missions. Neto and Sive told Smith that they had been recruited by Du Toit for the coup plot using a company called MTS and were told to report for training south of Johannesburg. Unfortunately, the two mercenaries missed the bus from Hotel 224 in Pretoria and were not allowed to join the team. Angry and disappointed, they tipped off Smith, who had served with them in 32 Battalion.

Smith had connections to the EG regime because of consultancy work he had undertaken there. After gathering more intelligence from Neto and Sive, he then warned the EG regime of the planned coup. He also felt obliged to inform the British and American governments 'because some of their nationals might be killed'. His report was sent to Michael Westphal, a senior Pentagon official, and to the personal e-mail address of two MI6 officers. 'I expected the US and British governments to warn EG or to stop the coup but there was no reaction,' recalled Smith.

Retaining the planning and logistical base in South Africa was a major blunder by Mann. He completely underestimated the capability of the South African intelligence agencies and their willingness to share their information with other African states. And buying the arms from the state-owned Zimbabwe Defence Industries only further jeopardised the mission. 'That blew it wide open,' said Steyl. 'They should have got the hardware from Eastern Europe, not a staunch enemy of the British.'

In fact, South African intelligence officials tipped off President Obiang five days before the coup and Zimbabwean President Robert Mugabe just as the mercenaries took off for Harare. Smiling with anticipation, the Zimbabwean security forces were waiting for Mann and his merry men. Despite widespread knowledge of the coup plot, Mann's 727 was allowed to take off for Harare and so in one sense it was a set-up. While holding no torch for Obiang, the South African government was keen to demonstrate that mercenaries could not use the country as a base to illegally overthrow other African regimes. Thabo Mbeki was sensitive to the criticism of the Afrikaaners that he was a 'black president of a white country' and not in control of the state. 'This is the new South Africa,' he said. 'We do things by the due process of law now.'[17]

The farcical, almost comic, feature of the coup was that so many people in South Africa (and even some British oil executives) knew about it. In Die Bosvelder (The Bushlander), a favourite watering hole in Centurion on the outskirts of Pretoria for apartheid-era Special Forces soldiers, the hard men, known as 'the Moustaches', said that the operation was an open secret for several weeks beforehand. Jokes about Mann 'going fishing' in West Africa or 'exporting agricultural equipment', accompanied by a nod and a wink, were all the rage. Many of these soldiers, who had seen some of the toughest fighting in Africa, advised the former SAS officer to pull out. 'Security was compromised and the odds were too high,' said one.[18] 'Every principle of warfare was contradicted in the lead-up to this operation,' recalled Johann Smith.[19]

The South African security services certainly knew that Mark Thatcher was in constant contact with those linked to the plot. Records show that Greg Wales called Thatcher on 11 occasions between 16 November 2003 and 24 March 2004. On the day the contract with Triple A Aviation was signed – 16 January 2004 – Wales called Thatcher in Cape Town and again the next day. The most significant call was at 6.20 a.m. on Thursday, 11 March, three days after Mann and his mercenaries were arrested and jailed. They spoke for nearly 15 minutes and discussed how to help Mann. As Thatcher had business contacts and knew influential lawyers in Zimbabwe, Wales suggested that he could use his connections. At first they debated whether their friend could be liberated 'in the usual African way' by bribing a government official, but that was discounted. 'OK, I'll get on the phone,' said Thatcher. But nothing materialised and it is unlikely that any calls to Zimbabwe were made.

At a time when planning of the coup was at its most intense, on 2 February 2004 – six days before Mann bought the weapons in Harare – Thatcher twice telephoned Ely Calil on his UK mobile phone. It is possible, of course, that they were discussing a separate business deal but the Lebanese middleman, a financial backer of Moto, was very close to Mann at this time and constantly talking to him, according to telephone logs.

Perhaps the best-informed person was Nigel Morgan, the affable British political risk analyst who was very knowledgeable about the activities of private military companies, diamond dealers and mining in Africa. A former member of Margaret Thatcher's speech-writing team during the 1979 election campaign, he was a close personal friend of both her son and Mann. Based in South Africa, Morgan was on the inside track partly because Mark Thatcher was alluding to Mann's activities but he was also well connected in the Mbeki government. On Thursday, 4 March, three days before the coup attempt, he had dinner with Mann at the Butcher's Shop restaurant in Johannesburg and told him that his operation was compromised. Morgan implored his old friend not to proceed and, concerned that Thatcher would be implicated, asked about his involvement. 'You know that whatever he does attracts media and intelligence,' he said.

'I wouldn't be stupid enough to get Mark involved,' replied Mann.

But Thatcher was very much involved and word of his investment in the military helicopter soon spread among the participants. A week after the coup attempt, Dries Coetzee, a former South African Special Forces officer and now a private detective, and a lawyer called Alwyn Griebenow, who was representing Mann and his men, flew to London. Desperate for funds to pay their legal fees and to help the prisoners, Coetzee approached the alleged plotters and claimed to have a mandate from Mann to obtain money 'from certain friends'. Over coffee at the Savoy Hotel, he told Wales, 'I am the only one doing anything about the welfare of the prisoners and they have to be paid.' He aggressively demanded the phone numbers of Calil and Fallaha, and snarled, 'We are going to come after you people.' His next phone call, on the afternoon of Sunday, 14 March, was to Mark Thatcher, who was in his study at home in Cape Town. 'We want $300,000 now,' he demanded. 'You had better pay up.' Taking the call on his mobile, Thatcher was relaxing, watching television. 'Look, Mr Coetzee, I tend not to give money to people whom I've never met,' he replied. 'I'm watching the Formula One, so why don't you just fuck off.'

A week later, Simon Mann, languishing in solitary confinement in Zimbabwe's maximum-security prison in Chikurubi, was becoming increasingly desperate. Instead of enjoying the power, patronage and unlimited wealth of EG post-coup, he was facing a long jail sentence or, worse, torture and execution if an extradition request from EG was successful.

Feeling isolated and deserted by his 'friends', Mann tore out two pages from a magazine and wrote a private letter to his wife Amanda, his personal assistant James Kershaw, Rebecca Gaskin, a lawyer and friend of Amanda, and his friend Nigel Morgan. 'Our situation is not good and it is very URGENT,' he wrote. 'They [his lawyers] get no reply from "Smelly" and from "Scratcher" [Mark Thatcher's nickname since school], who asked them to ring back after the Grand Prix race was over! This is not going well.

> What we need is maximum effort – whatever it takes – now . . . It may be that getting us out comcs down to a large splodge of wonga [British public school slang for cash]! Of course, the investors did not think this would happen. Do they think they can be part of something like this with only upside potential – no hardship or risk of this going wrong. Anyone and everyone who is in this – good times or bad. Now it's bad times and everyone has to F-ing well pull their full weight. What will get us out [of jail] is MAJOR CLOUT. We need heavy influence of the sort that Rebecca [Gaskin], Smelly, Scratcher, Nigel [Morgan] and David Hart [former adviser to Margaret Thatcher] [can exert] and it needs to be used heavily. Once we get into a real trial scenario we are F-d.

Mann concluded with the most incriminating detail: 'Anyway [another contact] was expecting project funds inwards to Logo [Mann's offshore firm which funded the operation] from Scratcher . . . If there is not enough, then present investors must come up with more.'

The note, written on 21 March 2004, clearly implicated Calil and Thatcher, and was in sharp contrast to Mann's earlier denials. This handwritten scrawl was the most honest account, partly because it was written from the heart. Both Mann and Du Toit later signed confessions that were produced by Zimbabwean officials but these were almost certainly obtained by torture and threats and so can be discounted.

The former SAS officer's worst fears were realised. Most of his friends had deserted him and the aggressive tactics of his lawyer Griebenow and his private investigator Dries Coetzee had alienated those implicated. 'All of his friends, of which I am one, are acutely aware that he is still incarcerated and care must be taken not to inflame the situation,' said Thatcher at the time.[20]

Mann became a pawn of southern African politics: Mugabe relished keeping the Englishman in a Zimbabwean prison and attempts to extradite him failed. It was no surprise when, on 22 July 2004, he was convicted on two counts of attempting to buy firearms illegally. He was sentenced to seven years in jail, later reduced to four years, and is due to be released in 2006.

After the failed coup attempt, the EG government accused Calil of plotting with Mann to overthrow their regime and sued for damages in the High Court in London. An irate Obiang was characteristically crude in his plans for the arrested conspirators. 'If we have to kill them, we will kill them,' he said.[21] The Lebanese trader vehemently denied that he was connected to the attempted coup and said the allegations were 'a set-up' to entrap Moto in a sting operation.[22] Now living in Beirut, Lebanon, Calil filed a counter claim in June 2005, alleging 'malicious prosecution' by President Obiang, who had accused him of financing the plot.[23]

As for Mark Thatcher, the net was closing in fast. When Crause Steyl returned to his home in Bethlehem, Orange Free State, in late March 2004, the police were initially quiet. Steyl was concerned that he might be prosecuted under the Foreign Military Assistance Act for his role in the attempted coup but the pilot remained convinced that Thatcher would leave the country and nothing would happen.

Then, in July 2004, Steyl was approached by the National Prosecuting Authority, the elite crime squad known as the Scorpions, and offered immunity from prosecution in return for his testimony and evidence. He agreed and for the next 15 days he disclosed everything he knew.

Based on Steyl's 220-page sworn affidavit, the Scorpions made their move. At 7 a.m. on 25 August 2004, 17 officers arrived at Thatcher's Constantia mansion and buzzed the intercom. 'We would like to talk to you, sir,' said the officer. Thatcher, still in his pyjamas, asked if he could have a shower and shave, and they agreed. He then opened the gates and was handed an arrest warrant. On entering his house, the Scorpions searched through documents, checked his mobile phones and swept the hard drive of his computer files while his wife, Diane, and 15-year-old son, Michael, looked anxiously on. The robust officers, with their trademark moustaches and crewcuts, explained that their search related to the attempted coup in EG. 'But I've been cooperating,' replied a nervous Mark, who had indeed been secretly talking to South African National Intelligence Agency officials. He had told them that he knew and liked Mann but he did not disclose everything he knew about the mercenary's activities.

At 7.40 a.m., confused and with a tone of panic in his voice, Thatcher called a friend. 'What the hell is going on?' he said. 'I've already told them what I know.' He had returned to Cape Town the previous month from a trip abroad specifically to brief South African domestic intelligence officers and so thought he was protected. But the Scorpions were acting independently of the security services, did not consult them or the government, and even Mbeki did not know about the raid and arrest. It was a shock to everyone. But, to some extent, Thatcher only had himself to blame. While he was in Dallas, the Scorpions left numerous messages on his mobile phone over several weeks but he did not return their calls. 'When he slipped quietly back into South Africa, he did not call us as we had instructed,' said Sipho Ngwema, a spokesman for the Scorpions. 'That's why we had to pay him a visit at his home.'[24]

For the next six hours, the police continued their 'search-and-seizure' operation before he was formally charged with contravening the Foreign Military Assistance Act. At 2 p.m., a stunned Thatcher was led away to a black police vehicle. He was not handcuffed and sat alone in the back. They travelled in convoy with two other cars, each displaying the crossed claws of the Scorpion's logo and the slogan 'Justice in Action'. Within ten minutes, they arrived at the bleak four-storey Wynberg Police Station in Cape Town.

Inside the holding cell, an element of farce was introduced when Thatcher was robbed of his jacket, shoes and mobile phone. At 4.10 p.m., he emerged blinking from a sunken stairwell into the middle of Wynberg Magistrates' Court, which was packed with journalists. With uniformed officers to his right, Thatcher characteristically shifted from foot to foot and impatiently fidgeted with his fingers as the magistrate, Awie Kotze, read out the charges. Wearing a dark suit with a smart blue-and-white handkerchief in his breast pocket, he nervously tapped a pen in the palm of his hand.

After a ten-minute hearing, Thatcher was released on bail set at £167,000 and his passport was confiscated. He was not allowed to leave the Cape Town peninsula and was required to report to the local police station every day between 8 a.m. and 4 p.m. 'See that you comply with those conditions,' warned Kotze. 'If you fail to comply with them, you know what the consequences will be.' After the magistrate gave him until 8 September 2004 to pay the bail, Thatcher smiled weakly and said, 'Thank you.' The court was then adjourned and he hastily disappeared back down the stairs without a word.

On arriving back at the iron security gates of his vast double-storey thatched house, Thatcher turned to his escorting police officers and said, 'OK, I'll talk to you if I need to go anywhere.' He was virtually under house arrest. He then sat down with his lawyers and at 5 p.m. a statement was issued through Lord Bell, his friend and long-time unofficial PR consultant: 'I am innocent of all charges made against me. I have been, and am, cooperating fully with the authorities in order to resolve this matter. I have no involvement in any alleged coup in EG and I reject totally all suggestions to the contrary.'

At first, his friends were dismissive of the charges and privately briefed journalists that Thatcher was not directly involved and the evidence was purely circumstantial. They claimed that his arrest was politically motivated and an attempt at revenge by the African National Congress for Margaret Thatcher's opposition to sanctions against the former apartheid regime. 'Mark was born guilty,' said one. But then Mann's letter leaked and details of his numerous meetings with Thatcher during the coup's planning stage emerged. 'It was clear that Simon needed both Mark's cash for the helicopter and his network of wealthy contacts,' said a source close to both Thatcher and Mann.

Margaret Thatcher was asleep in her hotel room in Richmond, Virginia, where she was holidaying, when her son was arrested. After being informed by telephone that morning, she immediately agreed to pay his £167,000 bail and returned to London the next day. Surrounded by five armed bodyguards, she refused to comment as she entered her house in Chester Square, Belgravia. Obviously distraught, she was then in constant contact by phone with her son, badgering him with questions about the case.

Mark Thatcher's sister, Carol, was in Zurich, Switzerland, at the time and only heard the news while listening to the BBC. She immediately flew to London to be with her mother. 'My real concern is for my mother because she is in America and I haven't spoken to her,' she told BBC News 24 at Heathrow airport. 'I don't know her reaction and I care about her.' It was a revealing reaction. She added that she was shocked by the allegations but had 'lived through scandals before'.

It was a humiliating ordeal for the family and the Scorpions reinforced the embarrassment by claiming that Mark Thatcher had been preparing to flee South Africa the next day because he knew his arrest was imminent. A police spokesman said that the raid took place after they learned that he had placed his house on the market for £1.8 million, arranged to sell four of his cars and bought his family plane tickets to the US.[25] In fact, according to two informed sources, Thatcher had already decided to move back to Texas six months earlier because his wife Diane wanted their children to be raised and educated there. It had nothing to do with the police investigation.

But as the daily headlines of televised court hearings, extradition applications and potential jail sentences compounded the family misery, the only relief seemed to be that Denis Thatcher was not a witness to the events, having died the previous year. 'Thank God my father isn't alive to see this,' Mark reflected. Virtually imprisoned in his Constantia mansion, he was angry and frustrated and only rarely expressed his emotions. 'I just feel in this particular case like a corpse that's going down the Colorado river and there's nothing I can do about it,' he told *Vanity Fair*.[26]

For his mother, the issue was more pragmatic: how to keep her beloved son out of prison. But as she discussed the case with his lawyer Ron Wheeldon and Lord Bell, Margaret Thatcher would have done well to reflect on a more profound issue: how on earth did her 51-year-old son end up facing a potential 10-year jail sentence? The answer lies not just in the fevered atmosphere of post-apartheid South Africa but over several decades when Margaret Thatcher evolved from being a fiercely ambitious politician into Britain's most controversial prime minister.

TWO

The Search for Eldorado

In Margaret Thatcher's eyes, there is nothing for which
Mark requires forgiveness.
  – Andrew Thomson, constituency agent to Margaret
Thatcher, 1982–7[1]

In late April 2005, Mark Thatcher flew from London to the tax
haven of Jersey on a very discreet visit to see his private bankers. It
was an unsettling and tense time in the turbulent life of the son of the
former prime minister. He had just been told that his application for
permanent residency in the United States had been refused and the
previous eight months had been dominated by court appearances and
relentless media scrutiny over his role in the attempted coup. As he
walked into the offices of HSBC Private Bank in Grenville Street, his
only certainty was the money that he could fall back on in a web of
intricate offshore accounts and trust companies.

For Jersey holds the key to unlocking the secrets of the Thatcher
fortune. With its generous benefits, the island is a refuge from the tax
authorities for wealthy international businessmen. Income tax has
remained at 20 per cent since 1940 and corporation tax is a mere
£300 a year. Jersey also serves as a base for overseas funds and by the
end of 2005 the island's banks had received about $90 billion in
foreign deposits.

Living quietly there in a large two-storeyed house in St Helier, the
capital of Jersey, is an unassuming 74-year-old bachelor and banker
called Dr Ian Hugh Thurston. Since the late 1970s, Thurston has
been the chief financial adviser to Margaret Thatcher and her son,

Mark. He has set up many tax shelters for the family and travels on their behalf. It is Thurston who knows the secret details of Mark Thatcher's riches, for he has devised a secret pattern of offshore trusts and companies in Jersey and in Switzerland to hide Thatcher the Younger's vast wealth. That pattern is so intricate that if Mark died in an air crash, only Thurston could unravel it. It also means he would inherit much of the loot. 'God forbid anything should happen to Mark,' he once remarked jokingly, with a wry smile.

Working alongside Thurston as the keeper of Thatcher's treasure is an accountant called Leonard Henry Day, who works barely two miles away at his well-protected Spanish-style £500,000 home in St Clement. He is also the treasurer of the island's Variety Club and a director of the Modern Hotels group. Together they manage Mark's funds through a network of Jersey companies, notably Zariba Management Ltd, Eastcoast Investments Ltd and Diversified Capital Ltd. Zariba is used to pay domestic and personal bills, while Eastcoast owned his house at 1 Tregunter Road, Kensington, west London, until the early 1990s. Diversified is a vehicle for moving funds for investments, notably for channelling money to the United States. Leonard Day is a shareholder of all three, while Thurston controls Eastcoast and Diversified.

In a very rare public comment, Thurston said that Diversified Capital is an investment holding company financed by Far Eastern investors. He did not refer to Mark Thatcher's involvement. But two former business partners of Thatcher have testified that this Jersey firm is 'the key' to his commercial operations. 'Mark said Diversified was his company,' said Jay Laughlin, former president of Ameristar, a US aviation fuel firm in which Thatcher, via Diversified, invested in the early 1990s. And Barnet Skelton, the lawyer investigating the bankruptcy of Ameristar, also said that the offshore company was controlled by the son of the former prime minister.[2]

Even Mark Thatcher's proposed commercial interests in Equatorial Guinea can be traced back to Jersey. In 1999, he set up Cogito Intelligence Ltd, registered and administered by Insinger Trust (Jersey) Ltd, which was controlled by his trusted aides Thurston and Day. The purpose of Cogito, whose principals were Thatcher and former British military attaché John Galt, was to provide private security advice and intelligence to diamond and multinational oil companies in Africa. It secured a contract in Angola during the UNITA–NPLA civil war and in 2000 approached President Obiang in EG and suggested that it gather intelligence on the brutal dictator's opponents, provide threat assessments and help draft repressive legislation to reinforce his grip on power. Thatcher saw the £134,000 contract as a way of securing lucrative oil concessions in EG, according to Johann Smith, a former director of Cogito.[3] But Obiang rejected the proposal.

However, it is in taxation that Thurston's secret services are most valuable, because that is where Margaret's son is most vulnerable. The banker–client relationship is not a warm one. 'Hugh does not like Mark because he sees him as a loose cannon and detrimental to his mother, whom he hero-worships,' said a source who has had business dealings with Thurston. 'He would help Mrs Thatcher with her tax affairs and then find that Mark had talked to her and changed her mind,' said a different source. 'This made Hugh very angry, which is unusual because he is a very mild-mannered man.'

The treasurer of Thatcher's fortune has a conventional background. Born in Balham, south London, in 1931, Thurston was educated at Wellington School in Somerset and Rotterdam Economics High School in Holland. He was seriously ill for much of his childhood. 'I have never been very tough, as a result of it,' he later reflected. 'I would have been interested in entering the political field in England but I think the life would have been too strenuous for me.'[4] Instead, Thurston turned to economics and accountancy. He worked for British and Commonwealth Shipping from 1956 until 1961, when he joined Bridor, Hamlyn and Fry, a firm of business consultants. As their economic adviser, Thurston set up their overseas network, including their branch office in Switzerland. 'Yes, I did know some of the Gnomes of Zurich,' he said.[5]

In May 1967, Thurston moved to Jersey and became an adviser to the government on the economic consequences for the island if the UK entered the Common Market. For the next six years, he was Jersey's economic adviser, helping to set up a special office to regulate locally registered companies, business licences and the vetting of licences of prospective wealthy residents.[6] In the mid-1970s, he returned to the private sector and became a director of Cope Allman International. More intriguingly, he joined the board of Jersey General Investment Trust Ltd, whose nominal share capital was £20 million. This company – whose aim was to 'deal with any stock, bonds, debentures, shares or securities' – changed its name to Pandale Holdings Ltd in July 1989. Three weeks later it was dissolved.

Thurston's main commercial job in the 1980s was as director of

Citibank, the American-owned bank well known for offering its clients offshore services. He was head of its Jersey office but ran into controversy during the Gulf war in 1991. The *Jersey Evening Post* wanted to publish an article about the transfer of staff from Citibank's offices in the Gulf to Jersey. This appeared to contravene the island's strict rules on hiring extra foreign employees and so would have caused some embarrassment for the bank. So it applied, unsuccessfully, for an injunction against the newspaper and Thurston represented Citibank in court. He is no longer on the board of Citibank but in 1993 became a director of the merchant bank Lazard Brothers and Co. (Jersey) Ltd.

Whenever there was a financial issue to be resolved in the 1980s, the prime minister's son would not hesitate to fly to Jersey to see his trusted banker. On one occasion, according to his Special Branch bodyguard who accompanied him during the trip, Mark Thatcher spent the whole day, including lunch, with Thurston at his Jersey home.

But when we approached Thurston at his expensive, antiques-filled home at Claremont Court, Jersey, he refused even to come to the door. His loyalty to the Thatchers remains resolute, despite severe misgivings about Mark. The other treasurer of Thatcher's gold, accountant Leonard Day, was also unforthcoming. When we arrived at his office to ask for information about Zariba Management Ltd, he was very nervous. 'You've been digging, you've been digging,' he said repeatedly, his hands shaking. When questioned about Zariba, he replied, 'It's a personal private company owned by myself.'

'Then why have you issued cheques on behalf of Diane Thatcher?' we asked.

'So what? What's wrong with that? Look, I have better things to do with my time.'

On the nearby Channel Island of Guernsey, other pots of Thatcher's gold are kept in three offshore accounts, according to City sources who have seen documents relating to his assets.[7] Telephone records obtained by lawyers in 2004 show that Thatcher frequently telephones these banks in Guernsey. One of the numbers he also called is the office of Harbour Trust Ltd, a trust company which has acted for Ken Bates, former chairman of Chelsea football club.[8]

If Thurston and Day are the secret trustees of the Thatcher family fortune, then the late Sir Michael Richardson was the financial strategist. An occasional visitor to Jersey, Sir Michael, the most powerful investment banker of his generation, advised and managed

Margaret and Mark Thatcher's money from at least the mid-1980s. An Old Harrovian who served in the Irish Guards just as the Second World War drew to a close, he was exactly the sort of tall, strapping, well-groomed, wealthy businessman that appealed to the prime minister. But Lord Lawson, one of her chancellors of the exchequer, was not an admirer. In his memoirs, he describes Sir Michael as 'an investment banker who owes his considerable success to manipulating people rather than money'.[9] And, true to form, Thatcher's favourite banker persuaded her government to award most of the lucrative advisory contracts on privatising state assets to NM Rothschild, where he was managing director.

A committed Thatcherite, the smooth-talking Sir Michael introduced her to the City and was her unofficial adviser on privatisation, despite the fact that his bank was bidding for advisory work on the state sell-offs. 'No one epitomised the links between Margaret and the City quite as much as Michael Richardson. If anyone was the bridge, it was he,' said Lord Wakeham, the former energy secretary. He also became, according to Thatcher, 'a great and good family friend'.[10] He took the prime minister to the opera at Glyndbourne and introduced her to his favourite charities, and she invited him to Boxing Day lunch at Chequers. In 1990, Thatcher rewarded him with a knighthood, which he rather ungraciously described as 'a minor title', and on the day that she was ennobled as a Baroness, the only two non-family guests she invited to lunch at the House of Lords were Sir Michael and Sir Charles Powell, her Foreign Affairs private secretary.

Margaret Thatcher remained a close friend despite Sir Michael's record for advising and working for corporate criminals like the late Robert Maxwell and Asil Nadir, who is still wanted for fraud offences over the collapse of Polly Peck. 'He is the Christine Keeler of the City,' said the chairman of a rival investment trust.[11] Sir Michael was chairman of Smith New Court, which acted as brokers during the controversial flotation of Mirror Newspapers and endorsed Maxwell's integrity and probity. Six months later, he was present at the disgraced publisher's funeral in Israel. In 2001, Sir Michael's career ended in humiliation when he was banned from working in the City by the Securities and Futures Authority (SFA). He had provided letters of credit for up to £246 million for a client who was a former bankrupt and been accused of involvement in advance fee frauds. Sir Michael 'acted in reckless disregard of information in his own files which should have alerted him that there could be above-average risks,' concluded the SFA in one of the most critical judgements in its history. His appeal was rejected.

Despite his reputation, Sir Michael remained a trusted financial adviser to the Thatchers. The friendship stemmed from the late 1960s when Mark was at Harrow with the son of the investment banker and they played cricket together. From 1980 onwards, when he was a partner of the blue-blood stockbrokers Cazenove and then managing director of NM Rothschild, Sir Michael kept a benign eye on and provided financial advice to the prime minister's son. Stressing that his consultancy work was unpaid, Sir Michael said that he would peruse Mark Thatcher's proposed investments, notably an oil and minerals scheme in September 1987, and they held meetings at NM Rothschild's office in London.[12]

After Margaret Thatcher left Number 10, her favourite investment banker became more active in managing her finances. He was intimately involved in negotiating her multimillion-pound contract to publish her memoirs, liaised with the Jersey boys – Thurston and Day – and oversaw the offshore trusts.

Sir Michael, who left only £1.7 million in his will, took Thatcher's financial secrets to his grave and left open the perennial question: how much is Mark Thatcher really worth? Mark himself has always publicly denied being in the Big Rich league. 'It would be significantly wrong to conclude that I am worth more than £5 million,' he told the *Financial Times* in October 1994. 'There is just nothing to support it apart from innuendo. This whole idea that I have had tremendous success is just a myth. If I had tremendous success, I would not be running around trying to do the things that I am doing. I would be sitting on my own private island in the South Pacific but I am not.'[13] When asked by the *Sunday Times* in 2003 whether he was worth their £60 million estimation, he replied it was 'wildly' off the mark. 'People who have got their heads screwed on do not comment on these things,' he said.[14] However, Thatcher's own banker had a different view. In 1991, one of Hugh Thurston's legal clients asked him, 'How much is Mark worth?' The Jersey banker paused for thought. 'About £40 million,' he replied. Since then, it is true that his net value has fallen rapidly, down to less than £10 million. This is due to ill-judged investments and Mark's habitually extravagant lifestyle. A rare commercial success has been trading in diesel fuel and gold in Zimbabwe during President Mugabe's regime, which has been highly profitable.[15] But it is a far cry from the lucrative days when his mother was prime minister.

The Mark Thatcher story really begins on 13 October 1925, the day Margaret Hilda Roberts was born in Grantham, a quiet market town in Lincolnshire. Grantham was the epitome of Middle England, priding itself on its ordinariness and old-fashioned values. Margaret's father, Alfred Roberts, personified that lifestyle. A tall, imposing figure, he had a profound and lasting effect on the future prime minister. 'I owe almost everything to my father,' she later reflected.[16]

Alfred Roberts ran his own grocer's shop and was a pillar of the community. A Methodist lay preacher, Rotarian and local alderman, he took life very seriously. He did not drink alcohol and believed in hard work, the Church and civic duty. There was not much fun or emotion in the Roberts household and that was where the Victorian values that later guided Margaret's political life were first nurtured. 'My father's view was that life was a serious matter,' said Margaret soon after becoming leader of the Tory Party. 'His maxim was that you did not sit idle.'[17]

Another favourite family saying was: 'Never be in anyone's debt'. Money was for saving not spending. Hence Margaret was brought up with few possessions or home comforts. There was no garden to play in or bicycle to ride. Holidays were rare. Yet this was due to her father's meanness with money rather than to genuine poverty. For the family business prospered as Margaret grew up. It was an austere and ascetic upbringing for the grocer's young daughter. But working in her father's shop had a lasting influence on Margaret. While prime minister, she used to say that 10 Downing Street was like 'living above the shop'.[18]

Her mother, Beatrice, a local seamstress, was, in contrast to Alfred, a mouse-like figure who appeared chained to the family shop and house and was hardly seen in the town. A gentle, unassuming woman, she was not prone to displays of emotion towards her children and appeared intimidated by her husband.[19] Margaret clearly did not regard her with much affection. She barely mentioned her mother's name in later life and it was highly significant that Beatrice Roberts's name was omitted by Margaret from her *Who's Who* entries. This was seen by some as proof of her anti-female, pro-male bias, which manifested itself in her attitude towards Mark's behaviour and activities.

From the age of ten, Margaret Roberts went to Kesteven and Grantham Grammar School. She worked ferociously hard and became a star pupil, excelling at almost everything, including games and drama. The only exception was art, largely because it was the

47

one subject not dependent on hard graft and swotting. 'Her contemporaries remember her as a model pupil of demure habits and tediously impeccable behaviour,' wrote Hugo Young, her most authoritative biographer. 'She never put a foot wrong, in the classroom or on the hockey field.'[20] She had few close friends at school, mainly because she took life so seriously and rarely joined in the fun and frolics of her peers. Even her adoring, ultra-earnest father said of her, 'Margaret is 99.5 per cent perfect. The half per cent is that she could be a little bit warmer.'[21]

Margaret's major outside interest was public speaking. She took private elocution lessons outside school hours. 'One simply must talk properly,' she told her father when she asked him to pay for them. He agreed but once her classmates noticed her new contrived accent they began calling her 'Snobby Roberts'.[22] Unperturbed, she was an active member of the school debating club, where she showed unusual self-confidence for one so young. Her style was more that of a steamroller than a Rolls-Royce, a ponderous, relentless delivery that wore down rather than inspired her young audience.

But politics was in her blood, actively encouraged by her father. Alfred Roberts sat as an Independent on Grantham Borough Council and so Margaret soon learnt the art of electioneering. Even at the tender age of ten, she was helping the local Conservative candidate as a runner during the 1935 election campaign.[23] She was a Conservative from her first day at Somerville College, Oxford, in 1943. This blue allegiance stood out in a sea of Labour red. 'She was to me extremely interesting because she was a Conservative,' recalled Janet Vaughan, Margaret's principal at Somerville. 'The young at that time, especially at Somerville, were all pretty left wing . . . If I had interesting, amusing people staying with me, I would never have thought of asking Margaret Roberts – except as a Conservative.'[24]

Margaret was painfully homesick at Oxford, particularly when she was teased about the shrill Lincolnshire accent she had not quite suppressed. One biographer, Chris Ogden, London bureau chief of *Time* during her premiership, summed up her personality at the time. His description is an uncannily accurate portrayal of her son, Mark, in later life: 'She knew almost no one [at Oxford] and kept to herself. Socially inept, awkward and totally lost with men, she was badgered by the other girls. Her references to "Daddy, the Mayor" didn't help. Nor did her frank admissions about aiming for big things. Her ambition was boundless, her candour guileless.'[25]

Despite her youth, Margaret Roberts was set in her ways. Political discussion for her tended to monologue rather than dialogue. She was not popular among fellow students, mainly because of an inability to smile and relax – another characteristic she shares with Mark. Her only friends were Methodists, Conservatives or those who shared her political views and undisguised ambitions. Despite her preference for the company of men, she had no romantic relationship at Oxford – her strict religious upbringing saw to that.

By the 1945 general election, Margaret was consumed by politics. She canvassed for Quintin Hogg (later Lord Hailsham) in his campaign for the Oxford City seat against Labour's Frank Pakenham (later Lord Longford). But the family's financial circumstances meant she could not seriously contemplate politics as a career until 1946, when the government increased MPs' pay from £600 to £1,000.

The following year, Margaret graduated from Oxford with only a second-class BSc degree, mainly because she devoted most of her time to politics and the Oxford University Conservative Association. She regretted studying chemistry. 'I should have read law,' she said. 'That's what I need for politics. I shall just have to go and read law now.'[26] But she could not afford to continue her studies, so in 1947 she went to work as a research chemist with British Xylonite Plastics in Colchester.

According to Penny Junor, whose biography is the best account of her early life, the grocer's daughter again did not fit in: 'Margaret found it agonising. She was quite incapable of communicating with the men on the factory floor in any way at all. Where her fellow females might ask, "Hey, Charlie, what about trying this, I think it might work," and play along with the odd nudge and wink, Margaret would stand rather awkwardly over the man, and in her well-modulated, and now perfected true blue accent, would say, "Mr So-and-So, would you mind trying it this way?" This method, as often as not, elicited the two finger response, and earned Margaret the nickname "Duchess".'[27]

Socially, Margaret Roberts was out of her depth, largely because she concealed her lower-middle-class background and her conversation was humourless and dogmatic. But when it came to politics, she was supremely confident and spoke fluently and convincingly. Her big break came at the 1948 Tory Party conference in Llandudno, north Wales. Among the delegates was John Grant, director of Blackwell's, the Oxford bookshop, who knew the young chemistry graduate well. There he met John Miller, chairman of Dartford Conservative Association, who was looking for a new candidate. Grant recommended the eager Margaret Roberts.

She was delighted, despite Dartford's being a safe Labour seat. She also felt at home with the middle-class folk of north Kent rather than in metropolitan London. At her interview, she dazzled the selection committee with a well-informed presentation, delivered without a note. In a political setting, she glittered and glowed, and on 28 February 1949, she was selected as the party's parliamentary candidate.

That evening, a dinner was held to mark Margaret's adoption. One of the guests was a tall, prosperous 34-year-old Kent businessman called Denis Thatcher. He was only attending the dinner to make up the numbers but he was immediately impressed by the young candidate. 'She was beautiful, gay, very kind and thoughtful,' he later reflected. 'Who could meet Margaret without being completely slain by her personality and intellectual brilliance?'[28] After the dinner, Denis drove Margaret back to London, where she took a train back to her flat in Colchester. Denis owned a sandy-coloured Jaguar and liked to drive fast, which did not impress the serious-minded parliamentary candidate. But they had enough in common to chat away. Their next encounter was at a Rotary Club meeting and, despite the ten-year age gap, their courtship blossomed.

Denis Thatcher's origins lie in the unlikely setting of Wanganui, a town on the west coast of the North Island of New Zealand known locally as 'the River City'. The Kiwi Thatchers were a more upper-middle-class family than the Robertses: 'the last of the Edwardian snobs', as Denis later described them.[29] But, like the Robertses, they were active in the local community and there is even a street in Wanganui named after them. Their money came from sheep farming and brewing but also from devising a special weedkiller that could be used on railway tracks. This was marketed abroad and firms were set up in America and Europe.

In 1908, Denis's father, Tom Thatcher, aged 28, settled in London to manage the British parent company, Atlas Preservatives Ltd. An extrovert and likeable character, Tom was a typical member of the Edwardian middle class. He became a Freemason, was a devotee of rugby football and an active member of the Kipling Society. He married Lillian Bird, herself an astute businesswoman whose father was a south London horse dealer.

On 10 May 1915, Lillian Thatcher gave birth to Denis at their house in Southbrook Road, Lewisham, south London. Eight years later Denis was dispatched to prep school in Bognor Regis and then, at the age of 13, to Mill Hill School, north London. It was an institution more interested in games and social control than in academic excellence. According to the school's 'Plan', each resident master was to 'watch over the morals of the boys, as with parental solicitude, and to take every opportunity of inculcating sound principles and good dispositions'.[30]

Growing up during the pioneering days of the British Empire influenced Denis profoundly. His world view was shaped by the heroic tales and patriotic poetry of Macauley and Kipling, which glamorised the annexation of 'lesser nations'. For Denis's class and generation, that was the bedrock of their way of life. It resulted in an imperialist right-wing brand of Conservatism that he always retained.

Denis was not a success academically. He was more interested in sport (a dogged cricketer and rugby player) and attending the annual Duke of York's camp, a curious neo-military event whose one rule was 'Play the Game'.[31] Denis was in his element. Clubbable by nature, he loved the comradeship and the patriotic atmosphere of the camp, with its emphasis on outdoor pursuits.

In 1933, aged 17, he left school and joined Atlas Preservatives Ltd, the family firm, which had by then incorporated paint and other chemicals. Denis's basic character was quite different from Margaret's. Unlike his future wife, he was self-effacing and diffident, and he retained a self-deprecatory sense of humour. Even later in life, he would describe himself as 'a not unsuccessful businessman' rather than a 'successful' one.[32] He was essentially a cautious conformist who respected his elders and authority, almost unquestioningly. But, like Margaret, Denis was not afraid of speaking his mind in sharp and colourful language.[33] He must have found it excruciating and frustrating to hold his tongue during his time at 10 Downing Street.

Like most of his generation, the Second World War had a huge impact on Denis Thatcher's life. Already a Territorial Army officer, he joined the 34th Searchlight Regiment of the Royal Artillery. However, because of poor eyesight he was a junior staff officer rather than an active soldier in the field. He served in France and Italy, and then became a staff captain in the 9th Anti-Aircraft Division.

It was during the most tense period of the war, in 1941, that Denis fell in love with Margaret Kempson, daughter of a Potters Bar jewellery designer he had met at an officers' tea dance at Grosvenor House. According to Diana Farr, author of the most authoritative account of Denis's early life, Kempson was beautiful, high spirited and 'bore an uncanny resemblance to the second Margaret

Thatcher'.[34] Margaret Kempson was also very exuberant, 'working terribly hard driving lorries, tearing about delivering Mosquito parts from the factory to dispersal points around the country'.[35]

It was a classic wartime whirlwind romance and within weeks they were married, on 28 March 1942, in Monken Hadley Church, Hertfordshire. Although they were initially very happy, the war prevented them from living together permanently. The marriage was a series of snatched moments of intimacy, staying in hotels during his leave and governed by their service requirements.

In July 1943, two days before Denis was dispatched abroad for Operation Husky – the invasion of Sicily – his father died. It was a devastating blow but he went on the mission and was later mentioned in dispatches for 'gallant and distinguished service'.

By early 1945, Denis's exceptional organisational talents were being put to good use and he was promoted to major. His great triumph was Operation Goldflake – the movement of thousands of Canadian and British troops from Italy to Belgium. Because they were scattered far and wide, Marseilles was used as a transit camp. It was a perilously exposed location and the troops' presence could easily have been detected by the enemy. Denis was based at the British HQ in Marseilles and he worked day and night to help coordinate the successful operation, which involved both the utmost secrecy and diversionary tactics.

Denis Thatcher was subsequently awarded the MBE (military). In her book *Five At Ten*, Diana Farr quoted from the citation: 'Major Thatcher set an outstanding example of energy, initiative and drive. He deserved most of the credit for the very fine message of appreciation which has been conveyed to me from Field Marshal Montgomery as to the excellence of the work done.'[36]

Denis enjoyed the camaraderie of military life and did not want to leave the army.[37] But when he returned home he was unexpectedly summoned to run the family business, Atlas Preservatives, and soon became managing director. His marriage was not such a success. The couple had drifted apart and they found they now had little in common. In 1948, an amicable divorce was agreed. 'It was one of those war-time marriages which never really got off the ground,' the first Mrs Thatcher (now Lady Hickman) said years later.[38] She later married Sir Howard Hickman, an Old Etonian baronet, and lived a long and quiet country life.

For 25 years, Denis and Margaret Thatcher never mentioned his first marriage. Margaret found the subject acutely embarrassing and did not even tell her children until 1976, when they were 23 years old, after journalists began asking questions. Mark and Carol were shocked by the news but Margaret was almost Edwardian in her attitude. 'One didn't keep it a secret he'd been married before,' she said. 'One wasn't asked. One just didn't talk about a thing like that.'[39]

Unlike Margaret Thatcher, Denis was gregarious and at ease with people. He was popular with the workforce at his office in Erith, Kent, and was genuinely interested in the welfare of others. While Margaret aspired to the aristocracy, Denis disliked the pomposity and pretensions of the upper classes. He also developed a saloon-bar sense of humour which made him an entertaining drinking companion. 'When I'm not absolutely paralytic, I play a little golf'[40] and 'He's about as much use as a one-legged man at an arse-kicking party'[41] are typical Denis remarks. As Diana Farr put it: 'By now he had slipped into the use of sporting and business terms to explain everyday reactions or more solemn matters, an eccentricity which remains with him today. He will speak, sometimes, for example, of unattractive propositions that present a "large downside risk" and "no upside gain", even when talking to women who cannot be expected to understand such jargon.'[42]

Denis's political views and world outlook were heavily influenced by the war. He had always been an old-fashioned Conservative. But the war accentuated the class system in his eyes. For Denis the world was divided into Officers and Men. He was an Officer and socially he was only really interested in mixing with other Officers. 'Loyalty, to me, is the one quality all men must have,' Denis said later. 'I learnt this in the army – loyalty to the organisation and loyalty to the man you work for. That's the indispensable quality in life.'[43]

According to James Montagu, who was a neighbour of the Thatchers in Kent in the mid-1960s, the standard topic of conversation when Denis and his friends congregated was their wartime experiences. 'Denis has never really cared what other people think of him,' said Montagu. 'Like a lot of other former officers, he took the view of "I confronted death and got through the war. Everything else pales by comparison. Who cares what other people think?"'[44] It was that independent spirit that later endeared him to so many people.

By 1949, Denis was firmly established in the north Kent community. He was an active member of the Dartford Conservative Association and was building up a successful family firm. Outside business, his chief interest was sport, particularly rugby union (he was to become a highly respected referee), golf and sailing. He was friendly, good company and prosperous, so it is not hard to see why the young Margaret Roberts found Denis an attractive suitor.

The Thatcher courtship was far from a whirlwind romance. Margaret was later asked if meeting Denis was a case of love at first sight. 'Certainly not!' she exclaimed.[45] Their relationship developed slowly but steadily. 'We dined out from time to time,' recalled Margaret, 'and went to the occasional cinema or theatre. But they were still rather dark days in 1949 and 1950. There wasn't a lot of gay life about.'[46] Denis was more set on a long-term relationship, particularly after taking her to a dinner-dance at his trade association. Towards the end of the evening, his company chairman leaned over to him and whispered, 'That's it, Denis – that's the one.'[47]

One common interest was money. Margaret admired Denis for his business experience and for running his own company. She liked his direct style of talking and they spent hours discussing politics and finance. She felt comfortable in his company and he was a Methodist, which helped. Denis also had a physical resemblance to Margaret's father – tall, broad shouldered and striking, with thick-lensed spectacles. But her exhaustive lifestyle, combining a job with food manufacturer J. Lyons and political activity in the evening, precluded any impetuous romance.

Most of her evenings were taken up by canvassing in Dartford for the forthcoming general election. The campaign in February 1950 was bitterly fought and even then Margaret Roberts's slogans were apocalyptic in tone. The election was a choice between two ways of life. 'One leads inevitably to slavery, the other to freedom,' declared the intense young candidate. Another favourite was borrowed from her father. 'A caged bird has social security. It has food and warmth. But what good is all that if it has not the freedom to fly out and live its own life?'[48]

Despite her defeat, the Dartford Conservatives were pleased with her energetic performance and she was readopted for the second election in October 1951. But this was a more low-key campaign. Margaret Roberts faced a 13,000 Labour majority and was not able to rekindle her enthusiasm. Besides, she was distracted. Denis had been courting her. He had always been more keen on her than she on him. But they had enough in common for Margaret to treat him seriously, if not passionately.

In September 1951, he returned from a trip to France and proposed marriage. Margaret's only doubt was that he had been married before. Divorce was strongly frowned on by the Methodist Church but in a rare act of social rebellion she overlooked this inconvenient fact. She accepted but was in the midst of the election campaign. When the result was declared in Dartford town hall, Margaret Roberts had lost but had cut Labour's majority by 1,000. She thanked her party workers, who were celebrating a national Conservative victory, and said she had some other good news. Then Denis took over the podium and announced their impending marriage.

Margaret Roberts became Margaret Thatcher six weeks later, on 13 December 1951, at Wesley's Chapel, a Methodist church in London's City Road. For their honeymoon, the couple went to Portugal, then Madeira, and finally spent a few days in Paris, where Denis indulged in a little business activity.[49] They then moved into Denis's rented flat at 112 Swan Court in Flood Street, Chelsea. Margaret began her law studies at the Council of Legal Education while Denis continued his job with Atlas Preservatives, in Erith, Kent.

For Margaret, it was far from a love match. 'He was in the paint and chemicals business,' she later remarked. 'He was on the financial side; I was interested in economics. We were both interested in politics and we had a lot in common.'[50] Denis's financial support was crucial in enabling the 26-year-old Margaret to pursue her political career without distractions. 'Denis's money got me on my way,' she later reflected.[51]

From the beginning, it was a marriage of two busy professional people. 'This is a deal that we have always done,' Margaret said later. 'Work is the most important thing, and it comes first, and therefore you do it.'[52] Indeed, it was a very modern relationship for such a Conservative couple. Despite her reliance on Denis's salary, Margaret achieved independence through her work and political ambitions. In many ways, she was a pioneering feminist, arguing that women could and should have careers. 'In this way, gifts and talents that would otherwise be wasted are developed to the benefit of the community,' she wrote at the time. 'The idea that the family suffers is, I believe, quite mistaken.'[53]

It was in this context that the Thatchers planned to have children, one of each sex. Their dream came true on Saturday, 15 August 1953, when Margaret gave birth to twins, a boy and a girl, seven weeks ahead of schedule, at Princess Beatrice Hospital, in Chelsea, west London. It was a long, arduous labour until her doctors decided on a caesarean delivery. The boy was born first at 2.50 p.m., weighing four pounds, and two minutes later his sister appeared. Margaret was surprised but ecstatic with her double offspring but had yet to choose names. Mark and Carol were selected. 'We just wanted simple names that couldn't be shortened,' their mother said. 'We didn't like nicknames.'[54]

Denis was not present for the birth. As the twins were not due until October, he went to the Oval for the Test match between England and Australia. That Saturday night, Denis and his friends went off to the pub. Naturally, he could not be contacted, so Margaret travelled to the hospital alone. '*Do* I remember,' she later told *Time* magazine's Chris Ogden in mock anger [her emphasis]. 'We couldn't find my husband anywhere. He had mooched off.' When Denis arrived at the hospital, he gasped and joked, 'My God, they look like rabbits. Put them back.'[55]

Despite his absence, Denis was delighted with the twins as a classic case of Thatcherite efficiency and object lesson in productivity. 'Typical of Margaret,' he remarked. 'She produced twins and avoided the necessity of a second pregnancy.'[56] He marked their arrival by buying their mother a double string of pearls, which she often wears to this day.[57] He had a double cause for celebration: four days later England beat Australia and won the Ashes amidst scenes of national jubilation.

As Margaret lay exhausted in her hospital bed for two weeks, she was already thinking about her future career. 'I was concerned, particularly with two [children], that I might be tempted to spend all my time on the household and looking after them and not continue to read or use my mind or experience,' she recalled. 'I felt I must really use the rest of me as well.'[58] She told another biographer, 'I remember lying there and thinking, "If I don't, now that I'm in hospital, actually fill in the entrance form for the final of the law, I may never go back to it. But if I fill in the entrance form now, pride will not let me fail. And so I did. That was really an effort of will.'[59]

Four months later, Margaret passed her final Bar exams and the more routine hours of a tax lawyer enabled her to spend more time looking after her young children. But she still needed outside assistance. So the couple rented the adjoining sixth-floor flat in Swan Court, knocked down the wall and installed a live-in nanny and housekeeper to look after Mark and Carol. 'You tend to need some sort of help with twins, who wake for feeding at different hours of the day and night,' she said.[60] Margaret found motherhood nerve-racking and exhausting: 'I worried all the time. Of course, 90 per cent of the time, you worry about things that don't happen, but still you worry.'[61]

For a brief period, politics took a back seat as Margaret concentrated on the twins. She was a very attentive if preoccupied mother. Although the nanny tended to comfort the children if they cried during the night, Margaret always devoted time to them. 'The pull of a mother towards her children is perhaps the strongest and most instinctive emotion we have,' she later recalled. She always dressed them immaculately and read to them before they went to sleep. On their fourth or fifth birthday, she spent two days making and icing cakes – one was in the shape of a fort for Mark, the other a car for Carol.[62]

There is no doubt that in their early formative years her children were her priority. But it was also quite a formal Victorian upbringing. There were no nicknames and neither Margaret nor Denis romped around or played with the kids for the sheer hell of it.[63] In some ways, she resembled an affectionate, benevolent teacher rather than a mother. 'She never shouted at them,' said Margaret's sister, Muriel, 'it was all sweet reason. I could have screamed at her sometimes for being so reasonable. Her attitude all the time was to teach the twins interesting things. Everything she did with *them* was teaching but always in such a kind way. They arrived at our farm once when we were in the middle of lifting potatoes and straightaway she said, "Oh good, we can teach the twins how the machine works." Again, one holiday I can remember us all going out in a boat. To me it was just a trip in a boat but Margaret immediately said to the twins, "Now you'll be able to *learn* how to crew" [her emphasis]. She was always so imaginative with them, so stimulating.'[64]

Denis also tended to have a formal relationship with the twins and left the parenting to his wife and the nanny. 'For God's sake, teach the children some manners,' he once snapped. According to Penny Junor's biography of Margaret Thatcher: 'He insisted on manners and correct behaviour, would never allow the children to keep pets, wouldn't tolerate slippers and insisted on everything being neat and tidy in the house. The only games he played were ball games in the back garden, where he had set up a cricket net, bowling Mark balls to hit.'[65]

Like Margaret, Denis was guilty of regular absences from home – either on trips abroad or not arriving from work until well after the children were put to bed. He generally preferred a quiet family life but could be assertive when the occasion required it. He raised his hand to the twins only once during their childhood.[66] During a cocktail party in the mid-1980s at 10 Downing Street, the conversation turned to the rearing of children. 'Never had any trouble with my two,' said the prime minister's consort proudly. 'They always got on so well together. I can think of only one occasion when we had a problem.' He paused for a refill of his drink. 'On the road to Portsmouth, it was. Carol and Mark started bickering in the back. So I put my foot down. I stopped the car and I said, "Right, you three – get out." So they got out of the car. And I said, "Right, Margaret! Deal with them."'[67]

Margaret doted on her children but her thoughts were never far away from the challenging male worlds of the law and politics. She was always rushing in and dashing out, rarely remembering to wave up at the nursery window as she left for work in the morning. Their needs were just one set of demands to be fitted into her manic, packed days and she did not like delegating. 'The children were going to need a lot of looking after,' she said later. 'And, of course, they do become the centre of your life and you live for them as you've never lived for anyone else . . . And yet, I knew that I had something else to give.'[68] At first, her assiduous search for a parliamentary seat was frustrated by prejudiced Tory selection committees, who claimed she should be at home looking after her young children.

Life changed abruptly for the Thatchers in early 1959, when Margaret was chosen as the parliamentary candidate for Finchley, north London. The family had just moved into Dormers, a four-bedroomed detached house in a residential cul-de-sac near Farnborough, Kent. It was a typical middle-class Conservative area, inhabited by the 'gin and Jag set', where the talk in the golf club bar was of money, sport, the war and how the country was 'going to the dogs'. The men commuted to London and their wives stayed at home to look after the children. Margaret Thatcher was very much an anomaly as she took the train every day to Lincoln's Inn to work as a tax barrister.

Their mother's absences meant Mark and Carol depended on nannies for maternal affection. It also meant they spent more time outside the house on their own, playing with local children, and would make short excursions on their bicycles. As the 1959 general election approached, the twins' unintentional isolation from their parents increased. Mrs Thatcher completely absorbed herself in the campaign, utilising her legendary energy, and on 8 October 1959 she was elected the Conservative Member of Parliament for Finchley.

Even at the age of six, her son was basking in his mother's glory.

'My Mummy's a Member of Parliament,' he boasted the next day as he was surrounded by a group of small boys in the school playground in Farnborough, Kent.[69] Later, as she became more prominent and family-style photo sessions were called for, Mark would jostle for centre stage while his sister tried to wriggle out of the frame. Mark has given varying accounts of how his mother's initial success affected him. 'I knew my mother was something special the very first day she became a Member of Parliament,' he said in 1974.[70] But in a later interview he said, 'It didn't really affect my life at all. In fact, I very well remember the day she was elected walking into the garage and seeing the car covered in blue ribbon and confetti. I couldn't quite work it out because the car never looked like that before but even though I was only six I can remember thinking, "She's really going places."'[71]

According to her biographers, Margaret Thatcher then began to distance herself from her home town of Grantham. She rarely visited her birthplace, now viewing it as tedious and small minded. Instead, her life was in London and the House of Commons was effectively her new home. She did her best to devote time to the twins, always driving them to school in the mornings. But the truth was that during the week she rarely saw her children, mainly because of late-night parliamentary sittings. She did make their breakfast early in the morning and telephoned them at 6 p.m. to say goodnight. But in their infant years they were brought up by their nanny and housekeeper, a devoted and extrovert older woman called Abby, who became virtually their surrogate mother. 'Ssshhh,' she would whisper to the twins in the evening. 'Your mother's working.'[72]

One topic concerning their children to which Margaret and Denis did devote considerable time and thought was their education. They decided on private boarding schools, partly because it was Denis's preference but also to separate Mark and Carol, who were not getting on. Their mother even used to say they were 'mortal enemies'.[73] Carol herself does not look back on their relationship with any fondness: 'The two of us used to bicker about small things.'[74] Mark's habit of saying things like 'I have to open all my birthday presents two minutes earlier than you because I am two minutes older' did not exactly endear him to his twin sister.

So in September 1961, aged eight, Mark was sent to Belmont, the preparatory school for Mill Hill where Denis had spent many happy years, near his mother's north London constituency. It was not an auspicious period for the local MP's son. Margaret liked it because she could take him out to lunch and was 'not too far away in case of emergencies', she later reflected. 'He was a very quiet boy,' recalled David Gee, his housemaster and form master. 'He was not clever, to put it mildly, and was overshadowed by his sister, Carol, who was much brighter. He was not that good at games and it seemed to me he had an inferiority complex a lot of the time. I would say he was happy enough but his school record was very average and he needed special tuition to get into Harrow.'[75]

A month after Mark's arrival at Belmont, on 9 October 1961, his mother was appointed a junior social security minister in charge of pensions in Harold Macmillan's Conservative government. That evening, the twins were given two new books and sat in bed planning what they would like for Christmas.[76] Their lives were going through another sea change. 'I then realised she had a very wonderful career ahead of her as a politician,' said Mark later. 'She was so busy one could only assume she was very successful . . . I'd always known that she was on the fast track.'[77]

Despite the long separations from her children, Margaret was a very diligent mother and would always make up for lost time. When Mark was ill at Belmont boarding school, his mother made regular trips to his bedside to read him stories. 'Mum just kept popping up,' said Mark later. 'I was amazed how much she managed to be there. And she was a minister by then. She has always been a really devoted mother and she still is.'[78] She became almost obsessed with his health. 'I was always worried about Mark, who at that time seemed to catch every germ that was going, including pneumonia one winter at Lenzerhide,' she recalled in her memoirs. 'One of the worst days of my life was when he had appendicitis and I had to rush him to the nearby hospital. I spent so much time with him in the weeks that followed that I began to worry that Carol might feel left out. So I bought her a magnificent teddy bear which was christened Humphrey.'

However, Denis believed she over-compensated for her absence by excessive fussing and worrying about the twins. She was fastidious and class-conscious about their clothes and appearance – as she was about her own – and spent endless hours knitting them royal-blue jersey-style jackets. Once, when the twins were invited to play with other children at the house of Margaret Hickstead, a family friend, Mark was dressed in little velvet trousers and a white satin blouse, and Carol in a pretty but over-decorative dress. At the party, Mark refused to shake hands with one of the boys, who was dressed more sensibly for the sandpit, because he was 'too scruffy'.

As they grew up, it was also clear that their mother favoured Mark over Carol. According to Penny Junor, she 'pampered him as a child, fetched and carried for him when she was at home' and, most significantly, 'seldom corrected him'. Even at the age of 18, when she was education secretary, she would bring him breakfast in bed. As a result, he behaved as if the world revolved around him. 'Why do we have Christmas Carols but not Christmas Marks?' he said as a young boy. Mark's upbringing was a curious combination of a formal, cold and detached boarding-school education and sudden brief but extravagantly intense binges of maternal affection.[79]

As a young boy, Mark was much more like his father. Some childhood friends say he almost hero-worshipped Denis, to the extent of imitating his voice. Unsuspecting telephone callers were often bemused, and not a little irritated, when Mark answered the phone by barking 'Thatcher' loudly into the receiver, trying to copy his father.[80] Mark was soon banned from answering the phone in this way. But he retained his adoration of Denis. 'Mark worshipped his father,' said James Montagu, a neighbour of the family. 'He wanted to be just like him and was always saying, "My Dad says this" or "My Dad does that".'[81]

Despite her own strict, temperate upbringing and disciplined approach to life, Margaret was curiously conciliatory towards her son and never shouted at him. It was all sweet reason. This was despite Mark being an often mischievous and disruptive child. A mother who knew the family well noticed this anomaly: 'When Margaret first got elected, the papers were full of headlines like "New woman MP calls for the return of the lash", yet she never raised a finger to the twins. Instead, she used that low hypnotic voice of hers at times when I would have belted my kids. I vividly remember her saying, "Now Mark, you mustn't poke that sharp stick into your sister's eye, otherwise she won't grow up into a pretty little girl." I'd have walloped him.'[82]

This was later confirmed by the twins. 'We weren't brought up very strictly,' said Mark. 'It was a sort of back-scratching operation. If I did the things she expected of me as far as work was concerned and behaved in a reasonably civilised fashion, it was fairly easygoing. If I misbehaved or did something idiotic, then it was trouble, just as it would be with any mum.'[83] 'I don't remember her being a tough disciplinarian – definitely not a shrieker,' said Carol. 'If she ever smacked me, I don't recall it. She had such a strict upbringing herself that she was conscious that ours would be different. But nor did I grow up in one of those homes where people climb into bed with their parents on Sunday morning.'[84]

Margaret Thatcher's benign indulgence towards her son was partly influenced by her father's approach to wayward boys and this, according to the psychiatrist Anthony Clare, explained her lifelong blind spot towards Mark. In her memoirs, she tells a prescient story of how her father, Alfred Roberts, had a row with a fellow parishioner over a young man from a respectable family. The son had slowly gone from bad to worse, spent all his parents' savings and then turned up pleading for forgiveness. The parishioner was rigid and clear: the boy was no good, would never be any good and should be shown the door. But the response of Thatcher's father was 'vivid in my mind'. A son remains a son and must be treated with all the love and warmth of his family whenever he turns to them.

Although by all accounts Mark was emotionally spoilt as a child, his mother did not bestow on him lavish gifts and unlimited pocket money. He did receive dancing, skiing and riding lessons, and the house was full of toys. But she never indulged him in a materialistic way. This was due, say family friends, to her ascetic and serious nature, encouraged by her own parents.

In 1963, the Thatchers sold Dormers and bought a flat in Westminster Gardens, just off Artillery Row in Victoria. As Denis hated London at weekends, the family also rented a cottage in Horsmonden, near Tunbridge Wells, while they looked around for a new country house. The rented house was on Shere Farm, part of the estate of Commander Christopher Powell, a powerful and influential parliamentary lobbyist who was a close friend and adviser of the Thatchers.

Two years later, in 1965, Denis became a wealthy man when he sold his family company to Castrol, earning himself £560,000. This enabled him to purchase The Mount, a reconstructed eight-bedroomed mock-Tudor mansion in Lamberhurst, Kent, five miles from Shere Farm. The house was complete with three acres of garden, a tennis court and an outdoor swimming pool.[85] Next door to the Thatchers lived William Montagu, a retired naval officer who owned a pharmaceutical company, who had told Denis about the availability of The Mount. His son James, a year younger than Mark, was a regular visitor to the Thatcher household, as he liked to use the swimming pool. James spent a lot of time with Mark but has no fond recollections. 'He was a horrible and unpleasant person,' said James Montagu. 'He was very bumptious and boastful, and behaved as if he knew better than anyone else. He had a knack of putting people's backs up. I'll never forget how forward he was to other parents. On one occasion he sat in the back of our car and began advising my mother how to drive.'[86]

From an early age, pomposity was a feature of Mark's character, according to Penny Junor, a biographer of Margaret Thatcher and the daughter of a close friend of the prime minister, former *Sunday Express* editor Sir John Junor. In her book, Junor recounts what happened when Margaret took the twins to visit an old friend who had children much the same age as the Thatchers: 'While the mothers talked indoors, the children all played together in the sandpit outside. When the time came to leave, Mark, dressed as he invariably was like Little Lord Fauntleroy, didn't volunteer any farewells to his host in the sandpit. When instructed to do so by his mother, he regarded scathingly this child who looked appropriately grubby for the end of a day in the garden, and said, "Oh no, Mummy, I couldn't possibly say goodbye to someone so scruffy."'[87]

However, a childhood neighbour from the mid-1960s, Eric 'Ricki' Laws, now a doctor in Southampton, has a different recollection. 'I actually got on with Mark and liked him because he was so thick skinned,' said Laws. 'I was always amused at his inability to understand the least subtle of hints. It is true he was bumptious and lacked social grace but I enjoyed his company.'[88]

By the time Mark entered his teenage years, Margaret was emerging as the dominant figure in the Thatcher family. 'She was definitely in charge,' said James Montagu. It was not for nothing that both Denis and Mark referred to her as 'the Boss' – a nickname Mark uses to this day.[89] An indication of this status was the choice of Mark's senior school. It was always Denis's hope that his son, like himself, would go to Mill Hill. But, according to David Gee, Mark's housemaster at preparatory school, Margaret Thatcher vetoed the idea because Mill Hill had an unofficial Jewish 'quota' of boys. The Finchley MP believed that if Mark was admitted, then it would have been perceived that she had used her influence with her Jewish constituents. Instead, he was sent to Harrow.

Mark Thatcher went up to Harrow (motto: 'May the Fortune of the House be Steered by the Faithful Stewardship of the Gifts of God') in January 1967, aged 13. Founded in 1572, it was originally a free grammar school for the study of classics by local boys and only became fee-paying and private with an influx of pupils with wealthy parents from outside the parish. More significantly, it became the training school for the establishment, rivalled only by Eton, whose headmaster, Lord Charteris, once explained its appeal: 'The boys discover very early that they've got to get round people to get their way. It's the ideal training ground for statesmen, politicians, entrepreneurs. And pirates.'[90]

Grooming the boys for greatness is the school's underlying philosophy – the future generation who are to sustain and preserve basic establishment institutions. Hence Harrow has created eight prime ministers, notably Winston Churchill, and between 1900 and 1985 eighty-three government ministers. Its current school governors include Lord Butler, cabinet secretary and head of the civil service, Sir Evelyn de Rothschild and the Duke of Westminster.

Over the years, the Harrow culture became immensely status conscious and class ridden, according to one of its distinguished former pupils. Lord Deedes, Old Harrovian, former Conservative cabinet minister, former editor of the *Daily Telegraph* and close friend of Denis Thatcher, recalls how he was taught to look up to authority, almost literally tugging his forelock. 'We were taught that to respect authority was the most important thing in life,' said Lord Deedes, 'and there were whole obligations to privilege.'[91] When Mark was a pupil in the late 1960s, Harrow retained those snobbish characteristics. It was one of those curious ironies that Margaret Thatcher should send her son to an elitist school run by an establishment class that she later opposed so bitterly and would dismiss as 'those grandees'.[92]

However, Harrow was going through a mildly transitional stage when Mark joined. The 'fag' system, whereby first-year pupils act as personal servants to sixth-form members, was being reformed. This meant that by the time Mark was in the sixth form, a new rule – 'boy calls' – was in place. If a sixth former wanted an errand run, he would shout, 'Boy, boy, boy,' and all the fags in the House would have to come running. 'The aim of the "fag" system,' one Old Harrovian told us, 'was that it taught boys a fair use of power, in that you experienced the position of the servant before becoming a master.'

In fact, it accentuated class divisions, so that anyone arriving at Harrow with even the slightest hint of an 'inferior' social background would become very insecure. This is exactly what happened to Mark Thatcher, who was essentially from a petty bourgeois or *nouveau riche* family. 'When he arrived at school, he was not comfortable with himself,' said John Pearson, a contemporary. 'He never let himself get walked over, though, as he stuck up for himself. But people formed the impression that he was a bit of an oddball.'[93]

Mark's misfortune was his native London–Kent accent, which was deemed 'common' and 'below stairs'. He was teased and mimicked mercilessly, as it contrasted sharply with the plummy aristocratic tones of his peers. The boys found it particularly amusing because it clashed with the refined, if affected, accent of his mother on television when she was shadow minister for transport. Consequently, he was nicknamed 'Mawk Fatcher' or 'Mork Scratcher' (because of his acne problems). Margaret's son responded, unconvincingly, that he had picked up the accent from workers on a building site near the family home in London. He also tried to deflate his embarrassment and divert attention by performing his Harrow party piece. This involved jumping in the air, clicking his heels and shouting ''Allo, sunshine' at anyone he regarded as socially inferior.[94] But this served only to focus attention on himself and his own insecurities rather than to amuse his fellow pupils.

Instead of laughing off the jibes at his accent and blending in, Mark adopted a pompous and bumptious stance towards his fellow pupils. This attitude coincided with the election of the Conservative government in June 1970 and the elevation of his mother as secretary of state for education. 'When she got a place in the Cabinet,' he said later, 'it really started to affect me. I was beginning to grow up and understand what it was all about.'[95]

However, some of the masters were not so quick to recognise his mother's status. One day she arrived at Harrow to talk to Mark's housemaster, Mark Tindall. On that particular day, Tindall was interviewing for new domestic staff, so she waited patiently outside his rooms. Suddenly, he opened his study door and noticed her sitting in the corridor. 'Ah,' he said, 'you must have come about the new under-matron vacancy.' Margaret Thatcher was not amused.[96]

Margaret wanted her son to adapt, adjust and behave like the other boys. But Mark had a tendency to conduct himself as though his mother were already prime minister.[97] This did not endear him to his fellow pupils. 'He had the reputation for being fairly conceited,' recalled Clive Staveley, who was in the same house (Bradbys) as Mark. 'He was awarded colours early on, which meant you were allowed to wear a coloured scarf on half-days. He went right out and bought his but wasn't allowed to wear it, as people took a dim view of youngsters wearing them. He was only allowed to wear it three years later, by which time I think it had moth holes in it.'[98]

His fellow teenagers took a delight in belittling the son of 'Thatcher the milk-snatcher' (her nickname as the minister who abolished free milk for schoolchildren). 'I remember with some glee playing in a rugby match against Mark's house,' said a contemporary. 'Mark was going for a try and I smashed him into touch. I really enjoyed it because he was the son of the milk-snatcher.' Mark dutifully defended his mother: 'I think she did the right thing because it gave her the opportunity to reallocate the £22 million to other educational programmes.'[99]

Having a famous parent was not Mark's problem at Harrow (the place was, after all, full of such offspring). The truth was that he just could not, or would not, acclimatise. 'He was a bit of a loner, who didn't fit into the British public-school environment,' said Andrew Blamey, now an executive headhunter, who was in the same house. 'He couldn't hack it in an institutional atmosphere and Harrow was a very institutionalised place because its purpose was to equip people to become part of the established institutions.'[100] Robin Ward, who had the room opposite Mark's in Bradbys House, agreed: 'He was a little different from the other boys in that he didn't fit into Harrow as smoothly as some . . . To be honest, Mark wasn't everybody's cup of tea. He had a very sort of confident and cocky manner, which was sometimes misplaced. He was not necessarily the sort of boy you'd expect to go to public school and he was never really gregarious with the other boys . . . A lot of boys there were a lot richer than he was. His background meant that maybe he felt that he had more to prove because of his humble origins. He did have a slightly unfortunate air about him in that he tended to upset people by his mannerisms. He did have a fairly quick wit, though.'[101]

Essentially, public schools are run on a collegiate, club-like basis, whereby loyalty to each other and abiding by the rules are more important than individual achievement. Mark was never clubbable. He was an outsider and his arrogant manner, social background and insecurities prevented him from being accepted. That is why he was never able to adapt, blend in and be truly happy at Harrow.

However, Mark was not an outcast and did have some friends. He was particularly close to Jonathan Prenn, former head of Lacoste Sportswear, and James Lepp, now a jeweller, but they refused to talk to the authors. One Old Harrovian contemporary, Philip Oppenheim, son of former Conservative minister Sally Oppenheim and later a Tory MP, is one of the few to have spoken well of him. Mark, he said, was 'a thoroughly nice chap'.[102] Others who knew him at school say he was pleasant enough on his own but his manner changed dramatically in a group of boys – a characteristic he retained in later life.

In Mark's defence, it is argued that his parents underestimated and misjudged the impact of their achievements on their children. 'It has been said to me that having two successful parents might put them [the twins] under a bit of pressure,' said Denis Thatcher while Mark was at Harrow. 'Their schoolmasters and schoolmistresses think so but I don't myself know that it's affected them, bless their little golden hearts. They certainly know what hard work means, there's no doubt about *that*' [his emphasis].[103]

In fact, the desire and underlying pressure to live up to his parents' expectations unquestionably did affect Mark. Although he developed a thick skin against mockery, Mark was never at ease and often on edge. 'He had a very hard time,' said Blamey, 'because he doesn't mix very well and is convinced that everyone is trying to rip him off. I'm sure that if I called him now – even if it was just to ask him to come to a school dinner – he would run a mile.'[104] 'He was very closed up as a personality,' recalls another old schoolmate. 'I would say he was almost neurotic. My abiding memory of him was that he used to run everywhere. "There goes Thatcher, running again," we used to say. He *always* ran everywhere, books under arm, head back, from lesson to lesson. Quite extraordinary.'

The one redeeming feature of Mark's time at Harrow was that he was a brilliant sportsman – an important quality at any public school. Encouraged by Denis, his prowess at games also made him more popular in his house. Mark excelled at racquets – a fast, dangerous game similar to squash but using a hard ball like a golf ball and special racquets. It is played mainly by wealthy people because the racquets break regularly and so new ones are frequently needed. 'Few people could afford to play,' said Robin Ward, 'and he seemed to be fairly well off because he once told me that he broke five racquets in one game.'[105]

Racquets is a game requiring skill, courage and fast reflexes. Mark was Harrow and national public schools champion with his friend Jonathan Prenn in his last year, 1970–71. His prowess was regularly chronicled in the school magazine, the *Old Harrovian*. One report also provided a hint of Mark's personality: 'Thatcher, who, as captain of racquets, has been outstandingly alert and capable, is as confident off the court as he is unpredictable on it. His game bears all the marks of an impromptu performance – shots beaten above, below and on to the board; last-second calls to his partner; expressions of disgust with himself or indignant queries to the referee. All this means that the result of a single rally, let alone that of the whole competition, is beyond the range of rational prediction.'[106]

Mark was also a very fine all-round cricketer. He was a member of Harrow's First XI two years running – no mean feat. In his last year, he was the team's fourth best batsman, amassing a total of 172 runs at an average of 15.63, with a top score of 51 not out. He was also a very useful spin bowler. His high point was playing against Eton at Lord's. Unfortunately, Mark would later spoil things by overstating the significance of his sporting record. 'I won something at the racquets championship,' he said. 'That gave me a discipline to set targets on an annual basis.'[107]

His sporting success pleased his father but his mother was not so impressed by Mark's academic record. He was more interested in cars than in books. 'He was considered by us to be a bit of a dunce, poor in classes and generally not very bright,' recalled Jan Kruse, now living in Spain.[108] Mark was not lazy, worked hard and wanted to please his mother, who was ambitious for him. But he just did not have an aptitude for the work and was nicknamed 'Thickie Mork'. In July 1969, he gained only three O levels – he had to retake them in November – and he later obtained only mediocre A levels. This was in contrast to his sister, Carol, who acquired seven O levels at the first attempt at St Paul's School for Girls. Mark's scholastic failure was a source of great disappointment to his mother, although she was careful to conceal it. 'Mark doesn't seem as academically ambitious as Carol,' she said at the time.[109]

Despite his sub-standard academic performance, Mark stayed on an extra term to study for Oxbridge. To the astonishment and disbelief of his fellow pupils, he said that he was offered a place at Keble College, Oxford. To this day, Old Harrovians are amazed that he qualified and achieved the required results. Neither Harrow nor Keble would provide any information about Mark Thatcher's academic performances. 'The Governors of Harrow have long had a policy of not releasing information about Old Harrovians and their achievements whilst at the school,' said the headmaster, N.R. Bomford.[110]

Mark decided not to take up his place at Keble. 'I think that Mummy and Daddy, in their heart of hearts, were terribly upset that one member of their family had chosen not to go to Oxford,' he said years later. 'But I thought I could use the time I would have spent at

Oxford better. Four years is a long time when you are 18. My parents do not force things through. Nor do they stride up to their children and say, "I told you so. Now you are in a mess, now you've got trouble." They simply told me, "You've thought about it and you've put forward a very good argument. If that is what you want to do, that is fine by us."[111]

Towards the end of his time at Harrow, Mark talked about being a professional sportsman. By then he had developed his interest in motor racing. 'I know that he wanted to become a racing driver or sportsman,' said John Pearson, who was in Mark's house and left school at the same time, 'but I'm certain his father and mother felt that he should get a professional qualification before getting into sport.'[112]

Mark does not have fond memories of his school years (although he later considered sending his son Michael to Harrow). Later, in 1993, he attended a stag-night dinner party for his fellow Old Harrovian Jonathan Prenn in a private room at Claridge's. Despite Prenn being a multimillionaire, Thatcher spent the entire evening looking glum during the speeches and barely spoke to any of the 30 guests. He has not been an active member of the Harrow Association and his response to a circular letter sent out in 1986, two years after he moved to Texas, did not endear him to Old Harrovians. The questionnaire asked for details of his school record and an up-to-date address. After a brief reference to his sporting achievements, Mrs Thatcher's son inserted as his address: '10 Downing Street, London SW1'.

THREE

Setting up Shop

But don't you know who I am? I am the prime minister's son.

– Mark Thatcher[1]

Mark left Harrow in July 1971 with a moderate academic record, a growing passion for motor sport and a keen desire to follow in his father's footsteps as a businessman. He talked to Denis about his career prospects and how to make money. 'I told Mark,' said Denis, 'if you want to run two houses and two motor cars, the only way you can do it is work.'[2]

Through his father's business connections, Mark went to Hong Kong. He worked as a trainee at the giant trading group Jardine Matheson there and then briefly at the company's South African subsidiary, Rennies. In October 1972, aged 19, he joined the stockbrokers Davis, Borkum and Hare, where he spent four months researching reports on the motor industry.

This 18-month period was clearly work experience, as in January 1973, Mark returned to England to train as a chartered accountant with Touche Ross. The move was very much part of his desire to follow in his father's footsteps. 'He was very keen to emulate his father in business,' said James Montagu, who knew Mark during his teens. 'That's why he tried to be an accountant, because Denis was a financial executive, knew all about balance sheets and had written a book on accountancy [*Accounting and Costing in the Paint Industry*], which he gave to my father [William Montagu].'[3]

Mark joined Touche Ross as a trainee in September 1973 at their

71

head office at 3 London Wall, near Moorgate in the City of London. His fellow trainees were surprised to see the education secretary's son, as the three-year course was strictly for graduates and Mark had not been to university. They argued that he could have gained entry only through the political or business influence of his parents. Mark saw his time at Touche Ross as a lay-by on the highway to wealth and fame, according to his fellow trainees. 'His general attitude was that the job didn't matter to him,' said Steve Brownson, a former Conservative councillor, who worked with him. 'He gave the impression that he was destined for greater things.'[4]

In the office, Mark was very aloof. He would drift in at 10 a.m. and often spend up to an hour on the phone, speaking to girlfriends or fixing up badminton games for that evening. After a leisurely lunch, he would wander back and check some audit figures. Former graduates can recall barely any conversations with him, apart from 'Pass that file'. He did not mix socially and would often sit alone in the common room in a corner reading a Frederick Forsyth novel.

Despite being paid only £1,500 a year, Mark seemed to have plenty of money. 'He used to carry a wad of £10 notes with him which he would peel off for taxi fares and expenses,' recalled one trainee. This was a curious observation as Mark later claimed, 'I haven't had a cent from them [his parents] since I was 21.'[5] This presumably meant his allowance was cut off midway through his course.

The overriding impression of Margaret Thatcher's son at Touche Ross was that he was 'a law unto himself', said Steve Brownson. This was reflected in his attitude towards the work. As part of the course, Mark worked on the audits of specific companies under the supervision of a group manager. One task was to calculate how much tax a firm was due to pay. He was told by his tax supervisor that he would need to present his results by 4.30 p.m. on the Friday. 'I can't be here on Friday afternoon,' replied Mark. 'I'm flying off to South Africa for an important business trip.' The manager and his colleagues were stunned into silence by the offhand way in which he spoke. But this became a regular occurrence, as Mark would often leave early on a Friday afternoon, saying he needed to catch a 4 p.m. flight from Heathrow. He said it was for 'business' but by 1975 it was more likely to be racing practice. On 21 July 1975, Mark told his manager he was ill and needed the day off. His boss was not amused to open the newspaper the next day and see a photograph of Mrs Thatcher's son taking a brilliant diving catch in the Commons v. the MCC cricket match at Hurlingham Club in Fulham.

While Mark's accountancy career was declining and in some jeopardy, his mother's political career was rocketing. On Tuesday, 11 February 1975, Margaret Thatcher was dramatically elected leader of the Conservative Party. Her son heard the news while he was at Touche Ross. It was a historic victory and a celebration party was held that night at the flat of William Shelton, a Tory MP and her main backer, in Pimlico. Mark attended and struck up a conversation with Airey Neave, her campaign manager. 'You realise that overnight you have been elevated to the superhuman league,' said Neave.

'Oh, I don't think so,' replied Mark.

'Overnight, everybody has far higher expectations of you,' Neave insisted.[6]

It was a prophetic comment but rather lost in the joviality of the occasion as the champagne flowed. Outside Shelton's flat, reporters were waiting eagerly for a comment from Margaret Thatcher as she left for the evening. One of them was Norman Luck, the award-winning *Daily Express* journalist. Luck had brought his precious white Fiat 850 car, which he had recently repaired and renovated with great care and affection. He parked across the street, behind an Audi belonging to Denis Thatcher, and joined the shivering reporters.

When Margaret, Denis, Carol and Mark finally emerged late that night, they posed briefly for photographs (characteristically, Carol kept out of the limelight while Mark courted it). But the new Tory leader refused to say anything to the assembled media. Much to the reporters' frustration, the family bundled into the Audi. But instead of driving away, Denis, who had been celebrating with some vigour for the past 45 minutes, reversed straight into the back of Norman Luck's beloved Fiat. Luck was beside himself. 'Look what you've done to my car,' he shouted at Denis. Suddenly Mark leapt out of the rear seat and approached him. 'I'm sorry but I'm sure we can sort this out,' he said. 'Dad's had a few and we don't want to get the police involved, do we?' But Luck was fuming and wanted to call the police. Eventually, Mark persuaded him to change his mind. 'Look, I'll have a quick chat with Mum and she'll give you a quote,' he said. 'Here's my card. Let's get together.'

The next day Luck telephoned Mark Thatcher at his Touche Ross office and they met for lunch. The journalist found the son of the new Tory Party leader an agitated, intense young man, lacking in confidence and unable to relax. He told Luck he was keen to secure a favourable public profile for himself. The conversation was hardly profound, as Mark talked mainly about his girlfriends. 'I suppose people will start trying to marry me off,' he said. 'It makes no difference whether I live in Chelsea or if we move into 10 Downing Street. I know the type of girl I am looking for.' That afternoon, Luck wrote a story which was published the next day: 'Overnight, Mark Thatcher has become one of Britain's eligible bachelors'.[7]

The Tory leader's son was a good contact for Luck, so they met regularly. They set up a secret arrangement whereby Mark would telephone the reporter the day before he was taking out a girl so he could be waiting there with a *Daily Express* photographer. Then Luck would telephone the barman late at night and Mark and his girlfriend would leave the nightspot, often Annabel's, and she would be shocked to find her picture being taken. This started barely ten days after Margaret Thatcher's accession to the leadership, when Mark took Maryon Gill, a 20-year-old student nurse, to Mirabelle's for dinner. As they arrived at the restaurant, there were Norman Luck and photographer Tom Smith waiting. The next day, 'Only in the *Express*', the story began: 'Handsome Mark Thatcher, snowed under with fan mail since his mother became Tory leader, last night revealed his "Cinderella" romance with a student nurse.'[8]

Two days later, Mark telephoned Luck when he took out Caroline Lepp, the 17-year-old sister of James, whom he had known at Harrow. 'Mark wanted me to smooth his image,' recalled Luck. 'He loved being in the papers and lapped up the attention. He liked being in with journalists and would call me the day after the story appeared and say thank you. He loved the publicity. It was only when things got tough later on that he started hating journalists.'[9]

The delicious irony of Mark Thatcher consorting with tabloid newshounds was not lost on Peter Tory, then the *Daily Express* diarist. 'He used to lounge around the old William Hickey office and supply rather weak gossip about other politicians,' said Tory.[10] He also continued to supply the paper with a running account of his own love life – 'Mark's Coalition with a New Girl'.[11]

While Mark merrily continued secretly to feed and cooperate with the *Daily Express*, publicly he complained about invasions of privacy. 'When she was elected, it was a source of very great pride to me – God, I can't tell you how proud I was,' he said in 1978. 'The press, however, had found a new toy for a couple of months and I soon learnt that I had to be very careful. One evening I went to a restaurant with some friends and took along a girl who I'd known for some time. Afterwards, we went on somewhere else for coffee and I picked up the first editions of the newspapers. Wham! I was horror struck, there on the front page was a large picture of myself and this girl walking into the restaurant. Of course she did her nut and I can't blame her.'[12]

Despite her busy parliamentary schedule, Margaret Thatcher found time to monitor her son's phone calls because she wanted to know about his girlfriends. She was particularly concerned about a Romanian girl and occasionally withheld money to prevent him spending it on ambitious young women. Mark was a very young 23-year-old and for years later would bring his laundry home. A friend recalls a party that he hosted in the mid-1970s one night at home in Flood Street. The rooms were dominated by paintings, photographs and statues of the new Tory leader. During the evening Mark took a phone call. 'Yes, Mummy, no Mummy, thank you Mummy, no we're all right Mummy', he kept saying. 'I presume that was Mummy', said the friend when he escaped from the phone. 'Yes, she wants to check that we have everything we need and if she could come round and help.'

During the aftermath of his mother's triumph, Mark began contemplating its implications. 'For the first six or seven months after it happened,' he later reflected, 'I used to think, "What makes me so special to be the son of the Leader of the Opposition? I've done nothing to deserve it, nothing at all." I realised that suddenly I was in a different league, where I was expected to behave in a certain way otherwise I'd get crucified by the world outside. So I try and fulfil other people's expectations of me.'[13]

At first, he even talked about a political career. In May 1975, he delivered a speech to the Hendon Rotary Club and Chamber of Commerce on 'Freedom of Choice and the Common Market', as it was just before the referendum on whether Britain should remain in the EEC. 'Mother will probably see my speech,' he said. 'She has given me a lot of encouragement but it really is all my own work.'[14] Later on, he speculated about applying to be on the official list of prospective Tory candidates at Central Office but nothing came of it.[15]

When asked about a political career, Mark never ruled it out but said, 'I had other priorities.'[16] But he used to boast about knowing what was happening inside government. 'He told me he was involved in helping to draft his mother's speeches and advising her on her campaigns,' said Nick Faure, who knew Mark during his motor-racing career. 'It sounded like bravura and bluster, and I didn't believe him.'[17] Mark's political ambitions were 'pure fantasy', according to one of his closest friends. 'He knew nothing about politics and it was the one area where she would not have taken him seriously. It was the kind of thing he said to impress girlfriends.' This seemed to be confirmed by Mark himself when he said in 1991, 'It was never suggested that I should go into politics.'[18]

In April 1976, after failing his Intermediate and Part One accountancy examinations, Mark went to Manchester for a six-week crash course to prepare for his retakes. He was happy that the course was in Lancashire because he genuinely believed that people north of Watford were more stupid and hence he would have a better chance of passing. 'The grades and marks are always lower outside of London,' he said soon after his arrival at the London School of Accountancy, a firm of private tutors. This did not endear him to his new colleagues, who found him haughty and pompous. 'He thought he was royalty,' recalled a fellow trainee who sat behind him in class. 'The first time I saw him he was on the telephone. He turned to me and said, "Be a good chap, get me a coffee," as if I was some kind of servant . . . He was a terrible name-dropper and always bragging about going through the VIP lounge at the airport on his way to some motor-racing event in Paris or Frankfurt.'

Mark's colleagues remember him as always being on the telephone and asking inept questions in a loud voice – a far cry from his surly, taciturn presence at Touche Ross two years earlier. 'There are two kinds of people that sit in the front of the class – the bright ones and the gobby ones. He was a gobby one,' recalled the trainee who sat next to him throughout the six weeks. 'He behaved as if he knew better than anyone else. He used to turn round and lecture the class. If the lecturer was making a point, Thatcher would turn round and explain it loudly. The problem was that he was thick, quite frankly, and so he would often get it wrong.'

The lecturers were also irritated by this habit. During one seminar a tutor was discussing one of the questions in the previous examination. 'Yeah, it was *simple*,' interrupted Mark (his emphasis). 'Why did you fail, then?' responded the lecturer, quick as a flash, who clearly enjoyed humiliating him.

Mark's behaviour reflected an arrogance beyond his 23 years. It was based more on his perceived newly inherited 'status' as the son of the Leader of the Opposition than on any mature self-confidence. 'He just thought he was better than us and was destined for higher things,' said a fellow trainee who is now a successful accountant. 'That was quite ironic, really, because there were six of us in the front row of the class. Five of us passed and he didn't.' The reason for his failure was self-evident – he did not work but spent most of his time planning his racing excursions. After an initial flurry of enthusiasm, his lack of diligence became apparent when he walked out of tests halfway through, unable to answer all the questions.

Despite this disappointment, Mark Thatcher soldiered on and eventually passed his Intermediate and Part One examinations at the third attempt. The next year, he sat Part Two of his finals but was unsuccessful as he passed three but failed two of the exams. For his retakes, he was sent to the Financial Training Company, a firm of accountancy lecturers whose deputy chairman was the convivial Jeremy Hanley, later Tory MP for Richmond and Barnes and former chairman of the Conservative Party. 'I taught Mark Thatcher and I found him extremely hard-working, pleasant and energetic,' said Hanley, then the adopted parliamentary candidate for Lambeth Central.[19] Despite passing the exam taught by Hanley, Mark again failed his finals.

Shortly after he received his results, Mark invited Hanley over to Flood Street to discuss his future with his mother. The budding Conservative candidate advised that her son should continue his accountancy studies and try again in six months' time. Margaret Thatcher agreed. 'She wanted him to continue because she was very keen for him to have a professional qualification,' recalled Hanley. Mark disagreed and felt he did not need to pass his finals to make his way in the business world.

His professional prospects were left unresolved at the end of the meeting. But privately Mark had already decided to quit accountancy because by early 1977 he told friends he was already receiving potential business offers and keen to launch his motor-racing career. A month later, he called it a day and left Touche Ross.

Margaret was not pleased with the outcome but hardly condemnatory. 'You know, the trouble with Mark is he just can't pass exams,' she said at the time.[20] 'Margaret was disappointed that he did not qualify and regretted it,' said a former cabinet minister. 'She would have liked him to pass but just thought that whatever he did was right.' Denis was much more dejected. 'Failing to complete his accountancy studies was the thing that disappointed him most,' said a former Tory minister and a close friend of Mark's father. 'He was unhappy that Mark did not have a serious professional career or occupation.'

Mark's unhappy period as a trainee accountant later returned to haunt him. Five weeks after his mother became prime minister, in

June 1979, a press statement was released, announcing Mark's participation in a charity motor race at Brands Hatch. It stated that he 'returned to this country in 1973 to commence his chartered accountancy studies, qualifying in 1977'.[21] After the press handout was delivered, the radio news bulletins described him as 'a chartered accountant', a term which newspapers had used for some years. This, of course, was misleading but remained uncorrected, much to the fury of his Touche Ross colleagues who had passed their exams. Even the prime minister's office was economical with the *actualité*. 'Yes, he is an accountant but he is not fully qualified,' said a spokesperson in 1979. 'He works as an accountant but it is not technically correct to call him a chartered accountant.'[22]

While he was still at Touche Ross, Mark devoted a considerable amount of time to his first love, motor racing. For many years he had set his heart on racing as his career and he drove in several races in South Africa. 'My mother is a little apprehensive about my ambitions to be a top-class racing driver but she respects my judgement and would not stand in my way,' he said at the time.[23] In fact, Margaret Thatcher was never keen on his chosen career. She had never been interested in cars and always saw them as a means of transport rather than recreation. However, it was during his early attempts to establish his driving credentials that he met Stephen Tipping – later his most important business partner and confidant during the Downing Street years.

Stephen William Tipping was born in Deal on the Kent coast on 27 October 1951. His father, Geoffrey Tipping, was a sergeant in the Royal Marines. After leaving the Marines, Geoffrey had an assortment of jobs, from taxi driver to antiques dealer. He also stood unsuccessfully as a Conservative candidate in local elections. Steve spent most of his early years in Dover, Kent. The Tippings are a close family of dealers and traders, and Steve was no exception. He started out working in the family garage and filling-station business, Monteagle Motors Ltd, in Yateley, near Camberley, Surrey.

Steve's passion was motor racing and that is how he met Mark Thatcher. A racing driver from the age of 19, Tipping competed in the Super Vee Class, a similar category to Formula Three and established by Volkswagen. In 1973, he came third in the championship, collecting £1,000 in prize money. But he was always handicapped by lack of funds and back-up staff.

The following year, Tipping was competing in Zolder, Holland, when he was forced to change the tyres by himself during the race. So he advertised in *Motor Sport* for a mechanic and within a few days Mark Thatcher telephoned to apply for the job. Mark was not qualified and pretended he knew more than he did. Tipping soon realised this but was won over by his boyish enthusiasm. And so Mark became Tipping's mechanic. More importantly, the two became firm friends. Tipping admired Mark's middle-class, public-school self-confidence, while Thatcher liked Steve's streetwise business savvy and sense of humour. It was the beginning of a close friendship and a happy business partnership, which later led to Thatcher being godfather to Tipping's son, named, appropriately, Mark. They also shared a fanatical enthusiasm for motor sport.

In March 1975, Tipping and Thatcher decided to step up their racing careers. They launched Mark Thatcher Racing, originally to compete in Formula Three but ultimately intended to propel them into the big time. However, they soon realised they needed £20,000 sponsorship cash for the season. So they placed an advertisement with a box number in *Autosport* asking for fundraisers. They recruited Nigel Hart, a 20-year-old biochemistry student and racing enthusiast, who met Tipping in his flat in Yateley, Surrey. 'They wanted me to find sponsorship and raise money,' recalled Hart. 'I worked for them on the basis that if I got the sponsorship I would receive a percentage. I then wrote a number of letters to companies on specially headed notepaper which used his mother's name by implication rather than directly.'[24]

The basic idea was to offer companies guaranteed press coverage by ensuring their name would be blazoned across Mark Thatcher's car. 'The deal was that we would offer certain newspapers special inside information about Mark Thatcher Racing with photographs on an exclusive basis,' Hart told us. 'This would give an incentive for companies to sponsor us because they knew they were getting press coverage out of it. We were acting like a public relations agency for ourselves but it didn't work out because I don't think the companies were convinced about it.'[25]

One company Mark approached was London Rubber, manufacturers of the contraceptive Durex. He wrote to them asking for sponsorship but the marketing director, Mike Broadbridge, was not impressed by his application. 'Our venture into Formula One racing was very successful,' said Broadbridge, 'so we decided the next step should be to sponsor young drivers with winning potential. We decided, however, that Mark Thatcher did not really fit into that category . . . Durex is such an emotional product. We didn't want to get in a political hassle with the Leader of the Opposition or future prime minister.'[26]

The firm Mark used to promote his sponsorship drive was CSS Promotions Ltd, a sports marketing and PR agency that specialised in motor racing. A successful and effective company, their activities included promoting Marlboro cigarettes in Grand Prix racing and representing the late James Hunt, then world champion, and Mario Andretti.

For Mark, motor sport was almost like a release from the tensions of his life. 'I found a thrill in driving a racing car that I had not experienced before,' he said later. 'I felt completely comfortable in it and driving it. It is something you have either got – or you haven't. A racing car is where I feel at home. When I am racing there is a sort of metronome in my brain. As it goes faster and faster, my brain says, "Be careful, you need to watch this" and "Look out for that." . . . I find motor racing a form of relaxation. I take three or four days off every few weeks and do something totally different from my normal business life. Racing flushes all those other problems out of your mind.'[27]

As regards his career prospects, Mark saw racing as 'a very serious hobby . . . I approach it very seriously and it's something I enjoy doing very much, but that's as far as it goes.'[28] He considered himself 'a gifted amateur'[29] but believed he was capable of being a high-calibre driver. 'I have a well-developed competitive sense,' he said. 'I am hungry, ambitious and competitive.'[30] All he needed was financial backing and this could be obtained by high-powered media promotion for himself and potential sponsors. That was why CSS Promotions were hired, on an ad hoc basis. 'It was fairly obvious that he wanted publicity and to get known because he could not get sponsorship,' recalled a former senior CSS director.[31]

Mark Thatcher Racing lasted just over two years. It failed because Mark and Steve Tipping were unable to persuade major sponsors to provide enough cash. 'They wouldn't sponsor him because he just wasn't good enough,' said a former CSS director. That is a harsh judgement, according to Andrew Marriott, the former CSS commercial director. 'It was much more complex than that,' he said. 'Some companies were a little afraid to sponsor him because it would appear too overt an attempt at currying favour with the government.'

And so in the summer of 1977, Tipping and Thatcher temporarily went their separate ways. Tipping decided to become 'an entrepreneur' and set up his own trading company, SW Tipping (UK) Ltd. Based at the back of his house in Yateley, it was essentially an import–export business. His chief interest was the printing and selling of T-shirts through a chain of companies – Wizard Design Ltd, Go-Gear (London) Ltd and Biscotin Ltd. Within two years he was importing 250,000 T-shirts a year from Europe and Hong Kong, as well as buying from British wholesalers.

Tipping also became a director of Hudson Armoured Car Security Services Ltd (intended as a UK base for an American company but never incorporated), Caterland Ltd (selling gas-fired barbecues from Dallas into the UK), and Daco Office Equipment Ltd (a furniture, equipment and stationery company). These were all potentially highly profitable enterprises but they eventually collapsed.

In the meantime, Mark was struggling. He was unemployed and his racing career was in neutral. Then, in the autumn of 1977, he secured a job in a Manchester jewellery shop owned by L.J. Jewellery Import Ltd, part of the Lepp chain of companies based in Altrincham, Cheshire. Mark was hired because he was friendly with John Lepp, who had introduced him to motor racing, and his nephew Jamie Lepp, who had been at Harrow with him in the mid-1960s.[32]

The Lepp family became fabulously wealthy as manufacturers and wholesalers of upmarket luxury jewellery. L.J. Jewellery Import Ltd was owned by Sessna Holdings Ltd, incorporated in the Isle of Man, and their offshore connections were strengthened when Jim Lepp, Jamie's father, moved to Guernsey in 1977. Now retired and still living on the Channel Island, Jim Lepp would talk to the authors only if he received remuneration. 'How much are you going to pay me?' he said. We refused.

John Lepp, a lifelong friend of the Thatchers, declined to talk to the authors without Mark's permission. His reluctance is perhaps not surprising given the uneven progress of his company. In 1986, John Lepp sold his Altrincham shop to J.T. Cottrill and Sons Ltd, another successful Cheshire jeweller at the time.

Mark, then 24, was a sales manager of one of their wholesale jewellery shops and did some on-the-road selling. He was an enthusiastic worker. 'He was a very good salesman,' said his former boss, Anthony Kliger, who visited Asprey's and Garrard with young Thatcher in tow. 'If he had kept at it, he could have made his mark. I think it might have been beneficial for him if he had stayed in the business. However, his eyes were on higher things.'[33]

Another businessman who knew him at the time was Clive

Kandell, who had a shop on the King's Road, Chelsea, and introduced Mark to his Romanian girlfriend. One day the Opposition leader's son walked in and introduced himself. 'I'm selling jewellery,' he said. 'I live round the corner, so I can always come in and see you. The name's Thatcher.' 'You mean you're related to her?' asked Kandell. 'Yes,' replied Mark. The Chelsea businessman eventually bought jewellery from the keen young rep but was irritated by his aggressive sales pitch.

However, the jewellery job was a sideshow. Mark Thatcher's mind was always on motor racing and he left in the summer of 1978, barely nine months into the job. Those late summer and early autumn months saw him at his lowest ebb. He had no career prospects. He was often seen engrossed in *Motoring Weekly* but his racing prospects were bleak. Even his decision not to go to university was under question. 'There were times, say two years ago, when I thought I had made the wrong decision,' he said in 1980.[34]

Despite his anxiety, he remained full of bravado with people. Sarah Standing, who twice went out to dinner with him during this period, recorded her impressions in her diary: 'Mark means well and seems a nice enough man, but alas, it's all "me, me, me" and his dialogue is riddled with brash boasts. On being top dog. On naming prices and then on securing a "money-no-object" image. He is what used to be considered a playboy but at the same time he says he deplores the term. Uses words like "honking" a lot and calls his mother "Mummy" all the time.'[35]

Carol Thatcher, in the meantime, was prospering. In January 1978, she left England for Melbourne, Australia, after completing her legal training, and worked for Peter Jansen, a flamboyant and wealthy New Zealand businessman and socialite with interests ranging from goldmining to motor racing and horses. 'Carol was wonderful,' recalled Jansen. 'She was highly intelligent and the hardest worker I ever employed. I have the highest respect for her.'[36] She also later worked on a cattle ranch, as a journalist on the *Sydney Morning Herald* and for a television current affairs programme. 'I loved Australia,' she said later. 'I was my own person – rather than my mother's daughter.'[37] But her hostility towards her twin brother remained. Whenever his name cropped up in conversation, she would say, 'Oh, yes,' and change the subject abruptly.

It was Carol who inadvertently rescued Mark from his latest crisis. At a dinner party in Sydney hosted by Peter Jansen she met Gordon

Barton, chairman of the International Parcel Express Corporation (IPEC), a highly successful Australian conglomerate with interests in transport, property, insurance, publishing and hotels. Barton was impressed by Carol and he became a friend of the Thatcher family.

In the summer of 1978, Gordon Barton was invited by Margaret Thatcher for Sunday lunch at their Kent retreat near Lamberhurst. Just before lunch, Denis Thatcher approached Gordon Barton when Margaret was out of earshot. 'I don't know what I'm going to do about the boy,' he said, exasperated.

'Well, if I can help you I will,' replied Barton.

'If there is anything you can do, I would be most grateful,' said Denis.

According to one of the other guests present, 'Denis made it crystal clear, without actually using the precise words, that Mark was a problem and needed a job to settle him down.'

Barton did not have a vacancy at the time but an opportunity arose three months later when he commissioned a feasibility study into launching IPEC in Europe. The IPEC chairman needed freight depots in European ports, so he thought this was the moment to give Mark a job, as he planned to set up a British base.

At the time, the Barton family happened to be on holiday driving around Europe in their luxury Mercedes Sedan. When they reached Rome, Gordon Barton saw an ideal opportunity for Mark to learn the business from Ron Devonish, a rough, tough Australian brought over to do the feasibility study. The Mercedes needed to be returned to London while the Bartons flew on to Greece and then back to Australia, so Gordon suggested that Mark Thatcher and Ron Devonish drive the car back to London together and discuss their forthcoming business project during the journey.

Within barely fifty miles it was clear the two travellers did not get on. In fact, they hated each other. Known as 'the Rock Spider' to his colleagues back in Australia, Devonish was a no-nonsense, take-no-prisoners Aussie, who bristled when Mark wittered on endlessly about the saintly qualities of 'Mummy'. Also, Mark drove as if he were competing at Brands Hatch. By the time they reached Switzerland, Devonish could stand it no longer. He baled out of the car and told Margaret Thatcher's son he could drive the rest of the way alone while he, Devonish, flew back to London. However, the trip went from bad to worse when Mark crashed the Mercedes in Amsterdam and the car was wrecked.

Despite this inauspicious start, Devonish and Thatcher set up an office in the Bartons' London apartment in Three Kings Yard, just behind Claridge's Hotel in Mayfair. It was a curious setting for a feasibility study into a new transport company. The flat was emerald-green, with green walls and carpets, and had previously been used by Lord Lambton, the infamous Conservative defence minister, to entertain prostitutes in the early 1970s.

Mark was basically a gofer and office boy for Devonish. But the Tory leader's son saw his job in a rather grander light. 'I am to be the London representative of a Far East firm with a very large annual turnover,' he announced to the *Daily Express* in October 1978.[38] 'I'm working for a Far East conglomerate whose head comes over here five or six times a year,' he told the *Daily Mail*. 'Getting the job had absolutely nothing to do with who my mother is.'[39]

However, according to former senior IPEC managers, his duties were far less glamorous. 'He was employed as a runner, which basically meant doing research when we were planning to acquire a new company,' a former IPEC executive told us. 'My impression was that he thought the job was beneath him and he should have been higher up in the company. He also seemed more interested in what new car he was racing than working for us.'

Mark was a competent employee but he was constantly trying to use his mother's position as Leader of the Opposition. On several occasions when IPEC executives discussed the problems of moving freight quickly and dealing with government agencies like Customs, Mark said, 'Don't worry, Mummy can plug us in there.' According to an IPEC manager who was present, the company saw this as naive and ham-fisted as well as wrong.

It was not long before Ron 'the Rock Spider' Devonish, his immediate boss, had the boy's measure. One day an IPEC executive walked into the office to witness a sight which is forever imprinted on his memory. Devonish was sprawled across the sofa with a can of Fosters in his hand, barking out orders in his best Aussie drawl. Mark was standing by a blackboard and writing out what 'the Rock Spider' called 'Thatcher's Ten Commandments'. Among the most prominent was 'Thou Shall Not Mention or Use Thy Mother's Name In Vain!!'

In early 1979, IPEC was looking for a European services branch and bought Sayer Transport Ltd, a highly successful trucking firm, for £3.5 million. Mark became personal assistant to Ian Sayer, the 26-year-old founder of the company, and continued his job as a 'runner', driving around the country inspecting IPEC haulage depots.

Sayer, who was known to be an avid collector of Nazi memorabilia, was impressed by his assistant's connections and the two men became friends. He went to drinks parties at Flood Street and Thatcher stayed at his house on the Wentworth golf estate. But he later became a sharp critic. 'If Mark's mother wasn't prime minister, he wouldn't be anything,' he said many years later. 'In a way you could describe him as a second-rate Arthur Daley.'[40] Sayer now says he cannot recall anything about Mark's work for him until the 1979 general election. 'Everything changed after Mrs Thatcher became prime minister,' he told us.

Margaret Thatcher's victory at the 1979 general election was the pivotal moment in Mark's life. At the time, he was walking a treadmill at IPEC-Sayer, expending a lot of energy but not going anywhere. During the campaign itself, he accompanied his mother occasionally, trailing after her almost like an appendage to her retinue. He dutifully appeared at set-piece rallies but did not make much impression. 'Nobody took much notice of him,' a senior former Tory Central Office official told us. 'He just did not have the personality. All I can remember is that he would make excessive demands like always wanting to be in the lead group of cars.'

Unlike Carol, who had returned from Australia to work on her mother's campaign, Mark was only sporadically involved. 'I shall go out with her at strategic times,' he said.[41] 'I'm canvassing about two nights a week and at weekends but I won't be speaking.'[42] Instead, he continued to work at IPEC-Sayer, although there was an embarrassing incident on the evening of 23 April 1979, when he was noticed at a Mayfair casino. 'I really shouldn't be here,' Margaret's son said, nervously looking around. 'I came with a business associate who is a member.'[43]

On election night, Thursday, 4 May 1979, Mark appeared briefly in his mother's constituency at Finchley town hall for the count and then drove home to 19 Flood Street, Chelsea, to watch the results on television. At the moment when Alastair Burnet announced on ITN that the Tories had secured an absolute majority in the Commons, Mark recalled Airey Neave's remark four years earlier when Margaret Thatcher became Tory Party leader: 'You realise that overnight you have been elevated to the superhuman league.'[44] And as the news that his mother was to be prime minister sank in, Mark became more emotional. 'I sat there inwardly crying for joy for her,' he said. 'I remember going up to her, almost bursting into tears, and saying . . . well, *how* do you say what you feel when a member of your family is elected to the highest position in the land? You are speechless, it is unbelievable' [his emphasis].[45]

At noon the next day, Friday, 5 May, Mark, Carol and Denis accompanied the new premier to Conservative Central Office to celebrate the victory with champagne and slices of a huge chocolate cake made in the shape of the 10 Downing Street door. After lunch, the Thatcher family retired to Margaret's office to await the summons from Buckingham Palace. Denis was dozing quietly when the telephone call came through from Sir Philip Moore, the Queen's private secretary. Margaret took the call in another room and then reappeared. 'Right, we're off,' she said briskly. Denis straightened his tie. Mark put his arms around his mother and said, 'prime minister'. 'Not yet, dear,' replied Margaret. 'The car may break down,' suggested Denis helpfully.[46]

As they walked downstairs, Mark strode ahead and opened the door of the car which drove Mrs Thatcher to Buckingham Palace to be 'invited' by the Queen to form a government. A smiling son ushered his mother into the car and patted his father on the back as he got into the back seat. 'Opening that door was the proudest moment of my life,' he said later. 'I have a photograph of it. It's my greatest treasure.'[47]

The implications of being the son of the prime minister were not lost on young Thatcher. Three days after the election, on 7 May 1979, the address on some letters arriving at his office was scratched out and marked, 'Redirect to Penthouse Flat, 10 Downing Street'. He also began receiving dozens of telephone calls from 'friends' and people he barely knew.[48] But his mind was on other matters.

Mark's master plan, once his mother was ensconced in 10 Downing Street, was graphically spelt out to a Thatcherite minister at a drinks reception soon after the election. The minister, one of the original eight disciples who orchestrated Mrs Thatcher's Tory Party leadership triumph in 1975, was standing next to Denis and Margaret when their son commented, 'I have set myself a target. I want to make a million by the time I am 30.' The expressions on the faces of the premier and her consort barely flickered. But the minister, who would serve in the government for six years, was stunned and looked across at Charles Price, then the US ambassador in London who was equally startled and later recorded the remark in a telegram to the State Department. 'When he [Mark] said that, I thought to myself, "To do that you need to remove a few fingers from people's hands," recalled the minister.

Amputation of businessmen's fingers was not quite what Mark had in mind. But he was keen to set up his version of Mark Thatcher Enterprises. 'I had always known what I wanted,' he said later. 'Success in business, to be as successful as both Mummy and Daddy had been. They helped – we have always been a close, helping, caring family – but I haven't had a cent off them since I was 21.'[49]

His commercial outlet was launched six weeks after the election, when Mark Thatcher set up a business partnership with his best friend, Stephen Tipping. On 19 June 1979, Monteagle Marketing (London) Ltd was incorporated as a 'marketing consultancy company'. It acted as 'marketing consultants and agents for and on behalf of any person, firm or company in respect of any goods or services whether in the UK or abroad'.[50] Within a week, international businessmen were expressing interest. On 30 June, Mark flew by Concorde from Switzerland to New York and then by private jet to Greenville, South Carolina, for a lunch reception with local businessmen. They believed his presence was a 'business booster'.[51]

Mark formally became a director of Monteagle Marketing on 9 August 1979, describing himself as a 'company director'. Tipping was chairman and joined the board on 8 October 1979, as 'a managing executive'.[52] The next day, the first day of that year's Tory Party conference, the company commenced trading. Mark owned 99 per cent of the shares with Tipping retaining 1 per cent. The company's closeness to Margaret Thatcher herself was illustrated by the fact that they shared the same accountant: Philip J. Gee of Lithgow and Nelson, a relatively small firm based at 127 Clerkenwell Road, London EC1. Gee is also a trustee of the Margaret Thatcher Charitable Trust.

Monteagle Marketing was a very low-key, secretive operation. At first, the premier's son refused to disclose even basic details about the company – its name, his business partner, its location, how many people he employed (one) or even its general nature. It even had an ex-directory telephone number. Based at Forge Court, Yateley, Surrey, the office was in a converted seventeenth-century coaching house and consisted of a tiny reception area and one first-floor office used by Mark, Steve and Brenda Sanger, the company secretary.

During the company's infant months, the atmosphere inside the office was one of frenetic activity. Mark and Steve conducted business as if every day were their last. 'They were always rushing around,' a business associate told us. 'Steve in particular was very manic and intense. They have both calmed down now but I would guess that's because they have made all their money.' There was also a feeling that they had a limited amount of time, because in the early years it was unclear for how long Margaret Thatcher was going to be prime minister. 'I remember Steve telling me that we've only got about five years before she goes,' said a former director of one of Tipping's companies.

Some – but not much – money flowed in initially, as Tipping and Thatcher paid themselves an annual salary of only £10,000 each, although that was far from derisory by 1979 standards. 'Mark opened the doors on the deals,' said a source who worked in the office at the time. 'It was always known that he did not have the business acumen and so Steve sorted out the detail and the nuts and bolts.' This was, in effect, confirmed by Mark: 'He [Tipping] watches the shop while I am away and I trust him implicitly. I consider that I have many weaknesses, so he stands right behind me and tells me when he thinks I'm going wrong.'[53] A former business associate, Paul Carter, confirmed the relationship. 'Steve was the front man for Mark, who was paranoid about not being linked directly to their deals and he rarely told his father what he was up to,' he recalled. 'Mark told me that if I was speaking to Steve, it was the same as talking to him.'

Monteagle Marketing had various functions. Essentially, it was a conduit for Mark Thatcher and Tipping to be marketing agents, middlemen and consultants for corporations. Or, as one wit later quipped, 'an upmarket sandwich board'.[54] This description was, inadvertently, confirmed by Brenda Sanger, Thatcher's personal assistant and the company secretary. She said Monteagle's work was commercial 'catering'. 'By catering, we mean knowing the right people. Somebody who knows somebody who can put them in touch with somebody else,' she said.[55] It also exported British luxury cars and there was an associate firm, Monteagle International, which consulted on property deals, notably a shop and office complex in Southampton. 'The services are not desperately sophisticated,' a spokesperson for one of their future clients, Cementation International Ltd, commented.[56]

Mark saw the company in a more grandiose light. He said Monteagle specialised in 'turn-key' operations: 'Turn-key means that, for example, if a prospective buyer needs a cement plant, I will go along with my clients, persuade them that we are the people they need, then design, finance, build, train their staff and run it until an agreed takeover date. Then, all they have to do is turn the key and walk into a ready-made concern. It's the sort of thing I had always wanted to do. I had to wait for the right opportunity and when it came along, I grabbed it. I own the company, pay the wages and generate the income.'[57]

However, former business associates who spent time in the Monteagle office, though not employed there, cannot recall any clients that fit this description. Instead, they say, Mark and Tipping were spending most of their time abroad, mainly in hotels in Zurich. Mark confirmed this. 'I don't have to stay in this country to earn my living. All my marketing consultancy business is overseas,' he said in February 1980. 'I can do it from the south of France, central Europe, the Middle East or Hong Kong.'[58]

As a company, Monteagle was never the enterprise Mark hoped it would be. It was consistently late in filing annual accounts and financial returns, once only just avoiding prosecution after repeated warnings from Companies House. The accounts showed either small pre-tax profits or that losses and liabilities exceeded assets. It was a long, long way from being the respected family firm that his father, Denis, had nurtured.

FOUR

Racing Days

The episode [Mark getting lost in the desert] did have one benefit. We could relax a little, for Mark had hung an occupied sign on the family's 'embarrassing relative' slot.
– Carol Thatcher[1]

His mother's ascendancy to the premiership not only transformed Mark's business interests but also revived his flagging racing career. Margaret Thatcher never shared her son's fascination with fast cars and privately was horrified by his racing ambitions. But, as with almost everything he did, she could never bring herself to ask him to stop. 'Mum's a bit worried about me,' said Mark, 'but that's a mother's natural protective instinct. When I told her I was going to race she said, "Are you sure you know what you're doing?" But she didn't try to talk me out of it. She trusts my judgement and ability.'[2]

Two weeks after the 1979 general election, Mark Thatcher Racing was revived and he began training at Brands Hatch racing school. He made his debut on 10 June, racing a ShellSport Sunbeam Ti to victory in the annual Commons v. Lords race. Under the tutelage of John Webb, head of motor-circuit developments at Brands Hatch and Oulton Park, Mark's career suddenly took off. He acquired two important sponsors, Marlboro cigarettes and Playboy Toiletries For Men, whose maroon and gold livery he displayed on his racing overalls and car.

Mark's first major international race was in September 1979, when he competed in the seven-hour Hardie Ferodo 1,000-km road race around the 6-km Mount Panorama circuit in New South Wales, Australia. It was also his first major spot of controversy. The trouble started on 17 September at Heathrow, when he boarded a JAL flight to Tokyo en route to Australia. 'Get the Japan Airlines bag in the picture. They've given me a good deal,' Thatcher snapped at photographers at the airport. 'No airline bag, no pictures!' He travelled first class, paid for by Toyota cars, for whom Mark was driving alongside Kiyoshi Misaki, the Japanese national champion.[3]

However, the fact that the prime minister's son was driving a Japanese car at a time when the British motor industry was in crisis caused a mini-furore. 'I was asked to drive for them by the chap who runs the Toyota team because he thought I could drive, *not* because of who I was – even though that gave them a bonus,' responded Mark [his emphasis]. 'Let's face it, if I hadn't been any good and I'd injured or killed myself, that would not have been any good to them at all.'[4] Unfortunately, it was not a successful debut. After 12 laps, despite leading their class, Mark and his co-driver had to retire when the distributor drive-gear broke.[5]

The Australian trip marked a turning point in the way Mark dealt with people in business and social situations. It was almost as if he had just discovered the true potential of being the prime minister's only son. One businessman who met him in Sydney and on other occasions said, 'He is the biggest user of people I have ever come across. When you met him at parties, he would stop at nothing to hustle for money, mainly for his racing career. If you talked to him, he would never look at you. It was always at starboard or port to see who was more important. I remember being at a party once with him and I noticed he was looking across the room. He then said, "I say, she's rather nice. Why don't you ask her what she's doing later and see if she will have dinner with me later?" I told him to do his own chatting up. I wasn't his bloody pimp.'[6]

The relaunch of Mark Thatcher Racing coincided with a closer relationship with CSS Promotions Ltd, his PR and marketing agency. This was crucial, as Mark desperately needed sponsorship funding and that would be forthcoming only if he could guarantee media exposure for the sponsors via himself. The CSS arrangement was on an ad hoc basis. When Mark was offered a race, he telephoned the agency's office and asked for promotional work to finance it. The plan was to plug Thatcher's name everywhere, with photo opportunities, and press packs were widely distributed. But in those days, he was often short of money and never paid CSS himself.

When he was asked to settle invoices, they were covered by Monteagle Marketing Ltd.

CSS's strategy worked as the sponsorship offers flowed in but Mark's chequered racing career was still impeded by funding problems. As a result, he often seemed indiscriminate in his choice of benefactors. On 12 February 1980, he signed an agreement to promote the multinational Japanese textile company, Kanebo Ltd. This included modelling the company's clothes, except in Britain. In Europe and the Far East, he was to appear in press and billboard advertisements wearing Kanebo products, mainly synthetic-suede garments. One publicity photograph, taken in the south of France, showed him wearing an imitation antelope-skin coat sold in Harrods. Another showed him posing alongside Isabella Rossellini, daughter of the actress Ingrid Bergman, in an artificial-leather racing suit.[7]

Mark also agreed to wear Kanebo's name and symbol, embroidered in gold, on his racing overalls and jacket. The company then used photographs of him decked out in his racing gear in their advertisements, which were released to the media. However, the British people were deprived of seeing Mark's modelling work unless it was directly related to his racing activities.

In return, Kanebo provided 'personal sponsorship' by paying him £10,000 to cover his living and travel expenses while racing a Formula Three car at Japan's Suzuka circuit and in Formula Atlantic at the Macao Grand Prix.[8] The money was paid in a curious way, according to Nigel Hart, then working for Mark and Stephen Tipping. Hart recalls being with Tipping at a Heathrow airport hotel waiting for the prime minister's son, who was flying in from the south of France after posing for some publicity photos. 'I remember Stephen picking up Mark from the airport,' said Hart. 'He then came back to the hotel with a travelling bag full of cash. We then drove off to a Lloyds Bank branch in Blackwater, Surrey, and converted the money into a banker's draft.'[9]

The Japanese sponsorship deal resulted in brief but intense controversy. Gerald French, director of the British Clothing Manufacturers' Federation, condemned it as 'shameful and shameless' and issued a furious statement: 'Any kudos accruing to the family because of Mrs Thatcher's position as prime minister should surely be used to boost Britain and not Japan. We are particularly upset because at this moment the British clothing industry is struggling desperately just to keep alive and could do with any helping hand held out to us.' The National Union of Tailors and

Garment Workers, which had lost 15,000 jobs in the previous five months, partly because of Japanese imports, took a similar line. 'People in the public eye have a major responsibility to Britain and this displays a distinct lack of concern and even shortage of patriotism,' said Neil Kearney, the union's head of research and information.[10]

Thatcher responded by saying he had spent £1,000 over two months trying, in vain, to persuade British companies to sponsor his driving. He had lobbied Unipart, a subsidiary of British Leyland, then a publicly owned corporation. 'I was swiftly shown the door,' he said. So he turned to Kanebo. 'The Japanese clothing industry got off their backsides and asked me and put a very good package to me to do it,' he added.[11] 'It is no good British industry bleating about foreign sponsorship deals. They should get off their fat backsides and do something about marketing their own products. British companies are very bad at supporting sport, particularly motor racing.'[12]

Mark did not consult the prime minister about the Kanebo deal and she was not amused. On the afternoon of the agreement's announcement, Monday, 12 February, Mark said confidently, 'I don't know what my mother's attitude will be but she is not aggressive about this sort of thing and will doubtless see my point of view.'[13]

But when interviewed the next morning at the family home in Flood Street, he had a different view: 'She must be particularly upset about this and I wouldn't blame her. I'm sure she'll go up the wall . . . She'll think I've made a big mistake and blame it all on me. She might tell me either to give up motor racing or leave Britain. I wouldn't be at all surprised if she said that. In that case, I'd leave Britain like a shot. I expected there might be a little fuss but I never expected people would be so vindictive. If the row doesn't blow over soon I'll leave this country for good . . . My work as a management consultant is all abroad, so it would be easy to move. It would also be advantageous for tax purposes. But I'd only leave because I've been hounded out of this country.'[14]

Within a few hours of his comments appearing in the press, Mark finally discussed the Kanebo deal with his mother. She told him the situation was not serious enough for him either to leave the country or to give up motor racing. But she suggested he should be more cautious in his remarks to journalists and not pose for photographs.[15] 'There has been no acrimony,' said Mark defensively. 'There were no big scenes and we agreed what is done is done. It is not her or my way of doing things to sit down and have big post-mortems. Family life with us is the bedrock of our existence.'[16]

Kanebo's motives were made crystal clear by their London representative. 'Our head office are delighted to have signed Mr Thatcher and are ready to bask in the reflected glory from the prime minister's son,' he said. 'He has no personal charisma so far as I am concerned. I wouldn't recognise him if I saw him.'[17] In Japan, the company seemed pleased to have hired him cheaply. 'Thatcher has more news value than a drunken singer or a playboy type image and since he's not a professional model we don't have to pay him as much,' said a Kanebo representative.[18]

Eventually Mark said '*sayonara*' to Kanebo, claiming that the use of his family name by the firm was 'in breach' of his agreement. He issued a curt two-sentence statement from 10 Downing Street: 'I will not now be driving in Japan as previously planned. I have now signed to drive for an all-British team based at Brands Hatch.'[19] 'I had to buy out the contract,' he said a year later. 'It cost me a very large amount of money – much more than the deal was worth in the first place. Looking back on it, it is possible I made an error of judgement. Certainly there could be no question of my driving for a Japanese car company as long as my mother is prime minister. That would be as out of place as a pork pie at a bar mitzvah.'[20]

At first glance, the Kanebo episode was a disaster for Mark. He lost £20,000-worth of British sponsorship money immediately and the bad publicity hardly endeared him to the racing fraternity. It did not help matters that in almost every interview he said he would 'emigrate' if his critics did not 'lay off'.[21] However, publicity is vital in attracting sponsors and, ironically, the Kanebo saga resulted in interest from new benefactors.

One offer that was taken seriously came from Paul Raymond, the millionaire strip club owner and publisher of soft-porn magazines. On 14 February 1980, three days after his deal with Kanebo was announced, Raymond sent a telegram to Mark Thatcher's Chelsea home offering him £25,000 a year to join his new *Men Only* Racing for Britain team. 'I was amazed to hear that no English company would sponsor him,' said the Soho businessman and owner of Raymond's Revue Bar. 'I thought it was appalling that a young man of his education should have to go abroad for sponsorship rather than stay in Britain.' He added that Mark would not have to pose with naked women but his car would be required to advertise *Men Only* magazine on its side.[22]

The next day, Mark Thatcher and Paul Raymond met for an hour at the Windmill Theatre, Soho, to discuss the deal. It was a bizarre venue for the prime minister's son to attend a business meeting. There were entertaining sideshows for the photographers and reporters waiting outside. As they gazed at the posters for the theatre's latest production – *Rip Off, The Erotic Experience* – they were kept busy by the locals, usually women in high-heeled brown leather boots, asking them if they would 'like some action'.[23]

Eventually, Mark emerged from the theatre, smiling sheepishly, but he refused to say whether he had accepted the offer. 'I have nothing to say,' he declared. When asked what he thought his mother's reaction would be to his latest sponsorship solicitation, he replied, 'She's on tour at the moment.' Raymond was more forthcoming: 'As far as we are concerned, he is well worth sponsoring and we sincerely hope he will be a new James Hunt. I would like to boost Britain . . . I think that all young guys should be given every opportunity to stay here.' Before driving Mark away in his chocolate-brown Rolls-Royce, Raymond added that the £25,000 'might well be worth more than that in the long run'.[24]

Another meeting was scheduled for the weekend and Raymond expected a contract to be signed on the Monday. But then the proposed *Men Only* deal was abruptly cancelled. Mark had spoken to John Webb and other officials at Brands Hatch, who did not approve. 'I was told that he has various contractual obligations with Brands Hatch and they are not in favour of the deal with me,' said Raymond. 'It looks as if they want to keep in control of Mark themselves.'[25] Certainly, Mark seemed happy dealing with the soft-porn king. 'I think his [Raymond's] publicity machine handled the event in a way that was in my best interests,' he said.[26]

Despite Mark's talk of a 'media witch-hunt' against him, the publicity did not harm his financial prospects.[27] In the midst of the Kanebo row, John Creasey, managing director of the clothes firm John Peter, said, 'We will pay him the money to further his racing career if he will advertise our products. We would certainly not get £10,000-worth of business through signing him up. But it would be far better than the British textile industry getting another kick in the teeth from foreign competition.'[28]

Within a week, Thatcher secured £40,000-worth of sponsorship. His main benefactors were Kelly Girl Service, the temp employment agency whose slogan was 'If you're good – you're Kelly!'; roller-skate manufacturers Morris Vulcan Group; Shell Oil; Talbot Motor

Company; Wendy Wools; and the Truck Development Company. This package was cleared with 10 Downing Street. Previously, the prime minister's office would merely comment: 'It's nothing to do with us. Mark Thatcher is a private individual not a member of the Government.'[29] But now they were taking a close interest, according to Brands Hatch officials.[30]

On 28 February 1980, Mark was able to call a press conference at Brands Hatch to announce details of his race schedule for the year. The invitation stated that his 'all-British car racing programme was supported entirely by British-based companies and incorporating feminine interest'. But the media call was not without tension. Mark was nervous and edgy on the public platform. Journalists were told they could not ask questions about the Japanese Kanebo deal. When a BBC reporter did so, Mark refused to answer and passed the microphone to John Webb, head of Brands Hatch, who gave a bland response about nearly all drivers seeking sponsorship. Mark did later talk about his mother's attitude but it was clear that mention of foreign sponsorship of his racing career touched a raw nerve.[31]

Nevertheless, it was an impressive seven-month programme and Mark did seem to have resolved his sponsorship problems. His colleagues at Brands Hatch were also building up his chances. 'He's going to be very good, if people will leave him alone to get on with it,' said Jackie Epstein, then a Formula 5000 team owner and consultant to Webb. 'He's very courageous, although tending a little bit at the moment perhaps to try too hard.'[32] John Webb agreed: 'He's a very aggressive driver with a great future ahead of him. But he is not a potential world champion and nobody here is trying to pretend he will be. We see him as a very good long-distance driver who could eventually win the Le Mans 24-hour race one day.'[33]

The prestigious Brands Hatch programme was a real morale boost for Mark. But this served only to make him even more self-conscious about his unique proximity to the heart of government. His friends were quick to notice the change in manner. One of his marketing agents at the time, who liked Mark, recalled telling him about a sponsorship proposition. 'That seems a good idea,' replied Mark. 'I shall have to refer that to the prime minister.' 'No, you'll have to refer that to your mother,' said his agent caustically, who thought he needed bringing down to earth. This exploitation of his new-found status was confirmed by Mark himself. 'When we are alone together, she's just Mum, of course,' he said. 'But if I introduce anybody to her, then I call her prime minister.'[34]

Others who knew him at the time were less charitable. 'The point about Mark,' said Nick Faure, a fellow racing driver who spent a lot of time with him in the early months of 1980, 'was that the only thing he could do was cash in on the fact that he was the prime minister's son, and he's been very successful because he had this ability to project himself in that way.'[35]

Faure would go for dinner at the Thatchers' house in Flood Street, Chelsea, and invite Mark down to his home in Aldershot. 'He admitted to me that he was going to make as much money out of being the prime minister's son as he possibly could,' recalled the racing driver. 'He used the words "cash in" and that is exactly what he has done.' Faure claimed Mark was motivated almost entirely by money. 'The guy's got profit stamped all over his brain,' he said, 'but I have to say it was mainly his insecurity. He had a lonely upbringing and I actually have some sympathy for him because his mother was nearly always away and he must have had a difficult time growing up.'

Despite the successful relaunch at Brands Hatch, Mark Thatcher continued to seek sponsorship for his racing career. He struck lucky with Dr Jo Erhlich, an eccentric elderly Austrian millionaire, who funded him more for publicity purposes than for talent. But within three months he had written off two cars and blown an engine, and he never once thanked the Austrian tycoon for his support. 'I've never been more abused by an individual than by Mark Thatcher,' Erhlich later recalled.

One fundraising method used by the premier's son was to promise companies media coverage. 'He only got on the racing track because he could almost guarantee sponsors press and television coverage,' said Faure. 'He was a 100 per cent publicity seeker. He thrived on the media and loved every minute of it.' This obsession was confirmed when Faure was invited over for dinner in March 1980 at the Thatcher family home in Flood Street, Chelsea. The racing driver was stunned when Mark proudly played him a home video compilation of every single television bulletin and newspaper clipping about himself, including those that merely mentioned his name in passing. 'He wanted to show me what a big publicity vehicle he was for sponsors,' said Faure, looking back on an incident rich in irony.

Like everyone else, Faure saw the advantage of using the prime minister's son to acquire sponsors. In April 1980, Mark agreed to be one of his drivers for that year's 24-hour Le Mans race and brought in Diagrit Diamond as one of the sponsors. 'The managing director was very excited about it,' recalled Faure. Mark was to drive with Lella Lombardi, the exceptional Italian woman driver, in a super-fast De Cadanet Lola T380 with a Formula One engine. 'It is a very tough race and I have not entered into it lightly,' he said. 'I have taken advice from experienced drivers who have told me that I am up to it.'[36]

As it turned out, Mark did not race for Faure and Le Mans was not a success. On Sunday, 15 June 1980, after 16 hours, Mark lost control on the approach to a corner and the car spun into a crash barrier. Although his car was only slightly damaged, it could not be restarted and Mark had to retire from the race. The crash occurred despite fresh tyres being fitted to the car. Arriving in the paddock tired and frustrated, Thatcher argued with Quentin Spurring, editor of *Autosport* who had written some mild criticisms of his performances. 'You are a boil on the arse of humanity,' he shouted at Spurring.[37]

In the pits, Thatcher was not popular among his fellow drivers. 'He was an arrogant bastard,' recalled Ian Flux who raced with him in 1981. 'He rarely spoke to other drivers unless it was absolutely necessary when we were being fitted for a single-seater car. He never showed an ounce of gratitude to the mechanics or his sponsors. In racing, you all get on with other people whatever your circumstances but he was above all that . . . He was more worried about the way he looked and would parade about the pits and paddock in a pristine driver's suit with a shiny brand new helmet under his arm, making sure everyone noticed him.'

There is some dispute among fellow drivers about Mark's racing ability. Nick Faure is dismissive. 'I would never have considered employing him if he wasn't the prime minister's son,' he said. 'He just wasn't good enough.' Others argue he was a capable and promising club racer, though never quite up to international standard. Brands Hatch's then chief press officer, Juliette Brindlay, was more benevolent. 'He was quick, courageous and didn't get into too much trouble,' she told the authors at Wentworth Golf Club. 'The other drivers gave him some stick but he stood his ground. But he needed more track experience to make it big-time. He only raced one full season [1979–80] and I got on well with him and went to Chequers a couple of times. He always did what we asked of him on the PR front.'

According to Barrie Williams, who raced with him and was a friend on the circuit, Mark had a lot of potential but never devoted enough time to practice. 'He was always so busy doing other things with his business deals and travelling about.'[38] Even Mark acknowledged this. 'The trick is to think ahead,' he said in 1980. 'But my weakness has always been my concentration.'[39] A trait which held back Mark's racing career was his impatience. 'I got on very well with Mark and liked him,' said Barrie Williams, 'but he was very bad at taking advice and acted as though he always knew best. To his credit, he was always in control when driving and he did listen when he was in trouble with the car. But he could also be very pompous and aloof, which didn't help because racing is all about teamwork and getting on with people. He had this habit of looking down at people – quite literally. He would stand right in front of you and stretch himself up on to his toes so he was peering down at you.'[40]

Another respected veteran of the racing circuit who knew Mark well was Peter Jopp, then secretary of the British Racing Drivers' Club. 'My feeling about Mark is that he was a good driver, a bit better than club standard but not international. But he was a user of people. He used his name to get sponsorship and would only be friendly with people when it suited him.' Jopp said that, once Mark's racing career picked up, suddenly he was too busy. 'Sorry, Peter, I haven't got time to talk,' he once said when approached by the driver. Then, when Jopp was commentating on the Macao Grand Prix, Mark literally followed him around because he was deemed important again.[41]

Despite qualified votes of confidence from some fellow drivers, Mark became prone to accidents. Soon after his mother entered 10 Downing Street, he crashed at Mallory Park in Leicestershire and was pulled from the blazing wreckage of his car. During one meeting at Brands Hatch, he crashed twice in the same race and had to retire.[42] On another occasion, he lost control on an S-bend and collided with the barriers. Then, at Hockenheim in West Germany, he had a lucky escape, receiving only minor scratches when his 140-mph Formula Super Vee car was wrecked during a practice run. But he was criticised by other competitors for driving too slowly on the racing line during the race.[43]

Mark always maintained his mother was happy about his racing. 'As long as I am not doing something incredibly stupid, she is happy for me to pursue my motor racing interests,' he said.[44] But Margaret and Denis were not happy. She alluded to this: 'I am always a bit nervous when I know he is racing and quite honestly he often won't tell me about it for that reason. I have never been to see him race because I feel that he would be doubly anxious to win and might do something . . . You can't stop your children doing these things if they want to do them and you mustn't.'[45]

The truth was that Margaret secretly urged Mark's friends and associates to discourage his racing career. 'It was made abundantly clear to me that Mrs Thatcher was keen for Mark to be kept away from racing,' said a marketing agent who represented Mark in the early 1980s. 'She was frightened out of her wits about his racing, so Denis very discreetly asked his business friends not to sponsor him. Think about it. If it had been made known by Mrs Thatcher that she was supportive of his racing, the sponsorship money would have poured in.'[46]

This was borne out by the way Mark was plagued by sponsorship problems throughout his career. But he often saw fundraising as a business challenge. In September 1980, he said that although he raced largely for fun he was also 'a commercial son of a bitch. I make it pay.'[47] So while he was a client of CSS, that was for media promotion and representation. When it came to the intricate world of persuading companies to sponsor him, Mark assumed he could do it himself because he believed he was a good businessman. 'I'm a good salesman, I have the gift of the gab,' he boasted. 'When I landed one particular account, even Mum couldn't believe it.'[48]

One of the businessmen Mark Thatcher pursued for money was David Thieme, a flamboyant millionaire American oil trader who had access to the oil sheikhs in the Gulf and Brunei and owned several super-tankers. Known as 'Zorro', because he always wore black, the mysterious Thieme sponsored Team Lotus racing cars, Mark's favourite automobiles, and the two met regularly. Thatcher frequently spent weekends with Thieme in Monte Carlo, staying at Hotel de Paris. The oil trader paid him for 'one-off projects' but they used each other for their respective contacts.

Thieme's main commercial vehicle was his company Essex Petroleum and he talked to Mark Thatcher about organising a special event that would promote Essex and Lotus. Mark agreed to help and offered to ensure the prime minister would appear. So, on Friday, 13 February 1981, CSS Promotions hired the Royal Albert Hall for an extravagant promotional evening. The historic hall was transformed into a nightclub, resplendent with silver palm trees, and an extra gallery was installed in front of the theatre boxes as a cocktail area. The orchestra pit was turned into a stage with two racing cars, including a Grand Prix model, displayed on hydraulic lifts. Ray Charles, supported by Sheena Easton, provided the musical entertainment, and even the food was specially commissioned. Top French chef Roger Verge created the first course, which was flown from Mougins to London; British culinary wizard Anton Mosimann cooked the main course; and the Roux Brothers did the dessert. The champagne, Moet and Chandon, cost a staggering £21,000. The total bill, met by Thieme, was about £1 million, although CSS was landed with the invoice for the champagne.

The event was ostensibly to launch the new Lotus Essex Elan sports car (one was given away in a free raffle that night) and to announce that Essex was sponsoring Penske at the Indy 500. But for Mark it was a perfect opportunity to introduce potentially useful businessmen to the prime minister. He had arranged for her to attend and was in a very excited mood that evening as 400 businessmen, mostly oil traders, packed into the Royal Albert Hall. Mark arrived in a Land-Rover, decked out in the silver, red and blue colours of Essex Petroleum, and strode in wearing a white tuxedo with a bright red handkerchief in his breast pocket, accompanied by two bodyguards. He then strutted around the hall with a police handset radio, barking orders to an additional four police bodyguards assigned to the prime minister. 'Right, I'm coming over to the car now,' he said loudly. This irritated the Special Branch officers on duty and Thieme's bodyguard asked Thatcher to stop grabbing the walkie-talkie radios and telling his colleagues how to do their job. But he refused. 'Give me the radio, sit over there and shut up,' said the security adviser.

'You can't talk to me like that,' replied a shocked Thatcher. 'I'll report you.'

'I don't give a shit. If you don't give it to me, I'll knock your fucking head off and kick the shit out of you.'

Thatcher handed over the radio.

As the evening wore on, Mark became more excited about the arrival of the special guest, the prime minister. 'Mummy is coming, Mummy is coming,' he boasted to the guests. When she arrived towards the end of the evening, her son ushered her upstairs to meet David Thieme and Colin Chapman, chairman of Lotus Cars (who was later accused of fraud over the collapsed DeLorean sports car company).

Mark then introduced her to two Swiss oil traders, one from Tamoil, who had specifically asked him to arrange the meeting. After chatting to Thieme and Chapman, Margaret Thatcher and the two oilmen retired to an outside room for a private talk. 'She wanted to meet them and they wanted to meet her,' said a former CSS director who made the introductions. 'It couldn't have been done openly, so we took them to a small side room.' The prime minister was also introduced to senior executives of Shell and BP, and to Marc Rich, the Swiss oil trader (later wanted by the US government on massive tax fraud charges and pardoned 20 years later). The other businessman keen to talk to her was Mansour Ojjeh, the Saudi Arabian son of the owner of TAG, the French aviation and construction group that sponsored Frank Williams Racing. This meeting was also arranged by Mark. His mother stayed for an hour and a half and then returned to Downing Street before dinner, with just her bodyguards as no officials accompanied her. When asked if her presence boosted her son's financial interests, a spokesperson said she was 'acting in a purely private capacity'.

Mark's pay-off for his promotional work was to cut a deal with Lotus. In return for publicising and promoting the luxury car, he was given a free Lotus plus expenses. The car was a blue turbo-charged Lotus Esprit sports car with red and silver markings. Then valued at £21,000, it was, Lotus at first claimed, 'a loan in return for promotional projects' on a month's trial basis. 'After that,' said Chapman, 'we'll see if we can come to some more permanent arrangement.'[49] In fact, Mark was allowed to keep the car and later bought it for only £11,000 – at least £10,000 less than the list price.

Six months later, Mrs Thatcher again helped promote Lotus, courtesy of Mark. On 5 August 1981, accompanied by reporters and TV crews, she flew to Norwich airport in a private Cessna jet chartered by Colin Chapman. On the tarmac waiting for her was a silver and red Lotus Turbo Esprit, resplendent with black and gold John Player Special cigarette logos. She looked over the car while Chapman explained its refinements.[50] She took the wheel and drove along a deserted runway, accompanied by Chapman, and then returned to where her husband, Denis, was standing. 'This is the car that Mark drives,' she said. 'It's lively, it's British and it's good for our exports.'[51] It was also a wonderful free advertisement for Lotus, who were indirectly paying her son.

Mark loved dashing around town in his Lotus, which he considered 'the perfect car for London'.[52] But he was still obsessed with motor racing and decided that one way of keeping on the inside track was to ingratiate himself with the Frank Williams team. Mark was used as a fixer and facilitator, particularly on resolving sponsorship problems for the prestigious team. He was never paid a fee but in 1981 Frank Williams gave him a Formula One racing car, a 170-mph FWO7C model, similar to the one driven by the 1980 world champion, Alan Jones. Then worth £100,000, at 2005 prices the car would be valued at about £750,000. 'It was a gift to curry favour,' said Charlie Crichton-Stuart, one of Frank Williams's closest advisers. The car was later donated to Lord Montagu of Beaulieu, for his motor museum.

Mark certainly responded to this inducement. He was keen to help because he wanted to race at the top level and saw Williams as his entrée. On one occasion, a government minister was astonished to be told by one of his officials that 'a Mr Mark Thatcher is downstairs and wants to deliver a letter'. The minister was furious and refused to see him. 'I thought it was outrageous that he was even in the building,' he recalled.

Like most Formula One racing teams, Williams was afflicted by sponsorship troubles at that time. Since 1978, the team had been sponsored by the Saudi royal family and a TAG subsidiary owned by the Ojjeh family, who were close to the Saudis. The Ojjehs were racing enthusiasts, attended all the Grand Prix meetings and contributed some £6 million to Williams, while the Saudi royals paid another £4 million.

But by the early 1980s the Ojjehs believed their funding had achieved its purpose – the Williams team winning 50 per cent of all Grands Prix – and they were unhappy that Frank Williams refused to sell them any equity. In a dramatic move, the Ojjehs transferred their sponsorship allegiance to McLaren. This caused a mini-crisis in the Williams team and consultants were asked to find new sponsors. One of those targeted was Gallaher Ltd, the company that made Silk Cut cigarettes and sponsored Jaguar cars. It was decided to use the Thatcher family to solicit the funding, so Mark was approached by Crichton-Stuart. 'Yeah, sure, I'll do it,' he said. Two weeks later, a meeting took place in the green reception room at 10 Downing Street, where Stuart Cameron, chief executive and chairman of Gallaher Ltd, met Mark and Denis Thatcher. The Thatchers asked whether Gallaher would sponsor Williams Racing but Cameron explained this was not possible because of long-term financial commitments to Jaguar. Mark and Denis tried to persuade him but it was to no avail. Cameron, later a director of Saatchi & Saatchi, was uncomfortable about the meeting but refused to talk to the authors, except through Gallaher's public affairs office. He confirmed that the meeting took place but would not comment on what benefits were offered to the company if they agreed to sponsor Williams Racing.

An experienced adviser to Williams on procuring sponsorship, Charlie Crichton-Stuart, said that Cameron was more hard-headed than most. He told us that Mark Thatcher was used by racing teams purely because people were susceptible to his name and influence: 'You have to remember that businessmen on the racing circuit – and I'm talking about chief executives and chairmen of major companies – are easily impressed by politicians and people close to power, and you could not get much closer than the son of the prime minister,' Crichton-Stuart told us. 'So we used Mark to soften them up but the problem for us was Mark's lack of sensitivity, and so when I introduced him to businessmen I would never leave him alone because he was about as subtle as a Chieftain tank.'

By the spring of 1981, Mark was marketing himself in a broader way. He was still besotted with motor racing. But he now believed he had a multi-faceted career. When asked by the *Sunday Telegraph* what he actually *did* [their emphasis], he replied: 'Basically speaking, there are what I call three parts to Mark Thatcher. There is Mark Thatcher the businessman. That takes up 75 per cent of my time . . . There is then what I call Mark Thatcher the personality, which is split into two parts. [The first] is my motor racing activities and the things that come from that. The second part of Mark Thatcher the personality, if you want, is the promotional side, whereby someone will come up to me and say, "We would like you to do this. Come and open a supermarket in Bury or something."'53

The prime minister's son was still on the books of CSS Promotions. But that was always a loose arrangement and he now seemed prepared to do almost any form of promotional work. On the day of Prince Charles's wedding to Lady Diana Spencer, Mark even gave an address on 'The Workings of the Parliamentary System' during a special luncheon at the Café Royal. 'He will be giving a speech on politics and parliamentary procedure in this country and an insight into it,' said Philip Hughes, director of VIP Entertainment, the organisers who had signed him up.

Hughes refused to say how much Thatcher was paid but said his contribution was part of a week-long series of events, including an optional visit to a gaming club, to celebrate the royal wedding. As tickets cost £1,995 each for the week (up to £3,500 for Americans), Mark's fee would have been not inconsiderable.54

Thatcher was also keen on breaking into the American 'celebrity' marketing business. In March 1981, he signed a long-term £50,000-

a-year contract with ProServe Inc., a management promotional company based in Washington, DC. Run by Donald Dell, the former US Davis Cup team captain, ProServe represents the commercial interests of sports stars. 'Our function is to help them earn as much as possible,' said Francis Craighill, one of their partners, 'and to conserve as much as possible. We put them on an allowance, develop a budget, pay their bills, analyse their investments, advise them on endorsements and offer assistance from A to Z.'[55]

The company was not reticent about why they were keen to represent Mark. 'He's promotable in the sense that he's a motor racer and he is the son of Mrs Thatcher,' said Stephen Disson, the vice-president responsible for marketing and special events. 'He's a rather bright and aggressive person, and we like that.'[56] Another ProServe executive was more explicit: 'Our job is to find him work. Because of his background he is a highly marketable commodity. There is no doubt that his name and the position his mother holds make people want him to promote their products.'[57]

Mark's first assignment was to promote and find outlets in Britain for American sportswear, mainly tennis outfits. He also appeared on television in the USA talking about how he wanted to break into motor racing and was paid £5,000 by NBC TV to commentate on the Las Vegas Grand Prix.[58]

Although it was a short-lived contract, ProServe Inc. did obtain one lucrative commission for Thatcher. This involved appearing in television commercials in Japan promoting Cutty Sark 12, a brand of Scotch whisky. As part of the advertising campaign, he also posed for photographs which appeared in Japanese newspapers and on posters, endorsing the whisky. The fee was estimated to be in the region of £40,000 but Mark denied it was that much. 'No, I'm not being paid anything like that,' he said. 'I mean, that is just light years away from the truth. But it is important to remember that it is a British product.'[59] A difference between this and his previous Japanese sponsorship deal – with the clothing firm Kanebo – was that this time the prime minister was consulted beforehand and gave her approval of the whisky promotion.[60]

Despite his mother's endorsement of selling Scotch to the Far East, Mark remained a source of anxiety within the family. It was his tendency to take money indiscriminately or consider commercial propositions from virtually anyone that caused most concern. Denis, with his sharp business antennae, was acutely aware of it from day one but kept quiet. His twin sister Carol also identified the problem but was more prepared to refer to it publicly, if only obliquely. 'We get on quite well but we aren't particularly close,' she said. 'I don't do many "Child of the prime minister" things like he does . . . Mark has done some things which were *bound* to land him in the papers [her emphasis], and I do think, "You silly boy, you're giving them the perfect ammunition." But what can I do? He's not keen on sisterly advice. If I ring up and tell him to pipe down, it's unlikely to be well received.'[61]

For a brief but emotionally fraught period Denis and Carol Thatcher's apprehensiveness about Mark's business activities was forgotten. Instead their anxiety was focused on an event which put him firmly in the public eye but also encapsulated the intensity of Margaret's relationship with her son – the six days when he was missing in the Sahara desert.

On New Year's Day 1982, Mark and his highly experienced French co-driver, 38-year-old Anne-Charlotte Verney, set off in their white Peugeot 504 to take part in the Paris-to-Dakar motor rally. Competing against 392 other drivers, they aimed to complete the gruelling 6,200-mile journey in about 20 days. However, by the time Mark and his crew reached the Sahara desert a week later, they had run into serious trouble. Their car's back axle snapped during the sixth leg of the race and they failed to turn up for a checkpoint at Timeiaouine, at the southern tip of Algeria. Then the organisers lost radio contact with the car and Mark, Charlotte and their mechanic, Jean Garnier, were stranded in the African wilderness, 43 miles north of Timeiaouine.[62]

At first it was claimed they had been spotted by reconnaissance planes and directed by nomadic tribesmen to safety. But these were false reports and Mark, Charlotte and Jean remained missing. By the end of the fourth day, Monday, 11 January, the prime minister was 'very concerned' as there was 'no trace' of her son or his crew and desert conditions could be very harsh. But then an Algerian news agency report that evening stated Mark had been rescued by helicopter. She even received a telegram saying he was 'safe'.[63] Relief turned to despair later that evening, though, when a two-line telex arrived, informing her that Mark was 'officially still missing' and the 'rescue' information applied to a different competitor. The prime minister later said her 'heart stopped' when she read that telex.[64] She immediately telephoned Algeria to ask for an official search.[65]

107

The rescue operation was hampered by two natural factors – heavy sandstorms and the barren and mountainous location, with no telephone lines for hundreds of square miles. It was also slow and dominated by confusing and conflicting media stories. Margaret Thatcher became even more worried on the fifth day, Tuesday, 12 January, when Derek Howe, her political secretary, came up to the Downing Street flat and told Denis and Carol: 'There's very bad news. Mark is still missing.'[66] Denis went pale. 'Christ, Margaret will go spare,' he said. 'We'd better go down to the study.' Troops and aircraft then joined the operation. But the prime minister's state of mind was not helped by French reports about political abductions and Mark being kidnapped by a guerrilla gang with 'possible Libyan links'.[67]

However, Mark was in 'no serious or immediate danger' and cars often got lost in this area, according to Thierry Sabine, the rally organiser. 'The desert is more inhabited than generally thought,' he said, 'and this time of year the climate is reasonable. Their car carries enough provisions and water to allow them to survive for a long time.'[68] The crew had also made a makeshift tent, in which they sheltered. 'Luckily, they did not try to go off into the desert,' said Ben Strachan, British ambassador in Algeria.[69] Mark later remarked that he passed the time by reading the same book twice – *The Fifth Horseman*, a thriller about a plot by Colonel Gaddafi to blow up New York City with an atomic bomb – and playing solitaire with pebbles.[70]

Still, the prime minister was increasingly distraught at the absence of positive action or news and, according to her daughter, was 'unable to function'. She repeatedly rang her friend and confidante Woodrow Wyatt, the newspaper columnist: 'What will I do without Mark? What will I do without Mark?' On the sixth day, reinforcements arrived. Early that morning, she received a telephone call from Sir Hector (now Lord) Laing, then chairman of United Biscuits and former joint treasurer of the Tory Party. Sir Hector was concerned and offered to lend his private jet so that Denis could fly out to the Algerian Sahara. Margaret was delighted and within hours the twin-engine eight-seater Beechcraft KingAir 200 aircraft was ready. Her husband was in the bath at the time and was astounded to hear his wife banging on the bathroom door shouting, 'Get out of the bath, Denis. The plane's there – you must go now.' Denis wearily and reluctantly bundled himself out of the 10 Downing Street flat, still dripping wet, and made his way to the airport at Denham, Buckinghamshire.[71]

While Denis was flying out to Algiers and then on to the oasis town of Tamanrasset with Ben Strachan, the British ambassador, Margaret was, understandably, extremely distressed. She had desperately wanted to accompany her husband to Algeria but was persuaded to stay in London. At midday, she arrived at the Imperial Hotel, Russell Square, for a meeting of the Federation of Small Businesses, accompanied by Ian Gow, her parliamentary private secretary.

Waiting reporters noticed how drawn her face was and her red eyes indicated she had been crying. 'I am afraid there is no news,' she said. 'I am naturally very concerned.' She walked into the foyer but broke down and sobbed for 30 seconds, her head low. Tears were streaming down her face as she leaned on the shoulder of one of her personal detectives. After recovering her composure, she walked towards the reception room. She broke down again, stumbling slightly, but then quickly composed herself and delivered her speech. It was the first time Margaret Thatcher had shown such emotion in public and indicated the extent of her anxiety.[72]

Meanwhile, Denis had arrived in the Algerian desert. He had flown out there, according to Barrie Gill, Mark's marketing and PR agent, to help and 'to stir things up' among the search organisers.[73] But when Denis telephoned his wife from the search HQ that evening to report back, there was not much news. He told her the French and Algerian air forces had called a temporary halt to the search as darkness set in, but would reconvene at first light. Denis also said the operation was plagued by false unofficial reports of sightings. The British embassy was reliant on the rally organisers for accurate information but they had drawn a blank – as had the Algerian authorities.

In London the next morning, Margaret Thatcher was waiting by the telephone in 10 Downing Street with her daughter Carol. 'It's all I *can* do,' said Mark's twin sister [her emphasis].[74] Margaret continued to work on her ministerial red boxes but would suddenly look up and say, 'I wonder if there is any news.'[75] But they did not have to wait long. At 11.30 the next morning, Thursday, 14 January 1982, Mark and his crew were found by a French pilot who was searching for minerals in his Hercules aircraft in the Sahara. They were discovered in Taoumdert, 50 km off the rally route, but were safe and well, standing by their Peugeot waving a shirt to attract attention.

That afternoon, Mark was flown to Tamanrasset but greeted his father rather too casually. 'Hello, Dad, what are you doing here?'[76]

Denis was furious and rapidly losing his temper, but held his tongue. When Mark mentioned that he would like to finish the rally, he replied, 'Not bloody likely'. Denis then announced the discovery on the lunchtime television news, watched by a much-relieved wife and daughter. 'When he was found, I just felt on top of the world,' Margaret said later.[77] When Mark met journalists, he looked relatively fit and well, if scruffy and tired. He shrugged off the six-day ordeal with 'Why the fuss?' and claimed to be 'simply staggered' by the media interest in his plight.

Back home, officials in 10 Downing Street braced themselves for a vintage Mark Thatcher performance. It was a mixture of bravado, condescension and insensitivity. 'We were not lost,' he announced at the Tahat Hotel. 'We knew where we were, although we weren't where we were supposed to be. I wasn't frightened at all. I would have liked a couple of ham sandwiches now and again but we were all right for water . . . We could have gone on for another 12 days. We had enough water, food and no problems at all. I planned on an eight-day stay. Then, when the rally plane didn't see us, I changed to a fortnight plan.'[78] As he spoke, Charlotte Verney, his co-driver, was being led shakily into a local hospital. 'All she's suffering from,' said Mark as she passed by, 'is air sickness and I think she drank too much water.'[79]

Foreign Office and 10 Downing Street officials winced at the premier's son's absence of tact and gratitude to those who had rescued him. So the next day, Margaret Thatcher herself telephoned Barrie Gill, Mark's PR agent and joint head of CSS Promotions, at his Strand office. 'Have you seen what is being said?' she said. 'Would you please to go to Heathrow airport and help Mark with his press conference? A car will take you and you will be allowed on the plane.' Her press secretary, Bernard Ingham, then spoke to Gill, because there was some concern about Mark's injudicious remarks. 'Tell him to be a bit more bloody diplomatic,' he added.

The PR agent was immediately driven to Heathrow with a bodyguard, just in time to brief his client as he arrived on the president of Algeria's personal jet. But when the prodigal son came out onto the freezing tarmac, he walked straight past his father and Bernard Ingham and snapped, 'Where's my detective?' A livid Denis and irritated press secretary then took him aside in a private room. When Ingham started to talk, Mark loftily dismissed his advice and Denis exploded: 'Will you for the first time in your life listen to somebody who might do you some good?' Stunned by his father's anger, he acquiesced.[80]

Minutes later, flanked by Barrie Gill, Mark gave the press conference. The tone and content of his remarks were amazingly transformed. Gone was the arrogance. Suddenly there was conciliation, almost humility. 'I am delighted to be back,' said Mark, 'and very sorry that a lot of trouble has been caused. I am only now becoming aware of the amount of concern that has actually been pointed towards me. I am simply amazed and embarrassed.'[81]

As for Anne-Charlotte Verney, she naturally got to know Mark quite well during the six days they were stranded in the desert. 'He likes being the son of the prime minister,' she reflected. 'He knows it helps him to do things he could never do otherwise. Mark has given in to the temptation of doing too much too soon – because it's easy for him as Margaret Thatcher's son.'

She was also amazed at Mark's relaxed disposition. 'He was very nervous when the car first broke down,' she said, 'but when he realised we could do nothing about it he accepted the situation and made the best of it. He was always very calm and collected and organised everything. We slept 15 hours a day to conserve energy, then we would read. After two days, I began to get worried inside. I began to think we might not make it but Mark made me feel safe. He was so confident.'[82]

It was this curiously laid-back attitude that increased speculation among racing experts and promoters that Mark exploited the 'lost-in-desert' saga as a publicity stunt. One senior executive of CSS Promotions, Thatcher's PR agency, believes his client may have taken advantage of the situation to create publicity for his beleaguered racing career. But another former CSS director disagrees and points out that it was not unusual for rally drivers to get lost in that part of the Sahara. Years later, Barrie Gill told a friend that his impression was that the prime minister's son was quite happy to be 'shacked up with a vivacious French blonde for a few days'.

There are indications that Mark was not completely stranded. For example, there was a curious incident when he was actually located on the fourth day of the search by Michael Bosi, a Swiss driver, but would not move. 'I got the impression young Thatcher was panicking,' said Bosi. 'He ignored my advice that they should get into my van and insisted on staying behind with his broken-down car.'[83] But it was Mark's remarkably composed attitude that led some to claim that he was far from lost and knew exactly the publicity implications of what he was doing.

Mark was eventually reunited with his mother at Chequers on the evening of his arrival. Margaret asked him not to continue his motor-rallying exploits. However, despite the enormous anxiety and emotional stress inflicted on her, Mark appeared reluctant to give up cross-country motor rallying. When asked about his future, he replied, 'I am contracted to drive cars next year and that is what I shall do.'[84] He later repeated his intention to continue rallying, much to Denis's irritation. 'I expect he'll get on with whatever he wants,' said Denis, 'but I hope it won't be rallying.'[85] Carol Thatcher agreed: 'I must say I hope this is the last of Mark's motor racing. Having seen the strain Mum has suffered this week, she can do without the additional hassle.'[86] Her twin brother was annoyed by this comment and told her to 'stick to her own business'.[87]

As for Margaret, she was characteristically reluctant to lay down the law. 'I am not that kind of mother,' she said. 'My son is grown up and in charge of his own life. You can't have grown men and women on their mothers' apron strings.'[88] She was also happy to pay part of the £200,000 costs of the rescue operation, which involved five Algerian aircraft, two helicopters, three French aircraft and over twenty cars. The prime minister paid the hotel bills of her son, her husband and the British ambassador in Tamanrasset.[89]

After the Sahara desert debacle, and much to the consternation of his family, Mark Thatcher was keen to resume his racing career. Within a week of returning to London, he announced plans to drive for the Goodwin Racing Team in the British Formula One championships at Brands Hatch. This was one of the most dangerous and difficult circuits because of the high speeds reached, often more than 200 mph. Experts also expressed surprise at the news because of Mark's inexperience at that level (he had not even driven a Formula One car before). Also, access to Formula One racing is very restricted and usually a driver needs to qualify through the junior ranks.[90]

However, Mark had been given a free car by Frank Williams and so felt confident about making the grade. He made this clear when he sent out a detailed file about his ambitious plans to 600 companies who might be interested in sponsoring him: 'I think it's reasonable to say my future motor sport activities will take place on circuits rather than the rough stuff.'[91]

The Thatcher family were again not pleased. Margaret let it be known, non-attributably, to political correspondents that she was 'not happy but accepts she could not dissuade him'.[92] Carol went on the record: 'Everyone knows her feelings about the dangers of motor racing.'[93] Unperturbed, Mark set off in pursuit of corporations who would collectively or individually sponsor him for the £250,000 needed for his Formula One campaign.

One of the people he approached was a wealthy Swiss businessman with a string of computer companies. In early 1982, the businessman was surprised to receive a dispatch postmarked 10 Downing Street, London SW1. It was a letter from Mark asking for an introduction to the Swiss commercial community. At first, the businessman was reluctant to cooperate but as the request came from the son of the British prime minister, he agreed to host a lunch of bankers at his home in Zurich.

As the lunch progressed, this Swiss executive became increasingly uneasy at what he saw as Thatcher's commercial opportunism. Mark came straight to the point. 'I need £30,000 for sponsorship,' he blurted out. The bankers looked at each other, embarrassed, and said nothing. 'Does your mother know you're seeking sponsorship money?' one asked. 'Of course, she knows,' Mark replied briskly. 'I've got six years to make my fortune and I'm bloody well going to do it.'[94]

The businessman politely declined to fund his racing activities. 'Oh, it doesn't matter,' Thatcher responded. 'One of the others I'm seeing here in Switzerland will give me the money.' He then handed his Swiss host a list of people he was meeting in Zurich. This enraged the businessman because he felt he had been tricked into meeting the prime minister's son. Bristling with anger, he telephoned all those on the list and advised them not to give the young entrepreneur any financial backing. Consequently, the prime minister's son left Switzerland empty-handed.

Two weeks later, the financier invited a British friend to stay at his Zurich home. Almost as soon as the visitor arrived, he was greeted with, 'I recently had lunch with the most objectionable young man I have ever met.'

'Who was it?'

'Mark Thatcher, the son of your prime minister.'[95]

Such an approach hardly endeared Mark to potential financial backers and so his corporate canvassing rapidly ran off course. He was scheduled to drive his Williams car for the Goodwin team on 9 April 1982 at Oulton Park, and three days later at Brands Hatch. But this arrangement was cancelled just two days before the first race because the sponsorship money never materialised. Some cash was acquired but not nearly enough to cover their costs.

Ivor Goodwin, who hoped to manage Mark's Formula One career, was mystified as to the reason. 'The recession has something to do with it,' he said. 'But I get the feeling the companies who were canvassed were very nervous as to what the public were going to say about it. We have had one or two bitter blows. One or two companies we thought were going to join in the sponsorship have left us high and dry. I just can't comprehend it at all. We had got so much television coverage lined up – I can't believe there are companies who could let so much publicity slip through their fingers.'[96]

Perhaps one reason was Mark's public comments on the performance of British companies. In March 1982, at the height of the economic recession and two days after the budget, he declared, 'If you sit back on your big arse and say, "It's no good, we've been hit by the recession," then it's a self-fulfilling prophecy. I would actually decry the notion that there is a recession. I mean, the people we do business with are only interested in work-rate and results. If you put in the necessary work-rate and have the commitment to succeed, then you will succeed, no matter what the business environment is. It's not difficult to sell British products overseas – it just comes down to work-rate. All the people who work for me are doers. They're very well paid and they perform. It's as simple as that. If they don't, then we have a look at it.'[97]

British industry was not amused at being lectured by the 28-year-old 'marketing consultant'. Unfazed, Mark continued his search for financial benefactors. But by late 1982, it was clear that the quest was fruitless. So he tried a different approach. As well as lobbying for cash, he attempted to persuade companies who were already sponsors of motor sport to allow him to join their racing team.

One businessman he set his sights on was Jerry D. Dominelli, whose investment advisory company, J. David, sponsored the Porsche racing team of British driver John Fitzpatrick. Mark had heard about the Californian financier from Fitzpatrick and was eager to meet him. So in January 1983, he invited Dominelli, based in La Jolla, near San Diego, to London. Over dinner they discussed the possibility of Mark's driving for the Fitzpatrick team. They could not agree terms but the investment adviser clearly enjoyed the meeting, during which they talked about Margaret Thatcher. 'Mark has a very strong fondness for his mother,' said Dominelli. 'We discussed his relationship [with her] and the pressure she was under during the Falklands crisis.'[98]

Dominelli, also known as 'Captain Money', was a typical example of the kind of businessman with whom Mark was associating in the early 1980s. At the time of his meeting with Thatcher, Captain Money was being investigated for embezzlement and theft. Since 1981 he had been running an investment racket called a Ponzi scheme. 'In a Ponzi scheme, investors' money is not invested in anything,' said Donald Bauder, author of a book on Dominelli. 'The early investors are paid off with money coming in from later investors. Thus the survival of the scam depends on the continuing recruitment of new investors. But with each new investor, the scheme goes further into the hole long-term. The roof has to cave in at some point.'[99]

Dominelli told potential customers that he could earn them a steady 40 to 50 per cent annual return on their investment on the foreign currency market. But the roof collapsed and the scam went horrendously wrong. Captain Money had spent much of the investors' funds on furs, fast foreign cars, jewellery and high living. The money disappeared.

In February 1984, a month after meeting Mark Thatcher, the robbed investors sued Dominelli to place his company in bankruptcy. Two months later, Captain Money fled to the Caribbean island of Montserrat, claiming he would pay back the money from there. Instead, things got worse. In late April 1984, he was arrested for illegal possession of firearms and sent back to San Diego for prosecution. He was convicted of fraud and sentenced to twenty years in prison. Two years later his crimes were compounded when he was found guilty of illegally channelling company money to fund a political campaign.[100] Jerry Dominelli now languishes in a southern California jail.

For Mark Thatcher, lobbying Dominelli was almost a last-gasp attempt to break into the big-time racing scene. Much to the annoyance of his family, he even returned to rally driving. He competed in one of the world's most dangerous cross-country motor races, the Baja 1000, an arduous 935-mile trip across the cactus-dotted Mexican desert.

A police helicopter, spotter plane and high-speed car were put on alert just for Mark and he did not disappoint them. As darkness fell early in the race, Thatcher and his co-driver went missing. An all-night 'priority alert' was ordered by the rally organiser, Ric Miller. 'We felt it was necessary because this is the most horrendous part of the course,' said Miller. 'It enables other drivers and checkers to be watchful for someone lost or in trouble. We have no idea why

Thatcher and his co-driver got out of touch.'[101] After eight hours Mark was discovered arriving at a designated checkpoint in his two-ton Dodge pick-up truck. He eventually completed the course but later said it was his last rally.

The Baja 1000 was effectively the end of his racing career. Its demise was due to his mother's increasing anxiety about safety and also to insufficient sponsorship. But he did make a successful, if brief, comeback in March 1988 when he came fourth in the European Touring Car championships. Driving a 150-mph BMW M3, he was praised by the professional drivers in the race. 'I'm very pleased, although I didn't drive as well as I can but then that's to be expected,' said Mark. 'I will be celebrating with a shower. I don't drink much. I will also be phoning my mother. I phone her every Sunday night without fail from wherever I am in the world.'[102]

Despite an accomplished fourteen-race series with BMW, Mark retired from competitive racing six months later. He finally came to realise that he could not step up a grade from touring cars. But the real reason was the amount of time racing consumed. As the Thatcher decade wore on and Mark's business interests blossomed, he simply could not devote the time to his favourite hobby. The premier's son had other things on his mind.

FIVE

Batting for Thatcher

Unlike my brother, I have never made swags of cash.
– Carol Thatcher[1]

In February 1981, Sayid Ahmad Halifah Suwaydi, a senior United Arab Emirates diplomat and former foreign minister, was asked by Mark Thatcher to Sunday lunch at the prime minister's weekend retreat at Chequers. The prime minister's son told him not to inform the Foreign Office or his embassy about the visit or to use his official car. 'This lunch must be kept strictly confidential,' he said. This was most unusual and troubled Suwaydi. When he arrived at Chequers, he was greeted by Margaret Thatcher and was surprised to find only three places set at the lunch table – for himself, the prime minister and Mark Thatcher.

Over lunch, Mrs Thatcher was keen to discuss business, not politics. Among various commercial projects she pressed him about was an order British Aerospace was seeking to sell Hawk aircraft to Abu Dhabi, one of the member states of the United Arab Emirates (UAE). After the meal, she withdrew and left him alone with her son. Mark immediately began talking about an oil deal he was involved in brokering between British Petroleum (BP) and the Abu Dhabi National Oil Company (ADNOC). BP had an agreement to supply crude oil to ADNOC and wanted to renew the contract and also to increase the supply by 5,000 barrels a day. He was representing BP's interests, without their official knowledge, on behalf of a third party – an oil trader based in the Bahamas. As they sat in the prime minister's official residence, Thatcher insisted that he wanted prompt

117

action on the contract, as he was working under commission – a potential $2 million spread over one year.

Suwaydi responded that he would need instructions from his government before such decisions could be implemented, as they were beyond his authority and competence. When he returned to his hotel, the Churchill Intercontinental in Portman Square, the diplomat was uncomfortable about Thatcher's approach. He was a politician not a businessman and felt he was being used. But he reported back to Sheikh Zayed bin Sultan al-Nahayan, ruler of Abu Dhabi and president of the UAE. A source in the UAE presidential court said Sheikh Zayed was surprised by Mark's request. But he was keen to help Margaret Thatcher and recommended that ADNOC back the BP course of action. Zayed then delegated Sheikh Sorour, president of his royal court, to inform ADNOC that they should sign BP's new agreement because 'Mark Thatcher was behind it'.

A few weeks later, Mark flew to Abu Dhabi, capital of the UAE, with Jamil Amyuni, a Lebanese businessman who was working alongside him. They booked into the Sheraton Hotel and prepared to continue negotiations. The next day, Mark arrived for meetings with ADNOC officials with a present: a portrait of his mother in a silver frame.

The UAE delegation were keen to please, as they saw it, the British prime minister and agreed to BP's renewal application for the extra oil supply. But the deal went sour when the BP executive arrived in Abu Dhabi to sign the contract and discovered Thatcher's involvement. The BP representative had flown in at almost the same time and even stayed on the same floor at the Sheraton Hotel. But he was unaware of Thatcher's presence.

At a meeting to finalise the details, a senior ADNOC director asked, 'Where is Mark Thatcher?'

'What's he got to do with it?' replied the shocked BP executive.

'I was told this deal was for Mark Thatcher,' said the director.

'I am sorry, we will have to adjourn this meeting until tomorrow because I know nothing about this,' said the BP executive. He then returned to the Sheraton and telephoned BP's head office, who instructed him to cancel the contract and return to London.

The aborted oil deal was the beginning of a long and prosperous relationship between Mark Thatcher and the Gulf states. It is an area of the Middle East where business is conducted on the basis of trust and connections, through personal and family introductions rather than through orthodox Western commercial practices; where the ruling Gulf families prefer to deal with brokers, middlemen and heads of state rather than being lobbied directly by grey-suited corporation executives; and where commission fees, based on a percentage of the contract's value, are paid through locally owned subsidiary companies.

It is a commercial culture that is ideally suited to the way Mark Thatcher likes to do business – secretly, using intermediaries and relying on political dynasties rather than being employed on a permanent basis by a company. The United Arab Emirates (incorporating Abu Dhabi, Ajman, Dubai, Sharjah, Umm al-Qaiwain, Ras al-Khaimah and Fujairah), Oman, Kuwait and Qatar are also geared to the business sectors that thrive and rely on the use of agents in negotiating oil, construction and arms deals. It was an environment in which the prime minister's son could prosper.

Mark Thatcher's original entrée to the Gulf was an informal meeting, just after the 1979 general election, with Victor Matthews, then chief executive of the conglomerate Trafalgar House plc. Matthews, a former property speculator, was a close friend and fervent supporter of Margaret Thatcher. As chairman of Fleet Publishing International, the Trafalgar House subsidiary which owned Express Group newspapers, he was in a key position to cheerlead her to victory. His papers, the *Daily Express*, London *Evening Standard*, *Daily Star* and *Sunday Express*, led the vociferous campaign to elect Margaret Thatcher. What's more, Trafalgar House paid £40,000 into Tory Party coffers in 1979 and organised a celebration lunch for the new prime minister at the Ritz Hotel on the morning of her triumph. The following year, Victor Matthews became Baron Matthews of Southgate.

So when the Trafalgar House boss arrived at 19 Flood Street, Chelsea, to see Margaret Thatcher, he was well disposed to help her. After he had chatted to the new premier, her son told Matthews about his work on two construction deals. 'I am looking for contractors,' he said. 'Do you know any companies that might be interested in two contracts I am involved in?' Matthews said he would arrange a meeting with William (now Sir William) Francis, chairman of Cementation International Ltd, Trafalgar's overseas construction subsidiary. Francis was told that Mark Thatcher 'needed some business experience' and 'wanted to get into the export side of industry'.[2]

On the basis of Lord Matthews' introduction, Mark was hired as a consultant to Cementation International Ltd. In early 1980, a contract was drawn up with Thatcher's company, Monteagle Marketing (London) Ltd, and he was placed on the payroll with a fixed retainer plus commission. He was immediately assigned to two highly influential Cementation consultants – Jamil Amyuni and Ghassan Shaker – who were to play a vital role in helping to accumulate the first major instalment of Thatcher's fortune.

Amyuni, the company's marketing director in the Middle East since 1967, was responsible for securing new contracts. While he held a Lebanese passport, he was also a British citizen and took Mark under his wing and educated him in the ways and means of doing business in the Arab world. They travelled together on overseas trips and Mark was introduced to the key players in the region.

But it was soon apparent that the prime minister's son was being used as an introductory agent and influence peddler rather than for his commercial acumen, according to former Cementation executives. Amyuni dealt with the middle managers and ministers but Mark was able to get them to see the heads of state, according to a former senior director. 'He was helpful to us as a door opener and gave us an extra lever to win contracts, but I would not have hired him as a corporate manager. He just did not have the business ability.'

The two worked very closely together and Amyuni met the prime minister on more than one occasion. He was introduced to her by Mark during a constituency dinner in the London Inter-Continental Hotel in October 1980, held to celebrate Margaret Thatcher's 21 years as the MP for Finchley. He was also a dinner guest at Chequers and 10 Downing Street, accompanied by Mark. Mrs Thatcher later admitted encountering the Lebanese middleman but only privately. 'I have not met him in any official capacity,' she said.[3] A 10 Downing Street statement confirmed the meetings but added that 'no business was discussed'. Amyuni, who later ran a string of property companies and retained a UK base, refused to speak to the authors. 'I have nothing to say,' he remarked. 'I'm not going to talk about it. There's no point.'

Mark Thatcher's other mentor at Cementation was Ghassan Ibrahim Shaker. A Saudi national with a Turkish father, Shaker was born in 1937 and educated at Victoria College, Alexandria, Egypt, at the same time as King Hussein of Jordan and the two became good friends. Of the middlemen who broker arms and construction contracts in the Gulf, Shaker is the most civilised. 'At least you can talk to Ghassan,' Sayyid Tarik, the Sultan of Oman's uncle, remarked to Malcolm Dennison, a British intelligence officer. 'He's a gentleman. The others are shits.'

Shaker is impeccably connected and was close to Kamal Adham, former head of Saudi Arabia's intelligence services. His brother, Ghazi, represented King Hussein on major defence contracts, notably the abortive attempt to buy Tornados. On the commercial front, he had a controlling stake in the Oman subsidiary of Joannou and Paraskevaides (Overseas) Ltd, owned by George Paraskevaides, a Greek businessman whose J. & P. Group is the largest construction company in the Middle East and was a major subcontractor to British Aerospace on the Al-Yamamah arms deal with Saudi Arabia.

Shaker played a vital supporting role in the acquisition of Thatcher's fortune as the 51 per cent shareholder of Cementation (Saudi Arabia) Ltd, a joint-venture company with Cementation International. It was as Cementation's agent in the Gulf that he was asked by a Trafalgar House executive to get Mark Thatcher 'on board' for major contracts. Shaker agreed and so in early 1980 Mark went to see him at his apartment at 17 Grosvenor Square, Mayfair, to discuss potential deals in the Middle East.

The focus of their attention was the oil-rich state of Oman, which lies in a key strategic position on the Gulf, close to the Straits of Hormuz. By 1980, its oil revenue was 44.4 million Omani rials a year. But little of this wealth trickled down to its one million people. Instead, much of the money – at least 50 per cent – was spent on military equipment for its armed forces. This was largely due to the country's strategic importance. Oman has the ports, airfields and radar to make it a very useful base for any British or American force keen to protect the lucrative oilfields.[4] For many years, Oman was also faced with an aggressive southern neighbour in communist South Yemen.

As any instability in the country could have serious repercussions for the West, the British have always retained a strong presence. Since 1798, they have been patrons of the sultans, intervening whenever required to prop up the regime. In the 1960s, SAS officers were used to crush a rebellion in the southern province of Dhofar. British military intelligence officers, or 'advisers' as they were officially described, were omnipresent in the Sultan's inner circle. In 1970, they were instrumental in the coup d'état in which the current Sultan overthrew his despotic father. At that time, there were at least 600 British soldiers in the Omani armed forces, most under contract but some on secondment.[5]

The Sultan of Oman, Qaboos bin Said, is heavily dependent on the

United Kingdom and Her Majesty's Government (HMG) for his throne and wealth. Hence, any approach by the Thatchers would be given a friendly reception. Ghassan Shaker, who had known the Sultan since the early 1970s and was a personal adviser, realised this and argued Oman was a promising business prospect. But so much was being spent on arms that it was short of cash (in 1974 the country nearly went bankrupt after buying an integrated air-defence missile system from British Aerospace). So they decided to consult Sheikh Zayed, president of the United Arab Emirates and the most influential figure in the Gulf.

Zayed was a very close ally of Margaret Thatcher, who agreed to help her son and Shaker. On 8 November 1980, she provided a handwritten and signed letter of introduction, underneath her photograph, for Mark to Sheikh Zayed: 'I have asked my son to convey to you my personal message of warm regards and good wishes.' The note, which we have in our possession, is evidence of how the prime minister effectively assisted her son's commercial interests.

Armed with this letter, Mark flew to Lausanne, Switzerland, to meet the sheikh. 'Go to Qaboos,' said Zayed, 'and ask him what he wants, and I will finance it from my purse.' During the meeting, Thatcher even discussed his mother's foreign policy, according to Douglas (now Lord) Hurd, a Foreign Office minister at the time.

When Mark approached the Sultan of Oman on behalf of Sheikh Zayed and Cementation, he was given a cordial welcome. But the cordiality was tinged with caution and scepticism. Qaboos distrusted Zayed and did not believe the funds would be forthcoming. Mark was conciliatory and asked him at least to consider the proposal. 'Well, we have designs for a new sports stadium,' said the Sultan, 'so that is something that would interest us.' Thatcher returned to Abu Dhabi to report back. Sheikh Zayed disapproved of the choice and said he preferred a project that would benefit the Omani population. The discussion ended with the sheikh telling Mark, 'They [the Omanis] don't need a sports stadium. They need a university.'

At first, Sultan Qaboos was resistant to the idea of a university because he resented Zayed's insinuations about his regime. But Cementation International Ltd, through Mark Thatcher and Shaker, managed to change Qaboos's mind by lobbying his advisers. The Sultan was won over because it was a prestige project and had the extra attraction of deterring young Omanis from seeking a Western education, in which they would be subject to non-Islamic and democratic philosophies. So he discussed the proposed university with Sheikh Amer, his education minister, who was enthusiastic. Amer, an Oxford-educated Anglophile, was then twice dispatched to England for discussions with eminent academics.

The obstacle was that Oman was short of funds and the university would soak up scarce resources. The government had spent so much of its oil revenue on arms that it had no budget for such a scheme. This was resolved when the UK Export Credit Guarantee Department (ECGD) guaranteed a £150 million loan, made available by a syndicate of banks led by Morgan Grenfell, to finance the contract.

Mark Thatcher was used to help secure this financial backing. It was such a delicate, secret operation that whenever he discussed it on the telephone he used code words and names – for example, the prime minister was referred to as 'Big John'.

In November 1980, on Oman's national day, the Sultan publicly announced the university scheme, to be built over five years. Enter Sadiq Ismail, a Zanzibari expatriate and an influential figure in Omani education policy. In February 1981, he travelled to England, under the auspices of the British Council, to conduct a fresh canvas of academics. The British Council in Oman arranged a meeting with Margaret Thatcher but it was cancelled because, according to Council sources, 'she had some political crisis at the time'.[6]

By now, the multimillion-pound contract was there for the bidding and the taking. Mark was to be closely involved because of his prior knowledge, and his immediate boss, Jamil Amyuni, was head of Cementation's negotiating team.

In March 1981, after Sadiq Ismail's visit to England, the Omani government released the official requirements that contractors were expected to fulfil. 'A reputable establishment renowned for its experience in building universities will be selected,' said the plan. The document spelt out that the contract would be awarded on the basis of competitive tendering, with sealed bids by rival firms: 'All government contracts are awarded through the Tender Board.' This system was based on a law passed in 1975 after Omani government advisers were found to have been securing secret business deals for foreign corporations.[7] 'The whole purpose of a tender board is to eliminate a behind-closed-doors system,' said Jeremy Cripps, a chartered accountant who scrutinised many contracts in Oman.[8]

And yet Cementation International Ltd, a subsidiary of Trafalgar House plc, was awarded the £300 million university design and construction contract by direct private negotiations. When the decision was made known, rival bidders like Costain, Wimpey and Taylor Woodrow were outraged, and two executives later went to see Ivor Lucas, then the British ambassador in Oman, after the contract was awarded. They were furious because the business had never been put out to competitive tender.

The contractors were especially resentful because Cementation had only just returned to Oman after a three-year absence, while they had maintained a permanent base in the country (Taylor Woodrow had built the Sultan's Salalah Palace). Apart from that, Cementation had never built a university before and had withdrawn its plant equipment. As it had its own plants in Oman, Taylor Woodrow in particular could have easily completed the project at a lower cost.

The construction executives also told Lucas that no independent architects had been hired to design the university. This was despite the fact that two fully qualified and experienced firms of architects – Robert Matthew-Johnson, Marshall & Partner (RMJM) and James Cubitt and Partners – actively sought to bid for the design contracts. After receiving a circular from the British Overseas Trade Board (BOTB), both companies submitted proposals to the Omani Education Ministry. They had high hopes after receiving a second circular on 11 May 1981, which stated: 'An architects' brief is being prepared . . . in preparation for design tenders being called in 1982.'[9]

However, in September 1981, the Omani government suddenly not only awarded the civil engineering contract to Cementation International Ltd but also allowed them to appoint their own architects. This design contract was given to another Trafalgar House subsidiary. The negotiations had clearly taken place without the knowledge of the interested bidders. 'The whole deal was a stitch-up for Cementation,' an angry rival contractor later complained to Ivor Lucas, sitting in the British embassy in Muscat, the capital of Oman. Lucas found it impossible to disagree and reported their grievances to the Foreign Office and the Department of Trade. The ambassador's dispatch was noted but nothing was done.

The story of how Cementation secured the £300 million university contract by secret private lobbying lies at the heart of the way Thatcher's gold was acquired. For the deal was done largely through a coterie of well-placed middlemen and the use of political and family influence and patronage at the very highest level.

It started in early April 1981, two weeks before an overseas tour by Margaret Thatcher. As part of her preparation, she was briefed by the British Council on the academic and design aspects of the proposed university in Oman.[10] 'I knew of the announcement of the Omani government in 1980 that it had decided to establish a university,' she said, 'and of the opportunities for British industry which this might represent.'[11]

The Oman trip was just one leg of an extensive trade mission by Margaret Thatcher. On 14 April 1981, she flew to India, where she spent five days in negotiations with Prime Minister Indira Gandhi over quotas on textile imports. But major defence contracts were soon occupying her attention. Accompanied by Sir Ronald Ellis, her chief of defence sales, Thatcher then flew to Riyadh, Saudi Arabia.

For the next three days, she was locked in discussions with King Khalid and Crown Prince Fahd over future arms deals. Dressed in a costume specially devised for a female prime minister visiting Saudi Arabia, she looked like a modern version of the late Queen Alexandria. Thatcher told the Saudis that Britain had neglected the region but she 'intended to put that right in the future'.[12] During her stay, she also made a speech to British businessmen in Riyadh. 'Gradually one has come to see,' she said, 'that there are times when the battle is not necessarily between company and company but between country and country.'[13]

The next afternoon, Tuesday, 21 April 1981, Margaret Thatcher flew into Abu Dhabi and attended a party at the British embassy to celebrate the Queen's birthday. During the evening, her private staff were surprised to see her son arrive. There was an embarrassing moment when Mark failed to withdraw discreetly when UAE diplomats wanted to talk politics with his mother. Journalists were prevented from attending the reception but he was noticed by Herbie Knott, a freelance press photographer, who asked him whether he was part of the official party. 'No,' was the characteristically curt response.[14]

Mark had just flown in by Gulf Air with Jamil Amyuni, Cementation International's marketing director. The company was seeking a contract to build a giant irrigation scheme in the desert oasis of Al-Ain in Abu Dhabi. After meeting his mother, he stayed overnight at the Sheraton Hotel. The next day, Mark and Amyuni were engaged in negotiations with UAE officials. These were only partially successful. A Trafalgar House specialist subsidiary, Cementation Frankopile Overseas, did later obtain work in the area.

But the al-Ain contract faltered because test borings showed there was not enough water available.[15]

That same morning, 22 April 1981, the prime minister had a meeting with Sheikh Zayed. They spoke mainly about arms sales but there was also clearly a bond between them. He flattered her and solemnly told her that he had gained more insight into her foreign policy from her son than from the British ambassador. 'Sheikh Zayed spoke for all the world like an Arab poet and was a man of great charm,' Margaret Thatcher recalled in her memoirs.[16] She then called on Crown Prince Khalifa, his son and deputy commander of the UAE armed forces. Those discussions laid the foundation for the sale of 18 British Aerospace Hawk aircraft worth £60 million. Despite the welcome export order, British Aerospace would not have made much profit from the deal as at least 9 per cent commissions were paid out to agents in the Gulf and London.[17]

After a lunch hosted by the Abu Dhabi government, Margaret Thatcher and her entourage went to Dubai for the afternoon. That evening, she flew to Muscat, the capital of Oman, with her party, which included Douglas Hurd, the Foreign Office minister of state, Sir Ronald Ellis, head of defence sales, Bernard Ingham, her press secretary, and Denis and Carol Thatcher. The prime minister stayed at the royal palace.

The following morning, 23 April, Margaret Thatcher visited the British embassy, where she met the staff and businessmen over coffee hosted by Ivor Lucas, the ambassador. She then went upstairs to the private sitting-room with Lucas for a 15-minute meeting. They did not see eye-to-eye on Oman. Lucas, in his understated, diplomatic manner, was critical of the Sultan's regime. 'The Sultan is spending too much on defence and on the city of Muscat,' he told her, 'and not enough on economic development for the majority of his people in the villages.'[18] He argued that Qaboos needed to make democratic concessions to ensure stability, otherwise political unrest would threaten British trade and strategic interests in the Gulf. Mrs Thatcher, who was in a restless mood and did not appear to be listening too intently, disagreed fundamentally. She replied that she thought the Soviet threat was more important than the way the Sultan ran his country. Consequently, she argued, Oman needed to build up its arsenal and buy strategic defence equipment.

Her preoccupation with communist encroachment was noted by the *Times* correspondent Robert Fisk, who reported on her visit: 'Mrs

Thatcher – sitting in a cane chair at the edge of a 2,000-feet precipice – peered with concern into the impenetrable bank of cold mist and fog that obscured South Yemen. The Marxist enemy may have been invisible but there was little doubt that she could identify it.'[19]

The prime minister's attitude to Ambassador Lucas's views was noticed by her aides. 'She was dismissive and unhappy about his analysis,' recalled one. 'It was as if she was already receiving advice from others close to the Sultan,' said another source. This tense, impatient mood lasted throughout the tour. During her stay in Oman, she telephoned Sir Kenneth Clucas, the permanent secretary at the Department of Trade. She harangued him over the arrangements for the Oman trip and wanted more support from his department. She seemed even more highly strung than usual and Sir Kenneth, a diffident, quietly spoken mandarin, withstood the verbal barrage with some dignity. When he put down the telephone, he turned to a colleague and said in classic *Yes, Minister* tones, 'Prime ministers should take a holiday during parliamentary recesses.'[20]

After her visit to the embassy, Mrs Thatcher and her party flew down to Salalah, capital of Dhofar, the southern province of Oman. Accompanied by Denis and Carol Thatcher, Douglas Hurd and Ivor Lucas, the prime minister was escorted in a convoy of armoured limousines with inch-thick bullet-proof windows and they lunched at his state guest house, built by Taylor Woodrow. Just as the guests sat down for lunch, Mark Thatcher suddenly arrived. He had flown into Muscat at 10 a.m. that day on a Gulf Air flight to Muscat and then on to Salalah on the Commander of the Omani air force's plane. 'He was a CIP – Commercially Important Passenger,' said Steve Lowes, a Gulf Air duty officer. 'An Omani minister on the incoming flight was telling me that he had just dined with Mrs Thatcher and I thought, "Oh, Mark must be off to meet his mum."'[21]

When Mark walked into the dining-room, Ambassador Lucas was shocked to see him, as nobody had informed him that the prime minister's son was going to be in Oman. Nor was he aware of Thatcher's consultancy with Cementation. Privately, Lucas was angry about the underhand way this occurred but he maintained his diplomatic silence. The main topic of conversation over lunch was the balance of power in the Gulf and the possible repercussions for the region of the Iran–Iraq war, which had broken out eight months earlier. Then Mark abruptly changed the subject and argued with his mother over his participation in the Nuremberg car rally. He was very keen to race but she was not happy about his competing and expressed her displeasure. The university project was not discussed, according to an official who was present.

Before lunch, the prime minister had an involved private talk with Sultan Qaboos, which lasted just over an hour. She saw him as 'one of Britain's closest friends in the Gulf'. During their meeting, they discussed the 'Sultan of Oman's requirements for military equipment'. She suggested he purchase the ground-attack Hawk aircraft rather than the more expensive Tornado.[22]

By her own account, she also raised the university project. 'I was advised to raise the matter of the whole university contract with the government of Oman,' she said later. 'I did it. I believed in it very forcefully because I wanted the business to come to Britain.'[23] She denied that she specifically asked for Cementation to be awarded the contract. However, as Cementation was the only British company allowed to bid, she was lobbying for them anyway – de facto. The Sultan, accompanied by his deputy Prime Minister Qaid Al-Zawawi, replied that he intended to award the contract to Cementation.

In the meantime, Mark Thatcher was flying back to Muscat to meet Jamil Amyuni, Cementation's marketing director. Amyuni was very familiar with what made the country tick, according to John Townsend, a former chief economic adviser to the Omani government who knew the Lebanese businessman for ten years. Townsend, who visited Oman for over 15 years as a businessman and consultant, was later asked how the arrival of Mark Thatcher would have led to certain assumptions in the minds of government ministers.

Interviewed by Granada TV's *World In Action* programme, he was asked, 'Would Omanis assume if the relative was in the country, then the head of government expected the contract to go to the relative?'

'They would certainly assume that,' he replied. 'That would be normal practice.'

'Why is that?'

'They would say that it's a normal part of business. It is recognised as normal in the Arab world for people in positions of authority to use that position for their own business interests. They would regard that as perfectly normal for other people as well.'[24]

Once Mark Thatcher's presence was confirmed, the prime minister's private office became concerned. They were not aware that he was a paid consultant to Cementation International but it was no secret in Whitehall and the Foreign Office that he had commercial interests in the Gulf. 'Her son Mark was not part of her entourage but he popped up from time to time in support of his business interests and handled himself in a way which I found embarrassing,' Douglas Hurd, the former Foreign Office minister who was present during the trip, recorded in his memoirs. 'The prime minister, whose own behaviour was impeccable, could not be persuaded that Mark's commercial ambitions were mainly of interest to the Gulf rulers because he was her son.'[25] The British embassy in Oman was also aware. One of its senior diplomats sent a confidential letter, recently obtained under the Freedom of Information Act, to the Foreign Office about Cementation's prospects of securing the contract and added: 'I believe Mark Thatcher is also associated with this firm.'

Clearly, as Mrs Thatcher had identified her trip as a commercial hard sell on behalf of British firms seeking export orders, there was a potential conflict of interests – at the very least. One of her private secretaries realised this and spoke to her. 'I was aware that Mark Thatcher was involved in oil trading, although I did not know then he was working for Cementation,' he told us. 'I suggested that her son's presence created a potential problem. I said it would be perceived in the wrong way. She replied that she was sensitive to the situation and would take my advice on board. But I have to say she was besotted by Mark and there was a blind spot, so whether she said anything to him I just don't know.'

The prime minister, unlike the British ambassador, knew full well that her son was going to be in Oman at the same time. Her daughter, Carol, told Gordon Martin, a BBC correspondent covering the trip, on the beach in Salalah that Mark was flying in for 'a family reunion'.[26]

Later that evening, Thursday, 23 April, Mrs Thatcher attended a formal state banquet as the guest of the Sultan. There are conflicting accounts of what was said during that dinner. After *The Observer* exposed Mark's relationship with Cementation and his visit to Oman, the paper received a letter written by a British army officer serving in the Omani Ministry of Defence. Written from Bait al Falaj, a military camp near Muscat, it stated: 'During dinner, Mrs Thatcher asked the Sultan about the next five-year plan. The Sultan explained that most of the capital expenditure would be for civil engineering works, at which Mrs Thatcher remarked that she hoped the Sultan would bear her son in mind as he was involved with a British contractor, Cementation. It did not go unnoticed that the Sultan showed some surprise at the remark.'[27] Diplomatic sources say that she did press the Sultan on the contract but did not mention Cementation.

When questioned later about her lobbying for Cementation, the prime minister replied vigorously, 'I bat for Britain. I don't distinguish between British companies. When I'm trying to secure contracts it is to try to get business for British companies and not overseas companies.'[28] 'Batting for Britain' became her stock answer during the Oman affair. It was a phrase devised for her by Bernard Ingham, her press secretary, to counter growing criticism.

Whitehall also defended her. Officials briefed the press, arguing that as Cementation was the only UK company seeking the university order, the prime minister could not be accused of favouring one firm over another. But this only made her case less credible. First, the contract was never put out to tender, which made it illegal under Omani law. Second, if Cementation was the only British company bidding, then Margaret Thatcher was obviously lobbying for Cementation! As her son was on Cementation's payroll she was also 'batting for Mark Thatcher Ltd'. Given that her own civil servants and the Foreign Office knew of his commercial interest, it is inconceivable that she did not know.

On 24 April 1981, the morning after the state banquet, the prime minister was given a helicopter tour of the Dhofar mountains and visited the military units there. Just before noon, she had another meeting with Sultan Qaboos in Salalah, in his remarkable palace, furnished by Asprey's and where leather-bound volumes of Trollope and Dickens decorated each bedroom. Then there was a private lunch at Mamurah, the Sultan's farm. This was a very restricted gathering, which excluded the British ambassador, Ivor Lucas, but did include some of the Sultan's closest advisers. Later that afternoon, Mrs Thatcher returned to Muscat and flew back to London the next day.

It was the vital, pivotal role of the Sultan's inner circle of confidants and courtiers that ensured the contract went to Cementation. It was a back-door deal, done through a coterie of British security counsellors, construction middlemen and Omani ministers – all with direct access to Sultan Qaboos. Mark Thatcher was, of course, indispensable to them. He was representing the right corporation and was in the right place at the right time. The company has always maintained that it secured the order before the prime minister's visit. But even one of their most loyal senior directors conceded to us, 'The university deal was won by a lot of hard work by us months before Mark was in Oman. There is no doubt he helped but I would say it was a combination of factors.'

A clue as to the source of real power and influence in Oman lies in the guest list of a special lunch at 10 Downing Street hosted by Margaret Thatcher on 17 March 1982. The lunch was in honour of Sultan Qaboos as part of his state visit. But its significance was that it took place the day after the university contract was publicly unveiled as 'one of the largest overseas orders to be won by a single building contractor'.[29] The function was therefore a celebratory affair, with the guests including British academics who were consulted over the project, such as Peter Morice, a professor of civil engineering, and also Nigel Broackes, chairman of Trafalgar House, the holding company of Cementation.

Mark Thatcher, who was seated opposite Morice, had suddenly cancelled an appearance in a celebrity golf tournament in Spain in order to attend. 'I have learnt there is to be a state visit during that week,' he wrote to the tournament organisers, 'so I hope you will understand this has to take precedence.'[30] For the prime minister's son to be a guest at an official state function was, in fact, most unusual, as Buckingham Palace pointed out. 'Mark Thatcher seldom takes part in state visits,' said a spokesperson, 'so there's no reason why he should do so this time.'[31]

However, the most important guest was the little-known Brigadier J.T.W. Landon, the Sultan's shadowy special adviser and a close associate of the prime minister's son. Before Margaret Thatcher embarked on her 'batting for Britain' tour in April 1981, Tim Landon met both Mark and Denis at 10 Downing Street.[32] The brigadier was known to be strongly in favour of Cementation for the university contract. This was effectively recognised at the Downing Street lunch, when ministers and officials adjourned upstairs. At the Sultan's request, Landon was awarded an honorary knighthood – a KCVO (Knight Commander of the Royal Victorian Order) – for 'services to British exports' by the prime minister. Such were his access and closeness to 10 Downing Street that Landon and Sultan Qaboos had private meetings with Margaret Thatcher at Chequers, that were not attended by any civil servants. According to one of her most senior foreign policy advisers, these tête-à-têtes were viewed with 'disquiet and concern' by Foreign Office officials.

These secret meetings were confirmed to us by two of Mrs Thatcher's private secretaries, who served her in the early 1980s. Landon's proximity to the affairs of state was such that an associate was once given a London telephone number to call him and was amazed to discover it was in the Cabinet Office.

In Oman, he was known as 'the White Sultan', such were his authority and status. 'Nothing can be done in Oman without Landon's knowledge and approval,' said an Arab businessman with interests in the region. A Buddhist, the brigadier is a cold, unsmiling man who never relaxes and is rarely rattled. 'He is the ultimate control freak,' said a source who knows him well. 'Everything Tim Landon does is calculated and premeditated. Nothing is left to chance.' He is so secretive that when he is in London he travels around in a privately owned black taxi cab for the sake of anonymity.

Landon's unparalleled influence over Sultan Qaboos can be traced back to the late 1950s when they were close friends at Sandhurst and where the Briton protected the Omani from bullying. In 1965, their friendship was rekindled when the brigadier was seconded to Oman during the Dhofar rebellion as a desert intelligence officer. 'Tim made a point of getting to know the local people', recalled a former colleague. 'He learned their language and his information was reliable.' He endeared himself to the ruler and two years later, after a brief course in military intelligence in London, he returned to Oman as the chief intelligence officer for the Sultan's armed forces.

It was the 1970 British-inspired coup that established Landon's power base. As the senior intelligence officer, he was in a unique position to help Qaboos overthrow his hated, despotic father, Sayyid bin Taimur. One account of the coup says that Landon led the military assault on the palace and was one of those who confronted the Sultan at the top of the stairs. They began firing and Sayyid bin Taimur was twice wounded. He then locked himself in a room and shouted, 'I will only give myself up to a British officer.' But he then managed to shoot himself in the foot and surrendered, and he later reluctantly abdicated. After leaving hospital, he was installed in the Dorchester Hotel, where he died two years later. When two former aides visited him near the end of his life, he was asked what was his greatest regret. 'Not killing Brigadier Landon,' the old man replied instantly.

After the coup, Landon helped install Qaboos. The new, grateful, 29-year-old Sultan rewarded the brigadier by making him his equerry, special adviser and chief military counsellor, and by awarding him an Omani diplomatic passport. He was now by far the most powerful official in the Omani government. An indication of his influence was that the Foreign Office official responsible for Oman had behind his desk a picture not of the Sultan but of the brigadier.[33]

Part of Landon's duties was to build up the Sultan's armed forces, and in the next decade he helped transform them into one of the best small armies in the Middle East. Defence became big business and by 1980 the budget for military equipment was £400 million. The problem was that Landon had no business acumen. Fortunately for him, he was introduced to Ronald Cheeseman, then managing director of Cogswell and Harrison Ltd, Britain's oldest arms manufacturer, which held a prohibited-weapons licence from the Ministry of Defence. Cheeseman was an experienced arms dealer and supplied the guns, usually from the United States, and the brigadier helped to sell them to Oman. They would meet at Cogswell and Harrison's office at 168 Piccadilly, central London, where orders were placed and negotiations conducted.

Landon's chief business partner in Oman was David Bayley, a former army officer who had learned to speak Arabic while serving in North Yemen. Bayley had moved to Oman in 1971, just after the coup. According to Lieutenant-Colonel Johnny Cooper, a founder member of the SAS who served in the Sultan's armed forces, Bayley set up a private office in Muscat as an arms dealer. Working with Colonel Jim Johnson, he then bought weapons for the Omani elite Special Forces. Landon found him useful because of his connections in South Africa and Rhodesia, and they began facilitating arms sales – working alongside Sayyid Fahr bin Taimur, the Sultan's uncle and Oman's defence minister. Their market was largely southern Africa and Afghanistan, and they worked closely with French arms manufacturers.

The Sultan also took a shine to the flamboyant Bayley and gave him a chauffeur-driven Rolls-Royce and paid for his stays at the Hyde Park Hotel, Knightsbridge, whenever he was in London. But it was not long before Bayley could afford to pay his own hotel bills. By the 1980s, he was reaping rich rewards as one of the four directors of Gulf Aviation Services Ltd, an Omani company which received some £2 million a year in commission fees from foreign companies to secure contracts. One of Landon and Bayley's unofficial agents was Mark Thatcher. In the mid-1980s they consulted him on some arms deals and visited him many times in Dallas, Texas, according to Simon Sloane, a former business associate who worked closely with Landon and Bayley during that period. Sloane met Thatcher twice – once with Bayley at the Mirabelle restaurant in London in 1986 and then in the company of both his business partners at the Ritz Hotel in Paris in 1989. 'Mark Thatcher was asked to find prices and products in the States for us for armoured personnel carriers, tanks, spare parts and air-to-ground rockets,' said Sloane. 'In 1989, the Omani air force needed some particular ammunition and so I rang Mark in Dallas and asked him to get us a quotation in the US. He was very enthusiastic but was always late on delivery and the work was incomplete. Landon and Bayley thought he could be helpful because the Thatcher name was big in the States.' But Bayley, in particular, found it frustrating to deal with him. 'Mark is useful but a complete idiot. He is so incompetent,' the arms dealer once said during a drinks party at Doyley Manor, his former Hampshire country mansion.

Bayley and Landon became fabulously wealthy from their Omani exploits. But while Landon conducts business with a ruthless, brutal logic, Bayley is emotional and temperamental. He spends most of his time in France as a tax exile. A heavy drinker, he is an exhibitionist and when he walked into the Ritz Hotel in Paris in the late 1980s the staff reacted as if he was the Prince of Wales. 'I have never seen such sycophancy,' said an eyewitness. 'The hotel staff and waiters fawn all over him. He gets the royalty treatment because he tips them £150 a time. He is always trying to impress and craves the attention and recognition.'

Landon's fortune was based more directly on the Sultan's patronage. After the coup, the brigadier received a 'thank you' payment from Qaboos. The exact amount is disputed. One source is adamant that it was £6 million tax free. Others say it was at least £3 million. One Christmas, the Sultan sent the brigadier a card with a message which said that he could not think of anything to buy him. Attached to the card was a cheque for £1 million, according to John Beasant, author of *Oman: The True Life Drama and Intrigue of an Arab State*. Whatever the exact fees, Landon's vast wealth, which by 2003 exceeded the Queen's fortune of £275 million, is apparent from his properties, huge country estates and lifestyle.

In 1978, he returned to Britain as a senior counsellor in the Omani embassy and immediately bought Faccombe Manor, a 100-acre country estate near Andover, north Hampshire. It cost him £2 million, paid through a Liechtenstein company, Etablissement Landon Co., and Mark and Denis Thatcher would spend weekends there at pheasant-shooting parties. It was no coincidence that the mansion was only a few miles from Wargrave Manor, the Sultan of Oman's country estate in a Thames-side hamlet near Reading, Berkshire. Qaboos had bought the residence three years earlier for £800,000 from Nigel (later Sir Nigel) Broackes, chairman of Trafalgar House plc, Cementation's holding company.[34]

Apart from Faccombe Manor, the brigadier also owns the entire village, runs a town house in London's Wilton Crescent, which is also used to accommodate visiting foreign guests, and an office in Green Street, Mayfair. He owns land in Cyprus and the south of France, a farm in Scotland and a 40,000-acre ranch in Zimbabwe. In 1994, Landon was able to pay £10 million for Gunnerside, a magnificent 36,000-acre north Yorkshire estate previously owned by Earl Peel and owns some of England's finest moorland.[35] His fortune was also visible through his own yacht – the *Katalina*, named after his Hungarian princess wife – the joint use of a private Boeing 707 and his own helicopter, which he later gave to the wealthy property and newspaper tycoons Sir David and Frederick Barclay.

In the summer of 1980, Landon officially 'retired' from the Omani government. He set up business as a 'consultant for Middle East clients' with an office in Mayfair's Upper Brook Street and another in Washington, where he hired Chet Nagel, a former CIA officer. But Landon remained Sultan Qaboos's most trusted and influential adviser and confidant. This was demonstrated by a letter written by Richard Helms, a former director of the CIA, who knew the brigadier well. Helms made enquiries about Landon's status and on 5 January 1981, three months before Margaret Thatcher's visit to Oman, he wrote to an American businessman: 'He is still the most influential individual on policy matters with the Sultan. The latter consults with him constantly. In fact, the Sultan has kept Landon on as chairman of his Planning Review Committee, which is the group making military policy and plans in Oman. To sum up, Tim Landon still has a most influential position in respect to the Sultan of Oman.'[36]

By the time Margaret and Mark Thatcher arrived in Oman on 23 April 1981, Cementation International was confident of winning the £300 million university contract. Its agents say they already had a letter of intent. But the Sultan, a solitary and indecisive man, had not decided, and so access to and influence over him became the crucial factor. Nobody could provide that better than Tim Landon. And so it proved.

For Mark Thatcher and Jamil Amyuni, a swift introduction to Qaboos was vital and Landon was the door opener. Within 24 hours of arriving in Muscat, Thatcher and Amyuni were meeting the head of state. 'Mark was able to get us to see the princes and rulers,' a former senior Cementation director told us. 'That's where he was useful and that's how Jamil used him on the Oman deal. He had the access to the Sultan.' In later years, the prime minister's son looked back with gratitude. 'The Sultan treated me like a son,' he told business associate Gary Smith on 4 December 1987. 'I saw him about six weeks ago and it was obvious we have gone as far as we can go in Oman. Too many people had gone on about the Cementation deal. It's a pity because I really liked him, a lovely man. He was very pro-British, you know.'

Timothy Landon was not the only facilitator on the university project. Ghassan Shaker, from Cementation Saudi Arabia Ltd, who first introduced Mark Thatcher to Oman, was influential in the early part of the negotiations. He also knew Landon and Bayley. But when it was discovered he was looking for a very high commission, his role was substantially reduced. Fortunately for Shaker, he had a separate private agreement with Amyuni, which allowed for smaller commissions to be paid through a Swiss company they had set up and registered at the President's Hotel, Geneva.

The person who effectively replaced Shaker was Dr Omar Zawawi, a personal adviser to the Sultan since 1975, whose brother Qais was deputy prime minister. Zawawi, who was active in oil deals, moved in amidst anxiety about the slow progress of the contract and counselled Qaboos about the merits of favouring Cementation. Eventually, in September 1981, the Sultan formally awarded the order to Cementation International to build the university. Within days, on 9 September, the company activated its Omani-registered subsidiary, Cementation SICO Ltd, to represent its interests as a joint-venture agreement. Four Omani ministers owned 35 per cent of SICO, including two foreign affairs ministers – Yousef al-Alawi Abdullah and Salim Ahmed Khalfan – and Abdel Aziz al-Rowas, the minister for information. All four later sold their stakes.[37]

The business was originally worth £215 million to Cementation. This rose to £300 million when they also secured a hospital contract. Part of the deal was underwritten by British public money, as the Export Credit Guarantee Department (ECGD) guaranteed a £150 million loan provided by a syndicate of banks led by Morgan Grenfell. At first, the Treasury and ECGD were not persuaded to cover 85 per cent of the contract, as requested by Cementation. A letter from the Foreign Office to the Treasury, obtained under the Freedom of Information Act, reveals that the dispute in Whitehall about approving the financial underwriting was linked to the personal involvement of Mrs Thatcher. 'The decision to award this contract to a British firm [Cementation] was a direct result of the prime minister having discussed British interest in the project with the Sultan when she visited Oman in April,' stated the letter. 'The Sultan's decision, therefore, can be seen as a political gesture: the Omanis may well feel slighted if they learn that HMG is now demurring in supporting its side of the project. That the prime minister took – and no doubt retains – a strong interest in the Project is quite certain.'

On 23 November 1981, two months after the Sultan had chosen Cementation, the Export Group for the Construction Industry held its annual luncheon at the Savoy Hotel. The guest speaker was Margaret Thatcher. Also present were Denis and her son, accompanied by Jamil Amyuni. As the guests gathered, Mark spoke to Lord Matthews, chief executive of Trafalgar House, which owned Cementation. Matthews then took his place at the luncheon table, seated next to the prime minister on her left. Her speech was apposite and full of irony. 'I was down in the Gulf recently,' she told the construction executives. 'I sometimes wonder if I missed a vocation. I should have been a head salesman of a company, where I would be a jolly sight better paid than I am now. So long as I get the orders for you and so long as you go on putting me back where I am now [i.e. electing her] so that I can go on getting orders for you, that will be absolutely marvellous.'[38]

Lord Matthews now says he had not expected to see her son at the lunch. 'I was surprised to see Mark Thatcher at the Savoy lunch,' he said from his retirement home in Jersey. 'I knew Mrs Thatcher would be there, of course, but I had not expected her son to attend.'[39] Three months later, in February 1982, details of the Qaboos University contract were finalised and signed. Cementation was delighted and paid tribute to the 'keen interest in the negotiations' shown by the prime minister.[40] The next month, the Sultan came to London for a state visit and celebrated the deal with a lunch at Downing Street, attended by Mark Thatcher and Nigel Broackes, chairman of Trafalgar House.

Details of the subsequent payments to Mark Thatcher have never appeared in the accounts of Trafalgar House, Cementation International or Monteagle Marketing, his own company. One of the more detailed press reports stated that he received, via his firm, a retainer of £34,000 a year, paid in quarterly instalments of £8,500.[41] These were paid into Monteagle's Barclays bank account at 415 The Strand. The co-signatories to the account were Steve Tipping, Mark's business partner, and Denis Thatcher.[42]

Tipping later claimed that their fees would be published in

Monteagle's annual returns. 'The Omani money will appear in our accounts,' he said. 'There will be a queue at the door for the company's returns.' But this never happened, as the money was not accounted for in the 1981–82 returns. Instead, Thatcher's friends briefed the press that Cementation paid him only £59,000.[43] This amount is disputed by Gulf sources, who say that Mark would also have received a commission – normal practice on Middle East construction deals – as high as £3 million (or 1 per cent of the contract price).

A clue as to how he was paid is contained in a private and confidential memo by Alastair Brett, legal director of Times Newspapers, based on a lunch he had with Ian Sayer, a friend and former employer of Mark Thatcher. In early 1984, when Mark's relationship with Cementation in Oman was under public scrutiny, Thatcher drove down to see Sayer at his house in West Drive, Wentworth, Surrey. The prime minister's son had always admired the wealthy transport businessman. He was exactly the kind of young, self-made entrepreneur Mark aspired to be. A man of extreme right-wing views, whose huge Volvo trucks had been instrumental in strike-breaking in the 1970s, Sayer was thrilled to be part of the Thatcher golden circle. He loved going to 10 Downing Street for drinks parties. He was also a deft hand at tax avoidance and it was on this delicate topic that Mark came to ask his advice.

According to Brett's memo, Mark told Sayer he was worried about the tax implications of the commission fee he was paid by Cementation for the university contract. Mark then sketched out on a piece of paper in some detail how his fee was channelled by Cementation through a Swiss company. Brett accepts he wrote the document but has only 'a hazy recollection of the memo and the circumstances under which it was written'.[44] Sayer told the authors, 'I have met Alastair Brett over the years and have met him for lunch, but that account does not accord with my memory. To be honest, I just can't remember.' Eventually the transport executive rediscovered his memory. When pressed by Barrie Penrose, a former *Sunday Times* journalist, he said, 'I accept that Alastair Brett's memo is accurate.'

The Oman affair affected Margaret Thatcher deeply. Ever since Mark was a young boy, she had tried to compartmentalise her life so that her children were separate from her public duties. For her, Mark's business activities bore no relevance to her being prime minister. She resented what she saw as the intrusion into her private family concerns. 'She would arrive in Finchley,' said Andrew Thomson, then her constituency agent, 'and very occasionally complain how badly he [Mark] was being treated by the media. But this was said not as an encouragement to further conversation on the subject, more as a mutter to herself.'[45]

Colleagues, including supportive cabinet ministers, were astonished at how protective the prime minister was towards Mark.[46] 'She's very sensitive about the boy,' said Edward (now Sir Edward) du Cann, a senior MP and chairman of the Conservative 1922 back-benchers' committee who later acknowledged, 'Mark exploited his mother's position quite unashamedly, demanding services from Britain's overseas representatives and using 10 Downing Street for personal purposes.'[47] The late Alan Clark, a former defence minister and close ally of Margaret Thatcher, recorded in his diary after talking to her in the Commons during the Oman controversy: 'He [Mark] must be a source of anxiety.'[48]

For the prime minister, criticism of Mark was a personal attack on her. 'What was important to Margaret Thatcher during the entire affair,' said Andrew Thomson, 'was that she was being challenged not just as a politician but as a mother.'[49] It was this inability or unwillingness to understand how her son's private commercial interests conflicted with her role as prime minister that would later undermine her credibility among colleagues and friends. 'It was a complete blind spot,' said one former Downing Street aide who dealt with Mark at the time of the Oman affair. 'She just could not come to terms with the implications of what he was doing and how it could have affected her politically. None of us could talk to her about it. She just wouldn't listen.'

The key question which Mrs Thatcher never answered in Parliament or in the media is whether she knew at the time of her Oman visit about her son's consultancy with Cementation. When directly and repeatedly asked this by Sir Robin Day on BBC TV, she refused to answer and would only say, 'I answer for what I do . . . I don't mention the names of particular companies and didn't on that occasion. I said it was vitally important that the business comes to Britain.'[50] When asked in the Commons to state categorically 'yes' or 'no' whether she knew, she again refused.[51]

During her BBC interview, Thatcher said that the full facts of the Oman affair could not be made public because 'discussions between heads of governments are confidential', particularly on 'commercial contracts'. She added that they would be published in 30 years when government records were released.[52] However, this was incorrect, as she was later forced to admit. In a letter to Peter Shore, shadow leader of the Commons, she acknowledged that the government documents did not contain the information which she refused to give Parliament. 'No reasonable person would expect the public record to cover the matters in those questions,' she wrote.[53] Consequently, the papers released in the year 2011 will not reveal the truth of what happened in Oman.

Despite being repeatedly asked to account fully for her actions (23 times in all), Mrs Thatcher stonewalled. One former trade minister was bemused by her approach. 'The curious aspect of the Oman business was that she intervened at all in foreign contracts,' he recalled. 'I mean, in 1981 most of us were monetarists and we couldn't understand why she kept going on about "batting for Britain". Let the market decide was our view . . . I could understand she was upset because it involved her family but I felt she was a seasoned street-fighter and she was being over-sensitive about it.'

Mrs Thatcher's parliamentary replies were drafted by Robin (now Lord) Butler, then her principal private secretary and later cabinet secretary. 'That's the way to handle it, prime minister,' he told her in 10 Downing Street. 'We don't need to go further than that.' It was the time-honoured method of answering tricky Commons questions – provide just enough information to enable the prime minister to refer to previous answers.

'As part of my public duties,' she told the Commons in her first statement on the Oman saga, 'I make strenuous efforts to secure contracts for this country. I do not decide upon those contracts. The decisions are made by the governments which give them. I do not distinguish between companies in this country. My job is to see that we get the contracts and the business here. As a result of that particular tour, hundreds of millions of pounds' worth of contracts came to this country.'[54] After that initial answer, she blocked further questions by saying, 'I have nothing to add to what I said on this matter in the House of Commons yesterday.'[55] She also refused to set up an inquiry, make a statement to the House or issue guidelines to ministers who are seeking contracts when their children have a financial interest in the outcome.[56]

Her only substantial attempt to justify refusing to answer the charge that her son benefited financially was to argue that her family was entitled to privacy. 'I answer for my public duties from this dispatch box,' she said, 'and members of my family are as much entitled to privacy in going about their private duties as any other citizen. I hope we have not reached the stage when parents and their sons have to report everything to the authorities. If it comes to that, 1984 will be here.'[57]

Eventually, the prime minister did respond to the central issue when she was asked 'whether there was a conflict between her private family interests and her public duties on the Oman University deal'. But she chose to ignore the reference to 'private family interests' and replied, 'There was no question of conflict arising between my private interests and public duties.'[58] This, of course, did not answer the question. The issue was her family's private interests, not specifically her own.

Mark Thatcher only twice surfaced to comment on the controversy. In an interview with the *Sunday Times*, he confirmed his financial involvement in the university contract and that he had met his mother while she was in Oman. 'I played a very small part in a very successful British contract,' he said. He was unconcerned that the contract was not put out to tender: 'It is the prerogative of the client to decide the method of awarding the contract.'[59]

In a later interview with his friend Rodney Tyler, published in the *Mail on Sunday*, he was more defensive and emotional: 'I have done nothing wrong – nothing I should be ashamed of. So I don't have to stand up and answer questions about my private affairs. It's all innuendo and speculation . . . I suppose I have been naive. I have only ever been Mark Thatcher so I don't know what it is like to be anyone else. I grew up with my mother as she is, though I realise now I have been naive about it . . . Naive to think that this business was just to do with me and my partner and nothing to do with my mother. I see now how they have used me to get at her.'[60]

Friends and colleagues of the prime minister became increasingly concerned about the political consequences of Mark's business affairs. 'It was a time-bomb ticking away inside 10 Downing Street,' said one close associate. 'I can tell you without any reservation that we were very worried about Mr Thatcher's activities,' Sir Edward du Cann told us. Sir Edward had direct access to the Tory chief whip and the prime minister and was extremely influential within the party. 'I was receiving reports from Conservative MPs which disturbed me,' he said. 'I would say there were two phases. The first stage was when he was doing things that could embarrass the prime minister by associating with the wrong type of people. At the time I discounted this to some extent because he was a bit of a joke figure. But then there was a second stage where I was receiving reports about how he was trading off her office.'

Sir Edward was sufficiently concerned to make two formal verbal reports to two separate chief whips during the Thatcher years. 'Thank you very much for the information. Noted,' replied one of them in the time-honoured Tory way of receiving such representations. It is not known whether they discussed Mark's activities with the prime minister herself. But one of them, John Wakeham, was sufficiently perturbed to privately meet Tiny Rowland, then owner of *The Observer*, and discuss the situation. Even in America, the pro-Thatcher Reagan administration saw it as a crisis. A confidential telegram written by the US State Department to George Shultz, secretary of state, on 19 March 1984, stated: 'Most of [Mark] Thatcher's business dealings were predicated on the belief that he had only one asset – with a limited lifespan – his link to the British prime minister. He was apparently willing to offer the use of his name to anyone willing to pay the requisite substantial fee. The businessmen who found such an asset worth the price tended to be on the shady side and Mrs Thatcher is now being forced to pay the price of her son's avarice.'

Inside Tory Central Office, the anxiety level was equally high. 'The problem we had was that she [Mrs Thatcher] used to put up such a stonewall whenever anyone raised it, so the Mark Factor became out of bounds for us,' a former senior party official told us. 'I was very close to Margaret during one election campaign, and I saw that she and Denis had difficulties with regard to Mark. He was kept away from things, yet she was edgy and felt guilty when he was not around. I think it was very draining on her personally.'

A senior Conservative MP who was anxious about the situation was Ian Gow, Margaret Thatcher's devoted parliamentary private secretary from 1979 until the 1983 election. Gow was almost universally admired and respected in the party and was in love, politically, with the prime minister. He was a political intelligence officer and trouble-shooter who knew how to drink with the troops in the Commons after midnight. He retained the prime minister's confidence and saw her son's commercial activities as potentially extremely damaging. 'It's very serious,' he told a colleague. Gow used to have regular informal meetings with senior MPs on what he called political 'trip-wires' and 'elephant traps'. A recurrent topic was what he called 'the Mark problem'.

One incident which disturbed Gow occurred just after the 1983 election. It concerned a naval architect called Commander Peter Thornycroft who had designed a new boat for the Royal Navy known as the 'short fat frigate' (the S90). In the early 1980s, Thornycroft became embroiled in a long-running dispute with the Ministry of Defence, which was resistant to the project. Thornycroft and his company, TT Boat Designs Ltd, claimed they were being deliberately obstructed and victimised by MoD civil servants and the naval establishment.

By the summer of 1983, Thornycroft and his partners had been awarded a development contract for a programme of testing of the hull. However, they desperately needed to get approval for the building of the frigate. And so they needed all the political muscle they could acquire. In September 1983, Thornycroft thought his luck had changed. One of his supporters was a director of the Frank Williams racing team and offered to act as an intermediary and lobby on his behalf. One of the people he approached was Mark Thatcher, who was courting Williams at the time.

One Saturday, Thatcher turned to the intermediary and said, 'All this stuff about the frigate. Doesn't it depend on whether the tank testing will work?'

'That's right,' said the Williams director.

'Well, why don't you get Thornycroft to write a one-page memo on the testing and I will put it in front of my mother,' said Mark.

The intermediary told Thornycroft and his associates, who were very excited. Their initial enthusiasm was tempered with caution when they consulted Ian Gow. 'Be careful when you deal with Mark Thatcher,' Gow counselled. 'He is her Achilles' heel.' But then they spoke to Captain John Moore, a former controller of the navy, who told them about the prime minister's views on the Ministry of Defence. Moore had recently met Mrs Thatcher at Chequers. 'The place that bothers me more than anywhere else is the Ministry of Defence,' she told him. 'It's like a concrete bunker. If you give me a bomb, I'll put it in there.'

Armed with this knowledge, the naval architect realised that appealing direct to 10 Downing Street was the ideal way of bypassing the MoD. On 21 September 1983, he wrote a one-page memo entitled 'Tank Testing – The S90 Frigate', and attached a covering letter to his influential supporter. The note, which is in our possession, stated: 'I enclose an envelope addressed to Mark Thatcher inside which is a memorandum which I think may explain some of the misunderstandings over the way the Ministry of Defence are judging our results . . . If you happen to have a chance of passing this over to him when you next see him, I feel that this may help when consideration is being given to our S90 proposals.'

Thornycroft's eager anticipation was shown by a letter he wrote the following day to Holst Sørensen, a Danish shipbuilder. 'As regards the S90, I have written a brief memo,' he said. 'This memo is, in fact, for Mark Thatcher, the prime minister's son, in the hope that it may find its way on to Mrs Thatcher's desk . . . Mark Thatcher is to be a spectator at the British Grand Prix and has asked to have some information about the tank testing results of the S90.'

By early March 1984, at the climax of the Oman affair, such stories were being logged in the upper echelons of the prime minister's inner circle. Many of her courtiers were concerned about the effect her son's activities could have on her political credibility and public image. The most prominent was Tim (now Lord) Bell, her media guru and one of her most influential advisers. As managing director of Saatchi & Saatchi, Bell had masterminded the Conservative Party's advertising campaign during the 1983 election and had become a close confidant of Margaret Thatcher. He also became friendly with Mark and advised him informally, though not as a client, on his media relations. But this was done as a favour and out of loyalty to his mother rather than from any personal admiration.

Publicly, Margaret Thatcher's favourite advertising executive defended him. 'He is tenacious, hard-working and has never courted publicity,' said Bell. 'I respect him enormously.'[61] 'I think what has been happening is that the media has been trying to get at Mrs Thatcher through her son,' he told the *Sunday Times*. 'It is nothing more nor less than a vendetta. The poor man is not a public figure but he has been rubbished left, right and centre. Why should he have anything but contempt for the media?'[62] Privately, Bell had a rather different view of the misunderstood prodigal son. In the summer of 1983, during a birthday dinner party which was tape-recorded by an enterprising journalist, he remarked, 'Mark Thatcher is a twit. In my opinion, he has nothing to offer the world.'[63]

Despite his staunch public rearguard action, Bell was a shrewd strategist and knew Mark's commercial activities were politically explosive. 'Tim thought he was a bomb just waiting to go off,' said a political source close to him at the time. This resulted in Bell secretly coordinating a public relations operation on behalf of the prime minister's son to limit the damage caused by the Oman disclosures. Late one Friday night in March 1984, he telephoned David Boddy, the former director of publicity at Tory Central Office, who had worked closely with Margaret Thatcher during the 1979 election. He asked him to come over to his house the following afternoon. The topic for discussion was the media treatment of Mark Thatcher. Bell told Boddy that the prime minister had 'requested his assistance' in dealing with the press and television coverage of her son.

Boddy, who had left Central Office to set up his own private company, Capital Publishing, agreed and was hired on a one-month contract for a fee of £18,000. He was paid by Bell, who secured the funds from Conservative-supporting businessmen. But the PR consultant received only £5,000 and never saw the remaining £13,000. It was never disclosed who bankrolled the 'Save Mark operation'. When asked, Boddy replied, 'A group of senior Conservatives. They were not based at Central Office but they were connected with it.'[64]

Under Boddy's tutelage a small informal group was formed, including Michael Dobbs, a Saatchi & Saatchi executive, and the journalist Rodney Tyler. Sir Gordon Reece, another of Margaret Thatcher's media Svengalis, was also consulted for strategic advice. Their brief was to engage in 'crisis management'. Their aim was to keep Mark out of the newspapers and remove him from the news agenda; but, when there were press enquiries, to ensure questions were answered and statements released.

At first Mark cooperated. He called in when arriving at Heathrow airport so that photo opportunities could be arranged. But then he began to act irrationally and showed signs of stress. His moods swung dramatically – from anger to despair to persecution complexes. 'It's become "Get Mark Thatcher Time" in certain sections of the media,' he said. 'And they don't care how they do it.'[65]

This resulted in bouts of manic and unstable behaviour. One night he attended the Miss World dinner at the Grosvenor House ballroom. After the main course, he suddenly stood up and started throwing sugar lumps at the journalists covering the beauty contest, shouting obscenities at them. 'He was on the verge of cracking up,' said one PR aide who witnessed this spectacle. His neurotic psyche was noticeable during periodic stays at the Athenaeum Hotel on Piccadilly where he was 'hiding out'. He was seen dashing around the corridors, barking orders at the receptionists and concierge.

According to one Conservative operative close to Mark Thatcher at the time, the more heat the media and Parliament generated the more paranoid he became. 'I remember getting a phone call from

Mark on a Sunday afternoon,' recalled his friend Rodney Tyler. 'He had just arrived at Heathrow airport and his main concern was that he was getting Special Branch protection. He sounded absolutely frantic.'

It did not help that Thatcher was surly and suspicious of David Boddy and made it almost impossible for him to do his job. He was always late for appointments, he never responded to questions with a straight answer, and his PR adviser had to talk privately to Steve Tipping, Mark's business partner, to find out what was going on.

The major problem for the crisis-management team was that Thatcher and Tipping refused to disclose any detailed information or answer questions about the Oman contract. 'The press are out to get me,' was all Mark could offer and so Boddy was reduced to issuing bland, meaningless denials. This, of course, made it extremely difficult to defuse the situation and only kept Thatcher in the firing line – rather than out of it. The Mark timebomb continued to tick away underneath 10 Downing Street; it was only a matter of time before it exploded. Something more drastic than effective public relations was required.

SIX

Exile in the USA

There's nothing wrong with having a lot of money. It is not the fact of having money that is wrong, it is when it becomes the sole and the only thing in your life.
– Margaret Thatcher[1]

Mark's hasty retreat to the United States of America was due mainly to counsel from the prime minister's inner circle of advisers, friends and her husband Denis. They believed that 'the Mark factor' was highly damaging to the government and undermined her authority. 'There was a real problem and real cause for concern,' recalled one of her aides, who was also close to her son. 'We thought the stakes were very high. Some of us felt his activities could really hurt her.'

And so at the height of the Oman crisis, Tim Bell and Gordon Reece, her media advisers; Lord McAlpine, the Tory Party treasurer; and Denis Thatcher attended a secret meeting at 19 Flood Street, the family's Chelsea home. It was essentially a 'What to do about Mark' summit. They discussed the situation and realised that damage limitation was not sufficient and something more drastic was required. Denis suggested that he should talk to David Wickins, a business associate and family friend, about arranging a job for Mark, preferably overseas. He telephoned Wickins and a lunch at Chequers was arranged at short notice, also attended by Margaret Thatcher and Tim Bell. They agreed that Mark needed to leave the country. The deed was done.

Wickins, the king of second-hand-car auctions, knew Denis because he owned a 36 per cent shareholding in Attwoods, the waste-disposal company. 'I was a friend of the Thatcher family and Denis was on the Attwoods board,' recalled Wickins, speaking from his retirement home in Ibiza. 'What happened was that I was watching the Grand Prix in Detroit at a rooftop party. Mark was there with some people from Team Lotus and that's when I offered him a job.'

Mark did not need long to make up his mind. 'It makes sense to move away,' he told Rodney Tyler, 'keep a low profile for a while and pull out of most of my present commitments – if only to examine each one from top to bottom. I have made this decision to live in the United States not least to show how sorry I am for the totally unnecessary aggravation all this business has caused my mother.[2] He also knew Wickins well, as British Car Auctions had sponsored his motor racing by paying him £6,000 for at least a year.[3]

Within a few days, on 20 March 1984, Thatcher's company, Monteagle Marketing Ltd, had been closed down and he had resigned his consultancy with Cementation International Ltd. His secretary, Brenda Sanger, continued to work for him for a further three years but mainly part time. She now lives in Chesterfield and has a house in Florida. 'I cannot talk to you without Mark's permission,' she said.

Mark's mood was one of angry resignation. 'It's been twelve bloody weeks when they've slung every bit of mud at me they can,' he said. 'Twelve weeks when they've accused me of being just about everything from a crook to a con man . . . If my partner Steve Tipping and I had robbed the Bank of England of £20 million, Mum would not have been to blame. But they would have tried.'[4]

But he was hardly going to be destitute and in late March 1984 he flew by Concorde with David Wickins, his new boss, to New York, his new home for the time being. Thatcher was hired as a consultant to Anglo-American Auto Auctions (AAAA) Inc., a subsidiary of British Car Auctions, on a salary of £45,000 a year. Based in Nashville, Tennessee, AAAA Inc. was a second-hand-car company set up in 1982 and run by Mike Richardson, an expatriate Yorkshireman.

Two weeks earlier, Richardson had received a telephone call from David Wickins. 'David said Mark Thatcher was moving to America and would be joining the company,' recalled Richardson. 'He said Mark was very good with numbers and would be useful to us on new acquisitions. He didn't have anything to do with the running of the existing 12 car auction sites. But if we were looking at new auctions, I sent him off to look at the locations and he advised me if the business was worth acquiring. I found him a level-headed, sensitive businessman but his personality changed when he was faced with the press. He became a different person and just couldn't handle it.'[5]

Essentially, his job was to promote and advise AAAA Inc. throughout the United States. But favourable publicity and Mark Thatcher are not often mentioned in the same sentence. David Wickins was clearly mindful of this. 'I appreciate that some people think he's an arrogant sod,' he said at the time. 'But I'm sure Mark will be a great asset. What I have to do perhaps is to persuade him to calm down a bit . . . to teach him to be a bit less aggressive with people. I suppose that is a thing of youth and you can't really blame him for being so uppity. He comes over very well as an upstanding young Englishman and that goes down particularly well in the sunshine states.'[6]

Clearly, personality was a key factor in his new job. But Mark seemed relatively unconcerned about his charm bypass. 'Some would call it arrogance,' he said. 'Some do. I would say, arrogantly, that I tend to be short with people. I don't tolerate fools. Period. It's something I've got from my parents. Neither of them tolerates idiots easily – what I have to do is learn to be a little softer about it.'[7] But moving to America did not smooth over the hard edges. During one lunch in Detroit with Wickins, the prime minister's son was irritated with what he saw as slow service. 'Look, I am Mark Thatcher,' he told the waitress. 'I don't care if you are Mark Twain, you take your turn like everybody else,' was her response.

Thatcher also worked in some capacity for Lotus Cars. One report stated he was 'an associate director'.[8] The company denied he was on the Lotus payroll and said he was merely working for one of their US subsidiaries. But the confusion was caused by Mark himself, who publicly proclaimed that he was 'selling Lotus' in the USA and referred to 'the Lotus job'.[9] Whatever the exact arrangement, he was certainly involved in building a chain of dealerships for the luxury sports car across the USA and Canada in preparation for a North American sales drive in 1985 to promote the new X100 car. 'His name is worth quite a few motor cars,' said Wickins, who was by then also chairman of Lotus.[10] The company's managing director, Michael Kimberley, was more explicit: 'He helps establish dealer points and arranges wine and cheese parties, to which he brings the right sort of people.'[11]

Mark was indebted to Wickins. He saw it as 'a real responsibility and a chance for which I am grateful'.[12] But he was not short of self-confidence. 'The Lotus job is a great challenge and one where I intend to use my name ruthlessly to win orders for Britain – my name, that is, as a racing commentator and sports car expert,' he declared. 'People in the performance car world in America just don't give a damn who my mother is. They know me for my expertise and experience.'[13]

Thatcher had already been working for the company behind the scenes for over three years. 'Mark has been a very good friend to Lotus for some time,' said Alan Curtis, the company's deputy chairman.[14] Mark and Curtis became close associates. According to Gerald James, former chairman of the arms manufacturer Astra Holdings, the Lotus boss regularly spoke of his friendship with the prime minister and her son. 'He told me on more than one occasion how he would visit 10 Downing Street at "Slipper Time",' recalled James. 'This was after 10.30 p.m. when Margaret Thatcher liked a chat with her favourite industrialists over a glass of whisky.'[15]

Mark Thatcher shamelessly used his position to promote the Lotus product and on one occasion deliberately parked the car that he had been given outside 10 Downing Street when he knew photographers and camera crews were waiting to film his mother leave. Norman Luck, the *Daily Express* journalist who had been fed stories by Mark in the mid-1970s, recalls being telephoned by Mark. 'He told me he was trying out new Lotus cars in the West End of London,' said Luck. 'But when I arrived I was surprised to find Margaret Thatcher sitting in a Lotus Esprit promoting the company.'[16]

By late 1982, despite Mark Thatcher's efforts, Lotus was in desperate trouble. It was losing money and was in a bitter dispute with the Inland Revenue over protective tax assessments totalling £84 million. This was calculated as part of the Revenue's inquiry into missing money from the failed DeLorean venture. Lotus had received funds from DeLorean, the supercar manufacturer, to prepare production of its new gull-winged car. But the cash had disappeared and senior executives were being investigated for theft.

Colin Chapman, chairman of Lotus, who was the prime suspect and later accused of embezzlement, approached Alan Curtis, who had enjoyed a successful career at Aston Martin and just sold his shareholding there. 'Lotus needs to change its image,' said Chapman over lunch. 'We need to revamp the corporate side of the company and we're having trouble with the DeLorean business. Will you join us and help restructure the company?' Curtis accepted and joined the board. Two days later, Fred Bushell, the managing director later convicted of fraud over the DeLorean affair, telephoned to say Chapman had died.

For the first six months of 1983, Curtis and Michael Kimberley, the new managing director, worked day and night to rescue Lotus. The company was in crisis, often on the brink of being sold to the Japanese. In July, Curtis consulted Mark Thatcher and discussed the situation. Thatcher responded by setting up a meeting with David Wickins. Five days later, Wickins bought a 29 per cent stake in Lotus and became chairman, with Curtis as his deputy. 'If David had not invested, then Lotus would have gone under,' Curtis told us over coffee at the Savoy Hotel.

Mark Thatcher played an active role as a middleman, massaging people on both sides and acting as a facilitator for new investors. He was not paid a retainer during this period but did receive expenses and free use of a Lotus. 'He helped us a great deal,' recalled Curtis. 'He used his clout and opened up all the right doors in Detroit and all the right top people in the motor industry.'[17] Using the Thatcher name, Mark then introduced Lotus to the chief executives and chairmen of General Motors (GM) and Chrysler. The key move was in 1984, when Thatcher introduced Curtis to Robert Eaton, a senior vice-president of GM.

Eaton, Thatcher, Curtis and Wickins met for dinner at the Savoy, where the long-term future of the company was discussed. It was this connection with Eaton which paved the way for the successful friendly takeover of Lotus by GM. By late 1985, an initial list of thirty-two companies had been reduced to five (two American and three British) before GM was chosen. In a deal which valued the company at £22.7 million, GM bought 58 per cent of the shares, including Wickins's 29 per cent stake. The takeover was completed in January 1986 and Mark Thatcher resigned his consultancy with both Lotus Performance Cars and Anglo-American Auto Auctions. By then, he was settled in the United States, where other business activities awaited him.

Mark Thatcher's stay in New York was always likely to be temporary. He lived at the expensive Regency Hotel, Park Lane, in Manhattan and his job with Anglo-American Auto Auctions meant travelling throughout the United States. But it was a blind date in Texas four months earlier that precipitated his permanent move south. On 22 December 1983, he had flown down to Dallas to watch the Cowboys play the Washington Redskins at American football. That evening, he was having dinner with oil billionaire Perry Bass and his wife, Nancy, when he found himself sitting next to Karen Fortson, a stunning 24-

year-old brunette from Fort Worth, Texas, and one of the wealthiest and most eligible women in the South. She was the daughter of Ben Fortson, a multimillionaire from oil and cattle-ranching stock, and Kay (née Carter), who had inherited a fortune from her own family based on grain, insurance and oil. The Fortsons were the arbiters of Fort Worth's old-moneyed aristocracy, keen to add dignity and culture to their wealth, in contrast to what they saw as the brash, flash nouveau riche crowd in Dallas.[18]

Karen, who had worked in a New York art auction house, was conservative, introvert, rich, well bred, radiant and, above all, very discreet. Mark was attracted to her immediately. 'I was struck by her poise and beauty,' he said. Karen was equally impressed. 'I don't make a habit of blind dates,' she remarked, 'but I was intrigued to know what Mark Thatcher was like. My first impression was that he was nice and rather reserved. I'm quite reserved myself, so it's good to meet someone else like that.'[19]

Romance soon blossomed and Mark became a frequent visitor to the family's palatial mansion in Westover Hill, just outside Fort Worth. The house boasted a vestibule the size of a Greek temple – a symbol of the family fortune estimated at £100 million.[20] The couple became very close and Mark even turned down some driving offers. 'Karen isn't very keen on motor racing,' he explained.[21] Their courtship was very low key and they once cancelled a weekend party at a Fort Worth nightclub to 'stay out of the limelight'.[22]

Their relationship was tested barely a month after they met with the Oman revelations. 'Karen was an enormous support to me. I don't know how I'd have got through without her,' said Mark. 'Things haven't been easy for him,' she said loyally, 'but he's really pulled himself together and coped with the problems . . . I felt the pressures, too, but his must have been a hundred times greater.'[23]

In the midst of the crisis, on Saturday, 18 February 1984, Mark took her to Chequers to spend the weekend with his parents. That evening, they entertained oil magnate Perry Bass and his wife, Nancy, for dinner. In the morning, the couple and Margaret and Denis attended service at St Peter's Church in the Buckinghamshire village of Ellesborough. By pure chance, but with remarkably apposite irony, the service happened to focus on the evils of wealth. 'Wisdom cannot be bought with silver or gold,' the church warden Bill Mitton read from the Gospel of St Luke to the congregation. 'How blessed are you who are poor, the Kingdom of God is yours. Alas for you who are rich, you have had your time of happiness.'[24] Mark and Karen then joined the prime minister for an official lunch for Crown Prince Naruhito of Japan, at which the guests included Princess Alexandra, Angus Ogilvy, Clive Sinclair and political friends. A sensitive Margaret Thatcher paid the bill out of her own purse for her son and girlfriend.

Karen and Mrs Thatcher established an immediate rapport. 'I found her so warm and pleasant,' said the Texan heiress.[25] 'She makes you feel so warm and comfortable.' This was apparent when the prime minister invited Mark, Karen, Karen's twin brother, Ben, and her mother for Sunday lunch at Chequers. On the morning of 13 May 1984, the party flew in from Paris and posed for photographers, arranged by Mark's friend Rodney Tyler. 'Come on, hurry up,' he snapped, glaring at the cameras. 'We will be late for lunch.'[26] He then drove Karen to his mother's country residence in his silver Lotus Esprit while her family followed in their Daimler.

The lunch went well and Karen gave only a cautious denial of any wedding plans. It seemed marriage was only a matter of time, particularly when Mark moved to Dallas – a mere thirty miles west of Fort Worth, Karen's home town – six weeks later. On 1 June 1984, he moved into a one-bedroom rented apartment at Terrace House in the elite Turtle Creek area for $1,000 a month.

However, by mid-July 1984, his romance with Karen Fortson had rather abruptly wilted. 'Anyone waiting for an engagement is going to wait for a very long time,' she said caustically.[27] It was never clear why she broke off the relationship so soon after Mark arrived in Dallas. 'She thought it would be entertaining and glamorous to date him,' said a Fortson family friend. 'But she didn't know he wouldn't be socially acceptable in Dallas.'[28] Another view is that, 'He was getting too much heat from the British tabloids and old man Fortson didn't like it,' according to a Dallas social commentator. 'When they started to suggest that Mark was a fortune hunter, the shit really hit the fan and suddenly it was all over.'[29] From a source close to Mark Thatcher comes a different view: 'Basically Karen rumbled him. She saw through all the bullshit and realised he was always going to be on edge and paranoid. There was no way she could live with him.'

Karen herself is now married with children and living back in Fort Worth. At first, she appeared willing to talk and asked for a list of questions, which were faxed to her. But she then changed her mind. 'I have the utmost respect and admiration for the Thatcher family,' she told us politely. 'I am afraid I would rather not say anything.'

When Mark moved permanently to Dallas, he was relatively

friendless and short on business contacts. Publicly, he denied being banished to America. 'I know this is what my enemies are saying,' he said.[30] But privately he wrote home to friends signing off 'In exile', and felt he had been dispatched to the colonies. Margaret Thatcher also saw it in those terms. 'He's in exile, you know,' she remarked to the Tory MP Jeremy Hanley, Mark's old accountancy tutor.

The prime minister's son arrived in Texas, aged 30, with ambitions to accumulate a pot of gold. 'I have a very high success criterion,' he said at the time, 'and I don't think I will have been successful until I reach what I see as success in my own mind – to have achieved something. Monetary values come into it, because I like to live well and have to earn a lot. I'll become less hungry once I do.'[31]

For Mark, business success was dependent almost exclusively on political connections. He already knew oil billionaire Perry Bass. And it was through the Texan oil network, which included vice-president George Bush, that Mark became friends with entrepreneur Bruce Leadbetter and John Tower, the late senator for Texas.

Senator Tower, whose nomination as defense secretary by the president in 1988 was rejected by the US Senate because of his reputation as an alcoholic and womaniser, became Mark's mentor in Texas. He introduced him to his business partner, veteran lawyer Paul Eggers, who has remained a close associate of Mark's. 'Mark has got a tremendous feel for business and finely tuned political antennae,' said Eggers, who has twice sought the governorship of Texas. 'He could have a political career of his own. It's a pity he wasn't born in this country and could run for office here.'[32]

Tower and Thatcher became close friends and associates. 'He [Mark] has had many meetings with John Tower,' said Eggers. 'They talk to each other on the same high plane.'[33] The two were often seen lunching and dining together at the luxurious Mansion on the Creek Hotel or drinking in the Library Bar. So much so that when Mark attended the senator's birthday dinner party at the Mansion on the Creek, on 19 September 1989, it became a joint celebration as his birthday was the previous month.

The senator was one of those who came to Mark's aid when he was asked to vacate his apartment after fellow residents expressed concern that he was 'a target of international terrorism'. Margaret Thatcher had been the only Western leader to support the Americans' bombing of Libya shortly before and her son had received anonymous death threats. 'The national interest and the honour of Texas were poorly served by this action,' said Tower. 'It reflects on my state. I'm terribly embarrassed. We have a moral obligation to this young man.'[34] Mark then received round-the-clock protection from armed FBI agents and a month's grace before moving to a new apartment in Turtle Creek.

Tower was a useful potential business contact for Thatcher, not least in the arms field. In 1985, he retired from Congress and set up his own defence consulting firm, advising contractors on how to secure orders in Washington. His clients included Martin Marietta, Rockwell International and Textron. For two years, 1986–8, he also acted for the American subsidiary of British Aerospace. Tower was paid a total of $256,000 by the company to 'work the system' in trying to sell Hawk and Tornado jets and Rapier anti-aircraft missiles to the Pentagon. He resigned the consultancy as soon as he became a candidate for defense secretary.[35]

Another close association was with Richard Fisher, a Dallas investment banker who befriended Mark and Denis Thatcher in the mid-1980s. 'I think Mark is extremely bright and loyal to his mother,' said Fisher. 'I think he realises that great people can serve and then be forgotten and their offspring amount to nothing.'[36] Mark described Fisher as 'a family friend who has had a number of private meetings with Lady Thatcher over the years'.[37] But he was more than that, according to the investment banker. 'For three years [1988–91], I had the honour of having been drawn into Prime Minister Thatcher's circle of private advisers, usually briefing her on financial markets.'[38]

Despite these useful entrées to Texas, Margaret Thatcher was concerned about her beloved son's activities, so she arranged for Calman L. Donsky, a lawyer and partner with the Dallas firm of Garderra and Wynne, to look after his interests. 'There was an agreement that whenever Mark launched a new business project, it would be cleared with Donsky,' said a Thatcher friend. 'Margaret provided her private telephone number, so she could be reached at any time. It was a strange situation where she would not admit he needed looking after but she did everything she could to make sure he was.'

An example of this crisis management was when Mark wanted to set up a financial services company which would manage and coordinate investors' funds. The problem was that he had not approached the Securities and Exchange Commission (SEC) for authorisation and did not seem to realise that investment management firms were strictly regulated in the USA. His proposed company would have operated outside the SEC laws. Donsky was aghast, as he knew this was a criminal offence and the British prime minister's son could end up in jail. So he blocked the project just in time, despite Mark's protests. 'But why can't I run the company in this way?' he asked.

Mark was keen to be accepted in Dallas society. But what he failed to realise was that social acceptance needed to be earned by civic duty. According to prominent Texans, he did not pay his social dues because he believed it was a free ride. Mark thought that being the prime minister's son was enough and that he would be automatically accepted. For example, he was desperate to be a member of the exclusive Dallas Country Club, not least for its lush golf course, but his application was rejected. This was not necessarily because the leaders of Dallas society disapproved of him. More relevant was his lacklustre support for charities like the Jewel Gala benefit for the Northwood Institute in Dallas.

In social terms, Mark blew it and never recovered. He tried to impress them by boasting that he knew the royal family intimately (he did know the Duke and Duchess of York, but that was about it). He also loudly told friends and anyone within earshot that he would later need to be addressed as 'Sir Mark' (this would only apply, of course, after his baronet father died). But it was his standoffish behaviour that did not endear him to the talkative Texans. 'He's quite friendly to meet in private,' said John Haynsworth, Dallas's leading society photographer, 'but if you go to a party he's at, you'll see him walking around looking very aloof.'[39] 'I hate people who look down their noses,' said Caroline Rose Hunt, the owner of two luxury hotels in Dallas. She wasn't referring directly to Thatcher but the implication was clear.

Thatcher's obsession with secrecy and his paranoia also did not rest well with Dallas's friendly and open society, particularly after his treasure chest began to fill. 'He had suddenly become a big fish,' said a school friend who visited him in America. 'I remember having lunch with him and he kept hiding behind a huge pot plant because he was worried who might see him. He told me he used to get dozens of death threats and that he had eight armed guards protecting him. He was rather proud of the fact. I came away thinking that Mark Thatcher was locked into himself and couldn't get out.'[40]

The focus of Thatcher's social and business activities was the Mansion on the Creek, the most expensive and luxurious hotel in town. He stayed there for six weeks when he first arrived in Texas and was remembered chiefly for insisting that his car be driven to just a few feet from the hotel kerb, so he did not need to walk the extra distance. He often held business dinners and lunches there and hosted a private New Year's Eve party on 31 December 1992 in the wine cellar.

Dallas society came to see through him and soon his arrogant manner led him to be known in some quarters as 'White Trash'. This came as quite a shock to Thatcher. He was noticeably irritated when asked about this. 'No, I don't get involved with Dallas society,' he replied with a trace of what the Hong Kong *Tatler* described as 'his famous sneer'.[41]

Mark responded by associating with an altogether different social set – young, flash, racy, aggressive entrepreneurs, often in the oil, automobile and property businesses. They were very much the 'new money' crowd and included Taylor Boyd, Bruce Leadbetter, Bob Franklin, Forrest Germany and David Davidson, a real-estate broker who was later convicted of eight counts of bank fraud and jailed for six months.[42]

An indication of Mark's new social crowd was the new woman in his life. Diane Burgdorf was very different from Karen Fortson in almost every way. They were both bright 24 year olds when they met him but there the similarity ended. Diane was blonde and vivacious. She was also reserved, old-fashioned and very religious. The epitomy of the all-American girl, she was a cheerleader and often competed in local beauty contests. After attending Bethany Lutheran College in Minnesota, she received a degree in business administration from the Southern Methodist University in Dallas. She then worked for a real-estate firm before joining the Cornerstone National Bank in Dallas, where her job was to open new accounts for customers.[43]

Diane's family was very much part of the 'new dollar' set in Dallas as opposed to the 'old dollar' clique of Fort Worth. Her father, Ted Burgdorf, was wealthy but not by Texan standards. His millions were derived from being the owner of Uptown Auto Sales in Garland and Burgdorf Chevrolet in Pittsburg, Texas. He was also chairman of the Mary Miler company, which converts vans into 'recreation vehicles (RVs)'. A staunch believer in Thatcherite values – self-reliance, hard work and aspirational materialism – Ted Burghdorf approved of his daughter's English suitor. Diane lived with her parents at their house ('smart not swanky') on Yacht Club Drive in Chandler's Landing, just by the Sam Rayburn lake, a 30-minute drive east of Dallas. 'She's just an ordinary Texan millionairess,' said her father of Diane, but he added that underneath her shyness, 'She's a hell of a tough little lady in a crisis.'[44]

Mark was introduced to her by a real-estate colleague at a Christmas party in 1984 in Dallas hosted by a glossy society magazine. He was mesmerised by her and soon bouquets of flowers began arriving at her office. On their first date, Diane loved the way Mark, then 31, constantly talked about Mummy. 'I figured that anyone who loved his mother so much must have been raised well,' she recalled.[45] But it was many months before passion entered the relationship. When the couple first stayed overnight at 10 Downing Street in April 1985, while Margaret Thatcher was abroad, Diane's mother, Lois Burgdorf, said, 'My daughter Diane is a real Southern Belle. And good Baptist girls from Texas don't go in for hanky-panky before they get married.'[46]

Their courtship was a quiet affair and Diane did not seem to mind that his bodyguards were present during dinner dates. Mark was obsessed with keeping their romance confidential and was furious that their trip to London was leaked to the press. When first approached by British reporters in Texas, she replied, 'You know very well I'm not allowed to say anything.'[47] He responded by calling the Dallas police.

Even at the couple's first major social function together – the 1985 Cattle Barons' Ball – Mark was paranoid about secrecy. While they mingled with guests at Southfork Ranch, where the *Dallas* TV series was filmed, he was recognised by the photographer Akhtar Hussein. 'Can I ask, who is your escort, sir?' he said politely. Bizarrely, Mark tried to avoid him by adopting a loud, fake Texan drawl. This less-than-subtle tactic failed to work because Hussein knew exactly who he was and so turned to Diane. 'Just call me Mark Thatcher's mystery blonde,' she joked. Mark immediately turned on Diane and scolded her, ordering her never to talk to the media. After that, he would always withdraw on seeing Hussein at parties.

This incident typified his future relations with the press. On 5 March 1988, the couple flew to California to attend a charity lunch in Palm Springs, hosted by the Duke and Duchess of York. It was a typical celebrity event, attended mainly by media stars, including Victoria Principal from *Dallas*. The night before the lunch, Mark and Diane walked into the hotel lobby for a reception. Margaret Hall, who was covering the story for the *News of the World*, was among the waiting reporters. She had no intention of asking any questions but decided to introduce herself. She approached Mark, stretched out her hand and said, 'Maggie Hall, *News of the World*.' The journalists were then astonished to see the prime minister's son take off and literally run away, sprinting around the pillars and then down the corridor. Hall stared, shocked and open-mouthed, and turned to Diane: 'I just wanted to say hello.' Diane shrugged her shoulders. 'What can you do?' she replied.

The next day, Mark and Diane attended the lunch in the VIP marquee at the El Dorado polo club in Palm Springs. Mark seemed happy enough, if moody, sitting next to Walter Annenberg, the billionaire former US ambassador to Britain, and at the same table as the Duchess of York. But then, after lunch, a club official approached his table and asked him to move his limousine because it was blocking the other cars. 'I am the passenger not the chauffeur,' he sniffed, scowling at the 'impertinence' of the man. Much to the surprise of the other guests and watching reporters, Mark then drove off with Diane at full speed.[48]

The remarkable irony of his time in Texas was that Mark wanted to venture into public relations. One day, an experienced PR consultant based in Dallas received a telephone call from a distant relative, who told her that Mark Thatcher wanted to 'get into public relations'. She was asked if she could offer any advice. After catching her breath, she politely declined. It would be hard to find someone less suited to PR, she thought to herself after replacing the receiver.

Despite Thatcher's penchant for secrecy, his romance with Diane prospered. They visited London periodically – either to see Margaret and Denis at Chequers or staying at the Carlton Tower Hotel in Knightsbridge. They would then fly to Paris, where Mark rented an apartment and spent a lot of time in the mid-1980s. He also began introducing her to his English friends. 'This is Diane Burgdorf, of Burgdorf-Goodman, you know,' said Mark. This did not impress the friend who knew she was Burgdorf – the car dealers from Texas – not Bergdorf – the prestigious New York department store.

After initial doubts, Margaret Thatcher was won over by Diane's decent nature and sincerity, and on 12 November 1986 Mark announced their engagement. The Burgdorf family were delighted. 'We have a very high regard for Mrs Thatcher, despite her critics,' said Diane's grandfather, Paul Burgdorf. 'As a preacher, I myself have been taking a stand against Communism since the 1930s.'[49] Her father, Ted, was telephoned by the prime minister, who said she was 'thrilled by the engagement and adored' her future daughter-in-law. 'We are very proud to have a family connection with Mrs Thatcher,' said Ted. 'It's a great honour. I am looking forward to meeting Mrs Thatcher but I don't plan to capitalise on it.'[50]

However, even Diane's father let slip Mark's obsession with security, with which the family originally found it difficult to cope. 'Every time we saw him, he had his guards with him,' said Ted. 'The security guard was constantly in attendance and he went with them on dates. There was one time when we went water-skiing and one of his guards even came in the boat. It seemed very strange at first but we eventually got used to it.'[51]

Another revealing glimpse – and perhaps a warning signal to the family – of Mark's personality arose during the official photo call at 10 Downing Street, the day after the engagement announcement. Margaret and Denis beamed at the cameras while Diane and Mark grimaced and then stood stony-faced, only smiling briefly at the end of the five-minute picture session. When photographers asked to take pictures of Diane's engagement ring, Mark pulled her hand behind his back so that they could not see what looked like a diamond solitaire. 'It's a family thing,' he told them, much to the consternation of Bernard Ingham, the prime minister's press secretary.[52]

Having said that, Ted Burgdorf seemed genuinely happy at the time with his prospective son-in-law. 'I was impressed with him right away,' he said. 'He is a gentleman and has always treated our daughter like the princess we feel she is. We couldn't wish for a finer son-in-law.'[53]

Margaret Thatcher liked Diane, particularly as she saw her as a calming influence on Mark's volatile personality, and she was keen to have grandchildren. 'She's a very nice girl', she told a friend at the time on the day the engagement was announced. 'She seems very steady.' But she viewed his marriage as her precious little boy being taken away from her, despite the fact that he was 33 years old. This was noticed by Diane's family and close friends at a private dinner on Monday, 9 February 1987, five days before the wedding. The party for thirty guests was given in honour of the couple by Charles Price, the American ambassador in London, and held at his home in Regent's Park.

During the dinner, attended by BBC chairman Marmaduke Hussey and cabinet minister Cecil (now Lord) Parkinson, Lois Burgdorf, Diane's mother, said to a fellow guest, 'I've been here for three days and she [Mrs Thatcher] has not spoken one word to me.' When this was pointed out to the prime minister, she shrugged it off and moved to the other side of the room. She did see Lois Burgdorf and Diane the following evening at 10 Downing Street. But her behaviour at the dinner was a measure of her emotions at the time.

Later, she was to have a warm but formal relationship with her daughter-in-law, who would often refer to her as 'Lady Thatcher'. 'I have tons of admiration for the woman,' said Diane.[54]

Meanwhile, Mark was enjoying himself at his stag party in the wine cellar of the elegant Stafford Hotel, St James's. Among the twenty-eight guests were nine Texans; John Webb, owner of the Brands Hatch racing circuit; Tim Bell, his unofficial public relations adviser; Alan Curtis, chairman of Lotus Cars; and Steve Tipping, Mark's best man and business partner.[55] It was a high-spirited, bubbly affair, with Mark an engaging and amusing host. One of the guests arrived with 30 pairs of Groucho Marx spectacles and false noses, enough for the whole crowd.[56]

But it was also very much a *Boys' Own* occasion. Among the guests was a Top Gun pilot who was talking in a jocular way about flying. 'Helicopter flying is like masturbation,' he quipped. 'It feels good but looks funny to anyone looking on.' Mark, who had heard only the reference to helicopters, piped up and bragged, 'I've done 400 hours in a helicopter.' Everyone cracked up laughing.

The following evening, 12 February, the prime minister hosted a pre-wedding party at 10 Downing Street for 200 friends, relatives and political colleagues. The two-hour reception appeared to be dominated by the Burgdorf family, who arrived in two black limousines. But it was notable for the presence of several high-powered industrialists, with Lord Weinstock being the notable exception. One of the guests recalls observing the prominence of Lord Hanson and the late Lord White. 'The thing I always remember about that night,' he said, 'was Mrs Thatcher speaking to Lord Hanson on six separate occasions. I watched them very carefully. He was standing very upright with a foot on one of the pillars as if he owned a slice of the place. She spoke to him in an almost earnest way and then Mark twice went over to his mother after she broke off her conversation with Hanson.'[57] Another guest, Charlie Crichton-Stuart, also recalled the prime minister escorting Hanson, White and Bernie Ecclestone from the lounge where everyone was having drinks to a small side room for a private talk for ten minutes before rejoining the crowd.

Two days later, on Saturday, 14 February 1987, Mark and Diane were married at the Savoy Chapel, a sixteenth-century church that seats only 150 people. That meant several close friends and relatives of the families were not invited. Officially, this was for 'security reasons', so when the couple walked down the aisle, armed Special

Branch detectives were watching their every move. Trained marksmen mingled with the guests and travelled with the bride and groom and their families. They also checked out staff at the Savoy Hotel where the reception was being held.[58] Over the two days, two hundred and forty police officers were assigned to the event, at a cost of several thousand pounds.[59]

On the wedding day, the press tried to provoke Mark. One newspaper dubbed it the 'St Valentine's Day Massacre' and 'The Bride and Gloom'.[60] Another paper published a detailed street map for Mark to find his way to the chapel – as a less than gentle reminder of his being lost in the Sahara desert.[61] But Mark, after being spoken to by his mother, was on his best behaviour. He arrived 15 minutes early, providing a rare smile for the cameras. It was a simple service based on the revised prayer book, which meant that Diane, much to the groom's irritation, did not undertake to 'obey' her husband. Margaret was noticeably emotional when Mark recited his marriage vows. 'There were tears in my eyes more than once,' she said.[62] Diane wore a traditional white satin dress with a five-foot train, at a cost of $2,000 from Nieman Marcus.

After the ceremony the newly-weds got into a red Rolls-Royce which drove them to the reception at the Savoy Hotel, 200 yards away. The party was a grand affair, with 300 guests, including 70 Texans. But Mark Thatcher could not resist trying to use even this romantic occasion for commercial purposes. 'It was quite extraordinary,' recalled one businessman who was present. 'He was even using his wedding to hustle for deals. I particularly remember him introducing Steve Tipping to people, saying, "We do a lot together, you know." That didn't go down too well.' Mark's bride shared this view. During a dinner party hosted by Wafic Said in Marbella in 1992, a guest told Diane about his daughter's impending wedding. 'Well, don't make the mistake I made,' she said. 'There were 300 guests at my wedding and the bulk of them were my husband's business contacts that he wanted to impress.'

Two days later, Mark and Diane Thatcher flew first class on a Qantas 747 jet to Sydney, Australia, for a month-long honeymoon. The couple were driven to the airport in an armoured chauffeur-driven black Jaguar. The prime minister then picked up the £70 bill for their use of the VIP Hillingdon Suite at Heathrow.[63] Mark was back to his pre-wedding mood. 'I do not pose for pictures,' he told waiting photographers.[64] The couple were booked into the Regency Hotel in Sydney as 'Mr and Mrs Green' but Mark was soon recognised, much to his fury. 'He looks as if he's spent a month on vinegar and lemon juice,' quipped one Australian journalist.[65]

On their return to Texas, Mark and Diane moved into their new home in Fairfax Avenue, Highland Park, one of the most fashionable and prestigious parts of Dallas. The area is known as 'the Bubble', because the atmosphere is so rarefied only millionaires can breathe easily.[66] Mark paid $725,000 using a bank loan from Sueide Luxembourgoise de Banque S.A., for the neo-Georgian house, relatively small (4,260 square feet) but built like a fortress. He installed an intricate security system, complete with a black iron security gate and an underground bunker room in the basement known as 'the war room'. In the centre of this room is a vault into which Mark, his wife and two children can retreat at times of 'security alerts' or, perhaps, other forms of human threat.

An estimated £110,000 was spent on a separate flat for the nanny at the back of the property, a new hallway with Italian marble floors and a new annexe to the sitting-room. Mark also employed a Mexican housekeeper and a personal English valet, Graham Henderson, who travelled with him on many of his trips to London. But property records filed in Dallas show that he was not yet flush with cash, as in June 1988, he increased his line of credit to $875,000 and Diane signed as a guarantor. The house is currently valued at $1,059,430.

Unfortunately, the house became so cluttered that, when they hosted dinner parties, the numerous servants made the occasion resemble a scene from the *Keystone Cops*. Perhaps the most significant feature of the house is that when Mark is abroad, people passing by can see an imposing illuminated portrait of his mother above the mantelpiece in his drawing-room. Just in case they missed it, potential business clients at the time were reminded of her presence in his office on the 38th floor of the Texas Commerce Bank building in Houston, nicknamed 'Maggie's hall of fame'. Portraits of Margaret Thatcher stared down imposingly from the sunken library and on every wall to any visitor. Her son even framed the original handwritten notes of a speech she delivered to the Dallas Chamber of Commerce in 1991.[67]

Today, unlike his wife, Diane, Mark is not a popular neighbour in Fairfax Avenue. When he drives his BMW 735 saloon or black Porsche Carrera (bought for $78,000 from his father-in-law), he barely acknowledges fellow residents. 'They do have parties,' said one woman who lives opposite, 'but Mark picks one person – usually someone important to his business – and talks to them all night. He says good evening to the rest of the guests, then ignores them. I'm not real fond of him. One day, after I had just moved here, I turned round to find him all the way back in my bedroom. I had parked my car across the street and he didn't like it and told me to move. I stuck out my hand to introduce myself but he just wanted me to move, quick.'[68]

Mark's behaviour towards his wife has also attracted comment in the neighbourhood and Dallas society. Diane's reasons for marrying Mark have never been clear. 'I always figured I'd marry the typical boy next door,' she said, laughing. 'But I guess God had something different in mind.'[69] Friends have often wondered what they have in common. Certainly, they are both very conventional socially and like to live discreet, secluded lives. They are also both devoted to their parents and children. But it's difficult to point to other mutual interests. More sceptical sources say the celebrity factor was crucial. 'Diane thought she was marrying British royalty,' said a friend of the couple. Mark played up to this by telling her he was close friends with the royal family. But this was only partly true as he only knew the Duke and Duchess of York (they had met at a polo match in California in 1986).

Mark was as aloof and arrogant with his wife as he was with almost everyone else. This was noted on Sunday mornings after church when Thatcher liked to breakfast at the Mansion on the Creek Hotel. According to a fellow guest, his head would be hidden behind a newspaper for over an hour and hardly any conversation would take place. On another occasion, in 1987, the couple were in a helicopter owned by Wafic Said, the Syrian financier. Alongside Wafic was Charles Powell, then the prime minister's foreign affairs private secretary. Because of drizzling rain, it was a rocky flight with considerable turbulence and suddenly Diane's foot was pierced by her umbrella. The cut drew blood and on landing she was limping and clearly in some pain. Mark gave her no more than a cursory glance. 'That seems to be all right,' he told her. 'Why do you always have to make such a fuss?' and walked on.

At home, Mark behaves with a curious combination of petulance and imperial aloofness. According to house guests, he treats Diane more like a glorified domestic servant than a wife. 'He would bark orders like "Where's the breakfast? I want it now," and was unbelievably rude to her,' said one long-standing friend who stayed in the bedroom specially kept for Margaret Thatcher.

Diane responds by trying to calm him down by adopting a soothing, serene Southern belle tone of voice. 'Oh, Maaark, don't be so aggressive,' she would say when he went into his pugnacious, wide-boy routine in front of friends. She is also not without a mischievous sense of humour. In the summer of 1992, while attending a dinner party at Wafic Said's house in Marbella, she confided in a fellow guest about her marital problems. She said one of their disputes was over her cat. She was deeply attached to it; Mark, however, was not. He asked her to find it another home but Diane refused. She told the guest that she returned home one day to find her pet missing. When she confronted her husband, he told her that he had ordered some Mexican workmen – who were building an extension to the Thatcher home – to bury the animal alive in the wall. Diane denied this when we spoke to her in August 1994. 'No, that's not true,' she said. 'Mark didn't like my cat but my cat passed away from natural causes about two months ago. It was not my husband's fault.'

Perhaps it was Diane's strict religious upbringing that has led her to endure her husband's antics for so long. For many years she has been a devout member of the Calvary Lutheran Church in Dallas. Founded in the 1960s by her father and part of the Wisconsin Evangelical Lutheran Synod, and now with some 500,000 members, it is very conservative and strict, and is devoted to the ideas of Martin Luther. Her brother, Dale, is an elder. 'Diane is a Bible girl and she's not afraid to tell anyone,' said Paul Burgdorf, her grandfather.[70]

Mark was converted to the Lutheran faith after a twenty-week course of one hour a week, which included a section on ethics. The couple attend a Sunday-morning service whenever they are in town. 'We believe that the husband should be the head of the household,' the pastor, John Vieths, told us. 'That does not mean that he can behave like a monster. But wives are encouraged to follow his lead.' When asked by David Jones of *Today* newspaper what the Church's attitude was towards monetary wealth, Pastor Vieths replied, 'If God blesses you with a lot, that's fine. There are some rich people in the Bible, too. Some end up with more, some with less.' And Mark Thatcher? 'The Lord has blessed him, certainly.'[71]

Diane herself told us from her home in Dallas, 'I'm a Christian woman. I'm raising my children with the same upbringing that I was raised. I'm a Bible-believing person and I exercise the virtues of the fruits of the Spirit as much as I can – love, joy, peace, patience, kindness, faithfulness, goodness, gentleness and self-control. That's how I would like myself described. I don't have any personal vendettas against anyone. If they come after me, I just pity them . . . I serve my Lord, I obey his commands and I think he has blessed me abundantly in this life because of it.'

The Church has strict, ascetic rules on moral behaviour. Smoking and gambling are discouraged, and drinking permitted only in moderation. Abortions are strictly forbidden and divorce is allowed only in cases of adultery or 'malicious desertion'.

On 28 February 1989, Diane gave birth to a son, Michael, at the Presbyterian Hospital in Dallas. The baby was then baptised in the Calvary Lutheran Church in a ceremony attended by his godparents, Steve Tipping and Carol Thatcher. Margaret Thatcher was elated. Three days after the birth, she strode out of 10 Downing Street and proclaimed to waiting reporters and cameramen, 'We have become a grandmother. It is just marvellous and Denis is thrilled, too.'[72]

Mark's Dallas friends were equally delighted. One even suggested young Michael would make a future state governor. 'He's a solid little Texan all right,' said Paul Eggers, the influential lawyer. 'If he turns out like his father and his grandfather, he'll be just the sort of guy we'll need in the next century.'[73]

Two months later, Mark and Diane flew to London to present their son to Mrs Thatcher, who was celebrating ten years as prime minister. 'He looks like Mark did at the same age,' she said as she cradled the boy in her arms on the steps of 10 Downing Street.[74] Within four years, she was celebrating again, when Diane produced a granddaughter for her. Mark named his new child Amanda Margaret; she is a lively little girl, who soon became known as 'the Iron Baby'.

Despite being wealthy enough to afford nannies, Diane chose not to work during her marriage. 'Although I loved the intellectual stimulation and drive at work, I thought, "What's the point of marrying someone if you never see him?"' she said three years into the marriage.[75]

The problem was that her worst fears came true. Diane did accompany her husband on some trips to Hong Kong, New Zealand and France. But for the most part she stayed in Dallas while Mark travelled three continents. He was abroad for three months a year. 'I have three homes, one in Dallas, one in London – and one on a Jumbo jet over the Atlantic,' she said, only half joking.[76]

The result of her husband's endless overseas business excursions is that the couple have gradually grown apart. Mark has always been addicted to travel and saw no reason to change his habits to suit his wife. This led to considerable tension in the marriage and they began to lead separate lives. Diane wanted a normal family life but her husband was simply never at home. So she has carved out her own lifestyle. Driving her Chevrolet Equinox LS four-door sports wagon, she spends her days at the gym, attending Bible study classes and collecting the children from school. She also enjoys skiing in Aspen, Colorado, but is often alone, while Mark is on an aeroplane somewhere or staying overnight in Houston, where he moved his office.

What was worse was that Diane suspected her husband was spending time with other women on his overseas excursions. In 1989, she even hired private detectives to follow him during a weekend trip to London. She believed he was spending evenings with Sarah-Jane Clemence, the 23-year-old daughter of property millionaire Terry Clemence, at her flat in Wilton Crescent, Knightsbridge. Mark knew the family through their mutual interests in real estate and car dealing. 'He's a friend of the family, that's all,' said Sarah in 1994. 'I had no idea his wife was suspicious about me . . . I'm the victim of his wife's jealousy. Diane is not a very nice person. She is unhappy and suspicious.'[77]

In February 1994, he was apparently trying to charm a female American air force pilot at an exclusive health resort in Ashram, just outside Los Angeles. Mark was at the $1,500-a-week retreat to lose weight but seemed more interested in 31-year-old Sheila O'Grady, according to two of the trainers. 'During hikes, she would let him catch up then steam off like a rocket,' said Karin Solo. 'He was rather arrogant and I don't think she was that interested.'[78] 'Mark pushed himself just to be near her – he was really keen,' agreed fellow trainer Geo Moskios. 'I saw him chase her but never saw him catch her.'[79]

When we asked Diane about her marital problems in August 1994, she replied with polite candour, 'I have no comment to make but I will not deny that things are not sympathetic at this time. He travels an awful lot. I can handle it myself but I do feel sorry for my children. They love their father and they don't see enough of him. I once said, "What's the point of marrying someone if you never see him?" and I still hold to that point. I'm not going to speak unkindly of him. He is the father of my children but I think some of the reporting in the press has some truth to it.'

By January 1994, the marriage was in deep trouble and disintegrating. Diane was unable to cope with Mark being away so much, his treatment of her as an appendage of his personal staff and his aloof behaviour. But instead of just meekly accepting his antics, she began to criticise him regularly. On occasion she has refused to sleep with him and he has had to stay in the nanny's flat above the garage. 'I've seen them together many times,' said a friend of the couple, 'and Mark just shows no affection or warmth towards her. But what's worse is that there's hardly any communication between them, even when he's in the house. I would say Diane is suffering from lack of emotional support, that's the crux of it.' Which makes Mark's comment that 'you have to work at family relationships' rather ironic.[80]

This was confirmed again by Sarah-Jane Clemence, who first met the couple while she was on holiday with her family in 1989, staying at the Hôtel du Cap at Cap d'Antibes in the south of France. 'They were like Mr and Mrs Glum,' she recalled. 'They had their baby with them and joined us for dinner a few times . . . She didn't seem to like being with us. My two sisters are very pretty and she continually stared at them and seemed to be keeping an eye on Mark.'[81]

An exasperated Diane took solace in her Church and told her husband the marriage could only be saved if he undertook religious counselling. 'Her everyday decisions are influenced by her faith,' said a close friend of the couple. 'If there is anyone else involved then it is God. Diane is having an affair with God.'[82]

Mark was unable to deal with the situation and spent more and more time away from home. He was already commuting 250 miles to his new office in Houston, and from 1993 increasingly stayed overnight at the Omni Hotel, returning only at weekends. For Diane, an absentee husband was not good enough. She became increasingly unhappy and it seemed that the only factor preventing divorce was the disruption and damage it would do to their children. Publicly, Mark denied this. 'No divorce, and any speculation of it is just fanciful,' he said.[83]

However, by October 1994, the marriage was in such a precarious state that Lady Thatcher herself decided to intervene. During a visit to Texas that month, she spoke to Mark and offered to pay for a family Christmas. According to a source close to the family, he complained that his wife wanted an expensive holiday in the Bahamas. So she called Diane who replied, 'No, that's not true. I just wanted a quiet family Christmas at home. It's Mark who wants to go to the Bahamas.' Margaret Thatcher was shocked by such deception and became virtually resigned to her son's marriage breakdown. 'I don't want to divorce him,' Diane told her, 'but it may be the only way to live a normal life.' Their marriage has, however, almost miraculously, survived.

Although Mark has respected and accommodated his wife's strong religious faith, he has always worshipped at a different altar, namely, the pursuit of wealth; and Texas, USA, was the perfect church in which to continue his devotion to his brand of spirituality. 'My brother-in-law used to say that anyone worth their salt could come to Dallas, fall over in the street and get up with a mouthful of money,' said Mark Seal, a local writer.[84]

Publicly, Thatcher's vehicle for his American business interests was the Grantham Company. Named in homage to his mother's birthplace, Grantham must be one of the most secretive commercial outfits in America. It is unlisted in any business directory and not registered with the Dallas Chamber of Commerce. Until 1992, the office was on the 18th floor of the Lincoln Center on LBJ Freeway in Richardson, a northern suburb of Dallas. It contained little more than a nameplate, a reception desk and a small boardroom. The secretary, Debbie Milner, was under instructions not to disclose the function of the company.[85] Even Paul Eggers, a very close friend of Thatcher in Dallas, was unaware of Grantham. 'I know he has some offshore things in Europe but that's all,' he said.[86]

Although companies with offices in Texas are required by law to register in that state, Grantham has been allowed to keep its activities secret. It seems this is because it is structured as a partnership rather than a corporation and so is not obliged to file accounts. But that remains an incomplete explanation. What is known is that it was founded in the summer of 1987 after the general election in which Margaret Thatcher secured a 101-seat majority. Set up by Mark and Dallas-based financier Bruce Leadbetter, Grantham 'looks at investment opportunities, makes direct investments on behalf of the partners and brings in other investors'.[87]

One of its early projects was setting up a printing company in Mexico. David Wallace, a partner in Grantham, later said this firm operated and made money partly because goods and services were provided 'at lower wages'.[88] Later, Grantham looked at financial leasing in the telecommunications industry, real-estate development and the processing of health-care claims.[89]

It also acts as a consultant to corporations and in June 1987 was hired by Electronic Data Systems Inc. (EDS), the computer company formerly owned by Ross Perot, the wealthy tycoon and 1993 presidential candidate. Perot had befriended Mark when he was asked to leave his apartment because of fears that he was a terrorist target. The billionaire businessman arranged for Thatcher to live in a bungalow near his Dallas house and the two became acquainted.[90]

It was a transitional period for Perot. EDS had just been taken over by General Motors and he was looking to break into international markets. It was in that context that Mark and Grantham were hired. The two-year EDS contract was for Thatcher to develop marketing plans for selling their data-processing facilities in South-east Asia, particularly in Hong Kong, China and Korea, 'and to the exclusion of all activities directly or indirectly related to the UK'.[91] 'They were door openers and advisers for us,' recalled Roger Still, an EDS regional director of public relations.

Despite the UK exclusion clause, the consultancy was highly sensitive, because at the time EDS was bidding for a £1.6 billion contract with the British government to run a privatised National Insurance and social security system. It was also interested in a Ministry of Defence computer project worth £500 million. EDS staff had also been discovered by the Home Office to have obtained employment in Britain 'without the necessary authority . . . some EDS employees entered by deception'.[92]

And so when Sir Robert (now Lord) Armstrong, then cabinet secretary, discovered the EDS consultancy he was not best pleased. He had been informed by Sallingbury Casey, a UK lobbying firm acting for EDS, and immediately told the prime minister. Sir Robert was surprised to be told that she 'knew nothing of the links'.[93]

The cabinet secretary and his senior civil servants were uneasy about Mark's commercial activities. Bernard Ingham, the prime minister's press secretary for 11 years, was particularly concerned that they would damage her politically. In May 1987, at the outset of the general election campaign, Mark approached Ingham and asked him what he could do to help his mother's campaign. 'Leave the country,' the blunt Yorkshireman responded.[94] Thatcher promptly flew back to Dallas and returned to London only during the final week of the campaign. He was in 10 Downing Street on election night and joined in the celebrations. But it was clear he was not welcomed by her staff and was soon back in Dallas.

Four months later, Margaret Thatcher visited Dallas for the first time. Ostensibly, her trip was a private family occasion to see her son and daughter-in-law. But the visit had another agenda which Mark and his associates tried in vain to keep confidential – she was being used to entice some of America's most powerful businessmen to a dinner in Dallas, thereby promoting her son's commercial interests.

Margaret Thatcher had been attending the Commonwealth Conference in Vancouver but instead of returning to London, she flew to Dallas in a US government DC-9 jet. At 2.30 a.m. on Sunday, 18 October 1987, she arrived at Mark's house in Highland Park like an empress visiting her crown prince. Residents on Fairfax Avenue were woken to see her appear in a twenty-car convoy led by eight steel-helmeted motorcycle police. To complete the performance, a Dallas police helicopter hovered low overhead, aiming a dazzling searchlight.[95]

Mark and Diane then greeted Margaret and Denis Thatcher on their doorstep, watched by armed guards. After five hours' sleep, the prime minister went on an impromptu walkabout to the nearby Flippen Park. She was accompanied by secret service agents, carrying concealed machine guns, loaned to her by vice-president George Bush. Her son walked beside her, looking distinctly uneasy as she chatted to local people and posed with bemused children for photographers. When asked about her schedule by a local reporter, Mark replied that it was secret. 'I want to save everything as a surprise for her,' he said.[96]

Mark was unhappy about the attention, as he had naively thought that her two-day stay could be kept confidential. 'We don't know how it got out that she's even coming here,' said Paul Eggers, the Dallas lawyer and close friend of Mark. 'I took an oath of secrecy.'[97] The reason for such reticence was the main motive for the trip – the private banquet the following evening on the first floor of the Verandah Club in the luxurious Loews Anatole Hotel in Dallas. Mark had invited a staggering selection of America's corporate and banking elite, stating that the British prime minister would be the guest of honour. Clearly, it was a device to attract many of the country's most powerful and influential to his dinner table and hence potentially benefit his newly established Grantham Company. Margaret Thatcher, basking in the triumph of her third successive election victory, and by then one of the world's most influential politicians, was being used to enhance Mark's business prospects.

On Monday, 19 October 1987, the 40 guests flew in from Washington, London, Boston and New York. The all-male guest list, marked 'Absolutely Private and Confidential', can be divided into two sections. The first consisted of prominent industrialists and merchant bankers. They were Robert Abboud, chief executive (CEO) of First City Bankcorp; Andrew L. Lewis Jr, president of Union Pacific; Alvin V. Shoemaker, chairman of First Boston Corporation; Robert

Anderson, chairman of Rockwell International; Roger Smith, chairman of General Motors; L. William Seidman, chairman of Federal Deposit Insurance Corporation; Bill Schmeid, president of the Singer Company; Robert T. Daniel, CEO of United Technologies; Jack Moseley, chairman of US Fidelity and Guaranty Corporation; Allen Shepherd, chairman of Grand Metropolitan plc; Fernando Solana, director-general of Banco Nacional de México; Ira Harris, director of Salomon Brothers; Malcolm Forbes, proprietor of *Forbes* magazine; William A. Wilson, former US ambassador to the Vatican; Walter H. Annenberg, former US ambassador to Britain; Tan Kat Hock, chairman of Johan Holdings in Malaysia; John Thompson, chairman of Southland Corporation; the late Lord White, chairman of Hanson Industries; and last, but certainly not least, Wafic Said, the Syrian financier who was a broker on the Al-Yamamah arms deal.[98]

Then there were Mark Thatcher's own commercial and legal associates – Steve Tipping, his business partner; Hugh Thurston, his personal banker and a director of Citicorp; Calman Donsky, his Texas lawyer; and Bruce Leadbetter, his partner at the Grantham Company. Other close business friends included Alan Curtis, chairman of Lotus Car; Vester Hughes, a Dallas lawyer; Jay Pritzker, chairman of the Hyatt Group; and Joe Refsnes, vice-chairman of the law and brokering firm Rauscher Pierce and Refsnes.[99]

The event was hosted by Mark and the lawyer Paul Eggers. But all attention was on the prime minister. She was accompanied by Charles (now Sir Charles) Powell, her private secretary for foreign affairs, and her husband, Denis. At her table sat Roger Smith, Malcolm Forbes, Walter Annenberg, Robert Anderson, William Wilson, John Thompson, Jay Pritzker and Wafic Said.

Whether any business was discussed is not clear. The main topic of conversation was the dramatic developments that day, later known as 'Black Monday'. The UK stock market had collapsed, precipitated by a dramatic fall in share prices on Wall Street. Margaret Thatcher discussed the situation with the businessmen at her table, who argued that 'we are not about to see a meltdown of the world economy'. She blamed the high deficit run by the American government and over-valued stock.[100]

One of the eight lucky businessmen who sat at the prime minister's table was Jay Pritzker, a multimillionaire whose Chicago-based family owns the Hyatt chain of hotels. Pritzker was the leading investor in a company which many people, including Margaret Thatcher, wrongly believed was the source of Mark's fortune.

The corporation was Emergency Networks Inc. (ENI), founded in 1981. Its basic function was to buy cheap off-the-shelf security equipment, install it in the home and then charge a monthly fee for a monitoring service. It was an attempt to undercut the expensive early-warning alarm systems then sold to largely affluent homeowners. ENI realised a profit only once the customer agreed to continue the monitoring service after the three-year minimum contract ended. Its strategy was to sacrifice short-term profits and go for rapid expansion and long-term customers.[101]

The problem was that the company did not allow for high operating costs and was massively under-capitalised. By 1987, ENI was facing financial ruin. The two founders, David Stull and Scott Gurley, approached their banker, Bob Davenport of the Gateway National Bank in Dallas, for advice. They decided they needed new capital and so Davenport contacted his friend Bruce Leadbetter, a Dallas-based financier originally from Flagstaff, Arizona, and at the time Mark Thatcher's business partner in the Grantham Company. Leadbetter agreed to assemble an investment rescue package worth $1.5 million and discussed it with Mark. 'Bruce and I sat down and worked out what we wanted to raise and wrote out a list of people and got on aeroplanes,' recalled Mark.[102] They set up Xpart Inc., an investment consortium which would purchase over 50 per cent of the share capital of Emergency Networks.

Near the top of their list of potential investors was Hanson plc, the industrial conglomerate which has donated more than £500,000 to the Conservative Party since 1987. The company's chairman was Lord Hanson, a close friend, supporter and influential unofficial adviser to Margaret Thatcher. He was her favourite tycoon and had been a guest at her son's wedding earlier that year. His company agreed to invest as a limited partner in Mark's business scheme. A US subsidiary of Hanson plc paid $100,000 for a stake in Xpart and hence Emergency Networks. 'We knew that Mark Thatcher was involved when we agreed to make an investment,' said Martin Taylor, a Hanson vice-chairman. 'It was the only time we invested with him.'[103]

Another name on Mark Thatcher's target list was Li Ka-Shing, the powerful Hong Kong tycoon, who had also handed over substantial payments to the Conservative Party and who later pledged a donation to the Margaret Thatcher Foundation. Like Hanson, Li invested $100,000 in Emergency Networks via Xpart Inc.[104] Mark denied exploiting Tory Party benefactors. 'If the whole thing was funded by the *Who's Who* contributors to the party, then that would have been a different game,' he said. 'But for them to subscribe two-fifteenths of the investment, I do not regard that as significant.'[105]

Other investors included Jay Pritzker, who provided a seven-figure sum, Bruce Babbit (later US interior secretary) and Joe Refsnes (who attended the famous Margaret Thatcher dinner in Dallas that year). As for Mark Thatcher, he joined in and became a non-executive director of Emergency Networks Inc. He was also a shareholder, although his stake was never higher than 5 per cent.

The Thatcher–Leadbetter investment group, code-named 'Renaissance 5', was not a success and another $10 million was required. So Mark returned to Hanson, who invested another $300,000 in an interest-bearing debenture. The new capital enabled Emergency Networks to expand and by 1991 it had installed alarms in almost 200,000 homes and generated annual sales of $80 million. But the company, in which the Pritzker family had the controlling interest, was badly run. The new executives were paying themselves large management fees beyond what was reasonable, despite raising more investment, and the losses mounted up.

Even more seriously, millions of dollars of employees' tax were not being paid to the US Internal Revenue Service. On 27 May 1992, David Wallace, an investor and at the time Mark Thatcher's business partner, wrote a memo recording the situation. He stated that some $2.3 million had been deducted from employees' salaries on a PAYE basis, but had not been passed on to the IRS. According to Wallace, taxes had not been paid for the previous three weeks, the company was trading near insolvently and bankruptcy was not far off the horizon.

The following month, a last-gasp effort was made to inject more capital. On 24 June 1992, a meeting took place at the Dallas offices of Electronic Data Systems (EDS) to discuss their outstanding $8 million loan to Emergency Networks. EDS executives made it clear to Wallace and Stull that further loan advances would not be forthcoming unless this $8 million was resolved. Despite this precarious position, Wallace and other executives did not file for Chapter 11 bankruptcy, which apparently would have saved the company.

Instead, Emergency Networks continued to trade, holding out to attract extra investment. Stull and Scott Gurley, his co-founder and president of operations, remained concerned about the non-payment of tax. But when Stull and Gurley again demanded that the funds be transmitted to the IRS, they were sacked as officers and removed as directors by the board. As a farewell salvo, on 4 August 1992, they wrote a memorandum to Bill Moore, chairman, and Bruce Leadbetter. 'We strongly recommend the company's payroll liability be paid immediately from *all* available company funds,' they said. 'We consider the payment of all the company's past, present and future tax obligations to be the responsibility of you and the present management.'

EDS were again approached for a cash infusion but it was a financial shot in the dark. In September 1992, Emergency Networks Inc. finally called it a day and filed for Chapter 11 bankruptcy, with assets of $1 million and liabilities of $7.4 million. The court-appointed trustees noticed the apparently excessive executive fees almost immediately. 'The fact that management was taking out so much in salaries while other expenses were going unpaid was very troublesome,' said George McElreath, a US government trustee.[106] Even worse, the company also failed to pass on private health insurance payments which left dozens of former employees bankrupt or suffering severe financial difficulties over unpaid medical bills, according to a *Sunday Times* investigation. 'It wrecked our lives,' said Loretta Liquori, whose husband was an employee.[107]

It was only a matter of time before the equally serious allegation – the non-payment of tax extracted from their employees – was investigated. David Stull, president of sales, was always aware of this danger and made strenuous efforts to effect the payments. This did not prevent detection and on 10 December 1993, the IRS Criminal Investigations Office issued proceedings against six former directors and investors of Emergency Networks. They included Mark Thatcher and two of his former business partners and associates, David Wallace and Bruce Leadbetter.

The IRS claimed that these former directors 'willfully failed to collect, truthfully account for, or pay over to the USA . . . taxes for wages paid to the employees, and neglected, failed and refused to pay the full amount of the assessment'. The total claim was for $2,661,496.[108]

Mark Thatcher was quick to respond. On 18 January 1994, through the Dallas law firm Garderra and Wynne, he said he was not a responsible person in the company and denied all knowledge of the tax negligence. He 'further denies that he wilfully failed to collect

[and] truthfully account for' taxes due to the IRS. But when the case was set for trial in 1996, an out-of-court settlement was reached in Dallas with Thatcher paying his own legal costs.

Despite his protestations, Thatcher was closely involved in Emergency Networks – as an investor and leading fundraiser. He was ever-present as a director until July 1992 and even lent $1.1 million to the company. Through the Grantham Company, Thatcher and David Wallace 'spent a great deal of time on various Emergency Networks related matters' while it was expanding.[109] Thatcher's participation can also be gleaned from the bankruptcy records: one of the creditors, owed $750,000, was Diversified Capital Ltd. This was one of Mark's companies, registered in Jersey and controlled by his banker, Hugh Thurston, and his accountant, Leonard Day.

Mark Thatcher made very little money out of Emergency Networks. He sold his shares to David Wallace (his close associate at Grantham) and bailed out in 1990 – just before the storm broke – but continued as a director for two more years. This was confirmed by Bruce Leadbetter, his former business partner in Grantham and former president of Emergency Networks. 'We all lost a lot of money in the company, including Mark,' he said. 'No one got rich out of it . . . Mark resigned because he could see what the problems were. He could see the writing on the wall and he didn't have the time to sort out the problems.'[110] The prime minister's son was reluctant to admit the failure of this venture. 'I did make money out of Emergency Networks,' he said. 'I made in percentage terms a reasonable return on my investment.'[111]

The interesting feature of Thatcher's role in this ambitious but doomed home-security corporation was the way the prime minister, her political friends and two of her newspaper supporters portrayed it as a financial triumph. Margaret Thatcher has always been convinced her son is a commercial wizard. 'Mark could sell snow to the Eskimos and sand to the Arabs,' she told a friend. 'Wonderful salesman, but he will not learn to say "please" and "thank you".' For some reason she believed Emergency Networks was a shining example of her son's entrepreneurial expertise. 'He is a very, very good businessman,' she said. 'He's a born businessman, as indeed my husband was. He built up his own business and he managed to sell part of his interest in it . . . It's a big concern for security, the best possible kind of home-security systems.'[112]

Fleet Street went further and claimed the 'profit' from the Emergency Networks investment was the source of Mark's multimillion-pound fortune! On 2 January 1990, the *Daily Mail* stated he made a 'killing' and 'stands to put around $10 million in his bank account'. The next day *The Sun* reported that the company was sold for $50 million and Mark's shareholding was 20 per cent, therefore he made a profit of $10 million. The paper quoted an unnamed Thatcher friend who said: 'He [Mark] bought just at the right time and the firm took off in a phenomenal way.'[113]

This, of course, was pure fantasy. The whole company was worth barely $10 million and so it was inconceivable that Mark could have collected such a financial windfall. But the stories were left uncorrected and the premier's friends continued to brief the press, notably the *Financial Times*, that his US interests were the source of his vast wealth. This was deliberate misinformation and it served a very useful purpose. By that stage, late 1989, Mark really was piling up Thatcher's fortune. But the loot did not emanate from installing burglar alarms in Texas. It was derived from much more lucrative ventures – international arms deals.

SEVEN

Arms and the Man

Mark Thatcher was trying to cash in on the Al-Yamamah deal . . . In the arms business we met many people, royal hangers on. We called them 'Black Princes' and sometimes they had to be bought off . . . Thatcher was acting in the same way, as a kind of British Black Prince, but it was surely not the proper role for a British prime minister's son.

– Alex Sanson, former managing director of British Aerospace, Dynamics Division[1]

Mark Thatcher loves to travel. It's almost a compulsion. Soon after his mother entered Downing Street, he was on jet planes – jumbos, Concorde, anything that would propel him to countries that looked favourably on doing business with the son of the British prime minister. By 1981, he was flying four hundred hours a year, or eight to ten hours a week, and that continued throughout the decade.[2] He used to boast to his Special Branch detectives that he never stayed in the same hotel twice, and his sister, Carol, remarked how her brother always called her from a different airport.

When he arrived in the first-class departure lounge, Mark was always immaculately dressed in a stiff, almost military, style – usually in a dark blazer, a crisply ironed shirt and a colourful handkerchief in the jacket pocket. Airline officials recall that he often drew attention to himself, ensuring he would be recognised. 'Mark reminded me of a former Sandhurst army officer,' said one. 'He talked in that clipped, brisk way and expected everything to be perfect. I didn't mind that but he has no sense of humour so when anything went even slightly wrong he was very difficult to deal with.'

Despite his obsession with security, Mark would explode when airport staff asked to inspect his hand luggage. 'What are you talking about?' he shouted on one occasion. 'Don't you know who I am?' before reluctantly allowing his bags to be checked.[3] Another of his habits was to leave the Heathrow executive lounge through a secret route like a catering workers' exit.[4] He also used the code-name 'M. Teacher' when making airline reservations on commercially sensitive trips.

Mark usually flew either first or business class. On American Airlines, one of his favourites, he was always upgraded to first class. But he was not a popular passenger, according to stewardesses who flew with him. Just as some waiters flinched on seeing Mark enter their restaurant, so did the aircraft staff. One senior flight attendant who encountered him was Jeannie Kovascy. Her first experience was when she did her usual checklist in the first-class area. She did not recognise the prime minister's son by sight, so she had to check. 'Are you Mark Thatcher?' asked Jeannie. 'Of course I am,' he replied, as if he had been asked if he was the Prince of Wales. 'Who else would I be?'

As soon as the passengers were settled, Mark ostentatiously stood up to his full height of six foot, looked around and surveyed the other travellers. It was classic celebrity body language, according to the stewardesses. 'He seemed to want everyone to know who he was,' said one. 'He also treated the cabin staff as if we were inferior serfs and he was lord of the manor in medieval England. Nobody liked him but his wife was very different. She flew with us on her own with their son and was very nice. A lovely person.'

On many of his overseas trips he was accompanied by armed Special Branch detectives. Mark had wanted bodyguards as soon as his mother was elected prime minister. On Monday, 7 May 1979, three days after her general election victory, he drove to Scotland Yard, walked into the office for the prime minister's Special Branch personal protection and slumped into a chair. 'Well, I know I'm something of a hero,' he said with a straight face. 'But I really do think that Scotland Yard should be providing me with some form of personal protection.'

The Branch officers were stunned by such pretentiousness and his application was turned down. 'It got nowhere because I didn't pass on the message,' said one of the officers present. 'If I'd thought he was vulnerable, I would have done so. But that kind of protection would have needed special funding by the Home Office and it didn't warrant it. He just wanted bodyguards for his own self-aggrandisement and self-esteem, and that's how it turned out later on.'

Despite Scotland Yard's refusal, Mark was insistent and continued to request them. 'How can I get bodyguards?' he later asked Barrie Gill, his PR and marketing agent, at a racing meeting. Eventually, in early 1982, the Yard agreed that a Special Branch minder be assigned to him and that he should have the use of a Jaguar or an armour-plated Rolls-Royce saloon.[5]

The official reason why Thatcher received personal protection was that there was 'a very serious IRA threat to his life. The IRA had plans to kidnap him and deprive him of food so that he could suffer in the same way Bobby Sands [the hunger striker] suffered.' This was the explanation given to Sir John Junor, then editor of the *Sunday Express* and a close friend of Margaret Thatcher, by Sir David McNee, then commissioner of the Metropolitan Police.[6] There were also aggressive anonymous notes being sent to the newspapers.

However, some former Special Branch officers were sceptical about why he needed them. 'In my opinion, he just wanted them so that he could swan around and feel important,' said one. 'He loved having them around and got a real buzz out of it.' Carol Thatcher, who always refused to have a minder, was also dubious about their necessity. When asked why he warranted them, she replied dismissively, 'Oh, I don't know, he's had some death threat or something.'[7] It was not the only time she expressed doubt about his use of bodyguards.[8]

Mark's first major trip with Special Branch protection was on 27 March 1982, when he flew to California for the Long Beach Grand Prix. He was there to take part in a celebrity saloon-car race. 'The detective is going along to protect me,' he said. 'There is an IRA trial going on in San Francisco. I won't be going there but you can't be too careful.'[9] In fact, the extradition hearing had already been adjourned four days earlier, to 14 May 1982, but Thatcher retained his bodyguard who carried a Smith and Weeson .38 revolver and ten rounds of ammunition.

While Mark was in California, Argentina invaded the Falkland Islands and his mother ordered the mobilisation of troops. At first Mark responded flippantly. 'That's all we need just before Easter,' he said on being told the news.[10] Then he became more aggressive.

While a business associate was talking to Carlos Reuteman, an Argentinian racing driver, at the Long Beach Grand Prix, Thatcher rushed over and blurted out: 'I've just been speaking to the Boss. We're going to whip those dago bastards' arses.' He apparently had not seen Reuteman and his associate, an adviser to Frank Williams, admonished him: 'Mark that's very tactless.' But he just shrugged his shoulders.

Mark was not popular among most of his Special Branch minders. 'He loved us being around,' said one, 'but he was so bloody arrogant. He was always so sarcastic and treated us like domestic servants. He would stop in the middle of the road, chuck the keys at us and shout, "Park the car." I was with him once when he parked the car on a double yellow line. When a traffic warden came across, he just leaned out of the window and said, "You can't give me a ticket, I'm Mark Thatcher." Most of us hated him but we got good money because of the overtime.' On one occasion he came sprinting out of Heathrow with a girlfriend as if he were in an episode of *Miami Vice*. Spotting waiting journalists, he shouted at his bodyguard, threw his girlfriend into the back of a chauffeur-driven limousine and slapped the top of the car. As he slid into the passenger seat, he shouted 'Go!' at the driver.

Friends of Mark's also testify to the way he behaved towards his bodyguards. Jim Paterson, a Scottish businessman and farmer, knew him well and was a regular visitor to 10 Downing Street. He was once finishing lunch with Mark at the Dragon Inn restaurant in Gerrard Street, Soho, when his Special Branch detective approached the table and politely reminded him about a 3 p.m. appointment. 'I'll fucking make up my own mind when I'm going,' he snapped back. Paterson was appalled and leaned across the table. 'Mark, if you think that impresses me, you can forget it.'[11]

On another occasion, in 1986, he arrived at Singapore airport to discover that his personal detectives were not there to escort him. 'Where are my Special Branch guys?' he shouted. 'Do you know who I am? Do you know who my mother is?' An airport official tried to placate him. 'This is Singapore, sir. We do things differently here.' But Mark was unimpressed. 'I want my detectives.'

Eventually, he was persuaded to accept an elaborate security system in his bedroom at the Raffles Hotel. 'After you go to bed, switch it on,' he was told. 'If there is an intruder you will receive help within seconds.' That night, Mark was drinking in the hotel bar when he encountered a remarkably striking young lady. The two became instant friends and she took a note of his room number.

Thatcher then stumbled up to bed. Forgetting about his spontaneous invitation to the young woman, he switched on the security system. Within a few minutes, his new friend entered his room and slipped into bed beside him. Almost immediately, all hell broke loose. In a flash, the finest of Singapore's security services burst through the door, guns cocked, shouting and pointing at the bed – ready to defend the son of the British prime minister. But all they found was a bleary-eyed Mark Thatcher and his innocent lady companion, blinking in fear and confusion![12]

Mark continued to use armed Special Branch detectives when it suited him. His obsession with security did not prevent him from dismissing them and travelling alone, or discarding them when with someone whom he clearly did not want identified. However, when he did retain them, the cost was met by the taxpayer. For example, in August 1982 he travelled to New York City for a three-day business trip. Before the visit, a detective travelled to the USA by jumbo jet to make the 'security arrangements'. Then Mark and another bodyguard flew by Concorde to join him. Thatcher paid his own fare of £1,124. But the total cost in fares and accommodation for the two officers was an estimated £5,000, paid out of police funds.[13]

From then on, Mark was escorted by at least two detective sergeants, usually travelling business class. On one occasion, two officers had flown to Los Angeles to check the security arrangements but were left languishing in the Californian sun for four days because Thatcher twice postponed his trip.[14] The official cost to the taxpayer was £3,200.[15] Labour MPs claimed it was a 'scandalous waste of public money'.[16] But Margaret Thatcher responded resolutely. 'Both the form of protection and the resources deployed are directly related to the nature of the assessed threat,' she said. 'In the case of my son's recent trip to the United States, the police judged it necessary that he should be accompanied . . . It is not the practice to disclose details of arrangements of this kind.'[17]

By early 1983, Mark was being shadowed by three bodyguards and a police car. They seemed to follow him everywhere – when he played golf and even on visits to Annabel's nightclub. Two dinner-jacketed officers would watch him inside the club while another stayed in a Rover outside.[18]

As more detectives were assigned to him, the cost spiralled to about £50,000 a year. This extraordinary level of police attention was illustrated by the 1983 election campaign when he abruptly left the country. There was considerable unease about Mark being around. 'We felt he was trading too much off his mother's name,' recalled one former senior official at Tory Central Office, 'and so there was a move to keep him under wraps during that election because of the potential damage he might cause the party and her.'

During the first week of the campaign, Mark was accompanied by three Special Branch officers and attended his mother's adoption meeting in Finchley, north London. He then told startled friends that he was leaving for America and would be away for at least a fortnight. Just over a week later, on 26 May 1983, Thatcher flew out of Heathrow first-class on a Pan Am flight to New York. He was escorted by no fewer than eight plain-clothes police officers to the BA VIP lounge in Terminal 3 and kept away from journalists. When his flight was ready to board, police and airline officials virtually smuggled Mark out of the side exit and down the back steps from the VIP suite – normally only used by royalty, foreign heads of state and cabinet ministers. He passed through the suite to a waiting police Rover and was driven to the jet. The car circled the plane as the police tried to find a way on to the aircraft without being seen by the watching cameramen. But they were unsuccessful and, much to Mark's annoyance, his car was caught by the photographers.[19]

Airline officials said that this elaborate route was for 'security reasons'. Yet when he flew back to Heathrow ten days later, forty-eight hours before the poll, there was another police reception, usually reserved for royalty. When he left the BA aircraft, he had so many bodyguards waiting that there was a crush in the car ride back to the airport terminal. He was then met by another plain-clothes detective and two armed uniformed officers. Watching airport workers were amazed to see all five squeeze into an Austin Allegro police panda car to drive to the passenger building. As he was escorted through Customs, a reporter half-heartedly suggested Mark was a 'don't-know' voter. 'That is almost an insulting question,' he replied sharply. 'There is such a thing as family unity, you know.'[20]

Mark Thatcher retained his Special Branch minders until 1992 – two years after his mother left 10 Downing Street.[21] For a decade, he had been granted an unprecedented privilege, as only about 20 other people in Britain are given such police protection. It is usually reserved only for senior cabinet ministers and current and former Northern Ireland secretaries of state.[22]

Thatcher's request and unparalleled use of them was partly due to his deep-seated insecurity. But it was also an indication of his habit of exploiting the benefits of his mother's public office to draw attention to himself.

As he travelled the world with his bodyguards, Thatcher's relationship with the Foreign Office and overseas embassies became increasingly frosty and frictional. As soon as he arrived in the Gulf, the Middle East and Africa, Mark walked into British embassies and foreign government offices, expecting VIP treatment to promote his commercial interests. He was, of course, entitled to use the embassy facilities. But several diplomats were concerned about the way he went about it and the extent to which he was allowed to exploit his position. 'He had no scruples and would do anything that was asked of him to make money,' one Gulf diplomat told us. 'He would bring out blank 10 Downing Street notepaper and invite business associates to draft their own letters on it to suit their purpose.'

His favourite approach was to arrive at a British embassy and announce to the senior mandarin, 'I've got some business clients to entertain. I want access to your facilities. It will be good business for Britain.' This happened in South Africa in the mid-1980s. Mark arrived at the embassy in Pretoria and demanded introductions, immediate access to facilities and information to help his business interests. Soon after the visit, the chairman of a major public company was briefed about the incident by an angry diplomat. On his return to London, the businessman reported this, via his political contacts, to the Conservative Party whips' office. He also informed Ian Gow, then Margaret Thatcher's parliamentary private secretary. 'This needs to be watched,' the company chairman, who was a Conservative Party supporter, told him. 'Yes, I know there is a problem,' replied Gow.

On another occasion, Mark visited Jordan on behalf of Cementation International Ltd, as they were bidding for a contract to build an extension to a hotel. Mark went straight to the King's palace rather than the British embassy and began lobbying on behalf of his client. The ambassador became concerned about the type of businessmen he was dealing with during his stay in Amman. 'They were not the kind of people the son of the prime minister should have been involved with,' he told us. The ambassador then told a senior director of Cementation International, 'Do be careful about Mark Thatcher.'

The prime minister was judicious enough not to allow her son to attend many official overseas functions. He was present at a dinner given by the British ambassador, Oliver Wright, in Washington, during her visit to the United States in September 1983.[23] But, unlike her husband Denis, Mark never appeared in an official capacity during her overseas tours.

That did not stop him complaining bitterly about the Foreign Office and British embassies after returning to London. This was music to Margaret Thatcher's anti-Foreign Office ears. In 1981, she harangued a ministerial meeting about what she saw as the Foreign Office's ineffectiveness. 'My son, Mark, has just been out in the Gulf and had a lot of trouble with our embassies,' she said. 'The clear implication of what she was saying,' recalled one cabinet minister who was present, 'was that the Foreign Office was useless and Mark could run it better.' This was confirmed by one of the prime minister's foreign policy advisers in the early 1980s. 'Yes, he was reporting back about what he claimed were badly run British embassies,' he recalled. 'It was all nonsense but she believed anything he said.'

The consequence of Mrs Thatcher's stance was that her son secured considerable power and influence. This was demonstrated when the wife of Sheikh Zayed, the president of the United Arab Emirates (UAE), where Mark had business interests, visited London and wanted to see 10 Downing Street at short notice. Instead of the visit being arranged through the Foreign Office, who might have expressed reservations, Mark was asked to fix it. 'No problem,' he replied and a few hours later he telephoned back. 'Everything is fine.' The next day Sheikh Zayed's wife arrived at 10 Downing Street and received the red-carpet treatment.

The main source of anxiety among some British diplomats about Mark Thatcher was not that he was a businessman using their embassies. It was the nature of the commercial deals, his associates and the exploitation of the prime ministerial office that concerned them.

By far the most politically explosive and controversial was Mark's involvement in international arms dealing. This has always been denied by Thatcher's friends. Some of them admit he played a role in major defence contracts by acting as an intermediary and providing introductions between manufacturer and customer. But they contend he never actually sold the military hardware as such. 'He was only involved in those deals indirectly,' said Rodney Tyler, a close friend of the Thatcher family.

However, businessmen on both sides of the Atlantic insist he was more directly involved. This was asserted in the UK by two former senior executives of Astra Holdings plc, an arms and munitions manufacturer. Its former chairman, Gerald James, said that he was told by Richard Unwin, one of his consultants, on more than one occasion, 'If you want to get on in the defence world, then the one person you need to get hold of is Mark Thatcher.'[24]

This was corroborated by Christopher Gumbley, Astra's managing director from 1986 until 1990. During that period he had several meetings with Unwin to discuss making contact with Steve Tipping, Mark's former business partner, and Alan Curtis, former chairman of Lotus Cars. 'It was quite clear from those discussions,' recalled Gumbley, 'that in order to promote the interests of Astra and obtain more customers and contracts it was important to include Mark Thatcher.'[25]

James also points to an encounter in July 1988, during the Army Air Corps exhibition at Middle Wallop near Andover, Hampshire. As he was walking towards the Astra chalet, James met Unwin, who was accompanied by Mark Thatcher, Denis Thatcher, Steve Tipping and Alan Curtis. The Astra chairman was introduced to each member of the party. They exchanged civilities and moved on.

Unwin has been an active player in the defence arena. In 1985, his company, Unwin Pyrotechnics Ltd, was involved in supplying mortar-fire-simulators to the Nigerian army in a contract in which substantial commissions were paid.[26] However, he denies that he ever said that Mark Thatcher was useful in the arms business. 'I never said that,' he told us. But he accepts that he met Mark at the Army Air Show and again at the Savoy Hotel with Alan Curtis in 1990. Unwin also confirmed meeting Steve Tipping: 'He came to see me in about 1984 or 1985 when I had my fireworks company but I can't really remember what it was about. He was wheeling and dealing at the time.'[27]

Across the Atlantic, more direct testimony comes from Jay Laughlin, who from 1993 until 1994 was one of Mark's business partners in Houston (see Chapter Nine). Laughlin was president of Ameristar Fuels, which traded in aviation fuel, and in December 1992 was negotiating with Mark, who was interested in investing in the company. As part of his due diligence, Laughlin asked Mark about his resources. He assumed that Thatcher's wealth was derived from his parents through trusts: 'So you've got your money from your parents?'

'I've got more money than my father or mother combined,' replied Mark indignantly.

'How? In what sort of business?'

'I brokered deals. I also have a construction company.'

'What sort of deals?'

'I brokered deals involving military equipment.'[28]

One of Mark Thatcher's first forays into the world of facilitating the buying and selling of military equipment was through a chance personal contact. In early 1982, he was going out with a girl who knew Colonel Henry 'Jim' Johnson, an insurance broker who was very well connected in the security and defence arena. He was a director and shareholder of Saladin Security Ltd, a private security company, and was well placed, partly because of his friendship with the mercenary soldier Major David Walker.

At the time, Mark was working on a project to sell surplus RAF aircraft to South America and so he wanted to sound Johnson out. A meeting was set up and he visited Johnson at his home in Sloane Avenue, Chelsea. 'He [Thatcher] had a girlfriend that I knew and she introduced me to him,' recalled the security consultant. 'He came to see me and we discussed it. He said he had a contact out there and wanted my advice. But he was very much fly-by-night and nothing ever came of it. I was supposed to receive some letters but when they arrived they were late and incomplete, so we never got any further.'[29]

The prime minister's son never lost his interest in pursuing business in South America. His chief contact was an Argentinian commodity broker called Leonardis Walger, who also acted as a middleman and, many years later, was convicted of cocaine trafficking. Born in 1944, the son of a judge, Walger was a colourful operator whose influence and connections stretched throughout the continent. A qualified lawyer, he was a private secretary to President Juan Carlos Onganía in the mid-1960s and responsible for liaising with Córdoba province, the country's most industrialised and sophisticated area. Walger then became an active member of the Montoneros, a right-wing Peronist guerrilla group in Argentina. As their financial adviser, Walger was responsible for fundraising and the movement of cash, most of which came from General Manuel Noriega, president of Panama. But he grew disillusioned with the Peronistas and, in May 1974, left Argentina for England. For a brief period, he remained on the payroll of the Montoneros, who, he admitted to us, were bandits.

The Argentinian decided to set up shop in the commodities business. His first break was meeting Sandy Harper, a futures trader who was well connected in London society as a one-time boyfriend of Princess Anne. Walger had contacts in Paraguay, one of the crucial markets in the commodities business, and so in 1977 they joined forces. Based in a top-floor City office at 3 Lloyd's Avenue, off Fenchurch Street, the two ran a commodity futures company called Cominter UK Ltd, which had been a corporate front for the Montoneros. Dealing in coffee, sugar and cocoa, Cominter secured new investment capital from Paraguay and their business took off. In 1980, they were able to move into new offices at 79 Eccleston Square, Pimlico, and Walger bought a house for £200,000 at 2 Kensington Gate, near Hyde Park. He also owned homes in Peru and Uruguay.

Cash became readily available and much of it was spent on Walger's budding career as a Formula One racing driver. But commodity futures is a risky business. Essentially it is gambling and investors can win or lose a fortune. This was in tune with Walger's personality – adventurous, independent minded and a commercial risk taker.

When he met Mark Thatcher in the summer of 1981, the Argentinian was at the height of his financial success. The two had much in common. Their lives were dominated by dual passions – making money and motor racing. As self-styled entrepreneurs, they were looking for the main chance. At first, they were just social acquaintances. But then the silver market collapsed and it hit Cominter hard. They paid off their losses but were left penniless in terms of cash, if not credit.

Walger and the prime minister's son then started talking business, mainly international ventures. The South American saw him as useful for opening markets, because he knew the senior executives of several top UK companies. 'I had a commodity called Mark Thatcher,' recalled Walger when we met him in London in 1994. The 'commodity' in turn viewed Walger as a beneficial front for his activities – someone to represent him. 'I was an ideal pioneer for his marketing interests,' said the Argentinian.[30]

Their first joint project was to lobby Société Minière, a Belgian mining company which was interested in selling its minerals – gold, silver and copper. Thatcher knew their top executives and Walger had sources in Spain who were potential purchasers, so in October 1981 the two men flew to Brussels for a meeting. It was successful, though eventually the deal fell through because the Spanish would not pay enough for the minerals.

South America was the next commercial target in their sights.

The itinerary was Paraguay (railways), Colombia (sugar) and Peru (aluminium). They also devised a scheme, using the Thatcher name, to raise sponsorship funds for their plans to drive in the Le Mans race in June 1982. The Argentinian contacted potential benefactors far and wide seeking £70,000. He approached *Holá!* magazine, the Spanish equivalent of *Hello!*, for £35,000 and even travelled to Bogotá, Colombia. But it was all to no avail. Their sponsorship drive and business trip to South America were abruptly interrupted by the outbreak of the Falklands war. The British embassy told the prime minister's son it was 'too dangerous' for him to visit Peru.

On 4 April 1982, two days after Argentine forces invaded the Falklands, Walger received a telephone call from Argentina. Two days later, he was on a plane to Peru and while in Lima he volunteered for service as an interpreter. He was not required for duty but after the war he received a certificate signed by General Galtieri, thanking him for his offer to help recover the islands, which he proudly hung on the wall of his London home.

Despite the war, Thatcher and Walger continued to communicate, though not on commercial matters. A week after the invasion Mark telephoned his Argentine friend and said with a mixture of respect and fear, 'You've got no idea what my mother is like. She is going to give your people such hell. You should tell the Peruvian government.' They exchanged telexes, discussing their ideas on racing. Two of them were apologies for not being able to drive in the June 1982 Le Mans race because of the South Atlantic campaign.

After the Falklands conflict, Walger returned to London and resumed his business career and friendship with Thatcher. Within two months of the war ending, he used the prime minister's son in an arms deal that was as bizarre as it was controversial. Mark seemed unaware of the potential repercussions of helping an Argentine middleman in a weapons transaction, which was surprising in view of the political and personal importance of the Falklands war to his mother.

The origins of the deal lay in a visit to Peru in the summer of 1981 by Ian Smalley, a notorious London-based arms trader and bankrupt, also known as 'Dr Doom' and 'the Fat Man'. Smalley's personal assistant, a bogus 'Russian princess' called Natasha Boldero (real name Cynthia Anne Mitchell), had useful Peruvian connections and suggested they cultivate them. Her most useful contact was Dr Juan Antonio Azula de la Guerra, a former boyfriend, who was a well-connected middleman based in Lima. He was also Leon Walger's Peru consultant.

Boldero arranged a meeting in Lima between Azula de la Guerra and Smalley. The Peruvian explained that his government was looking to buy weapons for its elite Special Forces, the Sinchis. He asked the British arms dealer whether he could supply them. Smalley said he could and returned to London. On 25 September 1981, Azula sent a telex to Smalley with a list of requirements and requested a price list. The dealer responded with a cost breakdown for 170,000 rounds of ammunition and explosives.

But negotiations became fractious and so Smalley decided to bring in Dick Meadows, his US contact, a retired Special Forces major and a former security consultant to Ross Perot. Meadows was director of marketing for Peregrine International Associates Inc., a Dallas-based company formed in 1981 to promote private security, arms sales and counter-terrorist training. It was modelled on the British firm, Keeni-Meeni Services (KMS) – *keeni-meeni* is a Swahili word describing a snake's movement through grass – which employed former SAS officers on operations deemed too sensitive for direct government involvement. Peregrine operated in much the same way, as a private arm of US Intelligence. Its personnel worked as contract undercover agents for the US Customs Service, infiltrating illegal international arms deals and reporting back inside information to customs officers. They were also directed by the Defense Intelligence Agency's (DIA) Forward Operating Group.[31]

Peregrine, named after the falcon, was set up by Gary Howard and Ronnie Tucker, both Vietnam veterans and former federal agents and state police officers in Texas. They were later joined by Meadows and Charles Odorizzi, a former director of training for Delta Force. The company was geared up for arms deals with South America, mainly because the DIA had given it a list of countries where it could operate. At its peak, it employed over 20 agents.

As it happened, one of the arms dealers Peregrine was secretly investigating on behalf of US Customs, the CIA and the DIA just happened to be Dr Ian Smalley. Howard and Tucker were hired to run a 'sting' operation against him because of his alleged involvement in illegal arms sales to Libya, Iran and Iraq. Known as 'Houston III', it involved setting up front companies to entice Smalley into delivering anti-tank missiles to Iraq and tanks to Iran. Peregrine would then receive a 'moiety' – a percentage-based commission on the captured military equipment. So when 'Dr Doom' Smalley and

'Princess' Natasha Boldero approached Howard and Meadows about the Peruvian business, they were delighted.

Meanwhile, on the other side of the deal, Azula talked to Leon Walger about the proposed business with Smalley and Meadows. Walger was interested because he had excellent connections in the Peruvian government. The family of his then wife, Malena Prado, was the most powerful in Peru. Her father was the founder of the National Bank and an uncle was a former president. Even more useful was Walger's friendship with Celso Pastor, legal adviser to the Prado family, the president's brother-in-law and the Peruvian ambassador to the United Nations. Pastor was an *éminence grise* and fixer for the Peruvian government. He was a perfect channel for any defence contract.

Walger agreed to proceed, and his office in Lima was used as a base for the deal. On 14 July 1982, Azula met Meadows and Odorizzi at a Dallas hotel. The Peruvian briefed them on how his government was now in favour of buying weapons from America rather than the Soviet Union. Meadows replied that he needed introductions in Peru for the transaction to succeed. 'No problem,' said Azula, and he described Walger's credentials. He also, for the first time, mentioned Mark Thatcher's friendship with the Argentinian.

Azula was ecstatic about his meeting with Meadows. He reported back to Walger that the former Special Forces major was 'a super hero and a very impressive man'. A highly decorated Vietnam war commando, Meadows had just appeared on the cover of *Newsweek* magazine. The article described how he had slipped into Tehran undercover in 1980 to provide crucial on-site intelligence for the failed raid to rescue the hostages in Iran. The Argentinian was impressed by the major's reputation and record.

On 22 July 1982, Meadows and Odorizzi flew to London and met Walger at the Montcalm Hotel in Cumberland Place, central London. Through the State Department's Office of Munitions Control, the DIA had arranged an export licence for Peregrine to sell arms to Peru. This gave Meadows the authority to tell Walger that Peregrine could fulfil Peru's requirements. The Argentinian responded by sending a telex to Celso Pastor, Peru's ambassador to the UN, introducing Meadows.

Two days later, Walger met Mark Thatcher for a drink at his Kensington Gate home and told him about his meeting with Meadows. The prime minister's son was excited, because he had also just read about the Special Forces major in *Newsweek*. 'What are you

CAPTURED: *Private Eye*'s portrayal of the day Mark Thatcher was
arrested at his house in Cape Town for helping to fund an attempted *coup
d'état* in the oil-rich African state of Equatorial Guinea.
(By kind permission of *Private Eye*)

SOLDIER OF FORTUNE: Simon Mann (right), the former SAS officer who led a group of mercenaries in an audacious plot to overthrow the president of Equatorial Guinea. He was captured in Zimbabwe and is now in prison He is pictured above playing the role of Colonel Derek Wilford, a senior British army officer, in the ITV drama *Bloody Sunday*. (Right © Getty Images/ Above © Granada Films)

THE DICTATOR: President Obiang of Equatorial Guinea. The discovery of oil has made his tiny country a magnet for multinational companies. 'The oil has been for us like the manna that the Jews ate in the desert,' he said.
(© *Press Association*)

TWINS: Mark Thatcher, aged six, and his twin sister
Carol, shortly after his mother was elected MP for
Finchley in 1959. (© Press Association)

REJOICE:
Mark Thatcher
with his mother
at Tory Central
Office on the
night she was
elected prime
minister for the
first time in 1979.
(© Press
Association)

THE BANKER: Hugh Thurston, the Jersey banker who has been the personal financial adviser to Mark and Margaret Thatcher since the early 1980s. (© *Jersey Evening Post*)

PARTNERS: Mark Thatcher with Steve Tipping, his business partner during the early 1980s. Within seven weeks of the 1979 election, they had set up their own marketing company. (© Solo Syndication)

IN OMAN: Margaret Thatcher and the Sultan of Oman, Qaboos bin Said, arriving for a state banquet in Muscat, the capital, in 1981. During her visit, she was given a diamond necklace by the Sultan.
(© Rex Features)

THE BOSS: Chatting to Lord Matthews, chairman of Trafalgar House plc, whose subsidiary, Cementation International, retained Mark Thatcher as a consultant in 1981. (© Tomas Jaski)

MUTUAL INTERESTS: Margaret Thatcher with Sheik Zayed (on her left) during a state visit to 10 Downing Street. (© Rex Features)

ARMS AND THE WOMAN: Margaret Thatcher, who was directly involved in negotiations when British companies sold weapons to the Middle East, greeting King Fahd, ruler of Saudi Arabia, at 10 Downing Street in 1987. (© Press Association)

FRIENDS UNITED: From left – Syrian businessman Wafic Said, Denis Thatcher, Rosemary Said, Margaret Thatcher, Mark, his wife Diane and Said's son, at the premiere of *The Fourth Protocol*. (© Rex Features)

WITH THE AUTHORS: Wafic Said, who played a crucial intermediary role during the negotiations for the $20 billion defence contract between British Aerospace and Saudi Arabia, with the authors of this book. Mark Hollingsworth is on Wafic's left, with Paul Halloran on his right.

DYNASTY: The Thatcher family with Mark's children, Michael and Amanda. A cartoon on the wall of Mark Thatcher's house depicted Lady Thatcher meeting some wealthy Arabs with a little boy. 'As far as business is concerned, Mark's keeping a low profile at the moment, but have you met my grandson?' she asks them.
(© National Pictures)

THE RANCH: Mark Thatcher's 15,000-square-foot mansion in Constantia, Cape Town. He sold it in 2005.
(© Rex Features)

IN THE DOCK: Mark Thatcher outside the Cape Town High Court after pleading guilty to 'unlawfully attempting to finance mercenary activity' during the coup plot in Equatorial Guinea. He was given a suspended jail sentence. (© Getty Images)

doing with him?' he asked. Walger explained how he was facilitating a combined arms, anti-kidnapping and military training deal. 'I'm introducing him to the Peruvian government,' he said. 'Well, I'm very close to the Marcos family,' replied Thatcher. 'I can do the same deal in the Philippines. They have the same trouble with rebels and guerrillas.' Nothing came of it but Mark Thatcher's close association with the Marcos regime was confirmed by a source who used to work for him. 'I know there was a Philippines connection,' he said, 'because Steve Tipping went out there and was entertained by one of the Marcos sons.'

When Meadows returned to Texas on 27 July 1982, a telex from Walger was waiting for him at his office in Dallas. The telex outlined his commitment to the deal and introduced a new participant: 'Dr Azula has briefed me on your interests re: certain particular countries in which we are well connected and in which we might be able to help selling your ideas and/or equipment. I would also like to point out that I am a close friend and associate of Mr Mark Thatcher who, for obvious reasons, is also highly well connected in other parts of the world. Last night, Dr Azula and I unsuccessfully tried to contact you. We will try to call between 8 and 8.45 p.m. London time. This time, Mark will also be with us.'

The following afternoon, Azula and Walger did indeed telephone from London with Mark Thatcher in attendance, in a conference call which the Texans tape-recorded. 'We can do some good business together, Dick,' Walger told Meadows. The Argentinian then asked Thatcher to come to the phone. 'No, no,' said Mark in a very panicky, almost frightened voice. 'For Christ's sake, don't use my name.'

Gary Howard, Meadows' employer at Peregrine, read the telex and listened in on the telephone call. He was surprised but impressed by the Thatcher connection. 'That name definitely added credibility to the deal,' he recalled. 'No one would figure that the prime minister's son would be involved in such a deal.'[32]

Meadows confirmed Thatcher's role. 'His name was mentioned as a point of reference,' he recalled. 'Walger and Azula wanted me to know that they had connections in the British government and they had some authority. They wanted to do some business and Mark Thatcher was part of it, but I don't know how. I had daily liaison with them.'

At the time Meadows was sufficiently impressed to fly back to London with his deputy, Charles Odorizzi, for a more substantial discussion with the South Americans on the arms supply. The meeting, which took place at 2 Kensington Gate, was successful. Meadows told them their political connections added weight to the deal. 'We are using Thatcher simply because of his name and the credibility it holds,' replied Walger. 'He is not very bright and has to be instructed on what to do. But his name does carry a lot of weight.'

Walger wanted a commission of up to 18 per cent on the deal. But that did not deter the Texans and it was agreed to draw up a contract for Peregrine International to provide $30 million-worth of weapons for the Peruvian counter-insurgency forces. 'The sky's the limit on this contract,' Meadows wrote in a memo afterwards. He thought that the deal was worth $200 million but was instructed by the DIA that he could supply only about $100 million-worth of hardware.

Peregrine immediately drew up a 100-page inventory of weapons and support equipment, and Meadows contacted the State Department to obtain authorisation. A Washington law firm – Arent, Fox, Kintner, Plotkin and Kahn – then drew up a five-page draft contract and Charles Odorizzi went to Lima for a meeting with the Ministry of the Interior. Everything seemed to be progressing smoothly. On 21 October 1982, Meadows told Howard that the deal had the blessing of the DIA and he would stay on contract for another twelve months with no pay to see it through. But five days later Meadows suddenly resigned from Peregrine. He claimed it was 'due to internal disagreements'. In fact, the DIA instructed him to leave the company because they were on the trail of Smalley for arms offences and Meadows was to be a witness at the trial.

Howard continued to liaise with Azula and Walger. But progress was slow and Peregrine was perplexed by the lack of action. Its formal bid had been finalised and freight costs were calculated. So, on 1 December 1982, Howard telexed the Argentinian: 'Due to circumstances beyond our control we are unable to make contact with you. Should we now make contact with Mark Thatcher through our British associate?' Walger did not respond and now says he was cut out of the deal. This has some credibility, as Meadows continued to work quietly for the DIA on the Peruvian order by setting up Gavilon, a private company he ran with Monza Bilbesi, a Jordanian arms dealer.

Despite Meadows' best endeavours, the Peruvians never received their weapons. It was later claimed that the Peruvian president, Fernando Belaúnde, rejected the deal because it was 'too complicated'.[33] Reflecting on it 12 years later, Walger believed Peru simply did not have the money. 'I don't think they could afford it,' he said.

Howard strongly disputed both explanations, claiming that the contract was cancelled because Meadows was tipped off that the arms were going not to Peru but to Argentina. Although he had no hard evidence to support this allegation, it was based on his personal involvement in and knowledge of the deal. 'After our meeting with Walger and Azula in London, which occurred after the Falklands conflict (which had left the Argentine army in a state of disarray), the whole tone of the telexes from them changed,' Howard told us. 'Peru wasn't mentioned any more. They were talking about Argentina now, not Peru, and here was Thatcher's son possibly involved in a deal with a country that Mrs Thatcher had declared war on.

'Part of the deal concerned mobile training teams. This was anything military – from medics to parachuting to armoured cars. It was obvious from the telexes these teams were destined for Argentina. On the weapons list, items jumped out at you to show that these were not arms for Peru. One was 36,000 riot batons. I mean, 36,000 riot batons! Peru doesn't have as many people as that in its defence force. Argentina does. There was an awful lot of cold-weather gear too. The Argentinians lost their cold-weather gear in the Falklands.'[34]

Walger later appeared anxious to protect Thatcher when the story broke. 'Mark was totally unaware that I had named him in the telex,' he said. 'It was wrong of me to do so and I regret having mentioned his name.'[35]

It was no surprise when his business relationship with Mark was abruptly terminated. In 1984, Walger sold his Knightsbridge house, closed down Cominter UK Ltd and returned to Buenos Aires. Three years later, he resurfaced on the southern coast of Spain and became part of the Marbella jet set. On 16 January 1987, Walger arrived in Madrid with two metal boxes containing 347 grams of cocaine with a 48 per cent purity which 'a friend from Peru' had handed him. Needing a buyer for the drugs, he hooked up with a notorious local playboy. But the Argentinian was then caught in possession of 247 grams of cocaine, valued at £10,000. Two months later he was convicted of drugs trafficking and sentenced to two years in jail. He served fourteen months of his sentence. After his prison term, he returned to Buenos Aires, where he now resides.

Walger's lawyer, Dr Azula, also faded from the scene but still lives in Lima. The other 'Doctor', Ian Smalley, whose visit to Peru was the first episode in this bizarre tale, was eventually charged with arms smuggling but acquitted. It was claimed by Howard and Tucker, the

Customs agents on his case, that this was because of what Smalley knew about covert and illicit weapons shipments by the US and UK governments. Smalley eventually went to jail and died in Houston in 2004. His former personal assistant, Natasha Boldero, a.k.a. Cynthia Mitchell, fell out with her boss and got a job at Arabesk, an upmarket jewellery shop in Walton Street, South Kensington. She has cut herself off from the twilight world of arms dealing and is believed to be living in Greece. Dick Meadows continued to work for the DIA until his retirement to Florida. He died in 1995.

As for the prime minister's son, he was scared to death about his involvement with an Argentine arms broker being known, as the tape-recording proves. When it was disclosed by *Private Eye*, he rang Walger in a panic. 'Mum is going bananas,' he said. 'I was not involved. You've got to clear my name.'

At the very least, his association with Walger so soon after the Falklands war showed an extraordinary lack of judgement. It was a clear demonstration of Mark's indiscriminate choice of business associates. But what this episode revealed most of all was how Thatcher secured an entrée to the military-equipment business – through the motor-racing circuit. That was his introduction to South America. And it was originally via the Formula One Grand Prix racing scene that Mark acquired his largest sack of gold.

Mark Thatcher's largest commission payment was from the largest arms deal in history. Known as Al-Yamamah (Arabic for 'the Dove of Peace'), this contract to supply military equipment to Saudi Arabia was negotiated at the very highest level. Batting for Britain was the prime minister, Margaret Thatcher, and for Saudi Arabia, Prince Bandar, Saudi ambassador to the United States and King Fahd's most trusted envoy.

Mrs Thatcher has always been an enthusiastic exponent of selling British weapons abroad. She enjoyed dealing personally with Third World kings and presidents, trading in the very symbols and sinews of national power. Usually, the secretary of state for defence was the front man in the negotiations, but Thatcher relished leading the charge and beating the arms drum for Britain. 'I knew that I had only to ask my office to contact Number 10 to wheel in the heavy guns if they could in any way help to achieve sales of British equipment,' recalls former defence secretary Michael Heseltine. Her enthusiasm for selling weapons was apparent in April 1981 when she told Arab correspondents in 10 Downing Street, 'We are particularly good on aircraft. We have also been very good on tanks and on armour. We are absolutely outstanding on radar, avionics in aircraft, on some aero engines, on carbon fire . . . The development of jet was ours, radar was ours . . . The Harrier is perhaps the best plane in the world. The Tornado is very, very advanced. The Rapier is quite superb.'[36]

Thatcher herself set up many of the largest and most controversial deals, negotiating directly with King Hussein of Jordan, General Suharto of Indonesia and General Pinochet of Chile. She sweetened and lubricated these contracts by what she called 'soft finance' and aggressive use of the export credit guarantee scheme by which her government underwrote the financing of the deal if it collapsed. The Treasury was unhappy about this un-Thatcherite and extravagant provision of credit for weapons sales but Thatcher brushed aside their objections to such lavish subsidies. 'You must find a way,' she told Trade and Industry officials. 'You are accountants and accounting is all about taking a sum of money from one person and giving it to someone else. Sort it out.' The problem was that the taxpayer was short-changed when some of the countries, notably Jordan and Iraq, did not pay up and HMG was landed with the bill. By 1990, Iraq had defaulted on defence contracts worth close to £2.3 billion. In reality, the prime minister was subsidising British arms firms with vast sums of public money – a policy she noticeably refused to do for other areas of industry.[37]

The contract that most interested her was Al-Yamamah, worth a total of £40 billion. It was originally conceived in the early 1980s when President Reagan tried to sell some F-15s, a strike aircraft, to Saudi Arabia. The Israeli lobby, through Congress, vetoed the deal and so British Aerospace promoted their Tornado, a more advanced and menacing aircraft but also more expensive than the rival Mirage 2000. Conscious that the Saudi princes were easily intimidated and neurotic about threats from neighbouring states, the Ministry of Defence argued that the offensive Tornado would be an effective deterrent.

The Saudis agreed and in late May 1985, Prince Bandar, son of the Saudi defence minister, flew to London and negotiated directly and privately with Mrs Thatcher. 'What do you want?' she asked Bandar. 'Planes, ships, tanks? They're yours. Anything short of nuclear. No problem.'[38]

Prince Bandar, only 36 years old when the negotiations took place, was King Fahd's favourite nephew, chief diplomatic troubleshooter and an ambassador in more ways than one. He operates at the highest levels – bypassing the foreign ministers and dealing with their principals. His diplomatic secret is that he is bi-cultural. A Koran-quoting Muslim, he is extremely adept at making all the right chess moves in the intriguing and conspiratorial world of rivalry between the Saudi princes. Yet at the same time he is a Scotch-drinking, US-trained fighter pilot, who is also a poker player and a graduate of the School of Advanced International Studies, Johns Hopkins University, in Washington, DC.[39]

It is a remarkable combination of qualities but he also brought to the negotiations knowledge of commissions to intermediaries on major arms sales. This was largely because of his father's experience as the Saudi defence minister. Whether such payments were referred to during his often unscheduled and periodic meetings with the prime minister is not known. But the multibillion-pound order was only awarded to Britain, according to Nihad Ghadry, a former adviser to King Faisal and successive monarchs, once Margaret Thatcher agreed to keep the details of the order secret and to allow the Saudis to handle the contract in their own way.

Thatcher's role was pivotal and she immersed herself in the detail. In August 1985, she interrupted her annual holiday in Switzerland and drove to the house of the British consul in Salzburg, Austria. There to meet her was Prince Bandar, armed with a confidential letter from King Fahd, and a memorandum of understanding was drawn up. During 1985, she had at least six private meetings with Prince Bandar and made unscheduled stops in Riyadh to discuss the deal. A month later, on 26 September, the contract was signed in London by Bandar's father, Prince Sultan, and Michael Heseltine, then defence secretary, who said the prime minister's role 'cannot be overstated'.[40] But the negotiations then embarked on a mysterious course. Two days before the document was initialled, Britain's chief of air staff was told that the Saudis were buying not just 48 Tornados but also an extra 24 planes for 'an air defence role'. And just for good measure, they also ordered an extra 30 Hawk trainer aircraft from BAE. A deal of already awesome proportions had ballooned into something colossal and unprecedented. The final contract was formally authorised in Riyadh in February 1986.

Extreme secrecy surrounded the details. The Saudis were particularly keen on the confidentiality clause and the British government readily agreed, not wanting to jeopardise such a key contribution to its balance of payments. The contract was governed by what is known in the USA as 'a black defence program' – whereby commercial information is withheld from the public and parliament – according to a report by the stockbrokers UBS Phillips and Drew. This was later borne out when a three-year investigation of the contract, focusing on secret commission payments, by the National Audit Office, the government's watchdog on spending, was suppressed in 1992 and has never been published. Details were blacked out in a later 'strategic marketing' report by the Defence Export Sales Organisation (DESO) because 'public interest in the disclosure of this information is outweighed by the risk this could pose to the Al-Yamamah programme'.

One reason why the prime minister played a direct role in Al-Yamamah was its massive value – eventually £40 billion to its contractor, British Aerospace plc. It was also a government-to-government deal which had diplomatic and political benefits in cementing alliances. This was underlined by David Gore-Booth, the British ambassador in Saudi Arabia at the time. He described the kingdom as 'easily Britain's most important partner in the Middle East, whether politically, commercially or militarily . . . We have no intention of depriving our friends of the means to defend themselves.'[41]

'The Dove of Peace' developed into a 'wish-list' of defence equipment for the Saudi armed forces, with priorities and delivery varied to suit their requirements, plus the availability of funding.[42] The first order was for 48 Tornado GR1 strike fighter bombers, 24 Tornado F3 air-defence aircraft, 30 Hawk 60 series advanced training aircraft and 30 Pilatus PC9 basic training aircraft. The second stage, three years later in 1988, was secured by the prime minister at a stopover in Bermuda on her way to Australia. The Saudis agreed to buy another 48 Tornados, 60 Hawks, 6 minehunters (from Vosper Thornycroft), 88 Black Hawk helicopters (from Westland) and a large air base and an air-defence command and control system.[43]

Al-Yamamah was a gold mine for British Aerospace, as it was paid mainly in oil, although there were substantial multimillion-dollar cash payments as well. But it was not a pure barter arrangement – the equivalent of exchanging two goats for a pig. Under the contract, the Saudis delivered to British Petroleum (BP) and Shell 600,000 barrels of oil per day. They then refined it and sold it on the open market. The proceeds were paid on a monthly basis into a special London bank account administered by the Ministry of Defence, with BAE as the custodian. The account was then drawn on by British Aerospace as the arms were delivered. 'This, in effect, was a general slush fund for the Saudi Ministry of Defence,' Chas Freeman, former US ambassador in Riyadh, told us. 'They could debit anything they wanted against this account and BAE would do the procurement. And it was not subject to public scrutiny in either country. It was not part of the Saudi defence budget. It was off budget and because it was out of sight, it was peculiarly susceptible to corruption . . . The fact is that if you have an essentially limitless trust fund, you can buy anything you want from anyone you want with no one the wiser; no matter how honest or patriotic your initial instincts might be, the temptation for abuse would be large.'

The contract was a huge commission-generating machine. A large proportion of British Aerospace's hardware and spare parts were sold at a high premium – or a 'friendship price' as the Saudis like to call it. The difference between the 'normal price' and the 'friendship' version were distributed in various tranches to Saudi defence officials, members of the royal family and intermediaries. 'The opportunities for rake-offs were very large,' said Freeman. Former CIA officer Robert Baer claimed, 'Most of the commissions went to Prince Sultan, his family and a legion of middlemen'. Numerous sources calculate the secret payments accounted for 30 per cent of the contract.

British Aerospace files on pay-offs are held in a vault in a Swiss bank. But documents obtained by *The Guardian* in 2003 disclosed a £60 million BAE slush fund that was used to pay Prince Turki bin Nasser, head of the Saudi Air Force, during the latter stages of Al-Yamamah. 'Commission contracts are often written so that no one party can remove them from a bank,' said Major-General Kenneth Perkins, former British Aerospace marketing director for the Middle East. 'The contract requires both parties to be present before it can be removed. Any party can go in and make photocopies of the contract. But the party has to cut off any letterheads and signatures before he can take the photocopies out of the bank.'[44] A former executive of the arms company BMARC, David Trigger, confirmed that such payments were paid while giving evidence in the High Court during an unrelated court case. 'Commission was obviously paid but my understanding is that all my work connected with that contract [Al-Yamamah] is governed by the Official Secrets Act.'[45]

There is, of course, nothing unusual in intermediaries playing key roles in major arms deals. Quite the reverse, in fact. Business in the Arab world is often conducted on the basis of personal trust and recommendations. Many contracts are sealed with a handshake not a fountain pen. All the Saudi princes have their own agents, although they are often little more than chiefs-of-staff. In the West, the brokers are more sophisticated: they bypass the formal channels of communication and structures between the contractor and the governments. In Saudi Arabia, the role is performed by a front man and a large share of the commission is routed to members of the royal family – usually through a less visible Prince or a trusted individual.

The difference with Al-Yamamah is that the son of the British prime minister who negotiated the multibillion-pound contract was one of those middlemen who benefited financially. Mrs Thatcher's contribution 'cannot be overstated', said her defence secretary Michael Heseltine.

The origins of Mark Thatcher's involvement lay in his friendship with Mansour Ojjeh, a wealthy American-educated Saudi businessman and fellow racing fan. They met in 1980 when Mark was invited to the Frank Williams base at Didcot, Oxfordshire, and was introduced to Mansour, whose family sponsored the Williams Formula One racing team. The two became friends. Mark would visit Mansour at his home in Monaco and in turn invite his fellow car enthusiast to Lotus promotional events.

Mansour introduced Mark to his father, the late Akram Ojjeh, then procurement agent for the Saudi royal family on all key military contracts. Born in Syria, brought up in Iraq and educated in France, the picaresque Akram Ojjeh established his first arms-trading company in Switzerland in 1956. By that time he had also set up Saudi Arabia's first weapons factory.[46]

The next decade saw Ojjeh base himself in Paris and represent French defence firms like Dassault, selling their Mirage jets and Matra's missile systems in the Middle East, and he hired the legendary Saudi arms dealer Adnan Khashoggi as a consultant. Often under scrutiny by the French authorities, he created a new business vehicle in 1977 – the Geneva-registered TAG Group, otherwise known as Technique d'Avant Garde or the Trans-Arabian Group. By that stage, Akram Ojjeh had unrivalled access to and influence with the Saudi royal family on major defence projects. His main channel and entrée to the royal family was Khalid bin Abdul Aziz Al-Ibrahim, an unofficial advisor to King Fahd and the brother of his favourite wife. Ojjeh was particularly close to Prince Sultan, the defence and aviation minister. Such connections brought vast wealth – enough to own the *QE2*, a large ranch in Paraguay, houses in Paris and Monte

Carlo and to give £1 million a year to the Frank Williams racing team as sponsorship.

After meeting Mark Thatcher, Ojjeh cultivated him as a useful contact and lent him a car from the Saudi racing team. From 1980 onwards, the prime minister's son acted as a TAG introductory agent, flying on their BAC1–11 private aircraft to Haiti, among other places. He was seen as potentially useful in 1983, when a major contract became available in Saudi Arabia for the construction and equipping of two hospitals for the National Guard, in Riyadh and Mecca. The staffing and equipment orders were handled by the British Ministry of Defence and they entertained bids from interested firms.

Ojjeh was interested in acting for any of the bidding contractors and dispatched young Thatcher to work on the project. He approached Christopher Chataway, the former Conservative minister who was chairman of United Medical Enterprises UK (UME). At Mark's invitation, Chataway flew to Paris for a meeting with Ojjeh to discuss the tender but nothing came of it.[47] Instead, UME hired the Saudi-based Project Development Company.

Unperturbed, TAG represented a rival prospective contractor, American Hospitals International Inc. Ojjeh then used Mark Thatcher to lobby the Ministry of Defence on his behalf. This was not a wise move as the civil servants resented being approached by the prime minister's son acting on behalf of an American company. Despite the fact that UME secured the order, there was considerable disquiet inside the MoD about the episode.

When asked about his business relationship with Akram Ojjeh a year later (in 1984), Mark admitted meeting him on four occasions but played down the association. 'I know his son and he likes the same things I do, like cars,' he said.[48]

What Thatcher did not mention was that his friend Akram Ojjeh played a pivotal role in the crucial early stages of Al-Yamamah on behalf of British Aerospace. Ojjeh was in a very powerful position because of his long-standing record as a procurement agent for the Saudi government and royal connections. But his relationship with British Aerospace deteriorated when it was disclosed he was also the agent for the French company Dassault, a competitor on the deal. This was discovered by Alex Sanson, managing director of British Aerospace's Dynamics Division, who saw it as a conflict of interests. Ojjeh was sacked by Aerospace but was paid some compensation through Lebanese sources.

The person who benefited most from Ojjeh's removal from the

Dassault contract was Wafic Said, a flamboyant, wealthy Syrian financier who was the UK director of Ojjeh's TAG company. He succeeded his former boss both as a key middleman on the Al-Yamamah deal and as the chief courtier to the House of Saud. 'It [replacing Ojjeh] put Wafic in an embarrassing position but then he was really the master of ceremonies,' said Sanson. He also became very close to Mark Thatcher, who was his principal contact at 10 Downing Street.

Born in Damascus in 1939, Wafic Mohammed Said comes from a prominent Syrian family of pharmacists and traders. His father, Dr Redha Said, was an eminent eye surgeon and the education minister in the Syrian government. Wafic was only six years old when his father died after a long illness. It was a turbulent upbringing as much of the family wealth was lost in the mid-1950s when their business was nationalised. Despite being brought up as a Muslim, he received a European education: he attended a Jesuit school in Beirut and then read economics at St John's College, Cambridge. But he was not a gifted student and his prospects were not promising. He moved to Geneva to work as a banker but the highlight of his time there was meeting an 18-year-old English Catholic girl, Rosemary, who had just left Cheltenham Ladies College and was in Switzerland to improve her French. Despite the clash of cultures and religions, they fell in love. Both families were strongly opposed to the marriage. It took six years to win them over and the wedding took place on 14 June 1969, though their parents only attended after some angst. Rosemary has since converted to Islam.

At the time, Wafic was drifting and spent most of his days helping his brother Rafic run Caravanserai, a restaurant in Kensington High Street, decorated like an Arab tent with Lebanese dancers. A meeting place for Arab students, Caravanserai operated more like a club than a business. 'It was terribly fashionable,' recalled Wafic, 'but most of the customers were friends who did not pay their bills.'[49] But it was there that he met two fun-loving young Saudi princes, Bandar and Khalid, sons of Prince Sultan. It was a crucial connection.

Wafic's first break was in 1969 when an old family friend, Dr Rashad Pharaon, arranged a job for him in the Saudi government. Pharaon had been the personal doctor to King Saud bin Abdul Aziz, the founder of Saudi Arabia, and headed an influential Syrian clique.[50] Reunited with Prince Sultan's sons, Wafic prospered in Saudi Arabia, working long hours in the Ministry of Municipalities, responsible for construction and maintenance operations.

His link-up with fellow Syrian-born businessman Akram Ojjeh was Wafic's next smart move. In 1973, he became president of TAG Systems Construction SA in Paris and was soon brokering major building deals for defence-related projects. He was the agent for Raytheon, the US company that makes advanced anti-missile systems. Wafic's involvement with arms contracts was confirmed to us by Alex Sanson, the former corporate marketing director of British Aerospace. Sanson recalls having lunch with him at Harry's Bar, an exclusive Mayfair restaurant in South Audley Street. 'Wafic told me he had a personal relationship with Prince Sultan,' he said, 'and that they had completed a large contract with Raytheon for the supply of Hawk missiles to Saudi.'

Financially, Wafic's real coup was in 1979, when he secured a $200 million subcontract for TAG Liechtenstein from the US firm Litton Industries Inc. to construct the infrastructure for a command and control system for the Saudi Ministry of Defence. He was on his way.

Wafic saw financial power as a passport to social and political respectability. 'I understand the value of money,' he said. 'I believe it is like a two-edged sword which can be used either for good or for destroying people.'[51] His wealth was derived largely from well-placed investments in the early 1980s. His chief corporate vehicle was Saudi (later Strategic) Investment and Finance Corporation (SIFCORP), which he formed with Ziad Idilby, a fellow Syrian banker. SIFCORP was registered in Bermuda and controlled by the Said Trust, Wafic's holding company based in Luxembourg.

One of his investments was a 30 per cent controlling stake in Aitken Hume International plc, the financial services company, whose founder and deputy chairman was Jonathan Aitken, the former Tory MP. Aitken was also, until April 1992, a director of Al Bilad (UK) Ltd, a subsidiary of a Saudi parent company 'which received payments from contracts with Saudi Arabian royal family interests and government agencies'.[52] He became minister for defence procurement in April 1992, and two years later was made chief secretary to the Treasury. In 1995, Aitken resigned to sue *The Guardian* and *World In Action* over claims about his commercial interests in arms deals. His case failed spectacularly and he was jailed for perjury.

But it was Wafic's close friendship with Saudi princes that elevated him into the inner circle of influence. A measure of this was the award of Saudi citizenship in 1981 – a rare honour. That year, an incident took place that Arab observers claim cemented Wafic's relationship with the royal family. Wafic and his family went to Prince Sultan's home in Riyadh for the ceremony at which the citizenship award was made. Just before the ceremony, Karim, Wafic's ten-year-old son, drowned in the prince's swimming pool in a tragic accident after the security door suddenly snapped shut. According to Islamic custom, a death in such circumstances incurs a moral obligation on the part of the host. It was claimed that in this case the moral debtor was the defence minister, the creditor was Wafic, and this created an extra bond between the Syrian financier and the Saudi princes.

Wafic finds this analysis 'offensive and entirely misplaced'. He said, 'This fabrication is as insulting to my Saudi host as it is to me. What happened was a tragic accident, no more and no less. My friendships in Saudi Arabia date back to the early 1960s and have nothing to do with that accident.'[53] But it had a profound impact on Wafic. 'Before he had been a devout Muslim who talked about philosophy and culture and was generous to his family, friends and employees,' said his former aviation manager. 'Then he became just another greedy aggressive rich Westernised businessman.' What is not in dispute is that the Syrian financier became a confidant of key members of the royal family.

By the early 1980s, Wafic had taken over the personal and financial affairs of Prince Khalid and Prince Bandar, their wives and their 19 brothers and sisters. But he was much more than a moneyman, handling all their investments and properties. Well-mannered, engaging and sophisticated, Wafic became indispensable as their social envoy in London and Paris. But his relationship with their father, Prince Sultan, was more subservient. 'Wafic was virtually a servant to Sultan,' recalled a British defence consultant. 'I was at a dinner party at his house in Holland Park and he suddenly announced in the middle of dinner that he was leaving. Sultan had called and wanted to see him immediately. He already had a bag packed and he just left us and caught a plane at Heathrow. He was very sycophantic towards Sultan and would laugh uproariously at his weak jokes, slapping his knee as if it was the funniest thing he had ever heard.'

The smooth-talking, good-humoured Syrian became known as a man of influence. From that moment, the defence contractors began calling and knocking on Wafic's door. He had direct access to the defence minister and nothing was more valuable. In that context, Wafic was never an arms dealer. 'I have never even sold a penknife,' he protested.[54] But he was very much the facilitator. When the titanic battle between Britain and France to supply the Saudis with military planes intensified, he was the crucial intermediary. It was Wafic who arranged Prince Sultan's letter of intent and persuaded the Saudis to buy British. That was why Sir Dennis Walters, the influential former Conservative MP and well-connected Arabist said that he 'made a great contribution to British interests in Saudi Arabia'.[55]

The Syrian middleman also liaised directly with Prince Bandar, who was negotiating with Margaret Thatcher. An indication of their closeness was that Wafic helped Bandar purchase Glympton, a vast estate-village in Oxfordshire, for £8 million from the bankrupt Australian businessman Alan Bond. It is just a few miles from his own 2,000-acre estate, Tusmore House, near Banbury, where he hosts pheasant-shooting parties.[56]

One person who knew both the Syrian financier and the Saudi ambassador well at the time is Luther H. Hodges, former chairman of Washington Bankcorp while Wafic owned 27 per cent of that bank's holding company stock. 'I would bet anything on the strength of that relationship,' recalled Hodges. 'I was involved with Wafic Said and Prince Bandar in Washington on a few occasions. I think they were extremely close. Wafic saw Prince Bandar every time he came to Washington and at some points that would be with some regularity . . . In fact, the first time I myself ever met Prince Bandar was when Wafic Said took me to the embassy and introduced me to him to get some Saudi Arabian business for the bank.'[57]

Hodges is convinced that Wafic played an intermediary role on Al-Yamamah: 'While I was visiting Wafic's home in Marbella, I had conversations with people as to why he was in London. What was it that was so important? It became my understanding that it was the arms transactions between the British government and Saudi Arabia that he was working on.'

Wafic acknowledges that he was an adviser on Al-Yamamah, but maintains he was active only in the £2 billion offset programme. This involved British Aerospace reinvesting 25 per cent of the contract's value in 'offset' joint-venture industrial projects in Saudi. Based on his experience in the Saudi building industry, Wafic advised British Aerospace on this scheme. His participation was verified by Mike Rouse, managing director of Aerospace's Systems and Services Division, which oversees the Al-Yamamah project. But Rouse said his company has no 'direct link' with Wafic and refused to comment further.[58]

But the Syrian facilitator was more involved in Al-Yamamah than has so far emerged. 'He did all the contract work,' said his former aviation director at the time. During the deal's infancy, Wafic also met Sir Richard Evans, the British Aerospace assistant marketing director for Saudi Arabia and later chairman, at his home in Regent's Park (a property later owned by Prince Bandar). In 1986, the Syrian flew to Warwick, where the Tornados were being built for another private meeting with the British Aerospace executive.

A year later, Sir Richard moved into a luxury penthouse apartment in Roseberry Court, Charles Street, Mayfair, which was owned by a Panamanian company controlled by Wafic. It was run from his head office at 49 Park Lane, Mayfair. For ten years the British Aerospace executive paid rent but the council tax was paid by Wafic's accountants. The flat, worth an estimated £800,000, was made available to Sir Richard, who refused to say how much rent he paid. 'Wafic Said had the keys and I knew him to be the owner,' Charles Allworth, the concierge for the block, told *The Observer*. 'He used to come in a big car accompanied by bodyguards. To my knowledge, he never spent a night there. Mr Said told me that Mr Evans would be living in the flat. The two men were obviously good friends.'[59]

Wafic Said has always denied that he received a commission payment from this arms deal. 'I did not receive any commissions from the Al-Yamamah programme and nor am I an agent for British Aerospace,' he said later.[60] 'The agent for British Aerospace is the British Government and the contract was a government-to-government project. King Fahd and Lady Thatcher were responsible and we played a secondary role in trying to ensure that everything went smoothly . . . Due to my extensive contacts in Saudi Arabia, I played a very small role. The big role was played by Lady Thatcher.'[61]

Indeed it was, and just a few steps behind her was her son, Mark, and it was his extremely close association with Wafic Said that enabled him to act as a broker on Al-Yamamah.

Mark Thatcher first met Wafic in 1984 through their mutual acquaintance Akram Ojjeh, who at the time was still lobbying the Saudis on arms deals. They became 'good friends' through the racing circuit, said Wafic.[62] But it was more than a social acquaintanceship. 'Wafic was using Mark for intelligence,' said Adnan Khashoggi, the international arms broker who was also involved in Al-Yamamah. 'His value to Wafic was his name, of course, and that whenever he needed a question answered, Mark could go directly to his mother for the answer. He would pick up things unofficially.'[63]

This was confirmed by Mark's closest associates. Wafic and Prince Bandar needed direct access and a back-door channel to the prime minister. They wanted to bypass the official Foreign Office route and so they would ring Mark, who set up the meetings, either dinner at Chequers or a daytime meeting at 10 Downing Street. 'I know for a fact that on one occasion Wafic rang Mark, who then arranged for him to fly to Chequers by helicopter to see Margaret,' said Rodney Tyler, a friend of the Thatcher family. 'Mark was useful to ensure his mother was onside,' said a former British Aerospace consultant and friend of Wafic. 'If the negotiations were going slowly, BAE would tell Wafic who called Mark who would nag his mother and tell her to keep batting for Britain. The irony is that Mrs Thatcher's role was useful but the deal was already done because Wafic had already persuaded the Saudis to buy British.'

Wafic, who has given nearly £300,000 to the Conservative Party, was a fervent admirer of Margaret Thatcher and kept her picture on the wall of his office at 49 Park Lane, Mayfair, opposite the Dorchester Hotel. He first met her on 19 March 1987 at the premiere of the film *The Fourth Protocol*, based on the novel by Frederick Forsyth, which the Syrian businessman helped finance. Mark Thatcher and his wife also attended, two days after returning from their honeymoon.[64]

Three months later, in the early hours of 12 June 1987, Wafic was to be found in an emotional state in Aspinall's, the exclusive gaming club in Curzon Street, Mayfair, celebrating Mrs Thatcher's third successive election victory. Every time a Conservative constituency victory was flashed on to the television screen, an ecstatic Wafic raised his glass and cried out loudly, 'Bless you, Maggie. Bless you!'[65] Three years later, he was in a more sombre mood when his heroine was ousted from 10 Downing Street. Sitting in his private Boeing 727 jet, he broke down and cried his eyes out when he heard the news on BBC Radio 4.

The period after the 1987 election triumph was a busy time for Al-Yamamah. Negotiations were renewed about a further supply of Tornado combat aircraft. Eventually, on 21 October 1987, George (now Lord) Younger, then defence secretary, signed an agreement for extra Tornados worth £7 billion – the largest single export order ever secured by the British aerospace industry. Two days earlier, on the night of 19 October, as previously detailed, Margaret Thatcher had been guest of honour at a special dinner in Dallas organised by Mark. In attendance were many of the top American tycoons. Only eight of them sat at the prime minister's table. One of them was Wafic Said (see pages 171–3 for details of Dallas dinner).

Despite the 1987 agreement, the full requirements of Al-Yamamah 2 were still to be finalised. This involved further supplies, including aircraft, ships and military installations. Largely because of the sheer size, complexity and value of the contract, negotiations dragged on for another 18 months. And it was during this period that Wafic Said and Mark Thatcher met regularly. They would lunch together at Harry's Bar or have dinner at Claridge's. Sometimes they were alone, occasionally in the company of mutual friends like the Duke and Duchess of Kent. Mark was also a house guest at Wafic's palatial home in Marbella and would fly by helicopter to Glympton, his Oxfordshire estate, for a day's pheasant shooting. 'Their meetings and links were encouraged by Margaret Thatcher,' said Wafic's aviation director during this period. 'It was at her insistence.'

However, it was the purchasing of Mark's first British house that demonstrated that his relationship with Wafic was more than social. In the autumn of 1987, Mark instructed two London estate agents to find him a suitable property in Mayfair. He told them he could afford to spend about £1 million.[66] Two months later, he bought a house at 34 Eaton Terrace, Belgravia, for £800,000. He wanted to spend another £300,000 but was persuaded not to.

Mark paid for the property using an offshore company called Formigol SA, registered in the Bank of America building in Panama and incorporated on 19 October 1987 (ironically the same day as the famous dinner in Dallas). Formigol's registered office in London was the fifth floor of 49 Park Lane, London W1. This was Wafic Said's business address and the head office of one of his companies, Safingest Services UK Ltd.

The connection was strengthened further as the payment for the household bills at 34 Eaton Terrace was arranged by the law firm of Simmons & Simmons, then also representing Wafic. They helped settle Mark's domestic expenses by arranging for them to be paid by a client account, which was funded by a Swiss bank. It was certainly a strange way to pay the gas, electricity and telephone bills!

The solicitor who handled this arrangement was William Heard, who then left to become Wafic's lawyer and financial adviser, based at the 49 Park Lane office, and work for Safingest Services UK Ltd. 'Heard is very close to Wafic,' said a former executive. 'He was his trusted adviser and always on call. He also travelled with him to the Middle East.' When we spoke to Heard, who is also a director of the

Said Trust, Wafic's holding company, he refused to comment. 'We have a robust reputation for dealing with journalists in court,' he added darkly. 'I am well aware of your reputation, Mr Heard,' replied Paul Halloran, equally darkly, 'and I am totally unfazed by it.' Heard's former employers, Simmons & Simmons, later became Mark Thatcher's solicitors.

As for 34 Eaton Terrace, Mark lived there for barely two years. In March 1990, he sold it for £1.3 million, claiming it was 'a little too poky' for his tastes. Almost immediately, Wafic's short-lived Panama company, Formigol SA, was dissolved. But his dealings with Mark continued. The Syrian financier gave the prime minister's son a £14,000 Rolex watch, presumably to express his appreciation of his friendship.[67] More significantly, Wafic was one of the businessmen who placed funds in one of Thatcher's pooled investment schemes controlled by his Grantham Company in Texas.

One person who knows Wafic well is Ghassan Zakaria, editor of *Sourakia*, an Arabic-language magazine based in London. He recalled that in April 1988, he was returning from the United States and happened to be on the same flight as Wafic. They chatted away amiably enough. But when they arrived at Heathrow airport and walked off the plane, Wafic was greeted by Mark Thatcher and two bodyguards, who whisked him through the VIP lounge while Zakaria was obliged to go through Customs.

The summer of 1988 was a crucial time for Al-Yamamah. On 13 June 1988, Prince Sultan met Mrs Thatcher for an hour and a half at 10 Downing Street to review the contract. During his four-day visit to Britain, he also saw Lord Trefgarne, minister for defence procurement, to discuss the problems surrounding the offset aspects of the original deal. The Saudis were concerned about the slow pace of UK investment in their country.

But this seemed to be resolved in July 1988, when the prime minister and her secretary of state for Defence, George Younger, flew to Bermuda to agree terms on Al-Yamamah 2. This new agreement, worth £10 billion-plus, dubbed 'the arms sale of the century', was dependent on the offset programme being implemented. Apart from establishing a missile-engineering facility in Saudi Arabia, British Aerospace had also agreed to invest in an aluminium-smelting plant.[68]

For Wafic Said, business was thriving. On 24 June 1989, his wealth was extravagantly displayed with a lavish party at his £10 million home in Cornwall Terrace overlooking Regent's Park. Friends and business associates were amazed by the house's opulence, particularly the paintings by Renoir, Picasso and Monet. 'I must have passed £30 million-worth on the way to the drawing-room,' said one.[69] Among the 150 guests at the party, which cost £50,000, were Mark Thatcher, Frederick Forsyth, Sir Mark Birley (owner of Harry's Bar), several British Aerospace executives and two arms-dealing Arab middlemen, Baha Bassatne and Yashir Kutay. He later sold this house to move to an opulent apartment at 100 Eaton Square, Belgravia, and has since acquired two palatial villas in Marbella, Spain, a suite at 27 Avenue Princess Grace, Monte Carlo, and a 2,000-acre estate in Oxfordshire. Then there are the obligatory private jets – a Boeing 727, then a Gulfstream 2 and finally a Boeing Business jet.

Meanwhile, progress on 'the Dove of Peace' was slow. In its early stages, Al-Yamamah was ultra-profitable for British Aerospace and resulted in considerable cash surpluses. This was due largely to oil revenues exceeding deliveries of military aircraft and interest income accrued from the pre-payments. But then there were production problems with the Tornados and British Aerospace began to face serious cash shortfalls. Oil revenues were running behind their requirements by several hundred million pounds and so, in December 1989, the Saudis injected a special £2 billion payment.[70]

However, this seemed to be only a short-term solution. From the spring of 1991, refinancing again became a problem because of low oil prices and the cost of the Gulf war to the Saudi exchequer, estimated at $6 billion. Protracted negotiations continued through the rest of the year and British Aerospace's share price was adversely affected by the delay.

Eventually, on 3 April 1992, six days before the general election, John Major helped salvage Al-Yamamah. Major had intimate knowledge of the arms deal as chief secretary to the Treasury (1987–9), then foreign secretary for three months, and then chancellor of the exchequer until November 1990. He announced that British Aerospace would receive an extra £1.5 billion cash instalment from the Saudis. This was arranged, almost uniquely, as a 15-month loan through a consortium of Saudi banks, rather than as a direct payment from government funds.[71] The contract was effectively rescued by this funding, although Al-Yamamah 2 was not formally signed until 28 January 1993, after John Major visited King Fahd in Riyadh.

For the Saudi princes, the fact that the prime minister's son was a middleman on Al-Yamamah was not unusual. Most Arab countries are run by families. Their allegiance is quite often to their relatives rather than to their nation state or social class. So Mark was perceived as a Crown Prince and his role did not raise any eyebrows in the House of Saud. For them, his involvement was a source of comfort and reassurance that it was a real deal. An insight into the Saudi approach was furnished by Nihad Ghadry, a former adviser to the royal family. In February 1987, he visited Prince Bandar at the Saudi embassy during one of his regular trips to Washington, DC. Ghadry raised the subject of Al-Yamamah and the large commissions. 'Only a few people, including myself, know the whole truth,' replied Bandar. 'As in politics, in order to successfully complete commercial deals, you need to communicate directly with the Head of State . . . I myself delivered a personal and confidential letter from King Fahd to the prime minister, Mrs Thatcher. I told her that this deal is between us directly, between the two countries. It should go no further. Whatever is related to us is our concern and no one else's . . . I also told her that we are a royal family and around us are a lot of people and a lot of responsibilities. My conversation with Mrs Thatcher ended with her understanding what I meant.'[72]

The prime minister's instinctive understanding of Prince Bandar's carefully chosen words was born out of her long-held views. 'There is no such thing as society,' she said while she was prime minister. 'There are individual men and women, and there are families. And no government can do anything except through people, and people must look to themselves. It's our duty to look after ourselves and then to look after our neighbours.'[73]

Given that philosophy, perhaps it was not surprising that Mark Thatcher made money out of the largest arms deal in history. It was Thatcherism in action. Evidence of her son's commercial involvement in Al-Yamamah comes from multiple sources. Mark's former business partner, Steve Tipping, described it in characteristically earthy terms. 'I specialise in defence,' he told former business associate Gary Smith over lunch at the Savoy Grill. 'But I was never involved in Saudi Arabia. That was Mark's business. In the world of defence, Saudi Arabia is an essential market because you can make the silly rag-headed buggers buy anything.'

An equally compelling source is Alex Sanson, who was managing director of British Aerospace's Dynamics Division during the Al-Yamamah period. An Armenian Turk, he had joined the company's guided-weapons section in 1977 and rose through the executive ranks to be group sales and marketing director. In 1983, Sanson was promoted to be Aerospace's corporate marketing director under Admiral Raymond Lygo. But it was as MD of the Dynamics Division – the prime contractor for Al-Yamamah – that he became intimately involved in the deal. For example, he was responsible for the first sale of Tornado aircraft.

We interviewed Sanson, who has retired to Biddenden, Kent, four times over the telephone. He was guarded but decisive in his remarks. When asked about Mark Thatcher in general terms, he said, 'Well, he was involved in the Tornado deal.'

'How was he involved?' we enquired.

'Well, when we [British Aerospace] realised that he was sniffing around in the classic way as he has done before, we simply made it clear [to him] that he get out of it. But I don't think he ever did because that's where he made all his money. The amazing thing is that he has survived all this time.'

'Whom was he representing on Al-Yamamah?'

'Let's face it, he managed to climb aboard . . . He was very close to Wafic Said and Prince Bandar, the indestructible ambassador for Saudi Arabia, who is, by the way, a very, very fine chap . . . A number of people were aware that he [Mark Thatcher] was involved. He is bad news. He was a user of people to make connections. I don't think there is any doubt about it. That was his technique and with the image of his mother at the time it was a useful asset at the time.'

'What was the attitude of British Aerospace towards Mark Thatcher?'

'We were very guarded but that did not stop the fact that he had got his fingers in there with certain Saudis and there was no getting out of it.'

'So he was working for the Saudis?'

'Oh, yes, yes, definitely, once he got his connections there.'

Documents relating to Mark Thatcher's commercial involvement were compiled by the Saudi Arabian intelligence agency, Istakbarat. In 1984, during the early stages of the Al-Yamamah negotiations, they secretly recorded telephone conversations between some of the leading participants – arms dealers and agents representing the Saudi royal family. Translated transcripts of those discussions were shown – but not given – to the *Sunday Times* by Mohammed al-Khilewi, a senior Saudi diplomat. He was a first secretary at the United Nations in New York until June 1994 when, disillusioned with the Saudi regime, he defected, taking with him thousands of documents.

The taped conversations took place at a time when the Saudis were monitoring and analysing the various bids by Britain, France and the United States to supply the weapons. They focus on the prospective merits of two influential British middlemen with inside knowledge and government connections. One was referred to as 'John'. The other was Mark Thatcher.

The first discussion was between Abdel Aziz al-Ibrahim, King Fahd's brother-in-law and his chief agent in major arms deals, and an unnamed Arab middleman. The prime minister's son had a rival in 'John' as the Saudis' intermediary to the British government. 'Don't forget to tell him we are already in contact with John in Britain,' said al-Ibrahim, 'through Prince Turki bin Nasser [chief of the air force] and Manquour [Nasir Hamad al-Manquour, then the Saudi ambassador in London] and John's offer is excellent and the cost is less than Mark is offering us.' The Arab arms broker replied, 'I think you are right, but Mark is more in power and he has influence with the military group and the government.' He added, 'These people will sell their families for money.' The two Saudis concluded by agreeing that the commission payments should be deposited into either a Swiss or a Saudi bank.[74]

Al-Ibrahim then consulted Prince Turki bin Nasser. 'I think Mark has connections regarding the military equipment . . . [but] we can't compare it with John's connections,' said the Prince. Al-Ibrahim responded, 'Yes, but Mark has excellent connections with the government and he has good information.' He later observed, 'We have to make a decision quickly because we can't keep dealing with both of them at the same time. And Tawil al-Omar [King Fahd] is more comfortable with Mark.'

The King's choice for facilitating the biggest arms deal in history was decisive. The Saudis chose the British crown prince, the son of Queen Thatcher.

Mark Thatcher's commercial interest in Al-Yamamah was also being monitored in the United States. One senior government official who did this was Howard Teicher, head of the National Security Council's (NSC) Near East Section from March 1982 until May 1986. He then became the NSC's senior director of political and military affairs until his departure in March 1987. Teicher was a specialist on the Middle East and responsible for monitoring arms sales to that area. 'Any application of military power and arms sales to the Middle East was a responsibility of mine,' he said. 'It was incumbent upon me to coordinate the positions of the disparate US government agencies in an effort to work out a common position on when, what and how to sell in terms of major weapons systems to our friendly countries in the Middle East.'[75]

Between May 1986 and March 1987, Teicher read several documents, classified intelligence cables and diplomatic dispatches from US embassies in Europe that included details about the activities of middlemen in Al-Yamamah. 'They were arms dealers who were not necessarily known to us, but obviously individuals who made their living selling arms and living off the commissions on the transactions,' he recalled. 'It was quite clear to me that this group believed that their ability to make the sale to the Saudis would be enhanced by the involvement of a political member of the group like Mark Thatcher.'[76]

Detailed data on Thatcher's commercial participation in the arms deal were contained in diplomatic dispatches by the defence attaché at the US embassy in Saudi Arabia. The information was also contained in CIA and Defense Intelligence Agency reports from Saudi Arabia and Europe, and in diplomatic cables from other European capitals. 'I considered these dispatches totally reliable and totally accurate,' Teicher told Channel 4's *Dispatches* programme. 'I did not think that people would loosely accuse the son of the prime minister of being involved in such a transaction unless they were certain that it was the case. Also, the fact that I saw his name appear in a number of different sourced documents convinced me of the authenticity of at least the basic information regarding some measure of involvement on Mark Thatcher's part. When I say "involvement" I mean a business involvement. He was clearly playing some sort of business role to help facilitate the completion of a transaction between the two governments.'[77]

Interviewed in Washington, DC, Teicher reaffirmed his assessment to us. 'He was playing an active role in the arms transaction and it was unambiguous that he was involved in a business capacity,' he said. 'He seemed to have no specific role except that he was suggesting that he could get the job done. In my view, there was no way he was doing it for the love of his country.' He added, 'I surmised that his role was to facilitate the communications between the UK manufacturer and the buyer in Saudi Arabia. The role that someone like him would play typically would be to ensure that the buyer was confident that the other side was genuine, legitimate and able to deliver the goods. I had no reason to believe that Mark Thatcher had any particular expertise with advanced weapons systems or Tornados.'[78]

215

After reading the intelligence and diplomatic documents, Teicher went to the British embassy in Washington to talk to two diplomats about young Thatcher's activities. 'They just looked at the ceiling,' recalled the former senior NSC director. 'They were very polite and diplomatic but were not happy to talk about it. Their view seemed to be "You are not surprised, are you?"'

Teicher then discussed the issue with a fellow member of the National Security bureaucracy in the US Defense Department: 'I asked him if he was confident that Mark Thatcher was actually playing a role. He said that he was quite confident that Thatcher was involved and that this showed him that the British were extremely serious about selling these aircraft.'[79] These claims were later partly corroborated by a former insider of the US National Security Agency (NSA) which eavesdrops on international communications. The former employee disclosed that the NSA intercepted and monitored phone calls by Mark Thatcher which showed his involvement in Al-Yamamah.[80]

The prime minister's son has been typically bullish in his denials. 'The idea that I run around peddling Kalashnikovs or second-hand MiG jets is ridiculous,' he told *Today* newspaper in 1994. When asked point blank whether he had received any payments in any way from the sale of weapons, he replied: 'No, I haven't even sold a penknife . . . There were allegations of CIA documents to say that I had been involved and subpoenas were flying around. At the end, absolutely nothing happened. Nothing at all . . . My position on the supposed Al-Yamamah agreement is that the people I am supposed to have been involved with – that is to say Mr Said – have denied, on any number of occasions, that there's any link.'[81] More specifically, he said: 'Merely because I know this man [Wafic Said] does not mean to say that he is going to pay me £12 million because I am a nice guy.'[82]

But privately he did refer to his role in Saudi Arabia during business meetings with Gary Smith, the international oil trader. In April 1987, when asked about business prospects in Saudi Arabia, Mark Thatcher replied, 'I have a perfect channel there [a favourite euphemism for 'connection']. He is A1 and tops for me.' He did not elaborate. But eight months later, on 4 December 1987, he was more forthcoming. 'It [Saudi Arabia] is a backward, feudal country,' he told Smith over dinner at Harry's Bar in Mayfair. 'But it's paradise for doing defence deals, because spare parts have no limits in a country where commissions have no limits.'

The precise amount the prime minister's son was paid is not known. Even Mark's friends admit it was considerable. 'I was told it was an enormous amount of money, an eight-figure sum,' said one. 'It was certainly at least £10 million,' said a former BAE consultant and a friend of Wafic. 'The agreement specified that Mark Thatcher received a 6 per cent commission,' said Wafic's former aviation director. The fee was not paid directly by British Aerospace or the Saudi Arabian government. It was channelled through one of the seemingly countless Al-Yamamah middlemen and brokers who received lucrative pay-offs. Our sources state that Mark's share was an estimated £12 million.

Evidence for the payment is in a transcript of the taped conversation between al-Ibrahim, King Fahd's agent, and an unnamed Arab middleman in Riyadh, the Saudi capital. 'The important thing is that they [the British companies bidding for the order] have to do it by our conditions,' said al-Ibrahim. 'Also to agree with us to increase the costs of the bills.' This meant increasing the cost of the contract to accommodate the commissions. The Arab intermediary agreed: 'I'll talk to Mark today and I will confirm to him the money will never be more than $500 million [£400 million at 1984 exchange rates] for him and his group.'

It is perfectly legal in Britain for a defence contractor or foreign government to pay a commission to an individual on an arms deal – unlike in the United States where it is a criminal offence under the Foreign Corrupt Practices Act. In the Arab world commissions are part of commercial life and are always spread widely. This is why the size of the contract is often astronomical to those who do not understand this simple economic fact.

On Al-Yamamah, the commissions – estimated at between 10 and 30 per cent of the contract's total price – were so huge that they created cash-flow problems and delayed delivery of the weapons and aircraft. Indeed, one reason for Al-Yamamah's spiralling £20 billion-plus 'value' was the inflated kickback fees that were added on top of the actual cost of the equipment. For example, it was claimed that the Tornados were sold at £25 million each, about double their real value, allowing for extra money to be distributed to middlemen. Excessive shipments of oil for sale on international markets were also favoured. This activity took place alongside those genuine oil exports which were used to pay for the Al-Yamamah weapons.

The British and Saudis have always insisted officially that no commissions were paid on Al-Yamamah. It was such a sensitive issue that the Ministry of Defence was even asked by Saudi Arabia to write a letter denying their existence. They claimed that as it was a government-to-government deal, there was no need for kickbacks. It is true that senior cabinet ministers and diplomats did negotiate the contract. But it was also indisputably the case that Al-Yamamah was in a constant state of uncertainty and it took no less than eight years for the deal to be officially signed and sealed.

A more compelling argument that commissions were paid is the simple reality of doing business in the Middle East. 'When you sell to Saudi Arabia, you are really selling to the Saudi royal family – a limited company with 200 shareholders,' said one senior executive involved in Al-Yamamah. 'It is quite simple. In some countries you pay import duties of 30 per cent, in others you pay commissions.'[83]

Mark Thatcher knew, at the very least, many of these advisers. Apart from Wafic Said, one of his closest associates was Jean-Pierre Yonan, a Lebanese-born businessman based in Paris. Fabulously wealthy, Yonan has homes in Beaulieu in the south of France, Rio de Janeiro and Geneva. In the 1970s, he had a powerful commercial presence in Oman and then became close, like Wafic, to the Saudi royal family. Yonan was part of the bridgehead between the UK government, British Aerospace and the Saudis on Al-Yamamah 1. He once laid on an impressive fleet of cars for Sir James Blyth, then head of defence sales, on his arrival in Riyadh. The Lebanese arms broker also flew with the prime minister's son on his private 727 jet to Saudi Arabia as a way of impressing on the Saudis the fact that he was well connected. 'Yonan knew [Mark] Thatcher very well,' recalled Alex Sanson, British Aerospace's former marketing director.[84]

The crucial political factor, of course, was whether the prime minister knew that her son had enriched himself on the back of the epic arms deal which she promoted and negotiated. It was an issue she had consistently and repeatedly refused to answer over the Oman University contract. And on Al-Yamamah, she adopted the same approach. In October 1994, she said she was 'absolutely satisfied that the Al-Yamamah contract was properly negotiated . . . and proud that, after a great deal of hard work by ministers and officials, it brought thousands of jobs and billions of pounds to this country.'[85] Lady Thatcher (she had become a baroness in June 1992) again declined to say whether she knew her son was paid a commission.

However, her private office staff were certainly told – and were duty-bound to inform her – because British Aerospace executives became very concerned about what they called Mark's 'meddling' in the arms deal of the century. They knew that if his role was publicly exposed, the consequences would be disastrous. The Saudis, renowned for their distaste for public scandal and embarrassing publicity, might cancel the whole deal and negotiate instead with the French or the Americans.

Senior British Aerospace executives discussed the potential crisis. They decided that the prime minister needed to be informed in what, in a reference to *Macbeth*, was nicknamed the 'witches' warning'. And so Admiral Raymond (later Sir Raymond) Lygo, the company's chief executive and chairman, and Alex Sanson, corporate marketing director, went to see Clive (later Sir Clive) Whitmore, permanent secretary at the Ministry of Defence from 1983 until 1988. During this period Lygo met Whitmore regularly at the MoD to brief him on Al-Yamamah's progress and at one of their meetings talked to him about Mark Thatcher's 'interference'. Whitmore was especially close to the prime minister, having been her principal private secretary from 1979 until 1982, so it was perhaps easier for him to talk to Mrs Thatcher about her son in a 'nudge-and-a-wink way'.[86]

Admiral Lygo told Whitmore that Mark's business interests in the Middle East were 'dangerous for British industry' and asked him to inform the prime minister about the company's anxieties. 'This happened because we got very concerned about Mark Thatcher's interference in the Saudi Tornados deal,' Sanson told us. 'It was felt that if this matter came out, it could be exceedingly damaging to the prime minister.' The 'witches' warning' was duly delivered but Whitmore's former boss refused, as usual, to address herself to the problem.

When asked about this, Lygo confirmed meeting Whitmore 'at least once a month' but denied discussing the prime minister's son. 'I remember Mark Thatcher being mentioned in the office but whether that specific meeting took place, I couldn't really say,' he said.[87] Sir Clive, later a director of Morgan Crucible plc and NM Rothschild, declined to comment. 'I do not believe there is anything I can do to help you,' he said.[88]

Howard Teicher, the US National Security Council's former director of political and military affairs for the Middle East, confirmed that, at the very least, her senior and closest civil servants knew. 'I find it difficult to believe that Margaret Thatcher would not be aware that he [Mark] might have been playing a role,' he said. 'Certainly the senior officials in the British Ministry of Defence and

219

the British arms industry would have been aware of the role that he was playing. Is it possible that she might somehow be insulated from that kind of information? It's possible . . . Over a period of years Mark Thatcher's involvement, in my mind, certainly seemed to be something that officials in London would have been aware of.'[89]

Mrs Thatcher's friends often argue that she might have been informed about her son's business activities but she would have disbelieved the information. She was often in denial. 'Oh, that could not have happened,' she once responded after receiving a report about Mark, according to a family friend.

However, the difference with Al-Yamamah was that Mark helped arrange meetings for her with Wafic Said and Prince Bandar. So she could hardly shut her eyes and ears to that reality. Indeed, according to Wafic's former aviation director, Mark's dealings with the Syrian middleman were 'at Mrs Thatcher's insistence'. As with Cementation's contract in Oman, her son was a shadowy figure one step behind her while she helped British Aerospace to secure the contract in Saudi Arabia. Al-Yamamah was the payday that Mark Thatcher had been looking for. Now he could look further east to exploit the business interests and contacts he had cultivated in the early 1980s.

EIGHT

Far-Eastern Promise

My mother loved me, too, but she knew when I was being
a bloody idiot – and she said so.

– Thatcher Peer[1]

The Far East was an ideal commercial hunting ground for Mark
Thatcher. It is a continent full of lands of opportunity and the prime
minister's son was the ultimate opportunist. Business is conducted in
an uncluttered, unregulated market where money talks and contacts
are everything. For Mark, who has always found it difficult to work
in a corporate or structured environment, the Asian enterprise culture
suited the way he liked to operate. In opera terms, he was a *primo
uomo*: he was not interested in being part of the chorus.

Nowhere is the materialistic, money-obsessed ethos more clearly
exemplified than Hong Kong – the Wall Street of the Far East. The
British colony appealed to Mark Thatcher because many of its
inhabitants shared his pursuit-of-wealth attitude to life. 'The great
thing about Hong Kong is its enterprise and ambition,' he said in
1991. 'Less government is one of the reasons for Hong Kong's
success . . . It is one of the few places I look forward to coming to.'[2]

Mark genuinely enjoyed visiting the colony. He had worked there
as a trainee for Jardine Matheson in 1971 and had been treated well.
He liked the polite, deferential Hong Kong society, where he was
sought after as an honoured guest at dinner parties. He would stay at
the Mandarin Hotel and drink at the Hilton's Dragon Boat bar. Best
of all, businessmen were discreet and even the hated newspapers were
relatively sympathetic to him.

He made an excursion to Hong Kong in November 1977, driving in a major race in the nearby Portuguese enclave of Macao. He failed to finish but later competed three times at Macao for the Crown Motors Toyota team, usually driving a 1300cc Starlet in which he had moderate success.[3]

The 1981 Macao Grand Prix brought the first glimpse of Thatcher's business interests in Hong Kong. While preparing for the race, Mark was filmed wearing a smart green-striped Giordano sports shirt. It was part of a television commercial for the Hong Kong-based fashion label, later broadcast on the local ATV and TVB stations. The 30-second advertisement showed the British prime minister's son donning a shining silver catsuit with 'Mark Thatcher' blazoned across it. As the music soothed, he slowly zipped it up and put on his helmet. Then, after posing in the sports shirt, he smoothed his hands down his chest and body. At the climax, he stood beside a long red car, again with the brand-name 'Mark Thatcher' written on it, and a husky Chinese voice said, 'Giordano, every inch a man.'

Mark had been hired as a male model as part of a £100,000 advertising campaign by Giordano. 'He exactly fits the image of the shirts. Very sporty,' said Antony Chow, director of account services at the Hong Kong office of Young & Rubicam, the agency which made the commercial. It was broadcast in the summer of 1982 but was last shown on 20 September that year. The next evening the advert mysteriously disappeared from the TV screens, just as Margaret Thatcher was about to bid farewell to Japan on her way to China for delicate discussions over the future of Hong Kong. The commercial's absence was 'a complete coincidence,' said Chow.[4]

It was also through competing in the Macao Grand Prix that Mark Thatcher secured his introduction into the Hong Kong business community. In November 1979, he met Tony Zie, alias Chin Kwok Chung, one of the race's promoters and an ambitious financier. They became friends and Mark introduced Zie to his business partner, Steve Tipping. The three then set up various joint commercial projects.

Their first venture was Ulferts Services Company Ltd, incorporated in Hong Kong in February 1981 and set up to 'import consumer durables and sales promotion items', particularly furniture. Thatcher, Tipping and Zie were all directors, with Mark holding 30 per cent of the shares. His financial stake was later expanded to a controlling HK$30,000 as the capital of the company was increased to HK$100,000.[5]

The company was launched with a dinner party at Maxim's Palace restaurant and printed invitations were issued to guests on behalf of Ulferts 'to meet our chairman, Mr Mark Thatcher'. A holding company, Ulferts Services UK Ltd, was established in the UK 'to extend the trade, not only in the Far East but worldwide'.[6] But the two firms never traded and both folded after two years, with the Inland Revenue chasing the British parent for a notional corporation tax assessment. It was not an auspicious start to Mark's Far Eastern commercial career. He was strangely sensitive about his involvement with Ulferts. When asked later whether he still had an interest in the company, he reacted angrily: 'Absolutely not. Why do you have to mention Ulferts? I just happen to know some of the Ulferts people.'[7]

Within a few months of the collapse of Ulferts, Mark became chairman of Hon Hing Trivest Group, one of the largest commodities traders in Hong Kong – itself the third largest bullion market in the world. In the summer of 1982, the company issued a glossy booklet and distributed it to potential clients overseas, including Canada. It enclosed a signed statement by Mark, accompanied by his photograph. Hon Hing, he wrote, is 'supported by an extensive network of international offices specialising in commodity-based investments. This group has amongst its members specialists in practically every form of commodity investment.' He concluded by saying the company had 'a reputation of which we are justifiably proud'.

However, the group's reputation was far from unsullied. During the period that Thatcher was chairman, three of its subsidiaries were under investigation for financial irregularities. One of them was Yearcome Commodities Ltd, a subsidiary based in Vancouver, British Columbia, Canada. Between 1982 and 1984, the superintendent of Brokers, Investment and Real Estate of the British Columbian government (BIRE) and the police received numerous complaints about the company. This led to BIRE, the Royal Canadian Mounted Police and the Canadian Ministry of Consumer Affairs conducting an inquiry to trace missing money paid to Yearcome Commodities to invest overseas.[8]

The investigation was also embraced by the Hong Kong Securities Commission. 'We have attempted to establish whether the [investment] orders came through,' said Alan Mills, an assistant commissioner. 'They were specified in the loco-London market here. We're continuing to look into it.'[9] But Hon Hing, which means 'Chinese prosperity', refused to cooperate with the regulators as there was no law governing commodity traders, although one senior partner was interviewed.[10] No action was taken against Yearcome but in January 1984 it stopped trading.

Another Hon Hing subsidiary, Yearcome Pte Ltd, based in Singapore, was forced to shut down for financial offences after an investigation by police and the Singapore Monetary Authority. An inspectors' inquiry, held while Mark Thatcher was chairman of the holding company, resulted in a court order to close it for 'conducting its business in a manner detrimental to the interests of its clients'. The firm did not appeal against the ruling.[11]

The third subsidiary to be probed by regulatory authorities was another Singapore company, Trivest Bullion Enterprises Pte Ltd (TBE). A report by Singapore government inspectors stated that the firm's local directors had 'acted in concert with Hon Hing Hong to deceive the authorities'. The inspectors concluded that TBE failed to control their brokers, clients were tricked into giving brokers discretionary control over their accounts and that this control was abused by brokers who ordered unnecessary transactions to increase their commission payments.[12] It was recommended that TBE be closed by court order and this was granted.

Mark Thatcher maintains he was a 'non-executive chairman of Hon Hing Trivest for a short period' until he relinquished it in December 1982. He added that he 'had no involvement in the running of the company and was not aware of the brochure being circulated after he resigned the position'.[13] He also 'totally rejected' any suggestion that he should be linked to the financial irregularities of Hon Hing's subsidiary companies.

However, Mark was not quite the passive company chairman he would like to appear. On 7 September 1982, he opened a new gold-dealer branch for Hon Hing Trivest in Kowloon, flanked by his bodyguards and his close business associate, Tony Zie. The ribbon-cutting ceremony was conducted with some aplomb and fanfare. Every announcement began: 'Mark Thatcher, son of the British prime minister . . .' Local businessmen noticed that this occurred only a few days after Mrs Thatcher had paid an official visit to Hong Kong for talks on the future sovereignty of the colony. 'It is not what he is but who he represents,' said one observer.[14]

Mark's claim that he 'had no involvement in the running of the company' was further weakened by his attendance at a private meeting in early 1983 with the president of the Chinese Gold and Silver Exchange, Woo Hon-Fai. He was accompanied by John Kit, managing director of Hon Hing Trivest, and Tony Zie, at the time his fellow director at Ulferts. All three refused to talk about the meeting.[15]

A mere month before the two Singapore subsidiaries of Hon Hing Trivest were closed down for fraud, they were bought by a Hong Kong-based company called Emperor Investment Holdings Ltd (EIH). The affiliates were then renamed and traded on the gold market.

It was Mark Thatcher's direct involvement with EIH that was to prove the most controversial of his business dealings in Hong Kong. The bullion and commodities futures trading firm has a chequered history. It was originally owned by Marvellous Investments, a property and jewellery company which collapsed in the early 1980s after writs were issued for the repayment of debts totalling HK$250 million.

In early 1983, Emperor Investment Holdings was set free after Marvellous sold its 52 per cent stake in the company. It was then resurrected by Albert Yeung Shou-Shing, the chairman, a leading shareholder and one of Hong Kong's most controversial businessmen. He relaunched Emperor with a capital of HK$70 million and 10 million shares. 'It rose like a phoenix from burning ash,' according to one local analyst. Yeung had a strong desire to make Emperor a powerful and prestigious force, and spoke to Tony Zie about how to achieve this. Zie suggested recruiting the British prime minister's son and his business partner, Steve Tipping.[16] And so on 27 June 1983, two weeks after Mrs Thatcher's second general election victory, Mark Thatcher and Steve Tipping became directors of Emperor Investment Holdings, with an arrangement to be paid a slice of any future profits.

Emperor executives were not shy of explaining why Thatcher was hired. 'We are using his name because he is well known through car racing and his advertising here,' said Ho-Pak Kong at the time (he was the chief shareholder who bought Yeung's stake just before Mark joined the board). 'The fact that he is the son of the prime minister carries some weight.'[17] Looking back ten years later, Ho-Pak Kong has not changed his view. 'Mark was made a director because he was the prime minister's son and Albert [Yeung] thought it would add prestige to the company.'[18]

It showed an extraordinary lack of judgement to forge such a close business association with Albert Yeung. Emperor's chairman was not allowed even to be on the board because of his recent criminal past, which was well documented and widely reported. Just two years earlier, Yeung had been convicted and jailed for nine months for attempting to pervert the course of justice. The case involved Tony Cruz, a young jockey, who was charged with assaulting Wai Kin-Bong, manager of the *Tin Tin Daily News*. Yeung, a high-flying racehorse owner and watch dealer, was a close friend of Cruz and decided to intervene on his behalf. He approached Wai, introduced himself as 'the boss of Tony Cruz' and offered Wai 'up to HK$2 million' for not giving evidence against his jockey friend. Yeung added that he could 'fix up the police officers at the Shatin station' and there would be no further trouble. Another witness, Lau Tinchau, testified that the Emperor executive told him he would pay 'up to HK$10,000' as Wai's medical fees if the matter could be forgotten.[19]

At first, Yeung was given only a two-month suspended sentence, which caused such shock and outrage that when he lodged an appeal the judges increased it to nine months' imprisonment. As he was managing director of a number of companies, Yeung was allowed a few days' grace before he was taken away to Ma Hang prison, where he served six months. Tony Cruz later pleaded guilty to the charge of assaulting Wai Kin-Bong, whose injuries required him to remain in hospital for 18 days.

The Emperor chairman's criminal activities did not end there. In July 1986, he was convicted of bookmaking offences and sentenced to six months' imprisonment, suspended for two years. He was also fined HK$50,000. Yeung, a well-known gambler, and two associates were found in a Kowloon flat when police from the Organised and Serious Crimes Bureau raided the premises. They discovered two telephone units which were used to receive calls from people who wanted to place bets on races or check their winnings. One police officer later claimed she had been obstructed by Yeung but this charge was later withdrawn.[20]

After his conviction for trying to bribe Wai Kin-Bong, Yeung was disqualified as a director and banned from the Hong Kong Jockey Club. But that did not appear to concern Mark Thatcher. Not only did he join the board of Emperor Investment Holdings but he also became deputy chairman of Andrope Commodities Ltd, a wholly owned subsidiary. To launch his involvement, Mark co-hosted a cocktail party at the Hilton Hotel. All directors of Hong Kong government departments, civil servants responsible for the futures and securities business and several journalists were invited. Several of them were introduced to Thatcher.[21] He was enthusiastic about his participation in Emperor and its subsidiaries, which he described as a 'gold futures trading operation'. He added, 'We make available to the man in the street the ability to trade in gold and gold futures. We write an incredible amount of business. I mean 20, 30, 40 million dollars is not exceptional. It's a very good little business.'[22] He also acknowledged his active interest in the company. 'I will look at each month's management report, balance sheet and will attend all the business meetings,' he said proudly.[23]

One of Emperor's most controversial subsidiaries was Gainsborough Holdings Ltd, an unlicensed offshore commodity-broking company registered in Guernsey. Incorporated in May 1983, a month before Mark Thatcher joined Emperor, its function was to act on behalf of speculators who wished to gamble on the price of commodities. Funds were accepted from Hong Kong and British investors to speculate in futures on the New York commodities exchange. Clients made a 10 per cent deposit to buy or sell gold, tin, cocoa or sugar at a price set months ahead.[24] Emperor in Hong Kong then charged a commission for placing these bids on their behalf. But it was a highly risky operation, as investors could often lose large amounts of money overnight. Commodity-broking was, said an Old Bailey judge at the time, 'a jungle . . . in which the small animal is gravely at risk'.[25]

Mark Thatcher's connection with Gainsborough Holdings was that his name was used as a 'selling point' for clients. For example, he was introduced to Alec McDade, a director of the company, at Les Ambassadeurs club, renowned for its casino, in Hamilton Place, Mayfair, by Andrew Chan, Emperor's managing director. At the time, McDade, a haulage executive from Wakefield, Yorkshire, was considering investing 'a very considerable sum' in Gainsborough. While he was negotiating this shareholding, he was informed by Uisden McInnes, a director of Emperor Investments and former head of the Hong Kong Securities Commission, that Mark Thatcher was a director of the parent company. McDade proceeded with this investment but later withdrew from the company. 'It was just gambling,' he recalled.[26]

Despite McDade's departure, Gainsborough continued to operate and remained an Emperor subsidiary. On 4 October 1983, newspaper advertisements were placed soliciting funds for 'investment purposes'. But there was little, if any, trading taking place and clients were becoming concerned about their money. Five weeks later, a saviour appeared at hand when City financier Robert Knight walked into Gainsborough's London office in Buckingham Palace Road, Victoria, and announced, according to a former employee, that he had 'bought the company'.

However, he was far from dressed in shining armour. At that precise moment, Knight was facing criminal charges of attempting to defraud financial institutions by trafficking in fraudulent Eurodollar bonds. He was also charged with defrauding his own company, Sturla Holdings, and was being sued for an outstanding debt of £115,000. Known as 'the Conjurer', Knight was a director of numerous companies. Two of the firms he had acquired were put into receivership.

Gainsborough fared little better. Its clients became anxious about the way their funds were being handled, particularly as their bids were not being placed in New York. Within two months, in January 1984, the firm had collapsed and this led to several complaints to the police. Almost immediately, the City of London Fraud Squad launched an investigation into Gainsborough Holdings – both during Emperor's ownership and while Knight controlled the company.

Mark Thatcher and his business partner, Steve Tipping, went to great pains to say that 'as directors of Emperor Holdings they were in no way involved in the business activities of Gainsborough Holdings'.[27] However, apart from Mark's business link with the holding company, there was a further connection which has remained undisclosed until now. Thatcher knew Robert 'the Conjurer' Knight and had had a previous commercial association with him.

This connection can be traced back at least until late 1979. At the time Knight was chairman of Tiger Securities Ltd, his private investment vehicle specialising in sport. He adorned the board with some influential figures. One was Sir David Checketts, former private secretary to Prince Charles and later a director of arms firm International Signal and Control Technologies. Another was George Magnus, later a senior executive in the corporate empire of Li Ka-Shing, one of Hong Kong's most powerful businessmen.

In late 1979, Knight was looking to invest money he had made in the Far East and spoke to Mark Thatcher about it. Mark suggested CSS Promotions Ltd, who were his marketing and promotions agents at the time. Knight agreed and so Mark spoke to his friend Barrie Gill, joint managing director of CSS, about the proposal. Gill was enthusiastic and told a fellow senior director, 'There is an opportunity for us to expand through a company called Tiger Securities. They have a lot of money from the Far East which they want to invest.'

Two weeks later, Gill and the director went to see Knight at his office at 78 South Audley Street, Mayfair. 'I would like Tiger to invest in your company,' Knight told them. 'In return, I have some sports stars I would like you to look after.' But the meeting was not a success, as Gill's colleague was not impressed by his prospective investor. 'Almost from the first moment, I knew I could not deal with him,' he recalled. 'He was flaunting his diamond and gold cufflinks and decorated his office in a ridiculously flashy way with two huge stuffed China tigers in the foyer.'[28]

Drawing on his extensive commercial experience, Gill's colleague instinctively felt that Knight was bent. 'We're not having anything to do with an outfit like that,' he said to Gill as they walked down South Audley Street after the meeting. 'I can't stand the man. He's not reliable.' His partner disagreed: 'But he's very wealthy and comes highly recommended as a respectable investor. Anyway, I'm sure Mark would not be involved with them [Tiger Securities] if there was anything dodgy about them.'

It seemed to CSS Promotions that Mark Thatcher was acting as if he were an introductory agent for Knight. As it turned out, Tiger Securities' proposals were so vague and indecisive that the investment never occurred. But Gill's colleague proved to be correct. Two years later, in 1981, Tiger Securities went bankrupt. In 1985, Knight was charged and convicted of conspiracy to defraud and was jailed for 12 months. He now lives in the Canary Islands.

Robert Knight and Gainsborough Holdings might have lost their way but another of Mark Thatcher's friends with a criminal record, Albert Yeung, prospered. His company, the Emperor Group, former owner of Gainsborough, expanded by mergers and takeovers, and by 1993 its assets had risen to over HK$2 billion. Its principal sectors of business are property investment, gold and securities, jewellery and overseas investments. The company was also awarded a licence to open a bank in Cambodia. Yeung is now fabulously wealthy and owns Hong Kong's most expensive car licence plate – the prized 'lucky' Number Nine, which he bought for HK$13 million.[29]

But he remains a notorious figure in the colony. On 11 December 1994, after an investigation by the Organised Crime and Triads Bureau, Yeung was arrested by police officers at 1 a.m. in the karaoke bar of the Happy Valley Hotel. He was accused of detaining Lam Yih-Jun, a rival businessman, against his will at the Mandarin Hotel and inside a room in the Emperor International Exchange office. The next day, he was charged with criminal intimidation and unlawful punishment.[30]

The Emperor chairman had also lost none of his knack of hiring political muscle to strengthen his sprawling business empire. In 1994, he recruited Bob Hawke, who until his replacement by Paul Keating in December 1991 had been Australia's longest-serving prime minister, as a non-executive director, largely to develop the company's racing and casino interests. 'I know the region well and the political and business leaders in the region,' said the former premier. 'I've been able to help them out with some introductions.' Yeung confirmed this role: 'Mr Hawke has introduced a lot of friends to me and he has a lot of connections.'[31] This, of course, was why the Emperor chairman had hired Mark Thatcher a decade earlier and the two were, according to one Hong Kong source, 'very friendly'.

Mark Thatcher's commercial interests in Hong Kong, particularly in Emperor Investment Holdings, led to concern among some Foreign Office civil servants about a potential conflict of interests. At the time (1982–3) Mrs Thatcher was conducting sensitive and decisive negotiations with China over the future sovereignty of the colony. It was argued that the prime minister's son could benefit commercially from inside information about the state of the Sino–British talks. This was because the price of gold was exceptionally vulnerable to reports about the state of those discussions. As Mark Thatcher was a director of a company that traded in gold futures in Hong Kong, London and New York, there was a possible conflict of interests. 'That's utter crap,' was Mark's characteristic response in 1984. 'We're open in Hong Kong for 20 hours a day and anyone can walk in and take a gold position on the Hong Kong market or the London, New York or Chicago exchanges. There is no way that Hong Kong lease negotiations can possibly affect the gold futures price in, say, Chicago.'[32]

However, his Foreign Office critics point to an incident which reveals how easy it was for him to be on the inside track during the Hong Kong negotiations. In 1983, a senior diplomat called on the prime minister to brief her on the latest developments in the colony. To his surprise, he found her son sitting in the room. According to two press reports, the diplomat waited uneasily while he thought personal family business would be disposed of and Mark would depart. But, much to his discomfort, Margaret Thatcher told him to continue his briefing while her son remained. 'It's only Mark,' she reportedly said reassuringly.[33]

More first-hand information can be derived from a remarkable interview Mark Thatcher gave in late 1983 to a reporter from *Ming Pao Weekly* in Hong Kong. Despite arranging and agreeing the meeting in advance, the Chinese journalist was told he could have 15 minutes on the street while the prime minister's son waited for his car, accompanied by his security guard. The reporter first asked about the nature of Mark's business interests. 'Nothing special, I just don't like to disclose,' sniffed Mark. The conversation then turned to Hong Kong.

'Do you talk to your mother about Hong Kong?' asked the journalist.

'Of course I do,' replied Thatcher.

'Are your views about Hong Kong the same?'

'She likes Hong Kong, too. Naturally, she is not as familiar with the place as I am. She has only been here two or three times. Of course, we often talk about Hong Kong, but this is only between us – mother and son.'

'Have you any intention of doing business in China?'

'Just taking a look. Many friends invited me to go. Perhaps I will accept their invitation in the future. China is a place really worth going to.'[34] (His commercial interest in China was as chairman of Couvin Ltd, a Hong Kong company that advised firms on doing business on the mainland.)[35]

'Does the reason for your affinity with Hong Kong have anything to do with China?'

'Definitely not. Hong Kong will not become better or worse just because of China. You can never see Hong Kong and China as two separate matters.'

The interview was notable for the candour with which he spoke about his relationship with the prime minister. 'My mother is perfect,' he said. 'She will support me 100 per cent, no matter what I do. We talk about virtually everything but this is strictly between my mother and me.'[36]

The depth and extent of Mark's conversations with the prime minister on Hong Kong are not known. However, by his own account in late 1983, 'we often talk about Hong Kong' and it was the one international issue he commented on. 'She fought very hard for the agreement,' he said in 1991. 'She feels a great affinity with Hong Kong. It has such self-reliance, adaptability and self-determination.'[37]

How much money Mark Thatcher made out of Hong Kong is in some dispute. The Hong Kong press estimated it at £100,000 a year but that seems very unlikely. Apart from Emperor, most of the companies that hired him were not a success and it is inconceivable that he reaped much reward from them. Tony Zie, his former business partner, who has since become embroiled in a series of civil lawsuits over control of the Jademan comics publishing company, later played down Mark's activities: 'He was rarely here. I used mainly to deal with Steve Tipping. Mark seemed more interested in the Middle East.'[38]

The last statement was certainly true but the first was not. Throughout the 1980s, Mark visited Hong Kong every three months. After delving into the gold and commodities market, he opted for the investment business. One of his main contacts was Robert V. Wang, chairman of the United Overseas Bank Group. He met Wang through Suntech Investments, a hugely powerful investment consortium dominated by six of Hong Kong's top ten business tycoons and controller of 35 per cent of the colony's capitalisation. 'He comes here fairly regularly to touch base and sniff around for business,' the banker said in 1993. 'When my company started, we looked at some of his proposals for mobile telephones and hi-tech equipment but we didn't go ahead because it was for an American market.'[39]

However, despite his mother's boasts about Mark being 'a born businessman',[40] his foray into the investment game brought him few, if any, financial successes. 'I would say Mark wanted to be an entrepreneur and an investment syndicator for different companies,' said the managing director of a Hong Kong investment company that deals mainly with middle-ranking Chinese businessmen. 'He is a man of tremendous energy but he wished to play in a finance and investment world which is an unforgiving environment in Hong Kong for people who are short on skill and Mark is lacking in wisdom, I'm afraid. He is more likely to have succeeded in marketing, sales and promotion.'

For Margaret Thatcher's son, Hong Kong was not the place where he acquired sacks of gold. As in many of his commercial adventures of the early 1980s, he found there was much Eastern promise but not much fulfilment. Considerable energy and activity were invested and generated but there is precious little evidence of much in the way of cash returns. His business record in the colony is summed up by an old Chinese proverb: 'The chap who sits on a hot cooker once learns. But the chap who does it twice is stupid.' Mark sat on the cooker several times and so decided to look elsewhere in South-east Asia.

In February 1994, Hugh Thurston, the personal banker to Mark and Margaret Thatcher, flew from his home in St Helier, Jersey, to Belgravia, London. He had been asked to make the journey by the former prime minister for a special reason. They spoke periodically, of course, but this time there was an urgent matter. According to a source close to the Thatcher family, she asked Thurston about the family finances: 'Are they in order, Hugh?' After being reassured, she then expressed fears about Mark's possible implication in a looming scandal – his involvement in an arms deal with Malaysia which she negotiated and signed as prime minister in 1988. Her anxiety was fuelled by the disclosure that millions of pounds of taxpayers' money, designated as aid for Third World countries, had been handed to Malaysia as a 'sweetener' to secure the £1.3 billion defence contract. This policy, confirmed by former defence secretary George Younger in early 1994, was particularly controversial, as Malaysia was seen as a wealthy country.

The origins of the deal lay in Margaret Thatcher's assertive and aggressive arms-sales policy in the Far East. Briefed by Sir Colin Chandler, head of defence sales, she was told that Malaysia could be a sequel to Al-Yamamah. It was ripe for an arms deal, as the country had laid plans and allocated a multibillion-pound budget to turn its armed forces into a tough fighting outfit by re-equipping all three major service branches by the year 2000. As a bonus, the deal had the advantage of restoring diplomatic relations with the country after a dispute over university fees for overseas students in the UK.

Malaysia's prime minister, Dr Mahathir Mohamed, was keen to pursue rearmament because of disputes with China, the Philippines and Vietnam over islands in the South China Sea. Defence spending cuts had taken their toll and so he welcomed Mrs Thatcher's approach, particularly as he admired her political and economic policies. The result was direct and intimate negotiations between the two prime ministers. They began with Dr Mahathir's visit to London in 1987 and culminated when Mrs Thatcher went to Kuala Lumpur on 6 August 1988.

A month later, on 27 September 1988, the two leaders signed a Memorandum of Understanding (MOU) in the Cabinet Room at 10 Downing Street. The terms of the MOU were not released for 'reasons of commercial confidentiality'.[41] But the essence of the document was that Malaysia agreed to buy from Britain twelve Tornado jet fighter aircraft, air-defence radars, artillery guns, two Oberon-class submarines and Rapier anti-aircraft missile systems worth £1.3 billion. Mrs Thatcher said the signing marked a new phase in their improved relationship, which showed their 'confidence in one another'.[42] It transformed Britain into the world's second largest arms exporter during her tenure in 10 Downing Street.

The prime minister set up a special unit in the Ministry of Defence in support of the deal. But negotiations were at first stalled by a dispute over air landing rights. The UK government had promised to grant Malaysia Airlines extra flights between Kuala Lumpur and London but this was not implemented. Mrs Thatcher intervened and an accord was reached on 10 March 1989 after British Airways was paid £1 million in compensation.[43] Detailed arms discussions then began between British Aerospace and the Malaysian Defence Ministry.

By the autumn of 1990, it had been decided that the Tornados were 'too costly' and Malaysia opted for the cheaper Hawks.[44] Eventually, on 10 December 1990, a contract was signed for Malaysia to purchase twenty-eight Hawk fighter aircraft, a Martello radar system and two frigates from Yarrow, a GEC subsidiary, for a total of £450 million. The deal was dependent, like the Al-Yamamah deal with Saudi Arabia, on an offset programme worth about £110 million. This included the transfer of technology from British Aerospace to Airod, a Malaysian-Lockheed joint-venture firm which performed all maintenance work on the Hawk.

The similarity with Al-Yamamah continued in its method of payment. The weapons were to be paid for partly in cash and partly by the sale of crude oil, natural gas and other commodities. Apart from using Britain's Overseas Aid Budget to sweeten the deal, Mrs Thatcher also offered the Malaysian government cheap loans to subsidise their arms purchase. Under 'Funding', the Memorandum of Understanding stated: 'In the event there is any shortfall in the funding, the UK government will assist in the arrangement of financial facilities provided by a UK bank or a group of UK banks and the UK will ensure that the interest to be charged will be at concessionary rates.' In other words, the British government was subsidising the arms deal by paying the difference between the banks' commercial rates and their concessionary interest rates.[45]

The role of Mark Thatcher in this massive military order was first alleged by two Malaysian MPs, Lim Kit Siang and Dr Kua Kia Soong, members of the opposition Democratic Action Party. In December 1991, they claimed (and they have since repeated the claim) that Mark was linked to the deal through a local company called Bakti Udara. They encountered strong denials from the Malaysian Ministry of Defence.

However, two major segments of the contract provided clues to the potential involvement of Margaret Thatcher's son. The first was the sale for £70 million of a top-secret Starburst laser-guided missile system, made by Short Brothers in Belfast. This missile was carried by British troops during the Gulf war and is highly regarded as an anti-aircraft device. The middleman who helped broker this deal on behalf of Short Brothers was one Stephen W. Tipping, Mark Thatcher's business partner since 1979 and best man at his wedding. Tipping represents Short Brothers in the Far East and it was confirmed by the Malaysian MoD that he was 'a facilitator' on the Starburst deal.[46] The ministry spokesman added that he understood Mark's best friend 'was influential with the Thatcher family'.[47]

Tipping acted as an intermediary by arranging and attending meetings in London between Alex Roberts, managing director and executive vice-president of Short Brothers, and Najib tun Razak, the Malaysian defence minister. He also visited Kuala Lumpur frequently, sometimes accompanied by Roberts. Between 1988 and 1993, he made over 30 trips, staying at least 169 nights at the Shangri-La Hotel, one of the most luxurious in South-east Asia.[48] He also based himself at the Oriental Hotel in Singapore. Razak has said that he met Tipping several times to discuss the Starburst contract and knew him as a 'friend of Mark Thatcher'. However, he denied that the prime minister's son had influenced the deal.[49]

Second, and more fundamental, Tipping was involved in providing parts for the British Aerospace Hawk fighter. This was consistent with his own policy as an arms fixer. 'The secret of defence deals is the engines,' he later told business associate Gary Smith. 'On the spare parts you can name your number.'

Tipping's direct commercial connection with British Aerospace was verified by his friend Sir Tim Bell, who also has a public relations contract with the Malaysian government. 'Tipping has a relationship with Dick Evans, chief executive of British Aerospace,' Sir Tim told the *Sunday Times*. 'He has either acted as an agent for British Aerospace in their negotiations with Malaysia or he has attempted to be involved in the BAE contracts. He certainly has interests in various contractual arrangements to do with BAE and Malaysia.' When asked by the paper to clarify his specific role, Sir Tim replied, 'What he does for a living is introduce people to each other.'[50]

The secret of Tipping's success in selling weapons to Malaysia is his cultivation of bankers, businessmen, brokers and politicians. One of his closest contacts was Harbhajan, an Indian. On 18 December 1989, Tipping wrote to a friend: 'Regarding Malaysia, Harbhajan is over for a few days over Christmas and I will have a long talk with him.' Another important associate was Mohamad Haji Hassan, who at the time was general manager of the Bank Bumiputra Malaysia. Hassan attended a reception with the English arms middleman at the Hilton ballroom in December 1990, just after the final contract to supply the Hawks was signed. The banker, like Tipping, was a keen golfer and they played together at Wentworth.

Perhaps more important in what became known as Thatcher's 'golden magic circle' of influence in Malaysia was Tan Sri Arumugam, a very close associate of Dr Mahathir, the prime minister. An Indian by birth, Arumugam controls GEC Malaysia, which was awarded contracts as part of the 1988 agreement. Both Mark Thatcher and Steve Tipping knew him as someone who could provide direct access to Mahathir. Arumugam, who is also represented by Sir Tim Bell, played a key role in the arms deal. Such was his close involvement in the deal that he stood behind Mrs Thatcher and Dr Mahathir when they signed the Memorandum of Understanding in 1988. Arumugam remains influential, and on 11 May 1992 he attended a dinner in honour of Mahathir, hosted by John Major at 10 Downing Street.[51]

However, Tipping's most significant relationship is with Najib tun Razak, the Malaysian defence minister, who was given prime responsibility by Mahathir for the Hawks contract which was signed on 10 December 1990. Razak shares Tipping's passion for golf and they spend as much time on the fairways and putting greens of Malaysia as they do in the ministry office.

Mark Thatcher's oldest friend has continued to broker arms deals since the 1988 agreement. 'I've just arranged the sale of six Sikorsky helicopters to Malaysia,' he told Gary Smith in October 1993. 'Mahathir is a good friend of mine and when the Malaysians come to England I fly them around all the golf courses in my private jet. I've done a lot of big defence deals in Malaysia. They were daft enough to buy MiG 28s from the Russians so I told them, "You had better check in case you buy toy ones!"' Tipping has always disputed this version of events.

Tipping's comment that the Malaysian prime minister was a close friend was no idle boast. In 1991, he attended a dinner at the Savoy Hotel to celebrate the birthday of Dr Mahathir's son. It was attended by Denis Thatcher, Alan Curtis, chairman of Lotus, and Alex Roberts, managing director of Short Brothers. The dinner, said one of the guests, was notable for Denis's remark that his wife regretted endorsing John Major as prime minister and that 'intellectually, he was just not up to the job'. But it also illustrated Tipping's Malaysian connections at the highest level.

The extent of Mark Thatcher's involvement in facilitating the supply of weapons to Malaysia is difficult to ascertain. Certainly Tipping's sales pitch to the Malaysian government was that he was connected to 'the Thatcher family'. He has also used Hugh Thurston, Mark's personal banker, to prepare the commercial papers on Short Brothers' military contracts with Malaysia.

In an attempt to distance Mark from the Malaysian arms deal, the Thatcher camp have sent out the message that Steve Tipping's business partnership with the prime minister's son ended in 1984. Consequently, say Thatcher's friends, Mark could not have been involved in the contract. Tipping himself has repeated this assertion – both to the authors and to *Financial Times* – claiming he departed after the liquidation of Monteagle Marketing Ltd in 1985.

It is certainly true that from 1985 onwards, Mark concentrated more on Saudi Arabia and Tipping devoted his time largely to the Far East. But as late as 1987, Mark recounted to Gary Smith, the oil trader, over supper at Claridge's how he had just visited Malaysia and dealt with an Indian consultant out there. Tipping has always disputed Smith's account.

But Smith claims that Tipping continued to be aware of several of Mark's commercial projects in the late 1980s. While their relationship no longer retained its Siamese twins character, they remained linked. This was demonstrated in August 1986, when Mark introduced Tipping to Gary Smith as my 'closest confidant'. He added: 'I do all my business with him. When you talk to Steve, you are talking to me. He is my eyes and ears in the business world.'[52] And at his wedding in 1987, Thatcher introduced his best man as someone with whom he discussed deals.

For the next 18 months, until the spring of 1988, Smith attended a series of meetings with both Mark Thatcher and Steve Tipping on a proposed oil deal in Nigeria (see Chapter Nine for details). According to Smith, it is beyond any doubt that the two remained, at the very least, business associates until the summer of 1988. And even in the early 1990s they continued to discuss investment propositions. In October 1993, Tipping had dinner with David Wallace, who represented Thatcher's interests in Ameristar, an aviation fuel company. They discussed 'the areas in which I [Wallace] feel you can assist' (see Chapter Nine for details).

Tipping also remained close friends with the prime minister and particularly with her husband. They share the same brand of right-wing golf club politics. 'If the Paddies, Jocks and Taffies want to go it alone, then that's bloody fine by me,' Tipping once remarked. A regular visitor to 10 Downing Street, he often spent late mornings with Denis Thatcher drinking gin and tonics. Early one morning, Tipping telephoned a business associate to arrange a meeting. 'Can we make our appointment lunch at 12.30?' he said. 'I'll need a meal by then because I'm seeing Denis in the morning.'

Margaret Thatcher saw Tipping as a moderating influence on her wayward son. He often saw her at 10 Downing Street and was a lunch guest at Chequers, particularly at Christmas. She once sent him a framed photograph of herself and signed it, 'To Stephen. Warm regards. Margaret.'

When asked to contribute to this biography, Tipping responded: 'Despite considerable provocation and temptation over the years, I have never discussed my business in public. I see no reason to change this habit of a lifetime as far as my own affairs are concerned; and certainly no justification whatsoever in talking about those of a friend and former colleague. I am sorry, therefore, to have to turn you down.'[53]

Stephen Tipping has come a long way from his days working for the family garage company in Yateley, Surrey, in the early 1970s. The Malaysian arms deal was the culmination of seizing the main chance in 1979 when he linked up with the prime minister's son. He now bears and wears all the trappings of his millionaire status. Since 1986, he has lived in a sprawling mansion in Fleet, Hampshire, with several garages containing his collection of classic cars. Many of his business meetings are held at the Savoy Hotel, where all the waiters address him as 'Mr Tipping, sir'. He also drops by at the St James's Club and the Lanesborough, London's most expensive hotel, for a drink when he is in town.

Mark Thatcher's business partner for almost ten years is now an immensely wealthy man. Like Mark, Tipping uses Hugh Thurston to look after his financial affairs. 'I have made more money than I think I can spend,' he told Gary Smith in 1993.

'Where do you bank it all?' he was asked.

'It's buried deep, man. Very deep.'

Stephen Tipping has consistently disputed the accuracy of the authors' sources for this account of his relationship with Mark Thatcher.

To the west of Malaysia, about 1,600 miles across the Indian Ocean, lies the tropical paradise of Sri Lanka. A mountainous, largely agricultural island – known as the 'Teardrop of India' – Sri Lanka has been experiencing an economic revolution. For 30 years, the country's basic utilities and industries have been state owned. But the early 1990s saw a sea change, with a programme of privatisation and industrialisation of its infrastructure. The process has been supported by the British government. Sri Lanka will be the 'Malaysia of South Asia within a few years,' said Richard Needham, the trade minister in the late 1980s. But the programme has been besmirched by allegations of corruption, including the misuse of financial aid from the United Kingdom.

It was to this once peaceful, neutral island that Mark Thatcher next turned his gaze in the Far East. His chief contact point was Ravinora B. Wethasinghe, a 32-year-old British-educated entrepreneur and aviation enthusiast. Wethasinghe is exactly the type of businessman Thatcher likes to associate with. Like Mark he is a car fanatic, owning eight Ferraris and a Lamborghini. A secretive man, for many years he preferred to hire a private jet and fly alone on his regular trips between England and Sri Lanka, rather than on a normal commercial flight. He owns two planes. One is a private executive Gulfstream jet, kept at the Osprey Aviation hangar in Southampton, for his own use. The other is chartered out to high-powered business delegations.

In his earlier years, Wethasinghe had been an arms dealer and supplied guns to the Sri Lankan government during the civil war with the Tamil Tigers. He also liked to have weapons for his own use. On 24 June 1989, he was convicted and fined £1,550 at West London Magistrates' Court for the illegal possession of 96 rounds of long ammunition and a high-calibre Ruger .22 semi-automatic combat rifle. Yet such was his influence in the Sri Lankan high commission that just two and a half weeks later he was a guest at a Buckingham Palace garden party, mingling with the royal family.[54]

Despite his criminal conviction, Wethasinghe has remained a powerful and wealthy business operator. In 1992, he secured a 600-million-rupee (£7.6 million) contract with the Sri Lankan government to supply 2,500 buses to a country which was in desperate need of public transport. Wethasinghe had set up a company, Latec

Engineering and Management Services Ltd, to facilitate the deal and manufacture the buses in Sri Lanka, based on imported parts and engines made by Duple Metsec Ltd, a Birmingham-based company. He had also persuaded the Department of Trade and Industry to provide an aid and provision grant of £2.65 million – 30 per cent of the total cost – for the project and acquired funding from the Sri Lankan government.

But the problem was that hardly any buses were actually built and the contract was heavily criticised for its high cost and overheads. One diplomat compiled a report entitled 'The Sri Lanka Bus Deal – How to Rob a Country'. Local politicians were also furious. On 17 June 1993, a Sri Lankan MP told parliament: 'The Duple Metsec–Lanka Agents collaboration has a sordid record in the supply of the earlier 600-bus-kit contract. The local businessman involved in the collaboration . . . has been fined in the British courts.'[55]

One of the executives whom Wethasinghe hired to promote the contract was Kate Roy, his communications manager. The project appealed to Kate because it provided much-needed employment for Sri Lankans and involved local people as investors. She was also a pacifist and a strong critic of Margaret Thatcher, whom she saw as promoting the arms trade. So when she first started working for Wethasinghe she made her views crystal clear. 'I have to know where your money comes from,' she told him. 'If it comes from arms or drugs I cannot work for you.' Wethasinghe appeared upset. 'Kate, I have to tell you that a few years ago I was involved in arms,' he said. 'It was lucrative, but I now want to put the money back into this project and change things in my country.'

Wethasinghe was not a political animal but he could see the value of politicians. 'I'm going to get Mrs Thatcher to open the factory,' he often said. 'Well, I'm not going to be there,' replied Kate. 'You'll have to get Babu [his security guard] to hold me down to shake her hand.' Wethasinghe laughed and teased her about her views. But his links with the Thatchers were no idle boast, according to Kate. Wethasinghe later telephoned to ask her advice on the best medical treatment for his father. 'He told me that when he flew his father from Colombo to London after his stroke he had dinner with Lady Thatcher,' recalled Kate. 'Ravi [Wethasinghe] said she was very kind because she introduced him to her personal physician and private clinic. She has been very helpful to [him] and she has been a good friend.'

By late August 1993, Wethasinghe's attitude towards Kate

changed. 'It's so difficult to make a living this way,' he told her. 'I'm going back to my old business.' Kate, who knew what this meant, replied, 'Well, you know we had an agreement. I will resign if that happens.' Suddenly Wethasinghe started making life in the company very difficult for her and on one occasion his staff tried to stop her entering her own office.

The reason for this behaviour became apparent five days later, on Thursday, 9 September 1993. Kate was sitting on the porch outside her office when she was stunned to see Mark Thatcher and Wethasinghe arriving together. She was introduced to Mark, who then entered the office and used the fax and telephone. 'I immediately thought, "All is lost," because it was obvious to me that they were doing some kind of business together,' she recalled.[56] She told Wethasinghe she was resigning because of the Thatcher association. 'Mark is a friend of mine,' he replied, 'and if you don't like the way things are done around here you should go.' Kate then returned to her hotel, packed her bags and flew back to England.

Mark Thatcher and Wethasinghe had met through a mutual passion for aviation. Mark has been a keen helicopter flyer since 1982 when he qualified as a pilot after being instructed at Blackbushe airport, Surrey, in an American-built Enstrom helicopter. He paid £5,000 for the 35-hour training course and at the time he said he did it 'just for fun'.[57]

Ten years later, in July 1992, Thatcher was able to buy a B206 Bell jet ranger helicopter from Skyline Ltd for £185,500 (he occasionally leases it back to them for commercial projects). He then spent £70,000 on its interior. 'It looked like the inside of a Ford Escort,' said film-maker Tim Cooper, who has flown in it. That same month, the helicopter was purchased through a company called Newbury International Ltd, based in the Isle of Man. Six weeks later, the helicopter's registration was transferred to another Isle of Man firm called Corporate Enterprises Ltd. This appears as the owner in Civil Aviation Authority (CAA) records as of 10 August 1992. However, this was a misleading CAA registration, because five days earlier, on 5 August 1992, Mark Thatcher's nominee directors had changed the name of the helicopter's owner to Newbury Aviation Ltd. Consequently, his declared CAA declaration is incorrect because Corporate Enterprises Ltd does not exist! Such a convoluted method of registering a helicopter is a classic example of Thatcher's secretive and intricate business methods.

The following spring, Ravi Wethasinghe also bought a B206 jetranger helicopter from Skyline and it was at their aerodrome in Booker, near High Wycombe, Buckinghamshire, that he first met Mark Thatcher in July 1993. 'Any dealings we had with Mr Wethasinghe and Mr Thatcher are confidential,' said former Skyline director Trevor Taylor. 'I cannot talk to you without their permission.'

But when Mark arrived in Sri Lanka two months later he was on a different kind of business mission. He was acting on behalf of American firms who were keen to bid for the state-owned Lanka Petroleum Corporation, other state-owned corporations being privatised, and contracts to supply equipment to the electricity-generating board. Mark needed introductions to the very top of the Sri Lankan government and Wethasinghe was the ideal facilitator. Wethasinghe used his chairman, D.S. Jayawickrema, to make the background enquiries. Jayawickrema asked Kate Roy to bring over brochures of British electricity companies that might be interested in bidding for the contracts.

Mark had flown into Colombo from Bombay, on a private British Aerospace 125 jet hired by Wethasinghe and leased from Osprey Aviation. The pilots were told that this trip was 'highly confidential' and ordered not to tell anyone whom they were picking up. If asked, they should say 'an engineer'. Mark stayed at the Ramada Renaissance Hotel and his bill was paid by Swiss Lloyd Ltd, a travel firm. Swiss Lloyd paid all the residential expenses for all Ravi Wethasinghe's employees and business associates, said Kate Roy. 'They paid all my hotel bills and Ravi then immediately reimbursed them, so there is no doubt in my mind that Ravi paid Mark Thatcher's hotel bill.'

For the next four days and three nights, Thatcher gained remarkable access to senior ministers and military generals. He met President D.B. Wijetunga at the presidential secretariat with Wethasinghe and his brother Gamini.[58] He also paid what was described as 'a courtesy call' on Prime Minister Ranil Wickremasinghe and the newly appointed military chief.[59]

On the first evening of his visit, Mark was a guest at a special dinner at the Ramada Renaissance Hotel hosted by Wethasinghe. The 12 guests included Ian Dallas, the commercial attaché at the British high commission; Scott Hamilton from Duple Metsec; Melinda Ekanayake, a director of Latec and managing director of Skyline Helicopters UK Ltd, which Wethasinghe had just taken over; Jacquie Fance-Wheeler, another Latec director; Latec's chairman, D.S. Jayawickrema; and Wethasinghe's brother, Gamini.

Officials at the British high commission were introduced to Thatcher and became increasingly concerned about his business activities in Sri Lanka. They were not informed about his visit and were particularly anxious about how he obtained direct access to senior ministers, while others had to wait or go through proper channels. His visit was also noticed by a Conservative MP with Sri Lankan connections who happened to be in Colombo at the same time. He was not happy. 'What the hell was that man doing there?' he said. 'I don't want to be associated with him.'

NINE

Black Gold

I am a millionaire. That is my religion.
— Major Barbara, **George Bernard Shaw**

Mark Thatcher's introduction to the oil business was a chance meeting with Gary Smith, a well-connected international oil trader, on a 7 a.m. British Airways flight from Paris to London in August 1986. The prime minister's son often flew from the USA to London via Paris, to avoid what he called 'the nurks' (journalists who met him at Heathrow airport by tracing his direct flights from Texas). He also had an apartment in Avenue Foch in Paris, which he used as a base to meet prominent Arabs.

But as he sat in the business-class compartment reading the newspapers, it was matters of a political nature that were on his mind. It was a time when the Conservative government was in trouble and the Labour Party (or 'the goons', as Mark liked to refer to them) was in contention for power. Suddenly, Mark closed his newspaper and turned to Gary Smith. 'What are you going to do if the goons get in?' he said without introducing himself. 'I don't know,' replied the oilman. 'Mum must be supported or the country will have all kinds of problems,' said the prime minister's son.

Smith then introduced himself formally and Mark began to chat away, particularly about the threat posed by 'the goons' and 'chief goon' Neil Kinnock.

'If I were you, I'd go and live in Switzerland like the rest of us will have to,' he said. 'In my opinion, Switzerland is by far the best place in the world.'

'I lived in Geneva for two years, which was very pleasant, but I prefer London because it's more vibrant,' replied the oilman.

'London is OK but Switzerland is where the dosh is,' said Mark.

The conversation then turned to the oil industry. 'A lot of politicians in nig-nog land [which Smith took to mean Africa and the Middle East] are creaming it off [making money] like crazy,' said Thatcher. Smith agreed and said that Saudi businessmen were the most avaricious. He added that he had helped put together a deal in 1984 which involved exchanging Saudi oil for aircraft. 'King Fahd was persuaded to insert an extra 36 million barrels of oil into a market which was over-supplied and huge commissions were paid,' said Smith. 'Sheikh Yamani had actually opposed these sort of deals.'

Mark was curious but not knowledgeable about the oil business. He was more interested in sponsorship for his motor-racing career. 'I would like to get sponsorship from oil companies for my racing cars,' he said. 'I'm looking at a minimum of $200,000, because my name has sponsorship value.'

Smith indicated he would be able to help.

'Good, I'll introduce you to my closest confidant, Stephen Tipping,' replied Thatcher. 'I do all my business with him. If he rings you, call him Steve as if you were talking to me. He is my eyes and ears in the business world and will know what to do if any really decent deal is on offer.'

Smith took 'decent' to mean profitable and said he would make some enquiries.

'I hate time wasters,' Mark added. 'I will need a lot of money to retire on, at least £5 million.' He then changed his mind. 'Well, £10 million would be safer because it's a tough world.'

Smith thought to himself that this reflected Margaret Thatcher's harsh view of the world. This was confirmed by her son's next remark: 'Life is short, brutish and nasty.'

As the BA flight descended into Heathrow airport, Mark handed Smith his business card, which read simply, 'The Grantham Company, Dallas, Texas'. 'Please call me in Texas or on this number at 10 Downing Street. I usually stay there when I am in London.' He then scribbled down the number 01–222 8141 (a direct 10 Downing Street line).

'Doesn't your mother mind if you do business from there?' asked Smith.

'Mum wouldn't have it any other way,' replied Mark. 'If you would like to meet my mother, I would be happy to introduce you.'

As they walked through Terminal 4, Smith said he would approach Swiss and German oil companies for sponsorship of his motor racing. Mark was appreciative and they began laughing about his getting lost in the desert. 'Mum was really worried about that,' he said. 'It shows what a wonderful mum she really is.' As they reached the end of the escalators of Terminal 4, Mark was met by four bodyguards. 'Everything OK, sir,' one said, and they went their separate ways.

That evening, Mark Thatcher rang Smith at his West Hampstead home. 'I am leaving soon for the States,' he said, 'but me and Steve [Tipping] have an oil deal which we would like to talk to you about.' Tipping strongly denies any involvement in this deal and Smith's version of events.

Three months later, the oil trader heard from Mark again. 'We're on track for a big oil contract in Nigeria,' he said. But again things went quiet. Then, in April 1987, Smith says he was invited by Mark to dinner at Claridge's, the elegant hotel in Brook Street, Mayfair, where he was introduced to Steve Tipping. At first, Thatcher recounted with great relish an episode when he was in Malaysia. 'An Indian I was dealing with offered me a pretty girl for the night,' related Mark. 'I told him, "No way. I am not that type," so the Indian offered me a pretty boy!' At this, he burst into raucous laughter, so loudly that a waiter came over to their table and asked, 'Is everything all right, sir?'

The conversation turned to commercial matters. 'I know nothing at all about oil, except how it works in cars,' said Mark repeatedly. 'That doesn't matter,' interrupted Tipping in his distinctive Kent accent. 'Mr Smith knows about oil. Connections and the right channels make the world go around.' Over coffee, the talk focused on which countries were ripe to do some business. Eventually, they reached Nigeria, if rather obliquely. 'We don't want Oman, we've done that,' said Tipping to Smith. 'We don't want Saudi, because that's your speciality. So, let me ask you. What's black, big and messy?'

'Nigeria?' replied the oil businessman hesitantly.

'Bang on, clever boy,' laughed Tipping, who added that they were working on a deal with an 'important' Nigerian chief. 'We will introduce you to him soon,' he said.

Marc Rich, the fugitive oil trader, was the next topic. Mark Thatcher, who said he had done some work for him in New York, thought that the Swiss trader was 'too big' to get entangled with.

'Marc Rich made so much loot by defrauding the Americans,'

remarked Smith, 'that if he squealed the whole Washington establishment would come crashing down, because so many top Americans were involved.'

Thatcher agreed: 'It's best left alone.'

The prime minister's son then made a remark which Smith found somewhat weird. 'Anyway, the Jews have Washington completely sewn up,' he said. 'My mother likes Jews a lot, especially their stress on family life.'

Tipping asked Smith: 'What do you think of Jews? Do you like them?'

Smith, somewhat taken aback by the question, replied that he lived in a Jewish area in north London. 'I have had no problems with them as neighbours,' he said.

'That's acceptable,' said Tipping quickly. 'It's important in our circle to like Jews, because Mark's mother likes them a lot, especially the members and officers in her constituency association.'

The dinner ended with Mark paying the bill and with a brief exchange on the importance of family life. The three agreed to meet again to discuss the Nigerian deal in detail. That happened a month later over a late dinner at Claridge's. The essence of the plan was that Nigeria had substantial oil reserves which it was keen to sell to pay off its foreign debts. Thatcher and Tipping saw a golden opportunity and had hooked up with Chief Bola Abimbola, who ran a trading company called Interocean Petroleum Nigeria Ltd. The chief was a controversial figure in the trade. From 1984 until 1986, he was the agent for Voest Alpine, the state-owned Austrian oil corporation, which was involved in a scam that lost the Austrian taxpayer millions of schillings. Its agents purchased crude oil from Egypt and Iran and then deliberately sold to traders at a loss in return for huge commissions.

Thatcher and Tipping saw Abimbola as their channel into oil-rich West Africa. The chief would use his influence and broker a deal with the state-owned Nigerian National Petroleum Corporation to sell 50,000 barrels of oil a day through Euravia AG, represented by Gary Smith. Euravia, based in Zurich, was a private distribution company which bought crude oil directly from countries like Saudi Arabia, the United Arab Emirates and Libya. It had offices in eight west European countries and Smith was their London manager, based at 37 Queen Anne Street, off Harley Street.

Thatcher and Tipping told Smith that 'Chiefy', as they half-mockingly called Abimbola, would deliver the contract for Euravia and everyone would 'get their cut'. Mark's role was to introduce Abimbola to Smith and help the chief lobby the Nigerian government. He added that Chiefy had a Scottish associate called James Lang, whose company supplied generators for the oil pipelines. Lang also became friendly with Mark Thatcher, despite being ten years older, and was a guest at his wedding. 'He's a nice guy,' said Mark, 'but he thinks the sun shines out of Chiefy's arse.' Tipping denies that these words were used and any involvement in the Nigerian deal. Unknown to Mark, Lang also became acquainted with the prime minister who asked him, 'to look after Mark and keep an eye on him'.

The second meeting at Claridge's was concluded by Mark's expressing confidence in Euravia, because they were 'cash-rich' and 'had the millions' to complete the deal. 'I have been told you are an acceptable name in the oil industry,' he said.

Six weeks later, shortly after the general election in late June 1987, the first set of negotiations took place, again over dinner at Claridge's. Gary Smith arrived first. Tipping then walked in and was greeted by the manager: 'Good evening, Mr Tipping.' He sat down next to the oil executive and pointed out the trio of elderly musicians dressed in eighteenth-century Austrian costumes. 'Wonderful thing is culture,' said Tipping, 'but they look as if they've been playing since the eighteenth century.'

Chief Abimbola and James Lang then arrived. The chief was in a jolly mood and said their proposed business was progressing well. He added that he was very close to Nigeria's president, General Ibrahim Babangida, who was 'all-powerful'. 'Absolutely correct, sir,' said Lang rather obsequiously.

Within 20 minutes Mark Thatcher and his wife, Diane, appeared. Mark was carrying a massive square briefcase of the type often used by architects. He passed it to the head waiter with instructions that it be kept safe because its contents were 'top secret'. He, too, was in a good mood and crowed about the large majority secured by the Conservative Party in the recent general election.

The group then moved to the adjoining restaurant for dinner. Smith sat next to the newly married Diane Thatcher. The oil trader found her a woman of happy disposition but the kind of person dependent on financial security. 'You cannot really enjoy life without money,' she said.

Tipping asked about the deal. Lang said that the chief could do anything in the oil business in Nigeria. 'We are all lucky to have his support,' he said. Tipping replied that Abimbola's influence was 'very much appreciated'. He then introduced Smith as the person who could market the oil and guarantee the commissions from Switzerland. 'The commissions are *the* most important issue,' said the chief [his emphasis]. 'My company is not the Salvation Army.' Thatcher agreed and said all commissions would be paid through the chief. 'He will look after everybody,' he said. Chief Abimbola concluded that he would ensure the Nigerian government would award the contract. The president, or 'IBB' as he referred to him, 'will push it through,' he said. Tipping again strongly disputes this account.

However, negotiations in Nigeria were slow and the next meeting did not take place for another five months. At 6.30 p.m. on 4 December 1987, Mark Thatcher and Gary Smith met for after-work drinks in the back bar of the Connaught Hotel, on the corner of Carlos Place in Mayfair. It was a regular and favourite watering hole of Mark's. 'Decent place,' he said. 'If the day winds you up, the Scotch at the Connaught can wind you down.'

When they arrived Mark was greeted by Lord Young, then secretary of state for trade and industry, who was sitting at the bar surrounded by a large entourage. 'Evening, Mark,' he said. 'Lovely to see you, Mark. How's everything, Mark?' Smith thought to himself that the repeated use of Thatcher's first name reminded him of a headmaster addressing a pupil whose parents were paying a large part of his salary. 'Fine, fine,' replied Thatcher. 'Good,' said Lord Young. 'I'll talk to you in detail at a more appropriate time.' Smith pondered about the cabinet minister's relationship with Mark. 'What do you think of Lord Young?' he asked. 'Tops,' replied Thatcher. 'He is one of Mum's closest advisers.' After a brief chat, the two left the Connaught with Lord Young shouting out, 'Bye, Mark.'

Thatcher and Smith walked around the corner to have dinner at Harry's Bar. Mark was given an equally sycophantic welcome. 'Welcome back, sir,' said the manager. 'How is Madam [i.e. Diane]? Is she joining us tonight?' 'No,' said Mark, 'she is back in Dallas because I'm in London on special business.' They were shown to a back table and it was not long before Thatcher spoke about the Nigerian oil deal. 'Everything is on course,' he said, 'and IBB is aware of the deal. The prospects are very good because he owes Mum a favour.' He did not elaborate, but it was no secret that Margaret Thatcher had assisted the Babangida government in its dealings with the International Monetary Fund (IMF) and the General was grateful. Her administration had also substantially increased overseas aid to

Nigeria, from an average of £5.7 million a year in 1984–8 to £67.7 million in 1989–90.

The 'favour' can be traced to her discussions with Babangida on 7 January 1985, during a visit to Lagos. 'He was a forceful, intelligent man,' she recalled in her memoirs, 'trying to put Nigeria's economy on to a sounder footing and in due course, we hoped, to create the conditions for a restoration of democracy. We had helped Nigeria in its dealings with the IMF and this was appreciated. General Babangida seemed to be open to my suggestions about the need to curb Nigeria's budget deficit, cut inflation and provide reassurances for foreign investors.'[1]

Margaret Thatcher returned to Nigeria on 7 January 1988, just five weeks after her son's dinner at Harry's Bar. She discovered that the General had taken her advice and embarked on a monetarist economic programme – even tougher than the measures she had advocated. 'With our support,' said Thatcher, 'Nigeria now had the approval of the IMF and its main Western creditors and had secured a rescheduling of debt to its public sector creditors.'[2] Nigeria is now a chaotic, corruption-ridden country plagued by civil unrest, and its economy is in dire straits.

Mark was clearly attempting to reap the commercial benefits of his mother's 'favour' to the Nigerian president. On this deal he was asking for a commission of $2 per barrel. Smith thought this was outrageous. The normal commission on 50,000 barrels a day was between 20 and 50 cents, unless it was something special. Thatcher was looking for a pay-off close to $2 million, based on 365 days of production. During the dinner at Harry's Bar, Smith told him this was 'unusually large' – even for Nigeria. 'It's not me who makes the rules,' replied Mark. 'Anyway, there are many mouths to feed and the president is unusually hungry. In Africa, they all have to make hay while the sun shines.'

Thatcher made it clear he did not like the country. 'I'm not going near the dump,' he said, 'but it's a good place to make a hoot [*sic*] of cash which is what matters most.' He added that Chief Abimbola was working out the contract details. 'Don't worry about Euravia's profits,' he concluded. 'Chiefy is protecting us.' (This was a euphemism for paying the commissions.)

The conversation then changed to oil deals in other parts of the world. Smith suggested Oman and described how the tiny Gulf state had supplied oil to South Africa during the United Nations embargo. Mark saw nothing wrong in it. His view was that, if it happened during the republic's 'down times', then 'good old Oman' because South Africa was pro-British. In any case, he said, 'my sympathy is with the struggling white community'. As to future petroleum business in Oman, he said it was a 'non-starter' because of the problems created by the Cementation university contract. 'Why not see what we can do in Saudi and Iraq?' he added more hopefully. 'There are plenty of big fish in the pond. Go for it.'

They then talked about his mother. Mark repeated his statement that he stayed at and worked from 10 Downing Street and that 'Mum wouldn't have it any other way.' After a brief chat about the political scene, they left Harry's Bar. The next day, Thatcher rang Smith and suggested drawing up a Heads of Agreement between Euravia AG and himself for future oil deals in Saudi Arabia and Nigeria. That afternoon, he visited Smith at his office in Queen Anne Street to say that he was returning to Dallas. Before he walked in, his Special Branch detective came into the office to check it out. 'Got to do this, because his Mum got back in,' he said.

After the Harry's Bar dinner, the negotiations speeded up. Smith reported back to Switzerland Mark Thatcher's comment about President Babangida owing the prime minister a favour. Thatcher began to visit Smith's office more regularly and even delegated his wife, Diane, to type out the contract letters. In Nigeria, Chief Abimbola was lobbying the minister of petroleum resources, Rilwanu Lukman, who agreed on the 50,000 barrels of oil a day. On 7 March 1988, he delivered their proposals directly to Lukman, who instructed his officials to appraise them.

In Switzerland, Euravia AG reluctantly agreed to pay the service fee (the industry phrase for commission). On 23 March 1988, Dr Erich Gayler, chairman of Euravia AG in Zurich, signed a letter in anticipation of the 'refine and sell' agreement: 'This is to confirm that Euravia AG will pay to Interocean Petroleum Nigeria Ltd, a service fee of $2 for each barrel of oil lifted and refined under such an agreement.'

The following month, Chief Abimbola returned to London and summoned the various parties to his UK residence, which he dubbed 'Obokum Castle'. Beforehand, Thatcher, Tipping and Smith met at the Connaught for a drink. Mark stressed that Abimbola was taking care of his commission. 'It's being dealt with by a separate letter between me and Chiefy,' he said. Tipping disputes that he was present at this meeting.

The three then drove up to Obokum Castle, which turned out to be not a castle at all but a large detached house in Totteridge Lane, Hendon, in the heart of suburban north London. An unimpressive dwelling, it was in a state of some disrepair. They were greeted by a Nigerian man who ushered them into a sparsely furnished room. The chief offered tea or beer but Mark was impatient. 'We need to move on and do the bloody deal,' he said. 'There has been far too much pissing about so far.' Tipping agreed. Smith responded by saying his letters guaranteeing the commissions were prepared and signed. 'Well then, the deal is ready,' said Mark. 'The ball is now in your court, Chief. You need to run with it.' The chief appeared uneasy. 'Things take time in Lagos,' he said. 'The president and the minister were both very greedy.' Thatcher was irritated: 'He [Babangida] owes my mum a favour and you should ask him to move his ass.'

Abimbola tried to reassure them. 'Don't worry, it will be OK.' But it was apparent to Smith that Abimbola lacked the finesse and resources of the other Nigerian middlemen he had dealt with in his trading days. Even the state of his 'castle' indicated that the chief was short of cash. Despite the documents he had sent from Lagos, it was not clear he could deliver the goods – quite literally. The deal was falling apart. Smith's superiors in Switzerland were also uneasy and losing interest, particularly in view of the size of the commission. In any case, they had their own connections and channels in Nigeria.

However, Mark Thatcher was hanging on. A week after the Obokum Castle summit, he telephoned Smith from his base at 10 Downing Street. The oil executive was out but returned his call that evening. He found Mark in angry mood. 'There has been too much delay on this business,' he said. 'If Euravia are not going to cover the chief with the $2 commission, then we'll forget the whole fucking thing. I don't want to piss about any longer.' Smith replied that Euravia was serious about the deal but its management were reassessing it.

As it turned out, on this occasion Nigeria's black gold was not sold, partly because the chief could not deliver, but also because of the massive commission fee demanded by Thatcher and his associates. This discouraged Euravia from further involvement.

Gary Smith continued in the oil business and later worked for Sonangol, the national oil corporation of Angola. He became increasingly disillusioned with West Africa as it declined economically, and virtually gave up on Nigeria. James Lang suffered great financial strain from his association with Abimbola and died from a heart attack in tragic circumstances in 1989. The chief, who had previously made a fortune from his oil exploits, lost all his money in a deal supplying crude to Guinea and Liberia. He went bankrupt and has since disappeared from the scene.

As for President Babangida, he was forced to resign in August 1993, after losing the June presidential elections. Known as a dictator with deep pockets, he was ousted largely because of the misuse of the vast wealth derived from Nigeria's oil. Babangida fled to Cairo, then Saudi Arabia, and for a time lived in exile in Jeddah, frightened for his safety as irate Nigerians want to know into whose pockets the oil revenue went. In the summer of 1994, Mark Thatcher was visiting Jeddah on business. Perhaps he dropped by to discuss that favour his mother had bestowed on Babangida all those years ago.

Africa was often viewed by Margaret Thatcher as dominated by nation states who could be converted to her political and economic creed. She saw herself as a missionary for Thatcherism in the Third World. 'I wanted to spread the message,' she recalled in her memoirs, 'that a combination of limited government, financial orthodoxy and free enterprise would work for prosperity in under-developed countries as well as it did in the prosperous West. I chose Kenya and Nigeria for my first African political safari. In both cases with good reason. Kenya because it was the most pro-Western, most free enterprise of the important black African states.'[3]

Its president, Daniel Arap Moi, was also pro-Britain, not least because it was the largest investor in his country and provided the most overseas aid. So Margaret Thatcher was made particularly welcome by President Moi when she flew to Nairobi on 4 January 1988, for a three-day visit.

Another member of the Thatcher family had a keen interest in Kenya. After the Nigerian deal collapsed in the summer of 1988, her son, Mark, and his partner, Steve Tipping, began cultivating channels into the prime minister's favourite African state. But there was nothing evangelical about their activities. It was, like everything they did, strictly business and very private.

Unlike Nigeria, Kenya was hungry for oil. According to Gary Smith, the oil executive who worked on the Nigerian deal, Thatcher and Tipping were keen to move into Kenya. Smith was not used on this occasion but was later told that their principal business contact in Kenya was Ketan Somaia, the country's most powerful and wealthiest businessman. An Asian entrepreneur, Somaia is a former motor trader who became a millionaire by the age of 36. His corporate vehicle is the Dolphin International Group, based in Dubai and registered in Bermuda. Worth about $120 million, its main interests are casinos, leisure centres, sugar plantations, car factories, oil and film-making. In August 1991, Dolphin bought the Kenyan and Mauritius subsidiaries of BCCI after the bank's collapse and changed the subsidiaries' names to the Delphis Group. But it was not an auspicious initial period of ownership. The following year Delphis was one of four banks to be investigated by the Kenyan Central Bank after complaints about their procedures were voiced by the IMF and Western aid donors.[4]

Somaia clearly felt he needed political muscle. In the autumn of 1992, Lord (Cecil) Parkinson, former energy secretary and close friend of the Thatcher family, became chairman of Dolphin. He spent a week in Dubai for a briefing on the company and then flew to Nairobi for a meeting with President Moi.[5] A year after his appointment, on 4 October 1993, Tipping had lunch with Gary Smith at the Savoy Grill and claimed, 'I fixed Cecil up with his job with Somaia because he was short of a few bob.' The appointment was confirmed by a separate source: 'Tipping introduced Parkinson to Somaia, because the Kenyan wanted a big name in the UK to be chairman of his company.'

Mark Thatcher's connection with Somaia was forged much earlier. No source can place a date on it but he and Tipping certainly visited Kenya in May 1989. Officially, Mark was there to open a car rally in Kisumu, sponsored by the Dolphin Group, but few believe that was the only purpose. Indeed, Tipping told Gerald James, then chairman of the arms company Astra, at the Savoy Hotel in April 1989, 'I am going to Kenya next month on business. If you supply me with your brochures, I'll show them to the people I'm meeting.' The commercial nature of the visit was also borne out by the fact that Thatcher, Tipping and Ketan Somaia had two meetings with President Moi at his state houses, one in Nairobi, the other in Nakuru.

On another occasion in 1988, Mark Thatcher and Tipping attended a meeting with Somaia at his north London house. Also present was the Kenyan finance minister, the head of Kenya's Central Reserve Bank, and influential Arabs. Somaia wanted introductions to wealthy Arabs in the Gulf, to advance his business operations there, but they were not impressed by the Kenyan's proposals and no substantial introductions were made.

When asked about Mark's links with Somaia, Lord Parkinson consulted with the Dolphin boss. Somaia said that he did discuss potential business with Thatcher but nothing came of it. But Tipping told Gary Smith, 'We've done some business with Somaia. I have to say he's done some stupid things. He once hosted a social function in Kenya but didn't invite any blacks. There were only Asians. That's just not on if you're aiming to make a few bob.' Tipping disputes this version of events.

Tipping continued to cultivate Somaia and arranged legal advice for him on how to base his company in Dubai. On 5 December 1990, he was one of the prominent guests at a reception arranged and paid for by Dolphin Promotions Ltd at the London Hilton ballroom. Gary Smith was also invited and when he arrived Tipping told him, 'Somaia is the key boy in Kenya. He is very close to [President] Moi.' The oil trader was intrigued and introduced himself to Somaia. 'I met Nicholas Biwott [the energy minister] in Abu Dhabi recently,' said Smith. 'Good old Biwott,' Somaia replied, laughing. It may have been a knowing chuckle because Biwott, known as 'Tricky Nicky', was later sacked by President Moi for corruption. Smith added that he had approached Biwott to supply oil to Kenya more cheaply than the complex, more expensive, deal already negotiated. But Somaia made no comment except, 'Talk to Steve about it.'

At the end of the evening Somaia went round the tables to shake hands and say goodnight. He sought out Smith and suggested a meeting in the New Year to discuss the oil business in Kenya. He then gave him his business card with his north London home address. Nothing came of it but they continued to keep in touch. So did Tipping. He continued to talk about Somaia in terms of oil and had meetings with him in London in late 1992. However, their relationship fizzled out and in July 1993, Steve Tipping telephoned Gary Smith: 'I have just spoken to Somaia, but he's not as hungry as he used to be.'

Despite his lack of success in Africa, Thatcher remained fascinated by the world's most valuable natural resource, especially aviation fuel. 'Mark is now into the oil business,' said Tipping in 1993. 'He calls it the stuff that goes into aircraft.' But for many years he did not have a commercial outlet for his ambitions.

The opportunity arrived fortuitously in the autumn of 1992, when Ameristar Fuels Corporation, which specialised in the sale of jet fuel, began looking for new investment. Founded in June 1990 by two enterprising Texans – Jay Laughlin, president, and Jim Swieter, vice-president and company secretary – Ameristar had a winning formula.

It provided a special facility by buying, distributing and selling fuel direct to airlines, charter firms and private pilots on a tax-exempt basis in North America. There was also a division which marketed petroleum to non-airline customers in South America.

It was a simple operation. Clients and customers simply presented their Ameristar card at the airport and were then able to buy the fuel at fixed prices. This undercut established outlets like Esso, BP and Shell, and turnover soared. Initially, the company operated as a 30 per cent partner in a joint venture with a competitor. After May 1992, Ameristar was successful enough to go independent and was financially flying with profits of £4 million a year.

For the 40-year-old Laughlin, a pilot and former commodities trader, it was a dream come true. Now he wanted to expand. That meant substantial extra investment and his deputy, Jim Swieter, believed he had the answer. He was friendly with David Wallace, a hungry, ambitious 32-year-old Texan, who was a junior partner in Mark Thatcher's Grantham Company and treasurer of the US Thatcher Foundation, set up by the former prime minister to promote her philosophy. When approached by Swieter, Wallace replied that he could facilitate the capital required through his associate, the son of the British prime minister.

A meeting was arranged, and in September 1992 Laughlin and Swieter flew to London. They stayed at the Number Sixteen Hotel on Sumner Place, South Kensington, where Thatcher booked in a number of business guests. The negotiations took place at his £2 million house at Tregunter Road, off The Boltons, and the Thatchers were generous hosts. They took the Texans out to dinner at their favourite restaurant, Formula Veneta in Hollywood Road, a 300-yard walk away. Laughlin and his girlfriend were also escorted to Ascot and Mark flew the Texan in his own helicopter to the Farnborough air show in Hampshire.

Although the trip went well, Ameristar's founder was in no hurry to agree terms that would bring extra capital into his company but also reduce his control. He owned 50 per cent of the shares and wanted time to think about it. But Thatcher was impatient and wanted him to sign a letter of intent quickly. When the Texan said he wanted more time to consider the proposals, Mark lost his temper. On the morning of 17 October 1992, in the garage connected to Ameristar's office in San Felipe, Houston, Laughlin repeated his request for more time. 'You'll sign now or there won't be a bloody deal,' Mark shouted, in a manner reminiscent of the Nigerian negotiations. 'Well, you can get in your little red rowing boat and row all the way back to England,' Laughlin shouted back. 'It didn't bother me,' he recalled later, 'but I was kind of surprised at [Mark's] manner.'[6]

Despite Thatcher's outburst, that afternoon the Texan partly agreed to his demand and a Management Agreement was signed between the Grantham Company and Ameristar Fuels Inc. The deal was for Grantham (Thatcher and Wallace) to provide 'financial services' for a fee of $16,000 a month plus expenses for 18 months.

Three months later, in January 1993, the investment agreement materialised. The deal was that Wallace provided capital of $500,000 on a certified deposit. This money came from Diversified Capital Ltd, one of Thatcher's offshore companies in Jersey overseen by his banker, Hugh Thurston, and his accountant, Leonard Day. The $500,000 was placed with the South-West Bank of Texas in Houston – as collateral for a loan, also of $500,000 – by Wallace, who acted as a 'messenger' for Thatcher's offshore firm. In return, Wallace acquired 20 per cent of Ameristar's stock, with an option for an additional 13 per cent if he brought in extra investment. He was also given control of the company's financial and accounting affairs.

Officially, Mark Thatcher did not hold any executive or corporate position in Ameristar. Rather bizarrely, a company spokesperson said he 'has never been involved with Ameristar as employee, director, shareholder, investor, anything'.[7] Yet Mark moved his Grantham Company from Dallas to their office at the Texas Commerce Tower on San Felipe Drive in Houston. His own personal office was right next to Laughlin's. To cement the connection, Grantham, whose plaque was placed alongside Ameristar's in the foyer, received the agreed $16,000 a month in management fees from the aviation fuel firm.[8] More significantly, the $500,000 investment capital was Thatcher's money. It came from Jersey and was channelled through Grantham. Effectively, Grantham played an active role in running the prosperous jet-fuel corporation and Mark was the senior partner. Wallace was simply a front man.

Laughlin certainly saw Thatcher as his partner, particularly as he attended board meetings. Mark was particularly energetic in trying to secure new business – with mixed fortunes. He went with some Chinese-American businessmen to Puerto Rico to buy an oil refinery. But there were environmental problems. He lobbied the Bahamas government for the contract to supply fuel to Nassau airport. But when prime minister Lynden Pindling lost the election, that failed.

In February 1993, Thatcher and Wallace travelled to Almaty, capital of Kazakhstan, to start up an air charter operation for the Kazakh oil industry. Before he set off, Mark said in the Ameristar office, in Laughlin's presence, that British Petroleum 'would help because my mother was owed favours by BP and the Russian [i.e. the former Soviet] government'. This materialised later that year when Lady Thatcher visited Kazakhstan and met President Nazarbayev. Her office confirmed the trip but said it was merely 'a stopover' and she met the president, a devoted Thatcherite, while her plane was refuelling. 'I agree with everything he [Nazarbayev] is doing,' said Lady Thatcher.

The Far East proved more encouraging. Mark targeted Indonesia because for some years he had cultivated close links with the family of President Suharto, who run the country. He is especially friendly with the president's son, who is a keen motor-racing fan. It helped that General Suharto was an admirer of Margaret Thatcher, whose government had sold his regime ground-attack aircraft and other weapons. In 1992, she was presented with an award from Indonesia for 'helping technology'. She replied, 'I am proud to be one of you.'[9]

Mark Thatcher's former business partner, Steve Tipping, had also been busy in Jakarta, the capital. 'Indonesia is big, man, big,' he said in 1993. He said the prospects for making money there are 'endless' because the country would become a net importer of oil in the year 2000. 'With our Middle East connections,' Tipping remarked, 'there should be a few shekels in it for us.'

However, Ameristar's office in Jakarta was more interested in providing charter aircraft to transport Muslims on the annual pilgrimage to Mecca. 'About three to five million people go to Mecca, and Garuda [Indonesia's state airline] does not have enough planes to bring them all,' said Anton Mandagi, the office administrator, in 1994. 'They are negotiating for Mark to supply planes to bring them all but we haven't got the answer yet.'[10]

Across the Indian Ocean in Malaysia, Ameristar International was also able to reap the benefits of Mrs Thatcher's legacy. In 1993, the company, based at Gatwick airport, secured a lucrative deal to distribute fuel to planes that land in Malaysia, supplied by Petronas, the country's state-owned oil corporation.[11]

As 1993 unfolded, the company was prospering. Gross sales amounted to $200 million a year, notably a lucrative fuel supply contract with Southwest Airlines. By the autumn, Mark Thatcher had become almost totally preoccupied by Ameristar. He had always been fascinated by aviation and it was now all-consuming. Privately, he began to view and even talk about it as 'his company'. For the first time, he believed he was in a position to build, manage and expand his own business, just as his father had done. After the failure of Monteagle Marketing Ltd in the mid-1980s, this was always his ambition. For all his millions, he wanted something tangible to show for all the years of 'brokering deals' and playing the middleman. But there was just one irritating snag: Ameristar did not belong to him. He was not even a director or shareholder. And its founder was not going to give it up easily.

The consequence, claimed Jay Laughlin, Ameristar's president, was that Mark and Wallace masterminded a carefully orchestrated operation to oust him. Their strategy, alleged Laughlin, was 'to suppress the actual state of the Ameristar entities' and engineer a cash crisis as a way of acquiring more of the shares.[12]

In September 1993, the Grantham duo informed Laughlin that outside capital investment was required to expand the company and increase profit margins. They claimed they could raise $10 million themselves. Their scheme was for the investment to be structured in the form of a 'limited partnership'. Controlled by Grantham, the various investors would be the limited partners. The partnership's principal asset would be a five-year senior secured-term loan note, as well as 25 per cent of Ameristar's equity. The prospectus, put together by Thatcher and Wallace, concluded: 'Having consideration to the [Ameristar] Group's sales and profit forecasts, the value of the warrants attached to the $10 million offering would provide prospective returns of greater than 30 per cent in the event of the Group accomplishing a public listing at very conservative multiples.'

Wallace and Thatcher immediately approached 23 potential investors in the USA, UK, Switzerland and Germany – bankers, fund managers, and even Wallace's own law firm, Akin, Gump, Hauer and Feld in Dallas, Texas. Others were asked on the basis that they might secure the capital on behalf of Grantham. Dmitry Bosky of MITRA Private Equity Ltd, based in Paradise Walk, Chelsea, was told by Wallace, 'As always, we will gladly discuss a fee arrangement and/or carried interest in this investment should you be able to arrange funding.'

An old favourite was also solicited 'to discuss a strategy for moving forward'. This was Steve Tipping. On 12 October 1993, he had dinner with David Wallace and their discussion clearly indicated that Tipping had retained his connections with his old friend. After the meal, Wallace wrote to his predecessor 'to describe several ways in which I think you could assist the company'. He added: 'The commission agreements presently in place generally provide for a percentage of the gross profit secured as to each particular transaction.' One of the sectors in which Tipping was asked to assist was privatisation of the jet-fuel divisions of state oil companies. 'We would have an interest in looking at their airport refuelling operations,' said Wallace. 'This would need to include the negotiation of long-term supply contracts and would generally depend on other competitive market forces at the airport.'

Mark Thatcher was equally engaged in the fundraising for the $10 million. In early November 1993, he was in Geneva on business and approached Claude Jourda of Aeroleasing for a half-hour meeting 'to explain the investment in greater detail'. He also approached Charles Wick, who was director of the US Information Agency under President Reagan throughout the 1980s.

As it turned out, only $1.25 million materialised. But Laughlin had agreed, on the basis of the proposed new investment, to reduce his stake to 25 per cent in return for the equity input. This enabled Wallace to secure a 50 per cent controlling shareholding. 'Having successfully reduced my share of ownership in the Ameristar entities,' Laughlin later stated in a legal petition, 'Wallace and Swieter [his former partner], along with others, concocted a scheme to freeze me out altogether.'[13]

Wallace's next device was to merge the various parent firms and form a new separate holding company called Ameristar Consolidated Holdings Inc. He then informed their president that the entire stock of all the Ameristar firms would have to be transferred to this new entity. Laughlin was given until 31 December 1993 to sign documents agreeing to the new corporate structure. He requested that this proposal be modified to conform with the shareholder agreements and by-laws of the Ameristar companies. Wallace agreed to make the changes and amended the relevant company documents. But, according to Laughlin, the finalised executed papers were never delivered to him.

Instead, unknown to the Ameristar president, Wallace had been devising a plan for Mark Thatcher to be the kingpin and dominant force of this new corporate structure. On 23 November 1993, Wallace wrote to Grantham's tax lawyers, Simmons & Simmons, about 'the role that Mark Thatcher will play in the ongoing operation'. He advocated: 'It is contemplated that Ameristar Fuels will be wholly owned by a company for which Mark Thatcher will be the chairman. It is not contemplated that Mark will hold any officer duties or other responsibilities. From an ongoing level of activity, Mark Thatcher would assist in various marketing efforts for both international and South America.' In effect, this meant he would have a service contract to market their international operations.

Wallace added, 'There are various matters that could affect Mark Thatcher and I would appreciate your guidance.' He asked about any 'ramifications' for Mark as chairman or shareholder of a holding company which had an office at Gatwick airport. Also, what were the consequences if 'Mark Thatcher actively solicits business' or was involved in its daily activities? In other words, Wallace was enquiring about the tax implications of Mark Thatcher playing an executive role in Ameristar and being based at its British office.

On 1 December 1993, the lawyer for Simmons & Simmons, who specialises in tax avoidance and offshore trusts, replied that it depended on 'the extent to which Mark Thatcher will be working in the UK'. If his time spent on Ameristar business in the UK was 'negligible', then there was no problem. 'However, if it is envisaged that Mark Thatcher will either be working in the UK, or for the office in Gatwick or in general for the promotion of Ameristar Fuels in the UK – then I would be concerned.'

Judgement day for Jay Laughlin came on 17 January 1994, the day of the Los Angeles earthquake. A board meeting was called at the office of law firm Fouts and Moore in Houston, ostensibly to discuss pending litigation. What transpired was somewhat different. When Ameristar's founder arrived for the meeting, he was abruptly informed of his removal as an officer and employee. Shell-shocked and stunned by the manoeuvre, Laughlin immediately drove back to his office on San Felipe Drive, anxious to collect his papers, which he believed would prove that the company had effectively been stolen from him.

However, as he was searching through his filing cabinet, two heavily built men burst through his office door. One was Mike Winton, a former British police officer and Mark Thatcher's personal bodyguard, or 'special assistant', as he describes himself. The other was Jay H. Olszewski, an armed off-duty policeman, who was head of Houston's Criminal Intelligence Division (one of his duties was to guard visiting dignitaries like Lady Thatcher). 'Please do not touch any property and leave the building immediately, sir,' said Winton threateningly. 'Otherwise we will have no option but to arrest you for trespassing.'[14]

Within minutes, Ameristar's president and founding father was taken away from his corporate baby and life's work. Laughlin had no choice and was escorted from the premises. He could scarcely believe it and was devastated as he drove home. 'This company was my hopes and my dreams,' he said later.[15]

Wallace argues that he had set up the new holding corporation to make a legitimate offer of $2 million to Ameristar's president to buy him out. 'The purpose of the merger company,' he said later, 'was to give Jay Laughlin his fair value for the stock.'[16]

In Laughlin's view, this was a miserly offer for a company which was valued at $20 million. He claimed Wallace, fronting for Thatcher, hijacked his company. So he decided to fight back. In June 1994, he filed a lawsuit alleging that Wallace and Swieter, using Thatcher's money, 'fraudulently induced him to transfer his entire stock in the various entities to the holding company'.[17] The writ also claimed that there was a breach of their 'fiduciary obligations of trust and care to the shareholders' to make 'all required disclosures' in the management of Ameristar's affairs. It concluded by alleging that 'the defendants fraudulently, maliciously and intentionally converted the assets of the Ameristar entities to their own personal use and benefit'.[18] Wallace countered that Laughlin was removed because he 'inadequately performed various management duties'.[19]

As part of the case, a subpoena was issued for Mark Thatcher to supply a deposition on the details of his wealth and business transactions, including a videotaped sworn statement. Publicly, he was unruffled and denied all the claims. 'He needs to be very careful what he's alleging,' he said. 'Mr Laughlin or anybody else can allege whatever they want.'[20]

But underneath the bravado, Thatcher was very worried. According to Laughlin, in July 1994, he received a telephone call from his former partner. 'He told me that if I put the Thatcher name on trial, he would bring all the power he could raise and go for me,' recalled the Texan. 'He also said that his father, Denis, was upset about the situation.' When asked by the *Today* newspaper about this conversation, Mark replied, 'Poppycock! That is totally untrue. It is fallacious. I mean, I wouldn't ring up and threaten Jay – good God. Why would I want to do it? I categorically deny it. That is exactly the sort of thing that Jay would do. God!'[21]

Whatever the truth about what was said on the telephone, Mark was very nervous about what might emerge during the litigation. He faced the horrifying prospect of appearing as a witness in Houston

County Court. Even worse, the proceedings would be recorded by video camera.

But then, just three weeks before the court case, Ameristar filed for Chapter 11 bankruptcy, which protected it from over 100 creditors, including Mobil and Shell, who were owed £12 million. Under American bankruptcy laws, Ameristar was allowed to continue to trade and operate. But it was obliged to make provision to pay off its debts. In one swift manoeuvre, the lawsuit was scuttled. With it sank any chance of Mark Thatcher's being cross-examined for the first time about the mystery of how he acquired his millions.

For Jay Laughlin, it was a devastating blow. 'The news of the bankruptcy sickened me,' he said. 'It was even worse because I heard it in a telephonic meeting of directors. Wallace just announced it. He then said, "Have a nice day, gentlemen," and hung up. It was all over in 30 seconds. This is a company that was my whole life. I built it up over four years and put all my money into it. When I left it, it was in a profitable state and the bankruptcy petition only makes me more determined to win it back.'[22]

Mark was delighted by this outcome and promised to stand by Wallace, who had effectively taken a fall for him. 'Because David is in difficulty doesn't mean that I or anybody else is going to run for the lifeboats,' he said. 'On the contrary, I am going to do everything I can to show that I'm supporting him personally – as a friend.'[23] It was more than personal, of course. Wallace's dependence on Thatcher was such that even his own house – 3318 Alcorn Crossing, Sugarlands, Texas – was owned by Diversified Capital, a Jersey-based company controlled by Hugh Thurston, Thatcher's banker, and Leonard Day, his accountant.

However, if Thatcher thought he had disposed of the Laughlin problem, he was very much mistaken. His former business partner continued to claim that his company had, in effect, been stolen from him. The dream of the prime minister's son to run his own business and emulate his father had turned sour.

Despite the failure of Ameristar, the lure of black gold was too enticing for Mark Thatcher. In the early 1990s, he was tipped off about the big money to be made in Azerbaijan, the former Soviet republic on the shore of the Caspian Sea. To the north lies Chechnya and to the south is Iran. A hotbed of intrigue, terrorism and coups d'état, Azerbaijan is regarded as the next oil-boom Eldorado. For traders, the stakes are high and the winnings are potentially enormous. Oil profits have been estimated at anything between $20 billion and $90 billion over 30 years from the mid-1990s, based on its vast reserves.

Known as 'The Kuwait of the Caspian', BP was quick to exploit Azerbaijan's potential and in 1992 began negotiations for exploration rights. But progress was slow and so the company enlisted Lady Thatcher to lobby on their behalf. On 7 September 1992, she stopped at the capital Baku during a flight from Hong Kong to London and met President Elchibey. During her visit, the former premier 'batted for Britain' on behalf of BP, according to her office. Eventually, in 1994, the foreign oil companies, led by BP, signed a $8 billion contract for drilling rights. Her son was fully aware of her involvement and implied that he played a part. 'We won the deal of the century for Britain,' he later bragged to his motor racing friends at a Grand Prix. 'No one knows what *we've* achieved for the country [his emphasis].'[24]

Captivated by its entrepreneurial new frontier energy and dark mystery, Mark Thatcher began visiting Azerbaijan regularly. During 1994 and 1995, he flew in once a month and stayed at the newly opened Hyatt Regency Hotel. Baku is very much his kind of town. In the early 1990s, it was invaded by shady arms dealers with bodyguards, commercial dilettantes with velvet-collared coats and oil traders with their wily interpreters – all looking to cash in on the oil boom and the reconstruction contracts fuelled by the petro-dollars. The streets were dominated by convoys of Rolls-Royces and Range Rovers cruising past the decrepit Stalinist buildings of a fallen empire. A new kind of robber baron had arrived. As the writer Simon Sebag Montefiore observed after a visit to Baku in 1995: 'In the British pubs and American sports bars, suits from Dallas and roustabouts from Louisiana and Scotland pull hookers and play cards. In the business clubs and restaurants and at the new Hyatt Regency Hotel, Russian agents, Iranian mullahs and Swiss bankers negotiate for their share of untold riches while spies plot coups. Baku and central Asia were once prizes in Victorian Britain's duel with Russia for the route to our Indian empire: this was the Great Game. A century later, we are again leading players in the Great Game, this time for the profit and power of oil.

'That spirit of swashbuckling adventure – and comic opera absurdity – was captured by George Macdonald Fraser in his classic best-selling novel *Flashman in the Great Game* which starred Flashman, the anti-hero of *Tom Brown's Schooldays*.'[25]

Just as Mark Thatcher's role in the attempted coup in Equatorial Guinea reminded his friends of the Tom Sharpe novels, so his presence in Baku invoked the spirit of nineteenth-century commercial turbulence and intrigue. In 1994, he opened a bank account and set up an office at the high-security apartment of Faina Miller, a tough 36-year-old Russian with an American passport, on Sheikh Shamil Street, where it is believed the CIA station chief also had a flat. The interior decor was a cross between a wealthy Azerbaijan national and 1970s functionalism, dominated by gilded Soviet furniture, state-of-the-art computers, orange sofas and a shiny boardroom table. Outside was a Range Rover which Thatcher used whenever he was in town.

The inhabitant, Faina Miller, was Mark's business partner in Azerbaijan. Together they ran Newbury International, an offshore company registered in the Isle of Man which was also used by Thatcher to buy his helicopter. Smartly dressed, but aggressive and described as being 'savagely rude' by one visitor, Miller never leaves her house without armed bodyguards or her fierce dog. Her apartment block was beset by gangland shootings and in October 1994 the deputy speaker of the Azerbaijan parliament was shot dead outside the complex.[26] When asked by Sebag-Montefiore about her commercial interests, Miller replied in an Americanised Russian accent, 'I don't speak to journalists. My business is secret.'[27]

But documents filed in Baku show that Miller, Thatcher and his business associate Graham Lorimer had an authority to act on behalf of Newbury International. Lorimer, a New Zealander, is an old friend who has partnered Thatcher in his rally driving and later worked closely with him on a deal to sell diesel fuel and gold to Zimbabwe. Business cards with Lorimer's name prominently displayed were printed and in early 1994 contacts were cultivated and trading began.

Thatcher was close to Natik Aliyev, head of the state-owned oil company; Rasul Guliev, the parliamentary speaker; and the director of Wahid bank, the largest private bank in Azerbaijan. Using a £30,000 loan facility granted by the president of the association of independent banks of Azerbaijan, Dr Yavuz Javadov of Azcom Bank, Thatcher clinched a deal to supply high-quality paper for security documents. But he failed to secure far more lucrative contracts to import computers and food and to print Azuri currency, share certificates and passports.

The son of the former prime minister found central Asia a more troublesome and complex political and commercial river to navigate. In the Middle East and Africa, he knew how to exploit the ruling dynasties and elites, but in the former Soviet republics closing deals was more intricate and convoluted. Barely four years after the end of the Cold War, the trading culture in Azerbaijan was more secretive, aggressive and crude, and business was conducted in an atmosphere of intrigue and skulduggery.

Fascinated by the enormous potential of Azerbaijan, Thatcher persevered and Lorimer said they were there 'for the long haul'. But the flood of lawsuits and tax investigations in the USA impeded their progress and South Africa became a more attractive country in which to live and invest Thatcher's fortune.

By 1988, Thatcher's opulent lifestyle began to provide clues as to the size of the treasure we have been hunting. He had always sought and craved the high life. Only now did he possess the money to pay for it. He was living in a plush £1.3 million house in exclusive Belgravia. He was travelling extensively, sometimes chartering private jets, and staying in the most expensive hotels. Suddenly he was seen lunching at Harry's Bar, dining at Mirabelle, drinking at the Connaught Hotel. Driving a black Porsche Carrera, Mark wore a gold Rolex watch, took holidays on the Riviera and drank vintage champagne. He even retained a personal tailor, Dimmy Major, whom he shared with the comedian Ronnie Corbett.

At weekends, he was visiting wealthy friends – shooting with Wafic Said or sailing with Sir David Gosling, chairman of National Car Parks, or a guest on the yacht of millionaire publisher Malcolm Forbes. Even at Chequers, the prime minister's son was noticeably star-struck by his mother's favourite tycoons. At one lunch for captains of industry, he continually muscled in on conversations, repeating things like, 'Gosh, $2 million.' This annoyed one of the guests, Alan Clark, then a trade and industry minister and a close friend and admirer of Margaret Thatcher. 'I got a bit sick of this,' he recorded in his diaries, 'and said, "That's not much" (which it isn't), but people affected not to hear.'[28]

Mark clearly saw himself as part of the new entrepreneurial Thatcherite jet-set, above and beyond ordinary people. 'I remember having lunch with him at the Dorchester Hotel,' said the financier Brian McHugo, who met him in 1988. 'I remember it because Mark had to sit at a particular angle so that his bodyguard could see him. Also he kept using the phrase "the great unwashed", which he said quite often. It was not said in jest and was not an expression I liked.'[29]

The most ostentatious symbol of Mark's new-found wealth was his hiring, in the summer of 1989, of a personal valet, Graham Henderson. Recruited in Texas, where such menservants can command salaries of up to £50,000 a year, Henderson waited on Mark, laid out his clothes, loaded his shotgun at shooting parties and flew with him during trips on a private jet.

When Mark stayed at the luxurious Claridge's Hotel later that year, the staff had to make special arrangements for his valet. This was a curious request as Claridge's is, of course, hardly the sort of place where a guest might need a valet. But Thatcher was insistent. While he moved into his £390-a-night suite, Henderson was dispatched to the servants' quarters for a mere £25 a night.[30] At dinner, fellow guests even saw his butler, rather than the waiters, serve him. This so embarrassed the *maitre d'hôtel* that he arranged for Thatcher to be seated in the restaurant's alcove, slightly hidden away. Those who saw them together say Mark treated his servant 'firmly but well, rather like an officer would treat a batman in the Army'.[31]

Later that year, in October 1990, Margaret Thatcher's son bought perhaps the most visible symbol of his fortune – a four-storey house in The Boltons in Kensington, one of the most exclusive residential areas of London. Among his neighbours are members of the Saudi royal family, the prime minister of Bahrain and the Sultan of Brunei. Many were astonished that he could afford to buy the £2.1 million property at 1 Tregunter Road from the financier Peter de Savary. 'If you can find out how he can afford a house in The Boltons, let me know,' said his sister, Carol.[32]

Semi-detached, with a double garage and a separate granny flat, the house was most notable for its extraordinarily elaborate security system. Visitors were greeted by two security cameras – one on the gate and another above the front door – with a video remote-control entry system. Just in case anyone escaped the surveillance, another camera was placed above the back door, marked 'Tradesmen's Entrance'. Mark also inserted bomb-proof windows, steel shutters and blast-resistant curtains. 'He was worried that he might be a terrorist target and he showed me the new security system he had installed,' said Jay Laughlin, his former business associate. 'He pushed a button and a metal grille came down over the windows to guard against a rocket attack.'[33] According to one regular guest, the house was 'climate-controlled' and 'bugged and monitored for sound'.

Once inside, visitors see a marble-floored entrance lobby. Off to the right is a 28 ft by 14 ft drawing-room with marble mantel and hearth and thick bottle-green carpets. The walls are hung with silk, with the dining-room featuring a mural by P.M. Rudelle. There are four air-conditioned bedroom suites and three reception rooms, and one of the bathrooms is complete with more marble, murals and gold taps. Outside there is a 140 ft garden. To accommodate his valet, there are separate servants' quarters with a housekeeper's flat. 'The staff are all locked away in the basement, which is jolly useful if you want to have an argument with your wife in the drawing-room upstairs,' said Andy Buchanan, the estate agent who handled the sale.[34]

Mark Thatcher spent £600,000 on 'improvements', notably the security devices, a Texas-style conservatory, a chiller unit in the garden, mahogany joinery in the drawing-room and a special television set that rises out of a box at the foot of the bed in the master bedroom. The house is dominated by gold and marble and was sold in 1997 after his move to South Africa.

The acquisition of 1 Tregunter Road in October 1990 was a sure sign that Mark Thatcher was by then a rich man. But the purchase of the property provided clues not just about the value of Thatcher's gold, but also the way the treasure has been handled.

The house was bought by Eastcoast Investments Ltd, an offshore company set up in January 1990 and registered in Jersey. The shares are jointly owned by Hugh Thurston, Thatcher's banker, and Leonard Day and his wife, Margery. Household bills, even Mark's poll tax, were paid using this Channel Island firm.

The ownership of his UK house by an offshore company highlighted Mark Thatcher's delicate and precarious relationship with the international tax authorities. His long years in Texas enabled him to secure non-residency status from the UK Inland Revenue. For most people that means they can spend only a stipulated, limited, number of days a year in Britain. It also requires that the individual does not own a UK property. Anyone found to have contravened either of those rules is liable to pay tax on his or her worldwide income.

As Thatcher owned a UK property and was spending several days a year in London, there was clearly a case that he was resident for tax purposes. This factor, plus his offshore companies and bank accounts, naturally brought him under the scrutiny of the Inland Revenue. He was petrified that he would have to pay tax at the top rate. Fortunately for him, the Revenue inquiry concluded that he would be exempt. In 1990, the prime minister's son received a certificate of clearance stating that for the previous six years he had been non-resident in the UK for tax purposes, because of his offshore status. Mark was delighted and promptly threw a champagne party at the Dorchester Hotel in Mayfair to celebrate. Thatcher's gold was safe – for the time being, anyway.

TEN

A Family Business

If Margaret Thatcher had a motto on her desk, it would have read 'No Cheques Accepted'.
– Paul Johnson, Historian and conservative columnist[1]

During the dramatic palace coup d'état which dethroned his mother as prime minister, Mark stayed at Chequers and, together with Carol, was a source of great emotional support for his mother. He attended the dinner given there, on Saturday, 17 November 1990, for her closest confidants – Sir Tim Bell, Sir Gordon Reece and Lord McAlpine – together with her campaign team.[2] It was a crucial summit meeting and, unfortunately for her, the atmosphere reeked of complacency. Mark was never a political animal and wisely steered clear of advising her on election tactics.

However, he was surprised by his mother's resignation. For during the tense and traumatic atmosphere following the first ballot – in the early hours of Wednesday, 21 November – he was on a flight home to Texas to take care of a business deal. The previous evening Mark had dinner at Buck's Club in Clifford Street, Piccadilly, with his father, who was despondent after the first ballot. Margaret Thatcher had secured a slim majority and announced she would stand in the second ballot but was facing certain defeat. 'We've had it,' said Denis. 'We're out.' His son tried his best to be upbeat. 'Don't worry, she'll win the next round,' he said.[3]

As soon as he landed at Dallas airport, Mark Thatcher telephoned London and was told her support was wavering. He immediately caught an American Airlines DC10 and flew back to Heathrow, possibly setting new records for transatlantic travel. When he arrived at 10 Downing Street later that day, his mother was incredibly busy but upset, confused and in disarray. She was shocked by what she saw as a calculated betrayal by her once-loyal cabinet ministers. 'It was treachery with a smile on its face,' she later remarked.[4] Mark comforted her and spent time with her. Even his many enemies conceded that he behaved with great care and compassion. That evening, he dined with Denis, Carol and Lord McAlpine at Mark's Club in Mayfair and, over large quantities of champagne, they did their best to look cheerful. But outside on Horse Guards' Parade, Denis, despite imploring his wife not to stand in the second ballot, could not restrain himself any more. He hugged Carol and cried, 'Oh, it's just the disloyalty of it all.'[5]

During his mother's final days in 10 Downing Street, Mark's mood changed from sadness to anger. When asked how she was spending her time, he snapped, 'She's doing what she always does on a Friday – running the country.'[6] His rage was barely concealed the following Wednesday morning when Mrs Thatcher finally left office. Mark was beside her in 10 Downing Street as she said a tearful farewell to her private staff. He then ushered her outside to read a short statement to the media. As he waited to drive her away, a cameraman noticed how Mark glared and glowered across at the journalists and photographers. It was as if he blamed the newspapers and television for his mother's dramatic downfall.

Mark's former business partner, Steve Tipping, was also in 10 Downing Street on that last day in office. He looked on, stunned and shocked, as the removal vans arrived to collect the Thatchers' possessions. He was upset at the prime minister's demise. This was partly because he was a genuine Thatcherite but also because he felt her policies benefited big business.

Tipping made his feelings clear the following Wednesday, 5 December 1990, when he attended a reception in the ballroom on the first floor of the London Hilton Hotel, Park Lane, Mayfair. It was on behalf of Dolphin Promotions Ltd, a trading company run by Ketan Somaia, the Kenyan businessman with close connections to President Moi and Mark Thatcher. Tipping was very depressed as he sat with Haji Hassan, a banker who worked with him in Malaysia, and other business associates, mainly Kenyan Asians. 'I've had a terrible week,' Tipping told the other guests. 'I've been sinking gin and tonics with Denis Thatcher.' 'Who was to blame for her downfall?' a guest asked. 'It was a Taffy Mafia that brought her down,' he replied, 'but at least

Heseltine didn't get the leadership, so it worked out well in the end. Major is one of us.' According to Gary Smith, the international oil trader, who was present, 'Mark and Steve were naturally unhappy about Mrs Thatcher leaving office but they felt Major was a satisfactory choice because it preserved the status quo.'[7]

Tipping and some of the other guests then retired to Trader Vic's bar downstairs. Once they had sat down with their drinks, Thatcher's former business partner became more reflective. 'I suppose we've got to admit we've all done well out of the Thatcher government,' he said. 'We've made our pile of money, so we can't complain too much. But things are going to be more difficult from now on. I suppose we're better off with Major than Heseltine.'

After leaving Downing Street, the Thatchers reluctantly drove to their neo-Georgian south London home at Hambledon Place, Dulwich, built by Barratt. They hated living there, mainly because it was so far from Westminster. 'A widow's house,' as Denis aptly described it, unsuitable for a woman cut off in her prime. Even the local political landscape was an eyesore to him. 'The disadvantage, and I shouldn't say this, is that it falls into the communist "whatnot" of Southwark,' he remarked.[8]

It was not long before the couple put the property on the market and eventually it was bought by Edward Nassar, a Swiss-based businessman, for £595,000 – £85,000 less than the original asking price. Nassar knew Mark Thatcher because both had commercial interests in Lausanne but was not keen to talk to us. 'I don't think it helps very much what you are doing,' he said from his office in Switzerland.

In the meantime, the Thatchers moved into an apartment in Belgravia's Eaton Square lent to them by Kathleen Ford, the widow of Henry Ford II, and looked around for a new home. Mark decided that he would be his mother's estate agent. But an early suggestion was not warmly greeted – a £7.5 million house in Tite Street, Chelsea, built by Lord Glenconner. His idea was that a grateful and adoring businessman would buy the property and lease it back to her at a favourable rent. Denis was comfortably off but Margaret would receive only an allowance of £59,600 a year and a £25,600 annual pension. Even with her projected earnings from lecture tours and memoirs, it was way out of their price range. More significantly, such a sweetheart deal would look like a pay-off to the former prime minister. But her son, unruffled, escorted his parents around the Tite

Street house, complaining loudly that the government had not done enough to help his mother adjust to life outside 10 Downing Street. The family then offered £6 million, but was £1,500,000 short of the asking price.

Carol Thatcher was furious about the idea and saw it as a futile expedition. 'When I heard about Tite Street, I knew it was a ridiculous amount of money,' she said.[9] Lord McAlpine, former Tory Party treasurer and a close friend of the Thatcher family, was more charitable and diplomatic. 'Mark's not a politician,' he said. 'He doesn't understand these things. Whatever Mark may have done was with the best intentions.'[10]

A more suitable property soon became available in the form of 73 Chester Square, Belgravia, two doors down from Tiny Rowland. It was owned by Sir David and Frederick Barclay, the secretive millionaire twins based in Monte Carlo who had made their fortunes during the Thatcher years. They offered the five-storeyed terraced house to the former prime minister for £700,000. The deal was arranged through the good offices of Sir Tim Bell, her long-time media adviser and confidant. But when her son was informed, he reacted petulantly. 'He told Tim that he wasn't going to have a couple of businessmen just walk in and buy up his mother like that,' said a Thatcher family friend. 'He implied that the Barclays were not fit to open the door of her Daimler. He was pretty offensive.'[11]

After Mark Thatcher's intervention, the property was sold to another buyer. But Bell was convinced this was the ideal home for the former prime minister. So a few weeks later he arranged for her to be shown the exterior as she was being driven through Belgravia. She liked it and, despite Mark's objections, asked the Barclay brothers to reconsider. They agreed, bought back the house, and in April 1991 sold it to the Thatchers for the original price on a ten-year lease with favourable terms.

Finding an office was equally difficult. At first, she set up camp at 27 Great College Street, Westminster, a seventeenth-century house kindly lent to her by its owner, Lord McAlpine. That was converted into a temporary base while Mark again played estate agent. One of the candidates was the head office of Sale Tilney plc, a mini-conglomerate, in Queen's Gate, Kensington, whose lease was up for sale. One day Dorothy Wyndham-Lewis, personal assistant to the chairman, was told that a VIP would be arriving to inspect the premises. 'Keep it under your hat,' said the estate agent.

The VIP turned out to be Mark Thatcher, who arrived with a

bodyguard and was shown into the boardroom. Sale Tilney's chairman then walked into the room to greet his visitor. Mark looked him up and down, readjusted his huge cufflinks and asked: 'And *who* are you?' [his emphasis]. Stunned by such impertinence, the businessman replied he was in fact the chairman and chief executive. He then escorted Thatcher up to the executive office, which overlooked Horse Guards Parade and St James's Park. 'You have a wonderful view,' he said. 'We used to be at Number 10, you know.' After inspecting the rest of the premises, Mark left.

Two days later, a black limousine drew up outside the office and two burly bodyguards stepped out, followed by a pale, weary-looking Margaret Thatcher, her son and an estate agent. The former prime minister, with Mark trailing sheepishly behind her, was given the same tour. She was impressed by the premises but decided against them and looked elsewhere. Eventually she moved into 35 Chesham Place, Belgravia, just across the road from the German embassy. Lady Thatcher rented the building from Chelsfield, a property company owned by Elliott Bernerd, and from Olayan, a Saudi Arabian investment institution, until 2000.

The choice of office for Denis Thatcher proved to be far more controversial. He moved into a suite at Westminster Palace Gardens, Artillery Row, near the House of Commons, on a part-time basis. Private decorators were hired to refurbish, decorate and repaint the office. The new furniture was 'worth thousands of pounds,' according to one of the contractors. But the Thatchers did not pay for any of the extensive renovation. The bills were paid by Ready Mixed Concrete (RMC) plc, which also covered Denis Thatcher's phone bill for the first two years and even his whisky glasses from Harrods. The payments were made by a Swiss subsidiary called Pelmark Project Management Services, under the supervision of Diane Camden, wife of John Camden, then company chairman. She said the work was done as a mark of respect for the Thatchers who they 'loved dearly' and RMC plc regarded the refurbishment as a gift. 'The company was quite proud to pay to help out the Thatchers when they had just been thrown out of office', said Diane Camden, a member of the North-West Surrey Conservative Association.

But the relatives of the 51 people who died on the *Marchioness* boat two years earlier were not so happy. In August 1989, the *Marchioness* was sunk on the Thames by the *Bowbelle*, a dredger owned by a RMC subsidiary. The families of the victims were angry because the Thatcher government consistently refused to hold a public inquiry into the disaster. In mid-1990 Cecil (now Lord) Parkinson, then transport secretary, consulted Margaret Thatcher and they refused to authorise the investigation. This was later confirmed by John Hayes QC in his report into the tragedy: 'The decision not to order an inquiry was taken at Number 10 Downing Street on advice from the Department of Transport, although earlier transport disasters on a similar scale had received a different response.'

Campaigners for the victims were furious because attention focused on what allegedly went wrong on the *Marchioness* rather than the *Bowbelle*. Within hours of the sinking, pro-Conservative newspapers were briefed that the cruise was a drugs party and in the wrong position on the river. The bereaved relatives claimed that there was a massive cover-up to protect RMC. The inquest, delayed until 1995, returned a verdict of unlawful killing – at odds with the official version. 'A lesson needs to be learned from the appalling manner in which the government has treated the Marchioness relatives,' said the solicitor for the families. 'The government cannot be relied upon to police itself.'

The bereaved alleged that the absence of a public inquiry was due to RMC's close links with the Thatcher government. From 1979 until the tragedy in August 1989, RMC plc had donated a total of £152,000 to the Conservative Party and one of its directors at the time, Sir Neil Macfarlane, was a senior Tory MP and former environment minister. More significantly, he was a close friend of the Thatchers, particularly Denis and had been his golfing partner for many years. And the benefits-in-kind worth thousands of pounds to the Thatchers so soon after leaving Number 10 gave the impression of a reward by RMC after they ratified the decision not to hold a public inquiry.

Lord Parkinson, who was transport secretary at the time, later said that he had decided not to hold a public inquiry because that was not the best way to establish the truth. 'Whether RMC had any connection with Mrs Thatcher or not, I wouldn't have known,' he said. 'What I decided was totally unconnected with that.'[12]

In the first two months of her exile, the atmosphere inside Lady Thatcher's new office was administrative chaos combined with the former premier trying to come to terms emotionally with losing power. The logistical problems were solved by hiring Andrew Bearpark, her capable former home affairs private secretary, as her chief of staff. But she also desperately needed sensible strategic advice if she was going to be a dignified world statesman and preserve her political strategy. The problem was that she was isolated and cut off from the trappings and levers of power. For the first few months, she relied on briefings from Sir Charles (now Lord) Powell, her devoted foreign affairs private secretary still at 10 Downing Street, but that stopped when he left government service.

The consequence of this vacuum was a private power struggle between Mark and Denis. 'They did not get on during this period,' recalled one of her closest aides. 'I was present when Mark was extremely rude to his father in front of Margaret, sometimes even in public, and she just sided with her son. Denis continued to give her emotional support but she turned to Mark to manage and organise her financial affairs and speaking programme.' When asked by *Vanity Fair* how her son was qualified to do this job, Mrs Thatcher replied angrily, 'Look, my children are not children any more. They know about life. I find he is one of the most businesslike people I deal with. You want something done, he does it quickly – there's no "Oh well, I'll do it tomorrow."'[13]

By late February 1991, Mark was running the Margaret Thatcher revue. For the first time in his life, his mother needed him – rather than the other way around – and he revelled in his new-found power and freedom of action. He became her aide-de-camp, financial adviser, literary and estate agent, tour operator, fundraiser and, it appeared, anything else that caught his fancy. One person he did consult was the international marketing agent Mark McCormack, who usually represents sports superstars. McCormack is the author of *What They Don't Teach You at Harvard Business School*, which contains the immortal Thatcherite advice, 'Never underestimate the importance of money.'[14] 'She [Lady Thatcher] certainly has complete and total confidence in Mark and that often outweighs a lot of alternatives,' said McCormack. 'He was speaking to us always on behalf of his mother . . . He decided he wanted to do different segments of her commercial activities with different groups of people. He was, as we say in America, the quarterback of the team, who plans the entire situation.'[15]

Mark's first act was to pour in some of his own private funds, acquired from contracts which his mother promoted and negotiated while she was prime minister. 'Now's the time to rally round and help Mummy,' he said, and paid nearly £1.5 million into her coffers. This was used for her initial expenses and also for the refurbishment and renovation of her new house in Chester Square. It later emerged that he had always planned to finance her later in life. 'We shall all have to help when she retires because she won't have much money,' he told her close friend Woodrow Wyatt in May 1989.[16]

A separate bank account was set up to handle the cheques that flooded in from big business. The early donations were for the Thatcher Foundation. This had been announced but as it did not yet formally exist the money was used, with the donors' permission, for running her office. Lord Hanson and Bruce Gyngell, the former chief executive of TV-AM, were among the early corporate backers who contributed some £250,000. Most of this money was used to pay staff salaries. Sir Michael Richardson, chairman of stockbrokers Smith New Court and a long-time confidant, became her unofficial financial adviser but it was Mark who controlled the Thatcher cheque book.

While her son looked after the money, Margaret Thatcher had grander designs. After the shock of her enforced abdication she decided to establish three lasting monuments to her political legacy – her memoirs, a foundation and a series of overseas lectures and speeches. This had the advantage of keeping alive the creed of Thatcherism and raising revenue. And Mark was a willing crown prince to the Empress Margaret to keep her legend alive – and prospering.

It was not long before Margaret Thatcher was off abroad. The trips were meant to be partly evangelical crusades for Thatcherism and partly fundraising for the stuttering Thatcher Foundation. Her beloved United States was to be a regular port of call, where she was greeted by ecstatic audiences. She was still worshipped there by conservatives, and there were plenty of willing congregations happy to pay handsomely for her ideological sermons.

Within a week of losing the premiership, she was approached by Harry Rhoads, head of the prestigious Washington Speakers Bureau, dangling untold riches on the international lecture circuit. He was in a position to do so, as his agency had just made former President Ronald Reagan the highest-paid speaker in the world. The previous year, Reagan had received a record $6 million fee for an eight-day speaking tour of Japan, although he later refused engagements unless they were less than an hour's flight from his California ranch.[17]

Margaret Thatcher was tempted but delayed her decision for two weeks until she had talked about the offer with her old friend Ronald Reagan. Over tea at Claridge's on the afternoon of 6 December 1990, the dethroned prime minister asked the former president and his wife,

Nancy, about the agency. They recommended acceptance, and the following month Thatcher signed an exclusive contract with the Washington Speakers Bureau. She charged $50,000 per lecture for a minimum of 30 minutes, plus another half-hour for a question-and-answer session. Then there was at least $5,000 for travel and hotel expenses for herself and her entourage. The fees were handled by her son, liaising with her full-time agent, Sandra Warfield.

Three weeks later, Margaret Thatcher flew to California on the private jet of Lodwrick M. Cook, chairman of the Atlantic Richfield Corporation (ARCO), for a week-long visit. After inspecting an ARCO oil refinery, she moved on to the principal reason for the trip, Ronald Reagan's 80th birthday party. Accompanied by Denis and Mark, she was the guest of honour at the Beverly Hills Hilton Hotel, Los Angeles. Among the friends and celebrities, paying £1,250 a head at dinner, were film stars, politicians and businessmen, notably media tycoons Rupert Murdoch and Barry Diller.

During their stay in California, Mark and Denis were entertained by Walter Annenberg, an old friend and former US ambassador to Britain. One morning Annenberg, one of America's wealthiest men and a great philanthropist, showed his guests his stunning new golf course on his Sunnylands Estate, specially designed by Jack Nicklaus. 'Well, what do you think?' he asked with undisguised pride. 'Marvellous,' replied Denis. 'Can't wait to get out there.' Mark, who plays an eight handicap to his father's sixteen, paused and then sniffed: 'Bit Mickey Mouse, isn't it?' He was not joking.[18] His comment has been confirmed by two other sources, both friends of the family.

The newly ennobled Lady Thatcher was the focus of celebration a month later on 7 March 1991, when she was awarded the Presidential Medal of Freedom at a special White House ceremony. President Bush praised the 'greengrocer's daughter who shaped a nation to her will'. The guests then retired to the president's private quarters for a lavish dinner party in her honour. Despite losing her crown, she was in her element. So was her son. Sitting next to Georgette Mosbacher, the flame-haired entrepreneur and wife of the then US commerce secretary, he held forth on his 'successful' business career and how he had 'made millions' in the home-security business. Mosbacher, no wilting flower, responded by describing how she had made her fortune in the cosmetics business. The two then sparred with each other for the rest of the evening about their respective commercial prowess.[19]

Lady Thatcher's next stop on her US tour was Mark's home town of Dallas. On 11 March 1991, she was the guest speaker at the annual meeting of the North Dallas Chamber of Commerce at the Loews Anatole Hotel. 'We sold out the biggest ballroom in Dallas and they loved her,' said Steve Taylor, president of the chamber. Arranged by Mark, 1,850 members and guests paid over $100,000 to hear her views on the Gulf war, crediting former defence secretary Caspar Weinberger and ex-US Senator John Tower with having 'kept our defences strong and our technology ahead of the others'.[20]

The Texas trip was, according to Taylor, 'a combination of business and pleasure'. That evening, a more intimate gathering assembled at the Mansion on Turtle Creek Hotel, where Lady Thatcher was staying at $1,000 a night. The 55 guests paid $5,000 each to dine with the former prime minister, raising $175,000 for the Chamber of Commerce. Mark negotiated her five-figure fee but only on the basis that her contract stipulated that the actual amount be kept confidential.

That event was hosted by Caroline Rose Hunt, the millionaire owner of the Mansion on Turtle Creek and the Lansborough in London, as head of the Rosewood Corporation. Before dinner, she hosted a drinks reception in the hotel's Pavilioni Room. All the guests were asked to wear name-tags. Mark Thatcher refused point-blank. 'If people don't know who I am by now, they never will,' he sniffed. Ironically, the truth was that much of Dallas society did *not* know who he was [our emphasis]. 'If Mark Thatcher walked into my office, I wouldn't recognise him,' said a local businessman.

Despite this act of petulance, Caroline Hunt was delighted with Lady Thatcher's appearance. She asked permission to be photographed with her, which was happily granted. So Hunt asked Wendy Strong, her PR consultant, to take a picture of herself and her honoured guest. Suddenly, just as Wendy clicked the instamatic camera, Mark pounced on her and yelled, 'You can't take pictures of my mother.' He then grabbed her left arm, dragged her away and tried to take the camera off her.

Mark looked around and there was an embarrassed silence. Lady Thatcher glared at him, stone-faced. Caroline Hunt looked away, mortified. Denis was also uncomfortable but tried to break the ice by laughing it off. 'Mark has always been like that,' he whispered to some nearby guests. 'He likes to be major-domo. We've always had problems with him.' Another guest was aghast: 'He was acting like a South African bodyguard. I've never seen anything like it.'

The guests, who included Charles Simmons, a Fort Worth oilman, and Rosewood Hotels president Atef Mankarios, were shocked but proceeded in to dinner. It was not long before the conversation turned to politics. In a discussion about social inequities, the chief executive of the *Dallas Morning News* dared to mention the existence of a class structure. 'Any reference to class distinctions is a Marxist concept,' snapped Lady Thatcher.[21]

Two days later, she was in the at-that-time-bankrupt Orange County, California. Dressed in royal purple, she arrived in a Costa Mesa mall with the band playing 'God Save The Queen'. 'You have come home to conservative country,' shouted her host, shopping magnate Henry Segerstrom. Later that evening, she addressed a dinner at which local businessmen paid $125 each to hear her. In return, she was paid $50,000 plus expenses. Mark did not attend and instead sent David Wallace, his business partner.

Her next trip was almost like a state visit. In May 1991, she flew to South Africa at the invitation of President De Klerk, with all expenses paid by his government. On her first day, she was presented with the Order of Good Hope (Grand Cross Class). Her son did not go but fixed the private plane and flights and arranged for her to stay with his friend Anton Rupert, a wealthy South African businessman and owner of Rembrandt Tobacco.

By June 1991, there was concern among some of her advisers and friends that too many of her overseas engagements were commercially rather than ideologically motivated – based on advice from her son. She was in danger of being famous for being famous and grubbily cashing in on her celebrity status. 'In the early weeks she was not paid for many of her trips or she would give the fee to charity,' one of her key aides told us. 'The strategy was that it would be partly free and partly financially rewarding. But later on it became nearly all commercial, because Mark wanted the tours to be run as a business proposition and purely as a money-making enterprise. We thought that could damage her and diminish her reputation as a world figure.'

Despite this disquiet, her son's view prevailed. On one occasion, Walter Annenberg hosted a special lunch and one of his guests invited Margaret and Mark. She attended and spoke at fairly short notice but Annenberg was shocked when approached by her son after the lunch. He asked the former ambassador for a contribution. A stunned Annenberg refused; another guest who entered was outraged.

One of Lady Thatcher's most lucrative trips was to the United States in June 1991. Eight carefully selected groups of wealthy businessmen and right-wing groups were addressed in exclusive private clubs. Six of her eight speeches were delivered in secret, with details not being divulged for 'security reasons'.[22] However, it has been possible to piece together much of her week-long lecture tour.

On 14 June 1991, she flew by private executive jet to the exclusive resort of Greenbriar, West Virginia, where she based herself. The next day, she addressed a food wholesalers group, sponsored by the Heinz Corporation. The following evening, Lady Thatcher dined and lectured the Chicago Council on Foreign Relations with 4,000 guests paying $15 each – total $60,000. The next day, she flew to New York to talk to 1,700 businessmen at the Economic Club; the lunch bill was $150 each – total $255,000. Those were the only public engagements and her estimated fees for both functions were $25,000.

The Thatcher camp then moved on to private meetings. Down in Atlantic City, New Jersey, she addressed IBM executives. In North Carolina and Ohio, $300 a head for dinner and speech was the going rate for 300 devotees. This took care of her fee of $30,000. Her rate for each lecture varied enormously – from $10,000 up to $60,000.[23] She also used the opportunity to solicit much-needed funds for the Thatcher Foundation.

One of her private seminars was at the Washington head office of Johnson & Johnson Inc., the huge US private medicare corporation. Executives and managing directors from their parent and subsidiary companies were specially flown in from all over the world for the occasion. Lady Thatcher spoke for an hour on the 'global market' and 'executive leadership' and then took questions from the star-struck executives. For two hours' work she was paid a cool $100,000 plus expenses. 'She was worth every cent,' said one of those present.

However, some aspects of the privatisation of Lady Thatcher bordered on the ludicrous as well as the lucrative. One organisation that was keen to market her name was the Richmond Forum, an organisation that arranges for celebrities to speak to Virginian audiences. In 1991, they distributed a brochure entitled 'How Having Dinner with Margaret Thatcher Could Be the Best $30,000 You Ever Spent'. It boasted: 'Converse with Mrs Thatcher. Ask General Schwarzkopf a strategy question . . . We're not talking about just getting to hear these people. We're talking about getting to know them. An opportunity for one-on-one conversation with some of the most important people in the world.'

Investing in Thatcher plc was clearly seen as profitable by the Richmond Forum. 'Imagine the lasting impression you could make on clients when you introduce them to someone like Margaret Thatcher,' advised the Forum. 'Join Richmond's leading companies and corporations in providing five unforgettable evenings of information and entertainment. And don't forget. An evening that starts with "Pass the salt, Mrs Thatcher" could end up with "Maggie, the next time you and your husband come to Richmond, stay with us".'

The former prime minister returned to more serious promotional appearances on 7 August 1991. She flew to New York to help out an old friend, Lord (Jeffrey) Sterling, chairman of P&O, which was a substantial financial donor to the Tory Party. That evening, she was guest of honour at dinner on board the *Regal Princess*, P&O's new 70,000-ton luxury cruise liner, to be based at Fort Lauderdale, Florida. The next day, Mrs Thatcher launched the *Princess*. Sterling paid her expenses and it was arranged as a tribute to her – co-hosted by Charles Price, the former US ambassador in London. When asked by *The Observer* why she was there, Lady Thatcher was uncharacteristically uncertain. 'Because I was invited,' she replied. 'Because I was asked by Lord Sterling. Because if I had been asked and not come, people would have . . .' Then she started stammering rather desperately and uncharacteristically – about the time of year and parliament being in recess.[24]

The Margaret Thatcher financial flying circus then turned to the Far East. On 1 September 1991, sponsored by Nippon Telegraph and Telephone (NTT), the Japanese telecommunications company, she flew to Tokyo accompanied by Lord Archer and Mark, plus entourage. For a week, she was treated as though she had almost divine status as she gave a series of lectures, attended private business dinners and granted interviews – 47 engagements in three cities. She was paid an estimated £50,000 a speech, bringing in a total of £1.5 million just for that trip, according to Lord Archer who made the bookings.[25] Privatisation was very much on the agenda as she had dinner with the presidents of Japan's leading privatised corporations in the airline, tobacco and railways industries. On her return trips, she was received by the Emperor and in 1996 was paid $150,000 for a two-hour lecture in the northern Japanese city of Sendai. It appeared the Thatcher magic was waning because some aggrieved residents sued the local council over the size of the fee.[26]

Like her recent US tour, her visit to Japan was also used to raise funds for the recently launched Thatcher Foundation. This was the case two days later when she arrived in Hong Kong. It was the first time she had returned to the British colony since signing the joint declaration on sovereignty with China in 1984.

But since leaving 10 Downing Street she had developed financial interests in Hong Kong along with her son, Mark. One commercial connection was with Moss and Partners, a firm of investment consultants and property developers, based in Tilney Street, near the Dorchester Hotel. One former employee was amused to learn that the company's secret codeword for Lady Thatcher's overseas financial correspondence was 'Roofmaker'.

As the former prime minister and her son descended on Hong Kong in their private plane on 13 September 1991, it was unclear how she would be received by local businessmen. 'Hong Kong is pretty ruthless and bourgeois about power,' said David Tsang, a prominent businessman who also raises money for the Conservative Party. 'Because of who she is there will still be interest in her, even though she is out of power. But if she is going there to raise money, she might find a lukewarm response. Everyone in Hong Kong will be thinking, "What's in it for me?"'[27]

Any doubts were immediately dismissed when she was greeted at the airport by George Magnus, deputy chairman of Cheung Kong Holdings, the giant property company owned by Li Ka-Shing. Before being whisked away in a stately Bentley limousine, Mark Thatcher said her visit was a 'private' matter. 'My mother has a lot of friends here,' he said. 'She will be renewing a lot of old friendships in the business world.'[28] His mother refused to comment. Instead she walked off to see Henry Kissinger, the former US secretary of state, whose private plane was on the tarmac just about to depart. He had been in Hong Kong on business for his own Kissinger Associates.

Li Ka-Shing was one of her strongest political supporters in the business world. He was also one of the most controversial. In 1986 a judicial tribunal concluded an investigation into insider dealing by one of his companies by stating: 'As to the degree of culpability to be attributed to Li Ka-Shing, we considered that it was high.' In Hong Kong, insider dealing was at the time not a criminal offence. The only sanction was public disgrace.

This did not appear to concern Lady Thatcher. In March 1991, she had flown to Vancouver with her son to launch the HK$16.75 billion Pacific Place community complex, a waterfront park. The project was run by Concord Pacific Developments Ltd, a Canada-based company in which Li Ka-Shing had a controlling interest. During her visit, Lady Thatcher and Mark had inspected the model of the park, accompanied by George Magnus and Victor Li, son of Li Ka-Shing and a senior vice-president of Concord Pacific Developments. She had then dedicated the project to David Lam, the first person of Chinese origin to become lieutenant-governor of a Canadian province.[29]

During her three-day stay in Hong Kong, the former prime minister and her son renewed their friendship with Li Ka-Shing, who also has interests in shipping and telecommunications. Mark stayed in the presidential suite of the Hilton Hotel, owned by Hong Kong's most powerful tycoon, while Margaret stayed in the Harbour Rooms at Government House.

After her only public appearance, as guest speaker at the Trade Development Council, she visited Li Ka-Shing's international container terminal by taking a trip on his boat in Hong Kong harbour. That evening, her final day in the colony, she was the guest of honour at a private dinner at the Albany penthouse of Baroness Lydia Dunn, chairwoman of Swire Pacific. The guests at what was billed as the 'Foundation Dinner' included top executives from Jardine Matheson and the Hong Kong and Shanghai Banking Corporation. It was intended diplomatically to solicit donations. One businessman who pledged a six-figure sum was Li Ka-Shing.

Her next Far East benefactor was Citibank, one of whose directors was her own personal banker, Hugh Thurston. Almost a year later, in August 1992, she flew to Taipei, the capital of Taiwan, for a three-day visit. Her party of seven, including two bodyguards, took up eighteen rooms on two floors of the Sherwood Hotel at a cost of £26,000 for three nights.

On 31 August, she had a private breakfast with Citibank executives and major clients and then delivered the bank's 'Leadership Series In Asia' lecture at the Hilton Hotel. That evening, she called on Taiwan, a country with the world's largest dollar reserves, to lift its remaining barriers against imports and foreign investment.[30]

This was a real money-spinning trip. 'Mr Gorbachev asked for a personal fee of £125,000 for one lecture and appearances. We put Lady Thatcher in that same pricing category,' said a Citibank spokesperson.[31] Her co-hosts, the United Daily News Group, paid a similar fee for their lecture. 'We had to pay a lot for the speech – but that was kept secret even from me,' said a spokesperson for the newspaper group. 'We were told we had to make a donation to the Thatcher Foundation.'[32]

Her next destination was Seoul, South Korea, where she was greeted by Kim Sang-Man, head of the powerful Dong-A Ilbo newspaper group. Kim donated £37,000 to the Thatcher Foundation. In return, she gave his newspaper an exclusive interview, spoke at one of its public meetings and attended a gala dinner hosted by the media corporation.[33] Another £12,500 was picked up after she granted an interview to KBS, the television station.

The Far East tours were well organised and even the donations were delivered in a relatively open way. But Lady Thatcher continued to attend and perform at functions, especially in the USA, which bordered on the evangelical. On 12 October 1994, she flew by a private jet, owned by right-wing property developer Harlan Crow, to Dallas for a charity lunch billed as 'A Conversation with a Living Legend'. An estimated 2,000 tickets, costing between $75 and $13,000, were sold. A year later her 70th birthday party in Washington, DC topped the fundraising charts. The former prime minister raised a staggering $2.4 million in ticket sales which was destined for the Thatcher Foundation. Invitations were sent to 800 personal and political friends and the party even included an 'international dinner committee' comprising former presidents Helmut Kohl, Giscard d'Estaing and Mikail Gorbachev. Under-written by US tobacco multinational Philip Morris, it was an extravagant evening. 'Even Caligula would be envious at the scale of the entertainment,' quipped a Thatcher family friend.

In Europe, the former prime minister rarely attended the House of Lords and instead assiduously cultivated the commercial lecture circuit. Her talks were more serious but they were still transparently money-making exercises. In June 1994, she spoke in London at the AGM of the Chase Manhattan Bank and was paid £60,000. She received the same fee in April 1995, when she addressed the AGM of the bank's European branch in Paris.

By cashing in on her premiership, Thatcher damaged her reputation. But one could equally argue that she was merely living out the ideological precepts that she taught as a politician. She was enacting the Thatcherite creed and receiving her just rewards for the enterprise culture which she promoted. 'Money is important,' said a former adviser. 'She always attached considerable importance to it and designed a society in which making money was one of the highest goals. It's a source of some satisfaction to her to be able to earn considerable quantities of it.'[34] And yet throughout her career, public service was also her watchword. She appealed to ordinary voters as one of them and often talked about her task which aimed to transform values and transcend material self-interest. Few prime ministers so completely and effortlessly abandoned public service in the pursuit of private sector wealth.

'My mother must have money,' said Mark soon after his parents left 10 Downing Street. Certainly, the allowances that former prime ministers receive compare unfavourably with those of other ex-world leaders. Besides, Margaret Thatcher was not retiring from public life nor departing from the political arena. So funding for her private office and activities was crucial. The real question was: who was she going to take money from? And to what extent were her paymasters going to use her unparalleled contacts and influence with governments?

Multinational corporations were soon lining up to persuade her to join their boards of directors. Executive headhunters were hired, largely by American companies, to secure her services. One of them was the Egon Zhender company, based in Switzerland. 'We have clients who would very much like to talk to her,' said John Gumbar, the head of its London office. 'A number of world-class corporations would give anything to have her on their board. I don't have a blank cheque but I do have several requests.'[35] They realised her international connections would enhance their commercial prospects as well as their prestige. 'This is seen as of enormous value to a company with a global strategy,' added Gumbar.[36]

One adoring businessman who approached her was Conrad Black, the Canadian owner of the *Daily Telegraph* and *Jerusalem Post* who has since been forced to sell his titles amid allegations of spending company money on his personal lifestyle. He asked her to join his international advisory board, which included such luminaries as Giovanni Agnelli, chairman of Fiat, and William F. Buckley, editor-at-large of the *National Review*. Mrs Thatcher politely declined the offer but did agree to be an honorary senior international adviser to his holding company, Hollinger Inc.

The former prime minister was selective as to which companies she joined. Perhaps she thought boardrooms were too restrictive an environment. Whatever the reason, she weighed up the offers very carefully but the one commercial proposition she did accept could not have been more controversial. In January 1992, she became a consultant to Philip Morris Inc., the giant global tobacco corporation and manufacturers of Marlboro, the biggest-selling cigarette in the world. Although the company also owned Kraft Foods and Miller beer, cigarettes accounted for 43 per cent of its operating revenues and 69 per cent of profits. Mrs Thatcher signed a contract worth $1 million over three years. 'She is doing consultancy work for us on geo-political concerns on a worldwide basis,' said a Philip Morris vice-president of corporate communications.[37]

Details of her services to the tobacco company were contained in an internal management memorandum, leaked to the *Sunday Times*. Written on 31 March 1992, by Geoffrey Bible, an executive vice-president of Philip Morris International, and circulated to 13 other executives, it said: 'We have the ability to use Mrs Thatcher's services and skills over the next few years. On the few occasions we have asked for her advice, she has provided very skilful help. However, we believe that we are not taking full advantage of all that she has to offer. As a result, I have attempted to summarise as many issues as I can think of where she may be able to offer guidance and assistance.'

Bible then listed the areas where Thatcher could use her influence. They were split into three areas. The first was the European Community. This included the advertising ban, lowering of tobacco tariffs and monopoly privatisation in Spain, France and Portugal. The second was non-EC international, which encompassed the Swiss cartel, Turkish pricing, distribution in the independent republics of the former Soviet Union, and entry into South Africa. The third was Asia and the Pacific, comprising China entry strategy, monopoly privatisation in Japan, Taiwan, Korea and Thailand, and legislation in Indonesia, Malaysia and Singapore.

Bible added: 'You will note that most of the points I have raised are skewed to tobacco where we tend to have more governmental issues. But I would very much appreciate it if you could reflect intensively on food issues where she could also be of assistance.' He concluded by asking his executives for a 'one-page summary on each of the points so that I can discuss them with senior management, finalise those which qualify for discussion with Mrs Thatcher and then meet with her to map out a game plan of how she might be able to help us over the coming years.'[38]

Essentially, Philip Morris was concerned about the decline in Western tobacco sales and saw the newly privatised markets in Asia and Eastern Europe as an opportunity to maintain profitability. But not all governments were accommodating and regulatory barriers were in place. 'Cigarette prices in many international markets are government controlled,' stated its 1993 accounts. 'Excise, other tax increases, higher costs and government price restraints in a number of markets have restricted the sales and income attributable to Philip Morris.'

Enter Mrs Thatcher. She was the one person who could help the company break into troublesome foreign markets and advise on the advertising bans and tobacco tariffs in the European Community. On the day that details of her contract were leaked to the *Sunday Times*, Lord Wyatt, a sycophantic friend and informal adviser, met her at Lord Archer's annual summer party in Grantchester, Cambridgeshire. 'I never would have become a director because of the legal liabilities,' she told him, and then let slip her real role: providing inside information about Europe. She is 'going to help them [Philip Morris] in relation to what goes on in the European Community,' wrote Lord Wyatt in his diaries later that day.[39] Philip Morris already had Rupert Murdoch as a director and shareholder. But the former prime minister could provide that extra political leverage which would persuade the presidents of developing countries to remove any regulatory and legislative obstacles.

Asia and the Pacific were the regions where Lady Thatcher was most likely to exert influence on Philip Morris's behalf. The massive untapped tobacco markets in the former Soviet republics and the Far East present golden sales opportunities. But the company was faced with significant government regulatory impediments – foreign ownership restrictions, monopoly privatisation and import barriers. Who better than the revered Lady Thatcher to lobby the presidents and rulers and open up access to those markets for her client?

Nowhere was this more paramount than Taiwan, the most anti-tobacco country in the Far East. This 20-million-strong island state off the coast of China presented a problem to Philip Morris. One out of five deaths in Taiwan is smoking-related and so in 1991 the government proposed a 'Law Governing the Prevention and Control of Damage from Tobacco Use'. This contained clauses banning cigarette sales through vending machines, restricting smoking in public places and banning all direct advertising and promotion of cigarettes.

Philip Morris was aghast. It immediately lobbied the US trade representative, complaining that the new law would have an adverse effect on its business. In public relations terms, the company was initially successful and boasted, 'We have successfully made this a trade issue rather than one of health.'

289

But there were serious negotiations to be conducted. Fortunately for the corporation, Lady Thatcher arrived on the island in August 1992 – on the eve of vital discussions between the Taiwanese and American governments about the planned advertising ban. She stayed at the luxurious Sherwood Hotel, where, ironically, she demanded that all the ashtrays and matches be removed from her suite.

Officially, she was in Taiwan to lecture and to raise funds for the Thatcher Foundation. But, according to a Philip Morris representative on the island, her presence was useful to the corporation because of her access to the highest echelons of government. 'She was seen by the president, who gave a state banquet,' the representative told Granada TV's *World In Action.* 'She had a private meeting with the prime minister and the foreign minister. She was accepted and seen at every level. She came at a very interesting juncture. The Taiwanese were addressing the issue of entering the world trading community. They were perhaps not clear which way they should go. But they got a very clear signal from her that this was what the rest of the trading world expected. It wasn't a lecture, it was a very friendly piece of advice.'[40]

In her main speech, Lady Thatcher called for the removal of all import barriers. 'The faster you go, the more positively the rest of the world will respond,' she said. It was sweet music to Philip Morris's ears. S. Chung, the company's Taiwan-based executive, said she had made 'a very good point'.[41]

Taiwan's proposed anti-tobacco law was scuppered and never reached the statute book. It was just one of several Asian countries – notably China, Korea, Kazakhstan and Japan – whose tobacco markets Philip Morris was keen on breaking into. And young teenagers were their target customers. In 1993, she flew to Kazakhstan, where she had a private meeting with President Nazarbayev. Shortly afterwards, he announced that he was selling a 49 per cent stake in the state-owned tobacco company, Almaty Tobacco Kombinat, to Philip Morris Inc. Later that year the *Wall Street Journal* reported that many of these privatised tobacco corporations in Eastern Europe became monopolies.

Lady Thatcher was a willing and active paid ambassador for their interests. Everyone who knows her testifies that her consultancy with Philip Morris was no passive affair. It was not in her nature to be laid-back and sanguine about a job of work. 'One thing you can be sure about,' said a friend, 'is that she has not been hired as some kind of ornament or decoration for the company.' For the tobacco giant, her consulting on what they called 'geo-political issues' was invaluable and they were happy to finance her lavish 70th birthday party in October 1995, which raised some £600,000 for her foundation.

For anti-tobacco campaigners, her $1 million contract was 'shameful'. The protests were long and loud. Among her critics was the Tory MP Roger Sims, who described her appointment as 'astonishing' and 'irresponsible'.[42] Doctors and cancer victims wrote to Mrs Thatcher requesting an explanation. None of them received a reply. The comedian Roy Castle, a lifelong Conservative who had campaigned for Margaret Thatcher, was shocked and dismayed. At an awards ceremony in November 1992, he refused to meet her. 'I would be accused of double standards if I shook her hand or posed with her,' he said. 'I'm very angry about cigarettes and what they do to young people in the Third World.'[43] In July 1994, Roy Castle died of lung cancer.

The great irony was not just that she was a non-smoker but she did not even like other people in the same room to smoke. In her memoirs, she rebuked her revered father: 'He smoked which was very bad for him because of his weak chest.' And while she was prime minister, she actively sought to protect vulnerable young teenagers from companies like Philip Morris. In January 1989, she launched a government campaign aimed at halving the number of young smokers by 1993. 'It is for me to emphasise, particularly to young people,' she said, 'the message that smoking kills. Smoking kills. About 95 per cent of those who die from lung cancer are smokers and for most the habit is acquired before adulthood.'[44]

The undeniable health hazards of smoking were graphically disclosed during the third year of Thatcher's consultancy. In May 1995, Philip Morris was forced to recall eight billion cigarettes – at a cost of $250 million – after discovering that a contaminant in the filters had produced a toxic chemical known as MITC, which can cause 'eye, nose and throat irritation, dizziness, coughing or wheezing'.

For some of her admirers, her choice of consultancy was, at best, politically inept. Their heroine could have spent her time more productively than promoting the sale of toxic substances and lethal cigarettes to teenagers in the Third World. But to any serious student of Thatcherism it should not have been too surprising. After all, she was merely lobbying for a company to operate in international markets. And being paid for it showed she had a market worth. Her speeches in the Far East imploring governments to abolish import duties and open up markets may have helped Philip Morris Inc. But she would argue she was simply promoting the Thatcherite creed. She wanted to preserve her legacy, not just for her contemporary political reputation but also for the history books.

On leaving 10 Downing Street, one of Mrs Thatcher's priorities was to write her political memoirs, a last monument to Thatcherism. Her first thought was of revenge. 'We knew that there were voices close to her from the very start,' said literary agent Michael Sissons, 'who were trying to urge her to write a short-term, splenetic book, whacking the ice-pick into the people who had been responsible for her demise.'[45] But she decided against the idea. 'No,' she told *ITN News* in June 1991, 'I will one day be able to write it but it would be too hurtful to too many people.' Instead, she chose a more considered approach. 'We are not dashing into the memoirs,' she said. 'We are making quite certain the memoirs will be a vigorous intellectual record of what we did and what happened.'[46]

However, the book was also lucrative. Every publisher was interested and a multimillion-pound advance on royalties beckoned. At first, the former prime minister was opposed to an auction and wanted to give the contract to her favourite media tycoon, Rupert Murdoch. 'She wanted you to do it because she felt she owed so much to you,' Lord Wyatt told the press baron in March 1991.[47] But she changed her mind and it went out to tender.

Finding the right publisher and deal required delicate, decisive and astute negotiation skills. Margaret Thatcher immediately appointed her son as her chief adviser and appeared uninterested in the financial aspects of the project. 'Let Mark deal with it,' she said, waving her hand impatiently. This was not greeted with great glee by her friends. On 4 January 1991, six weeks after she had left Downing Street, Alan Clark, the former Conservative minister and military historian, went to see her in her temporary office at Great College Street, Westminster. A paid-up member of the 'One of Us' club, he was a front-runner to write the book. But she had second thoughts and so during their talk Clark changed the subject to finance. He had heard from agents that multimillion-pound figures were being bandied about like Monopoly money. 'Apparently Mark has been winding her up,' Clark later recorded in his diaries, and saying the book's value 'could be as much as £20 million'. The former defence minister was uneasy about how it was being handled. 'I'm doubtful about all this,' he noted. 'It's tempting, I can see, to allow yourself to be regarded as a "property". But slightly demeaning for the premier politician of the Western world.'[48]

Two days later, a gathering of Mrs Thatcher's friends and confidants assembled for dinner at Alan Clark's magnificent home, Saltwood Castle, Kent. Among the guests were Richard Ryder, the Conservative chief whip; his wife, Caroline, a former secretary to Mrs Thatcher; Lord Deedes, former editor of the *Daily Telegraph*; and cabinet minister Michael Howard. Towards the end of the dinner, the conversation turned to the thorny question of the memoirs. 'There was some desultory talk about "the book",' recalled Clark. 'There was agreement on the general "problem" of Mark.'[49]

The subsequent negotiations were a protracted and unhappy saga. Initially, Mark agreed that his mother needed a literary agent. So he arranged for a 'beauty contest' of four prospective agents to be interviewed by 'Three Wise Men' – himself, Lord McAlpine, former treasurer of the Tory Party, and Sir Michael Richardson, chairman of City stockbrokers Smith New Court. After the literary agents were sent an elaborate questionnaire, an all-day meeting was arranged for a Saturday in London. The participants were sworn to secrecy. It was postponed several times but eventually cancelled by Mark. 'I can get a better deal than any agent,' he boasted.

In fact, secret parallel negotiations were already under way with Macmillan Scribner books, an imprint of the American firm owned by Robert Maxwell. They had a reputation for publishing high-quality non-fiction books and saw their list as the ideal home for Margaret Thatcher's account of her years as prime minister.

Macmillan was ahead of the pack because of an introduction by Lord Brownlow, a wealthy Lincolnshire landowner and close friend of the Thatchers. Brownlow, who once lent Margaret Thatcher a stunning silver plate collection worth £2 million while she was prime minister, arranged for her to meet Macmillan executives in mid-January 1991 to discuss the project. The meeting was a success. Mrs Thatcher got on extremely well with Robert Stewart, the commissioning editor, partly because of his knowledge of English history, and there was an immediate personal rapport. She also liked Macmillan because they had published the memoirs of George Shultz, the former US secretary of state, whom she had met at a dinner given in her honour at the White House. He recommended them.

The former premier was keen to proceed and outlined her view of the book. 'I want it to be a serious book which will contribute to history,' she said. She concluded the discussion by telling the Macmillan executives to negotiate with her son. 'Mark manages all my business affairs,' she said. She also informed them that Hugh Thurston, her banker, and Leonard Day, her accountant, would deal with the financial detail of the deal.

Stewart then had several conversations and meetings with Mark. 'What we found out fairly quickly was that he didn't know what he was doing,' recalled the editor. 'He didn't know how to be an agent because he had no experience and did not know what was involved in terms of planning a schedule for negotiations. It made those negotiations very difficult and vague. It was almost an attitude of "Take it or leave it".' The legendary American literary agent Irving 'Swifty' Lazar took the same view. 'The son is a fly in the ointment,' he said at the time. 'The son thinks he can be the agent. He's decided he knows all about publishing and he's an amateur.'[50]

Two weeks later, Mark Thatcher, Steve Tipping and Hugh Thurston flew to New York to meet Macmillan to discuss the book. A special lunch was laid on by the publishers, cooked by Maxwell's own chef. Mark dominated the conversation. He tends to babble when he is nervous and this occasion was no exception. He talked incessantly in his characteristic rapid-fire style, in between gulps of red wine. 'We want a great deal of money for this project,' he said. 'And I'm talking really big money.' He added that the book should be a monument to his mother. 'He was basking in her glory. He was also very imperious and sounded like a Saudi Arabian crown prince,' said a former Maxwell executive involved in the negotiations. Mark's attitude did not endear him to the Macmillan editors, who regularly dealt with former presidents and business tycoons. 'Genuinely successful people,' one said, 'don't need to boast about their achievements.'

Mark was Mrs Thatcher's principal agent but other members of her inner circle also became involved in the negotiations. Chief among them was Hugh Thurston, her Jersey-based banker. In March 1991, Thurston and Tipping flew to New York and met Maxwell himself at the Waldorf Astoria to discuss the financial aspects of the project. 'We don't want an agent, just a reputable publisher,' said Thurston. He told Maxwell that he wanted the advance payments and royalties to be paid into an offshore company, specially set up as a subsidiary of Macmillan. The publisher agreed. 'I would do anything to get my prime minister's book,' he told them. 'She is a wonderful patriot.'

But the negotiations were going painfully slowly because Mark continued to change his mind and shift the agenda. And so Jeffrey Archer brought in George Greenfield, the respected literary agent, as an adviser. Greenfield, a wily and highly experienced exponent of his craft, went with Lord Archer to see Margaret Thatcher, Denis and Mark at their Belgravia home in Chester Square. It was a frustrating meeting. Denis leaned against the mantelpiece pouring gin and tonic while Mark sat silent, keeping his countenance. Greenfield did his best to provide astute counsel but was constantly interrupted by Mrs Thatcher in clipped, acerbic tones, who fixed him with a blank self-absorbed stare. 'The extent of her ill-conceived ignorance at that time was only matched by the brazen vigour with which she expressed it,' he recalled.[51] He walked away from the meeting exasperated by her uncharacteristic indecisiveness. Still, they agreed with his recommendation that discussions with Macmillan should continue.

In April 1991, Robert Maxwell took over the negotiations for Macmillan. His stockbroker, Sir Michael Richardson, chairman of Smith New Court, telephoned the Macmillan office in New York from the Lyford Cay country club in the Bahamas, of which Mark was also a member. Sir Michael, a long-time confidant of both Mrs Thatcher and Maxwell, said her son was unreliable and he would play an intermediary role to smooth the path. He explained that he was also advising the former prime minister on the financial details of the contract. This was confirmed by Mark, who told Greenfield: 'If we reach any conclusions, Mummy wants to run them in front of her man, Sir Michael Richardson.' But this produced a conflict of interests which the stockbroker did not appear to grasp. During negotiations with Macmillan, Maxwell said, 'This sounds all right, but I must show my adviser Sir Michael Richardson.' After the meeting, Greenfield told Mark, 'He [Sir Michael) can't act for both sides.' 'Good God,' he replied. 'I never thought of that.'[52]

Maxwell was desperately keen to win the commission and was often in a state of tension and anxiety. 'I must have this book. I want my prime minister,' the tycoon once shouted. 'He was so desperate to be accepted and he saw the Thatcher book as a route to that,' said a source close to him at the time.

The crooked press baron had a close and curiously friendly relationship with Margaret Thatcher. 'Maxwell talked constantly about his respect and admiration for her,' said a source involved in the negotiations. 'He had done an important favour for her years ago and she was very grateful to him. He never said what it was but it was obviously quite significant.' Another source said, 'Maxwell was keen but he thought it unlikely that Mrs Thatcher would want him as the publisher. He liked her and said how helpful she was to big business in the 1980s.'

As for Mrs Thatcher, 'She told me she had no problems in being published by Maxwell,' said a Macmillan source. 'She said she admired Maxwell as a businessman and was not concerned about the attacks on her by the Mirror newspapers.' Her only public comment was after the publisher's death in late 1991: 'Mr Maxwell kept me informed about what was happening in Eastern European countries and what their leaders were thinking.'[53]

It was not difficult to see why Maxwell and Margaret Thatcher admired each other. They saw each other as self-made people, outside the class-ridden British establishment. She respected wealthy, flamboyant and powerful business tycoons who fought their way up. Maxwell dealt with her as a head of government rather than as leader of the Tory Party. He was also commercially grateful to her for two key policies. The first was her reform of the trade-union laws, which he applied ruthlessly to his own employees. The second was the privatisation of British Airways, which enabled him to buy British Helicopters International from the government for £30 million.

Although Mark was acting for Mrs Thatcher, Maxwell treated him like a domestic servant or medium-rank aide. 'Come along, my boy,' he would say, fussing over him. Yet Mark continued to play the primary role and remained in charge of the financial arrangements. 'My mother must have money,' he said. As usual, his urge to succeed and please his mother led to excessive demands. He wanted $10 million for world rights, apart from Japan. He proposed $1.5 million on signature of contract, $4.25 million on delivery of the manuscript and $4.25 million on publication of the book. On royalties, he wanted 17 per cent for hardback sales and 15 per cent for paperback.

The self-appointed literary agent held out on the $10 million figure as late as 22 May 1991. But the delays were diminishing the book's value. This enabled Maxwell to offer $8 million plus 'editorial and research expenses' for three books, two volumes of political memoirs and an illustrated history book entitled *England's Heritage*. This was accepted, and on 28 May 1991 a 'handshake contract' was agreed between Mark Thatcher and Robert Maxwell.

A secret undertaking was that Mark Thatcher wanted a commission or 'finder's fee', as he called it. 'I want to be specific about this,' said a Maxwell executive directly involved in the deal. 'We never actually said "plus one million for Mark". We called it expenses or something like that. It was never spoken openly but I knew Mark wanted a million dollars because this information was passed on to me. He wanted it as a finder's fee and so in a way there was nothing illegal about it.'

Macmillan drew up a draft agreement and on 4 June 1991 Mark Thatcher and George Greenfield met Maxwell and his executives at 10.30 a.m. in his penthouse suite at the Mirror Group offices, Holborn Circus. Ushered by a butler in full fig into a room dominated by marble and gilt furniture, their agenda was to close the deal. Mark made it clear that he was in charge of the tax provisions and financial arrangements. He said the Inland Revenue was happy with the advance and future royalties being paid into an offshore company. This was part of a complex arrangement to sell the copyright to the offshore firm. Maxwell confirmed his prior agreement. 'Now, we want a guaranteed, non-returnable advance of $10 million,' said Mark. 'I can live with that,' replied Maxwell. A five-page letter of intent was then signed by Greenfield and Mark, on his mother's behalf. They then shook hands and the delighted Macmillan team trooped off for a celebration lunch.

On Wednesday, 12 June, Macmillan formally agreed to the conditions. But suddenly, within 24 hours, the deal collapsed when Mark Thatcher received a fax from Robert Maxwell stating that the deal was off. Valiant attempts by Macmillan to recover the deal were then sunk. Just as well, really, as five months later Cap'n Bob took his final plunge. 'For a long time, I felt it was both ironic and inappropriate that the doubly corrupt hulk should be buried on the slopes of Mount Olive,' reflected George Greenfield.

Mark Thatcher, quite wrongly, blamed Greenfield for the Maxwell debacle and sacked him. The truth was that Mark and Sir Michael Richardson had been privately talking to Marvin Josephson, a high-powered New York literary agent, lawyer and friend of former president Ronald Reagan, and conducting discreet parallel negotiations. This was borne out less than a week later, on 18 June 1991, when Josephson signed up Mrs Thatcher as a client of his company, International Creative Management Inc.

Within a few days, publishers were invited to bid. Macmillan again entered the fray and in August 1991 offered $6 million. But Josephson would not even return Macmillan's telephone calls. Instead he went to Rupert Murdoch and cut a deal with HarperCollins for £3.5 million. Thurston was livid about the outcome because he believed the Macmillan proposal was excellent and he resented Mark's antics.

Other friends of Mrs Thatcher were also angry. They believed she could have secured a much better commission. 'We should have closed the deal in the first two weeks while people were being very silly indeed,' said Lord Archer. 'We could have got all the silly people in one room and made them bid against each other and I think we would have got a silly figure.'[54] Irving Lazar, the veteran literary agent, agreed: 'When [Mark] had the chance to strike he didn't . . . What [Lady Thatcher] doesn't realise is that there's a hot moment when you can get a lot of money.'[55]

Michael Sissons, a seasoned literary agent with Peters, Fraser & Dunlop, summed it up best: 'This was, unquestionably, the most saleable autobiography of our times. Not since de Gaulle has anyone been involved in world affairs at the very highest level for such an extraordinary length of time . . . So the project initially had enormous value and to see that frittered away was immensely depressing. The value just seemed to fade because of the bad publicity, the indecision and the aura that Mark Thatcher's involvement gave it.'[56]

The essence of the problem was that, as always with his mother's private affairs, Mark wanted to be major-domo, to use his father's apt description. Despite his non-existent knowledge of how to be a literary agent, he was adamant that only he could faithfully represent and protect Mrs Thatcher's interests. And so, far from master-minding the operation, he master-meddled. The result was an atmosphere of indecision, unreality and confusion.

Eventually, Mrs Thatcher settled down to write the book, assisted by her staff. By late December 1992, a first draft was complete and she flew with Mark, Carol and Denis to the Bahamas, partly to celebrate Christmas but also to work on the manuscript. She did not enjoy her stay in the sun-soaked Caribbean and would be seen sitting near the beach, impatiently tapping her fingers. But her son loved the Bahamas. He had been visiting the tax haven since the spring of 1991 and enjoyed rubbing shoulders with the 'big rich'. It was his kind of place. 'It's the Guernsey of America and a pirates' cove,' said one banker.

Apart from the casinos, the central focus for the tax-avoiding tycoons is the Lyford Cay Country Club in Nassau, whose members include Mohamed Al-Fayed. Mark Thatcher was desperately keen to join the exclusive club. 'It's a very money-orientated place and very snooty,' said one member. 'It is gutted with billionaires. Very few members are worth less than £10 million and the committee has to agree to your membership.'

Mark joined the club on the recommendation of Sir John Templeton, a multimillionaire financier knighted by Mrs Thatcher in 1986. Sir John, an active Christian and author of books like *Riches for the Mind and Spirit*, wrote a letter to the committee on her son's behalf and in the summer of 1991 Mark became a member. This caused some disquiet in the club, because his application was pushed through without consultation, but Mark was delighted. However, it was not long before he was indulging in some classic Thatcher Junior behaviour and alienating other members. 'I'm very annoyed with them,' he complained. 'They're not giving me prime starting times on the golf course.'

While Mark consorted with other wealthy visitors, his mother remained in her rented house completing her memoirs. She could not wait to return to London. *The Downing Street Years* was published in the autumn of 1993 and became both a bestseller and an enduring legacy of the former prime minister. But its success was despite rather than because of her son's involvement.

Lady Thatcher wanted her memoirs to be more than just a history book. She viewed them as a political instrument to promote her views and preserve her power base. But she also had secret commercial ambitions and it was to the Gulf that she looked.

The United Arab Emirates had always been one of Margaret Thatcher's favourite regions, both politically and commercially. She was a great admirer of Sheikh Zayed bin Sultan al-Nahayan, the imperious ruler of Abu Dhabi, and was a regular visitor, even after leaving 10 Downing Street. Her son also looked upon the region with some affection, as it was in nearby Oman that he had helped secure the university contract for his client Cementation International.

While prime minister, Thatcher cultivated her diplomatic ties with Sheikh Zayed, while assisting her son's business interests and connections in the Gulf. She had, after all, hand written a letter to Zayed, accompanied by her signed photograph, introducing her son as her unofficial envoy. 'I have asked my son to convey to you my personal message of warm regards and good wishes,' she wrote. The ruler of Abu Dhabi responded by helping her son with his commercial activities in the Gulf.

Mrs Thatcher also developed close ties with other UAE ministers. In 1982, she was visited at her home in Flood Street, Chelsea, by Dr

Mana bin Said al-Oteiba, the UAE oil minister. Al-Oteiba must have been keen to cultivate the prime minister as he gave her a Kutchinsky ruby and diamond necklace, then worth half a million pounds.

Dazzled by jewellery, Thatcher was well known for collecting expensive gifts from foreign heads of state. During 77 official trips to 54 countries, she amassed a vast treasure of presents and trophies. They included a heavy silver coffee pot from the Sultan of Oman which perched on the sideboard at 10 Downing Street, a jewelled desk set from Abu Dhabi, a perfect pearl necklace from Prince Khalid of Saudi Arabia and, in 1985, a glittering gold bracelet, encrusted with diamonds and rubies, from the Sultan of Brunei.[57] Under strict Cabinet Office rules for ministers, all presents valued at more than £125 become the property of the state unless the recipient buys them, so she was not allowed to keep the gifts and many of them languish in a vault at 10 Downing Street. They are available for use only by future prime ministers and their spouses.

One of Thatcher's favourite presents was a stunning diamond and sapphire necklace worth £200,000 from Sultan Qaboos of Oman. It was presented to her during her controversial trip to Oman in April 1981, when she lobbied the Sultan on behalf of Cementation International, which was bidding for the £300 million university contract. She was bedazzled by the necklace, which was made by Asprey's of which the Sultan was a shareholder. Liberally set with diamonds and sapphires and made of platinum, it was described by one member of the ruler's court as 'spectacular' and the prime minister often wore it at grand state occasions. But one Omani diplomat remarked cuttingly, 'It was more of a collar, actually, than a necklace and gave her the appearance of having won 'Best of Breed' at Crufts'.[58]

The prime minister remained captivated by the gift and was devastated when it was placed in the Downing Street vault immediately after her resignation in 1990. Barely six months later, shortly after the 1991 Gulf war, Lady Thatcher visited Oman to thank the Sultan for his support during the war but also to drum up funds for the Thatcher Foundation. During a private dinner at Bait Al Falaj, the principal barracks of the Sultan's armed forces in Muscat, she asked if a replacement necklace could be provided. The Sultan was 'visibly shocked' by the request, according to an Omani present at the dinner. It was a favour too far, even for such a pro-British head of state. He politely declined and suggested to the British ambassador that the necklace be discreetly returned.[59]

Eventually, the embarrassed Sultan let the matter drop and the original necklace remained in the vault. But Thatcher was besotted with the jewel and in November 1991, just before she visited the United Arab Emirates, she asked Hugh Thurston, her trusted adviser, to discreetly enquire whether the UAE would buy her a similar necklace from Asprey's. Her request was taken seriously by the UAE government, according to a source in the presidential court in Abu Dhabi. A meeting of Gulf diplomats took place in Paris but they could not agree terms and Lady Thatcher never received her beloved jewellery.

Even then the former prime minister would not let the matter drop. In 1994, she saw photographs of Norma Major wearing the same necklace during a banquet that the Queen gave for the Polish leader, Lech Walesa, at Windsor Castle and was enraged. The Iron Lady suffered a case of extreme metal fatigue and seethed with anger. 'That was given to me,' she told a friend at the time. 'It really is mine.' She then telephoned John Major in a fury and told him that the bauble was 'a personal favourite' and a private present to her from the Sultan and demanded that nobody else wear the necklace again. Her successor argued that the necklace was for the use of the incumbent prime minister and the government of the day. But Lady Thatcher aggressively insisted that nobody else should wear it. Eventually, Major backed down and agreed that his wife would wear a different necklace for future formal events. As one amused MP remarked, 'Thatcher obviously believes that diamonds really are for ever'.

Towards the end of her premiership, plans were laid to maintain her Gulf connections. There was speculation in Thatcher's inner circle as to what she might do after she left office voluntarily. The consensus was that she would lead the Conservatives into a fourth successive administration and then bow out gracefully. One of their most extraordinary ideas was to make her the president of the Bank of Credit and Commerce International (BCCI).

In the late summer of 1990, while she was still in office, her financial advisers and Mark devised a secret plan to take over BCCI. They believed they could run it better themselves. Clearly, they must have been unaware that the bank's other services included laundering drugs money, fraud, funding illegal arms deals and stealing customers' savings.

BCCI's fortunes were closely linked to and bound up with Sheikh Zayed, the Gulf's favourite Thatcherite. It was the dictatorial ruler of

Abu Dhabi who founded the bank in 1972 with Agha Hasan Abedi, a Pakistani financier. Zayed funded BCCI and was much more than its titular head. He supplied $6.9 million of the $10 million start-up capital and his family later held a 77 per cent controlling shareholding.

The crimes of BCCI were no great secret to the regulatory authorities in the late 1980s. Billions of pounds of investors' funds were disappearing down financial black holes and laundered through the Cayman Islands. But the biggest bank fraud in world financial history was not made public until 1991. 'BCCI was operated as a corrupt, criminal organisation throughout its entire 19-year history,' said Robert Morgenthau, the New York district attorney, on announcing the indictment against the bank. 'It systematically falsified its records. It knowingly allowed itself to be used to launder illegal income of drug sellers and other criminals and it paid bribes and kickbacks to other public officials.'[60]

Margaret Thatcher already had links with BCCI investors when she was prime minister. Her main contact was with Nazmi Virani, whose property and leisure company, Control Securities, was dependent largely on loans from BCCI. An Asian who settled in Britain after being expelled from Uganda, Virani made substantial donations to the Tory Party. 'I paid the money to Conservative Central Office over many years,' he said.[61] In 1986, he met Thatcher and Norman Tebbit, then Conservative Party chairman, on several occasions. She admired his entrepreneurial spirit, which had made him one of the richest people in Britain. 'Mrs Thatcher had a soft spot for Virani,' said one former BCCI official.[62]

Unfortunately, much of his wealth was accumulated by fraud and deception. In May 1994, Virani was jailed for two and a half years for seven offences – one of false accounting and six of furnishing false information to Price Waterhouse, BCCI's auditors. Essentially, he had conspired to help BCCI deceive the auditors into believing that the bank was solvent. In return, Virani received huge loans to prop up his companies and cash payments for himself.[63] Through Virani, Thatcher met several BCCI officials and investors.

Despite her lack of experience, her financial aides believed she had the aptitude and judgement to run an investment and commercial bank. In order to facilitate the deal, Sheikh Zayed needed to be approached because his family owned 77 per cent of the shares. His approval was crucial for both the takeover and this new version of BCCI.

The Thatcher camp's approach was received with some enthusiasm in Abu Dhabi. This resulted in a remarkable meeting at the Inn on the Park Hotel in Mayfair in the late summer of 1990. From Mrs Thatcher's stable were her son, Mark, and Hugh Thurston, her banker. From Abu Dhabi was Ali Shorafa, a former director of the sheikh's court, a one-time BCCI shareholder and the closest confidant and adviser to Sheikh Zayed. He was also one of the founders of BCCI. According to sources in Sheikh Zayed's court, the purpose of the meeting was to discuss concrete terms with Ali Shorafa and to persuade him that their proposals were realistic and beneficial to the bank.

Mark Thatcher and Hugh Thurston were very keen on the idea. Thurston presented an outline of the plan. He said the first stage was to conduct an extensive internal audit and due diligence into BCCI. This would take a year and cost about £3–4 million. At first Ali Shorafa was keen on the project and reported back to Sheikh Zayed. But sources close to the Abu Dhabi ruler say he was not happy and said the 'funds were not available' for such an investigation.

Unperturbed, the Thatchers proposed a new two-part deal whereby BCCI would enter into a joint-venture agreement with the Royal Bank of Scotland. This was because BCCI had lost a valuable ally when the Bank of America had dropped its corresponding-bank status with it, and was anxious to find a new partner. The idea was that the Royal Bank of Scotland should become the new corresponding bank. This meant they would introduce new business and clients to each other. A key figure would be Lord Younger, chairman of the Royal Bank of Scotland. As he had been Mrs Thatcher's defence secretary from 1986 until 1989 and her campaign manager in the 1990 Tory leadership election, her advisers were confident that he would agree to the deal. However, there is no evidence to suggest that the Royal Bank of Scotland or its officers had any knowledge of or were party to these negotiations.

The second stage was that Mrs Thatcher would become president of BCCI after she retired from public life and Sir Alan Walters, her former economic adviser, and other financiers close to her would then join her as directors. As part of this arrangement, BCCI would acquire a royal charter, which would have needed approval from the Queen (presumably it would have been known as the Royal British Bank of Commerce and Credit International!).

Ali Shorafa again responded with great interest and said he would need to discuss their proposals with Sheikh Zayed. But then he withdrew cooperation before the Bank of England closed down BCCI in July 1991 for fraud, corruption and money laundering. Zayed's decision caused much annoyance in the Thatcher camp, who were still enthusiastic about the idea. However, the truth was that the former prime minister had been saved from a humiliating commercial and political catastrophe by Hugh Thurston's astute decision to insist on a due diligence investigation into BCCI.

Mrs Thatcher herself remained enamoured of BCCI. In November 1991, four months after the bank was closed down, she met Sheikh Zayed during her tour of the Gulf. During their meeting, she told him she thought BCCI had been treated unfairly by the Bank of England and John Major: 'I believe you have been badly mistreated by my successor.' Their conversation was translated and a note of it was sent to 10 Downing Street.

Across the desert, Kuwait also had a special place in Mrs Thatcher's heart. She had been prime minister when Iraq invaded the oil-rich Gulf state in August 1990. And she was the politician who, according to President Bush, stiffened the allies' resolve during the build-up to the Gulf war. 'Remember, George,' she told him. 'This is no time to go wobbly.'[64] In return, the ruling al-Sabah royal family were eternally grateful to her. They named her '*Um*', an Arabic term meaning 'Mother of All' or 'Guardian of the Nation', and even named a street in Kuwait City after her. Mark was known as '*Um Quais' ah*' (pronounced 'Kissach') which means 'Son of a Great Mother'.

The Kuwaitis were equally grateful to President Bush and his government. In April 1993, after losing the presidency, George Bush flew to Kuwait with his wife, his sons Neil and Marvin, and entourage to be awarded the country's highest medal by the Emir. The al-Sabahs, most of whom had fled to the Bahamas when the Iraqi troops moved in, saw themselves as in Bush's debt. At official functions he was presented with dozens of expensive gifts, notably watches and necklaces, valued at thousands of dollars.[65]

The former president himself did not cash in on the spoils of war and returned to the United States. But his two sons had no such inhibitions. Neil was involved in two Houston oil-related firms – the Ultraflote Corporation, in which he was a partner, and the Link Group – who were both seeking business in Kuwait. His older brother, Marvin, was hired by Murphy and Associates, a Washington-based consulting firm, as a lobbyist for defence firms seeking a contract to build an electronic fence.[66]

Kuwait's infrastructure might have been wrecked by the war, but its massive oil reserves meant that billion-dollar contracts to rebuild the country were there for the taking. The Bush sons and former US public officials did not wait long before attempting to exploit the financial fruits of military victory. But others refused to do so. Norman Schwarzkopf, commander-in-chief of the allied forces, was offered hundred-million-dollar commissions by US defence firms to lobby their case in Kuwait. He declined. 'In the Arab world, your position in the government may get you through the door but it's the personal relationship that gets you the contract,' he told the *New Yorker*. 'I've developed that personal relationship in Kuwait. I know that all I've got to do is go to the Emir and say, "Hey, I want you to do this" and he will. There are people who have made use of such special connections and I don't begrudge them. But don't ask me to betray the trust these people have in me. I won't do it. American men and women were willing to die in Kuwait. Why should I profit from their sacrifice?'[67]

There were also opportunities for the Thatcher family to profit from the war dividend. But they were exploited in a different way. In October 1991, eight months after British and American troops drove Saddam Hussein's army out of Kuwait, the Emir of Kuwait visited London. He was anxious to see Mrs Thatcher to thank her for her steadfast support during the war. It was arranged that they would meet for breakfast at the Conrad Hotel on Chelsea harbour. Mark Thatcher then telephoned the Kuwaiti embassy and said he wanted the meeting to be at his mother's house in Belgravia. The Gulf visitors were offended by this brash request and so the breakfast remained at the Conrad. The meeting was a success and the Emir invited Mrs Thatcher to Kuwait. The only blemish was her son's abrupt manner, notably his insistence that non-Kuwaitis should be excluded from the room.

The following month, the former prime minister and her son did indeed go to Kuwait on a triumphant three-day 'state visit'. Again, Mark was prominent in the arrangements, running the show in his characteristically strident manner. Even the Kuwaitis found his behaviour difficult, to say the least. Apart from the gratitude bestowed on Mrs Thatcher, more tangible topics were discussed with the al-Sabahs. It was proposed that a 'Thatcher Committee' be established. This would consist of four Kuwaiti businessmen, four British businessmen and members of Mrs Thatcher's private office, including Mark. Its aim was to promote trade between the United Kingdom and Kuwait. But, according to a source in the Kuwaiti embassy, the Foreign Office expressed some disquiet about the idea, particularly about Mark's participation, and the project was shelved.

Mrs Thatcher and her son enjoyed the generous hospitality of the al-Sabahs and several introductions to the indigenous business community were arranged. One of the most prominent and influential was Souad M. al-Sabah, a very powerful businesswoman. She had created a successful career as chairwoman of Action International Consultancy Bureau Ltd, a firm of consultants based in Kuwait. Their clients include AT&T, General Dynamics, Marconi Space Systems, British Petroleum and construction firms Bovis and AMEC. Unsurprisingly, oil was Souad al-Sabah's speciality and well-placed Kuwaiti sources say commercial connections were forged with Mark Thatcher, or at least discussed.

During their visit, Souad al-Sabah introduced the former prime minister and her son to her managing director, Ahmed El-Mokadem, an Egyptian economist. As El-Mokadem had a house in Guildford, Surrey, they kept in touch and the Egyptian monetarist attended private dinners with Mark and his mother. 'I do know Mark and have met him several times but it has always been social,' El-Mokadem said in a telephone interview. 'There is no business relationship between us. We do not deal with wheelers and dealers. We don't operate in that way. We are a highly professional and serious company and in my opinion Mark Thatcher is not a good businessman.'[68]

It was no secret that Mrs Thatcher and her devoted son were also soliciting funds for an organisation that, like a newly born political party, was struggling and stuttering into life: the Thatcher Foundation. Kuwait was a good location to secure the funds. Grateful local merchants were falling over themselves to hand over large amounts of cash to 'Um', second only to George Bush as the saviour of their nation – and businesses. The most enthusiastic group of financial donors were the al-Ghanims, the second most powerful family in Kuwait and political and commercial rivals to the al-Sabahs.

As the agents for Ford and Bayer in Kuwait, the al-Ghanims were fabulously, and ostentatiously, wealthy. Some pledged hundreds of thousands of pounds each to the foundation. 'Lady Thatcher is now part of our nation's family,' said Fouad al-Ghanim, a BMW car dealer with construction interests. 'I could call 20 businessmen right now and each would give £100,000.' Fouad himself agreed to donate £100,000. Strangely, his money was not collected. 'Mark Thatcher was supposed to be in contact with our people but our fund organiser has heard nothing from him,' he said.[69] But other Kuwaiti donations were banked. Mrs Thatcher may not have been prime minister when British forces bombed Baghdad and helped liberate Kuwait City but her foundation was now reaping the rewards of her strong support for the war. And the way he amassed and presided over the gold filling up the coffers of her foundation would prove to be one of Mark Thatcher's most controversial deals.

Even before leaving 10 Downing Street, Margaret Thatcher envisaged the idea of a vehicle to preserve and continue her political vision. The foundation would have a dual function. It would spread the gospel of Thatcherism internationally, particularly in Eastern Europe. More significantly, from her point of view, the foundation would be a monument to her career and ideology. 'It will perpetuate all the kind of things that I believe in', she said. Her place in the history books has always been very important to Thatcher. And the notion of political immortality through Thatcherism living on beyond the grave has always appealed to her.

At first, some of her close friends questioned the need for a Foundation. Charles Price, US ambassador to the UK from 1983 until 1989 and a director of British Airways and Hanson plc, argued it was unnecessary and in the USA would face direct competition with countless other think-tanks. 'She could have put together a blue-ribbon panel of British businesspeople who would have helped her organise her office, get a staff and get it all done,' said Price. 'There were plenty of dynamic people around to help.'[70]

However, the former ambassador's advice was disregarded and the search for revenue began almost immediately. 'We've got to raise in excess of $20 million,' said Lord McAlpine, former Tory Party treasurer and head of the board of trustees of the UK Thatcher Foundation (other members included former arts minister Lord Gowrie and Sir Geoffrey Leigh, chairman of Allied Properties).[71]

As Mrs Thatcher had asked her son to handle all her financial affairs, he was the chief fundraiser. But his style did not endear him to even her most devoted business admirers. One chief executive of a major American corporation turned him down flat. 'If my company donates to the Thatcher Foundation, we will give a donation on the basis of a proper approach by Mrs Thatcher,' he said at the time. 'We are not going to give money after being propositioned by her son.'

Mark's attitude when he approached senior Conservative businessmen and financiers was that it was now payback time. Margaret Thatcher had been generous to big business. Now it was the turn of big business to be generous to Margaret Thatcher. At one fundraising meeting, he read out a list of high-powered chairmen and chief executives who had made their fortunes in the 1980s and asked how much they were donating. When informed of the amounts, he replied, 'Chickenfeed. My mother made them. Now they have to pay up.'[72] Just before her trip to the Far East, he telephoned a Hong Kong millionaire tycoon and told him, 'It's time to pay up for Mumsie.'[73] When one leading industrialist offered to raise £7 million for the foundation, Mark was dismissive. 'That's not good enough,' he sniffed contemptuously. 'I have someone else who can offer more.'[74]

By the second week of April 1991, chairmen and chief executives were reporting back these horror stories to the former prime minister's private office and her political friends. 'Our first thought was to talk to Margaret about him,' said one, 'because we felt his activities were preventing the foundation getting off the ground. But we knew she would not listen.' They were also scared to confront her, because of her usual stone-faced reaction. 'Some people have tried to do so,' said Charles Price, 'first questioning the wisdom of a foundation and then of having family members involved. It kind of goes into thin air.'[75]

As an alternative tactic, some of her closest disciples, notably a former senior Downing Street official and a former cabinet minister, briefed the *Sunday Times*. The result was a front-page story on 21 April 1991 with a banner headline: 'Mark Is "Wrecking Your Life", Friends Tell Thatcher'. An accompanying feature article contained strong criticisms of him – on a non-attributable basis, of course. Margaret Thatcher was horrified: not by the revelations about her son's antics but by its very disclosure. That Sunday morning, she telephoned her friend Lord Wyatt. 'Have you read the attack on the front page of the *Sunday Times*?' she asked. 'Yes, but I have read all that stuff before,' he replied.

'But it was terrible', said the former prime minister. 'It is bad enough when they attack me but now they are attacking my family and saying terrible things – that he is upsetting all my friends, interfering and spoiling the book. How can Rupert [Murdoch] do this to me?'

Lord Wyatt then spoke to Murdoch on behalf of his political mistress but he stood by the story. 'None of her friends dare tell her what a dreadful mess Mark is making of her affairs,' said the media tycoon.

'I certainly don't dare tell her,' replied Lord Wyatt. 'There's no mileage in it. She would just get angry and I would lose contact with her altogether. She dotes on him.'[76]

The secret briefing of the *Sunday Times* had little effect as Mark continued on his insensitive path of propositioning usually sympathetic businessmen. But industrialists who normally handed over thousands of pounds of shareholders' money to the Conservative Party over lunch at the Savoy Grill were not so happy to do the same for the foundation. 'Mark completely screwed it up,' said one foundation trustee. 'He behaved unbelievably badly. There were at least ten people who would happily have contributed a million had they not been approached by Mark.'[77]

The Thatcher stalwarts Lord Hanson and Lord King, then BA chairman, were conspicuous by their absence as donors to the foundation. BA was viewed as an almost automatic benefactor but when the airline's director of public affairs, David Burnside, was asked whether it would contribute, he replied, 'Not on your life.' The result was a potentially catastrophic shortage of funds, which threatened to sink the vessel before it was even launched. Officially, the delay was blamed on problems with negotiations over its plans for charitable status. But the truth was that Mark's lobbying tactics were dramatically counter-productive.

By June 1991, prospects for the foundation were bleak. There was no money, office, staff or even any headed notepaper. It was a woeful failure, particularly when compared to its nearest model, the Konrad Adenauer Foundation, which by 1991 had a worldwide staff of 1,700 and a budget of £230 million. But Margaret Thatcher was determined to proceed. On 28 June 1991, the day that she announced she was standing down as MP for Finchley at the next election, she said that branch offices of the foundation would be set up in several European capitals. 'It is going to embody all of those things which I've explained and believe in,' she said. 'How to roll forward the frontiers of freedom and how to bring it about. Educating people about what it is all about, giving practical help to the people of Eastern Europe who are trying to do it.'[78]

A 13-page colour brochure was compiled and produced by Sir Tim Bell's company. But even then the shortage of funds delayed the grand opening. This was decided for them on 22 July 1991, when a secretary inadvertently sent out the foundation's manifesto to the press. The glossy document outlined the basic idea of the foundation – to teach Thatcherism to the former communist states and developing nations. Backed by a £10 million budget, this would be realised by holding conferences, distributing grants and scholarships and commissioning research. The coordination and implementation of all this activity would be arranged by the branch offices in the capital cities of the various countries.

After its premature launch, the brochure was distributed to targeted Conservative businessmen with a discreet appeal for donations. Eventually, funds were forthcoming. But this was due to Margaret, rather than Mark, Thatcher. During her Far East tour in August and September, she secured donations from Li Ka-Shing and other Hong Kong magnates, the Sultan of Brunei and several corporations in Japan, Korea and Taiwan.

How these funds were handled by the US branch of the foundation would show just how dangerous it was for Mark Thatcher to be so influential in her financial affairs. As soon as she decided on the foundation, an application for charitable status was lodged with the UK Charity Commission. If granted, this would ensure tax relief and incentives for the donors and tax concessions for the foundation. The stumbling block was that the foundation would have to demonstrate that it did not have political objectives. Under the rules, 'A trust for the education of the public in one particular set of political principles is not charitable.' Clearly, for the Thatcher Foundation *not* to have political aims would be unthinkable, and it was no surprise that on 1 May 1991 the commission refused to grant charitable status.

Despite this setback, Mrs Thatcher's lawyers devised a plan whereby its financial backers could enjoy tax benefits. Six weeks after the Charity Commission's decision, on 10 June, the Margaret Thatcher Foundation Ltd, a company limited by guarantee, whose assets were held by trustees, was set up. The trustees included Lord McAlpine, Sir Tim Bell and Lord Gowrie.

Registered at the Mayfair law firm of Glover, this reconstituted version was used to channel its donations through the Charities Aid Foundation (CAF), a separate agency which acts as a fund manager for trusts. Essentially, the CAF was persuaded that some of the foundation's aims were charitable. This enabled donors to receive tax relief and the foundation to avoid paying tax on gifts deemed for charitable purposes. In return, the CAF is trustee of the money and 'content to act on instructions from our clients, in this case, the Thatcher Foundation'.[79]

This convenient new arrangement was confirmed on 22 November 1991, with the first official meeting of the UK Thatcher Foundation's trustees and members. Chaired by Mrs Thatcher at her new office in

Chesham Place, the meeting agreed the objectives and accounting procedures. One person who was noticeably absent as a trustee or even adviser was Mark Thatcher, who had been so prominent in its inception and attempted fundraising. He attended the celebratory lunch but it had been decided not to give him any official role. His friends said Mark was 'not interested' because he was 'neither a philosophical nor a political animal'.[80]

That was certainly true. But it did not stop him becoming an active president of the US Thatcher Foundation. In early 1991, Mark Thatcher telephoned Daniel Evans, an attorney with the Indianapolis law firm of Baker and Daniels. Evans was very much 'one of us'. In 1988, he had been chairman of the National 'Dan Quayle for Vice-President' Committee and he remained a close adviser to Quayle. Thatcher asked him to draw up the US foundation's articles of incorporation because his law firm specialised in representing non-profit-making far-right-wing think tanks like the Hudson Institute.

Evans agreed and applied for the US foundation to be granted charitable status by the Internal Revenue Service (IRS). Its aims were to 'promote the widest possible acceptance of the principles of economic and political freedom'. It also encouraged 'strong transatlantic links between Britain, Europe and North America' and would 'foster greater contact between Western nations and those of the Middle East'. Members of the executive advisory board include Charles Wick, director of the US Information Agency under President Reagan; Dwayne Andreas, former head of chemical giant Archer Daniels Midland; Timothy Forbes, son of billionaire publisher Malcolm Forbes; and Charles Price.

In May 1991, unknown to his mother's private office, Mark Thatcher secretly arranged for the Thatcher Foundation to be registered and run in the tiny state of Liechtenstein, a tax haven where financial donors can claim massive tax relief. Apart from Mark as president, the only trustees of the Liechtenstein arm were David Wallace, his business partner and later treasurer of the US foundation, and Cornelia Ritter, a local lawyer. Those three had sole signatory rights to the trust. This was arranged in such secrecy that the director of the UK Foundation, Julian Seymour, did not even know about it. 'I was not aware of its existence,' he admitted, and insisted that Lady Thatcher was also ignorant of the Liechtenstein trust.[81] In fact, the former prime minister not only knew but authorised it. 'It [the trust] required the written authorisation of my mother,' confirmed her son.[82]

Mark Thatcher also set up bank accounts for the US foundation in Liechtenstein and in Switzerland. This had the benefit of concealing the origin and size of the contributions. One trustee exploded when he discovered these accounts. 'Fortunately, the accounts were never activated, but can you imagine the scandal if it was discovered that Lady Thatcher was moving money through secret offshore and Swiss accounts,' said the foundation trustee. 'It was just unbelievable.'

Mark Thatcher's riposte was that the trust and accounts were set up in case the US or UK foundations did not achieve charitable status. 'We formed this one in Liechtenstein to have a fall-back position,' he said. 'If you examine the articles of incorporation, you will find they are bloody nearly word for word the same as the application to the Charity Commission and Charities Aid Foundation in the UK.' He claimed it was 'highly unlikely' that the Liechtenstein Thatcher Foundation would ever be used.[83]

In January 1992, the US foundation was awarded charitable status by the IRS, which meant substantial tax relief for its financial backers. Mark lent the foundation $15,000 to pay for legal fees to register as a charity. This made fundraising much easier, although in its first year donations amounted to only $448,229. The UK branch received £254,000 in outside funds, while Mrs Thatcher was paid an estimated £3 million during her overseas tours in 1991.

In Washington, it was not long before the IRS began preliminary investigations into the US foundation. Officials believed it was contravening laws on political activities. 'We don't care who they [the Thatcher Foundation] give their money to,' said Denis Broze, a specialist in tax-exempt organisations. 'What matters is the purpose of the donation. If the Thatcher Foundation is simply pushing out Margaret Thatcher's ideas, that may be a difficulty . . . If we're talking about the views of one person, that counts as political.'[84] On that basis, it is amazing that the US branch acquired charitable status in the first place.

More significantly, the US foundation became closely linked with the private commercial interests of Mark Thatcher. Although it was based in Washington, the foundation's registered office was 1850 Lincoln Center, 5420 LBJ Freeway, Dallas – the same address as Mark's Grantham Company. In 1992, when he moved his corporate office to 5847 San Felipe Drive, Houston, the foundation moved there, too. Mark remained president and spent one day a week on foundation business. The treasurer was David Wallace, his business partner in Grantham and other projects.

In 1992, Wallace was a 30-year-old ambitious financier looking for the main chance. A graduate of the University of Texas, with a degree in real estate finance, he had no professional or commercial training or qualifications. 'I'm trying to get my pilot's licence,' he said, 'but beyond that, I really can't think of anything.'[85] His first job was a three-year stint as a salesman with Equity Management, a real-estate syndication company which went bankrupt in 1986. He then became a consultant to the Dalfort Corporation, the parent company of Braniff Airlines. It was there he met Bruce Leadbetter, chairman of Braniff Airlines, and they joined forces on investment banking projects.

After the 1987 general election, Leadbetter set up the Grantham Company with Mark Thatcher, and Wallace came in later as a consultant. After Leadbetter left, Grantham was reconstituted as a separate outfit but using the same name, and Wallace became a full equity partner and later chief executive. He was an active director and shareholder of Emergency Networks Inc., which went bankrupt in 1992. One of his responsibilities was to liaise with its chief customer, Denver-based Alert Security, but that company also ended in insolvency, owing up to $18 million. His next venture was as chief executive of Ameristar Fuels. This corporation filed for Chapter 11 bankruptcy in 1994.

This was the commercial record of Mark Thatcher's latest business partner, who in 1992 became treasurer of the US Thatcher Foundation. The following year, Wallace became immersed in the affairs of Ameristar Fuels as a substantial shareholder and its financial officer. He was effectively fronting for Thatcher, according to Jay Laughlin, the company's president. It was during this period that the foundation and Ameristar became financially interconnected.

In October 1993, working alongside Mark Thatcher, Wallace approached several contacts to persuade them to invest in Ameristar Fuels. One of them was Robert Higdon, the $125,000-a-year director of the US foundation in Washington. Higdon was recruited into the White House in 1984 by Michael Deaver, then deputy chief of staff, who was later investigated for improper lobbying and received a suspended three-year jail sentence for lying about his business activities.[86] After his spell with Deaver, Higdon worked at the Library of Congress and as a fundraiser for President Reagan.

On 12 October 1993, a copy of the Ameristar prospectus arrived on Higdon's desk at the US foundation's office. Enclosed was a letter from David Wallace: 'Please give me a call after you have had an opportunity to review the enclosed.' Higdon, despite being the full-time head of an educational charity with strong political aims, was effectively being used on a commercial project. He responded by introducing Wallace, then foundation treasurer, to Frank Richardson of Westray Capital in New York and Robert Gray of Gray and Company in Miami.

That year, the US foundation was used in a more direct way to support Ameristar Fuels Inc., in which Lady Thatcher's son had invested, according to the firm's former president, Jay Laughlin. In February 1993, Laughlin had arranged for Mark Thatcher and David Wallace to meet Jean Baudois, a French banker from Caisse Nationale de Crédit Agricole. The meeting took place over tea in the lounge of the Carlisle Hotel, New York, where Baroness Thatcher was also staying. It was a long afternoon discussion, with Mark trying to persuade Baudois to invest in Ameristar Fuels. But when the $77 bill arrived it was charged to Mark's hotel bill, which, according to Laughlin, was paid for by the Thatcher Foundation. Ameristar Fuels later reimbursed the foundation for these expenses.

To what extent foundation funds were used to pay Mark Thatcher's business expenses is one of the questions to which the IRS sought to find answers in 1994 when it launched an investigation into the US foundation. The inquiry was no doubt given the names of the funders of Margaret Thatcher's US and UK 'charities'. This information has been kept secret from the public. 'I don't really feel comfortable talking precise figures,' said Robert Higdon, 'but we are not thinking small. It relies, you could say, on a great deal of generous support.'[87] In 1993 this amounted to $1.3 million in donations. There was increasing concern that the US foundation was spending far more on itself than it donated to the organisations that it was set up to support. In 1995, the accounts disclosed that out of the £676,751 received in contributions, only £40,175 was distributed to worthy causes. Instead, £500,000 was spent on 'administrative costs', salaries and 'fundraising expenses'. And the list of donors has also been withheld from the public.

The UK foundation has even utilised a legal loophole to ensure that only the barest minimum details of its finances are published. Under the 1985 Companies Act, small private companies are granted an exemption which allows them to file only abbreviated, limited accounts. Ironically, it was Margaret Thatcher who introduced this measure, designed to cut bureaucracy, while she was prime minister. As a company limited by guarantee, the UK foundation was able to take advantage of this useful clause. The 1993 accounts merely state they have £467,000 in cash and net assets of £452,000. What's more, the directors (trustees) opted to cancel annual general meetings and no longer present their accounts for inspection by foundation members.

The brief lives of the Thatcher foundations have not been happy. Some grants have been awarded – £30,000 to Enterprise Europe, £10,500 for a scheme to educate 53 students from the Eastern bloc in English public schools and $100,000 for Russian librarians to spend eight weeks in Washington. But by the mid-1990s, only £300,000 was available each year to pro-Thatcherite groups, mainly in Eastern Europe.

However, it could have been so much better. By 1994, only £6 million of the projected £10 million had been raised for both UK and US foundations after three years of lobbying. Fundraising was impeded because of Mark's inept, insensitive approaches to normally supportive businessmen. That brought what was supposed to be a philanthropic monument to Thatcherism into discredit and suspicion.

In the USA, donations were more forthcoming, with Walter Annenberg, the former US ambassador to the UK, and *Forbes* magazine being prominent benefactors. But that relative success was undermined by the use of foundation money to support Mark's involvement in Ameristar Fuels and the high costs and expenses of running the office.

Faced with a cash crisis, it took the former prime minister herself to help fill up the coffers. 'On occasion, Lady Thatcher will go and meet prospective donors and explain what she is trying to do,' said Robert Higdon, director of the US foundation. 'She never talks money with them. We ask them to donate, but don't ask for a certain sum. They write a cheque. She is very good at it.'[88] She has put some of her own money into the US foundation to 'keep it going', according to her friend and trustee Lord McAlpine.[89] And in June 1994, she flew to Abu Dhabi to see her old friend, Sheikh Zayed bin Sultan al-Nahayan. It was 14 years, almost to the week, since her son had been to see the benevolent ally of the Thatchers, armed with a letter of introduction from the prime minister. This time she was asking for a donation for her impoverished US foundation but it was not forthcoming.

By 2004, both the US and UK foundations were under review and their future looks precarious. They continue to fund scholarships and set up the Thatcher chair in entrepreneurial studies at Cambridge

University. But Lady Thatcher has retired from delivering public speeches and fundraising, it seems unlikely that it will be an active exponent of Thatcherite ideology.

In April 1991, Mark Thatcher took time out from his activities as the foundation's financial major-domo and his mother's business manager to fulfil a long-time aim – a commercial and residential base in Switzerland. His parents knew the country well. Every August for fifteen years they spent a two-week holiday at Freudenberg Castle, on the shore of Lake Zug, near Geneva, as the guest of Lady Eleanor Glover, the wealthy widow of former Tory MP Sir Douglas Glover.

Mark was also familiar with the country and used to half-joke about moving there if a Labour government were elected. He had been travelling to Switzerland since 1980, when he flew to Zurich to lobby bankers for sponsorship of his racing activities. He also had a Crédit Suisse bank account in Geneva. On 9 November 1987, Mark and Denis were spotted flying out of Heathrow on a private plane to Geneva.[90] It was a regular journey, for in the secret Swiss bank vaults of Geneva lies Thatcher's fortune, routed via Jersey to trust companies.

However, it was not until 1991 that Mark established a permanent presence in bankers' paradise. His motive was tax avoidance. An insight into his decision came to light on the evening of 3 December 1991, during a party in the Royal Suite at Claridge's hosted by Charles Price, the former US ambassador to London. Thatcher struck up a conversation with Lord Wyatt, his mother's confidant, and said that he had chosen Switzerland because it would never join the European Union or the single currency. 'Taxes will be enormous after the single currency comes in because they will be dictated by Brussels,' he said, 'so Switzerland will be the only place to be based to avoid Brussels' taxes.'[91]

Based in Lausanne, Thatcher became a consultant to Compagnie Financière Espirito Santo, a wholly owned investment subsidiary of the Portuguese-owned bank. Part of his contract was that his new employer would arrange his Swiss residency and work permit.

Banco Espirito Santo, which means 'Bank of the Holy Ghost', has a mixed reputation in the business world. Set up in October 1937, it became Portugal's most powerful bank, with the Espirito Santo family owning a 70 per cent shareholding in the company. The late 1930s and 1940s was a time of great prosperity for the bank. It became a conduit for flight capital as persecuted Jews and wealthy European aristocrats sought refuge in Portugal and planned their escape to South or North America. The family itself became aristocratically conservative and often played host to titled visitors, notably King Karol of Romania and the Duke of Windsor, who spent several months in Portugal during the Second World War.[92]

By the early 1970s, Espirito Santo was hugely successful, with deposits of about $2 billion and equity of $200 million.[93] But disaster struck in March 1975, when a socialist–communist coalition seized power from the military junta. One afternoon, Espirito Santo managers returned from lunch to find troops armed with machine guns in the lobby. Within three months, the banks had been nationalised, with senior Espirito Santo executives thrown in jail. They were charged with 'economic sabotage' but later released. The key family members regrouped in London, where they planned their comeback. They established a new holding company in Luxembourg and a bank in Brazil to look after the interests of Portuguese refugees.

By 1977, the Brazilian bank was sufficiently profitable to provide the capital to set up a new fund-management and private banking company in Lausanne – Compagnie Financière Espirito Santo (CFES). Ironically, it was the 1975 coup d'état that made CFES prosper, as wealthy expatriate Portuguese were looking for management of their money in Europe.

By 1991, when Mark Thatcher became a consultant, the bank's client base had expanded to 3,000 mainly private individuals of various nationalities. It supplied them with centralised portfolio and asset-management services, looking after $1.2 billion of funds. The investments are managed on a mainly discretionary basis and include international securities and gold and silver bullion.

The CFES consultancy was a useful arrangement for the son of the former prime minister. The financial benefits of living in Switzerland are well known, with income tax averaging 20 per cent and ultra-secret banking rules. Mark's salary was £80,000 a year after tax. This easily covered the £25,000 annual rent for his four-bedroomed penthouse apartment, which overlooked Lake Geneva and was only half a mile from CFES's glass-fronted office.

Mark Thatcher was allowed to spend a week in every month in Lausanne on a part-time two-year contract, shrouded in classic Swiss secrecy. When asked by a newspaper what services he provided,

Frederic Strittmatter, a senior CFES executive, replied defensively, 'We have other sons of well-known people working in our group as well as him. He is no exception. I don't see him very often but he is an international man and he travels a lot. There is nothing unusual about having more than one job. I know a lot of people in his position who live in Switzerland.'[94] But Strittmatter was a little more forthcoming when we spoke to him in Lausanne. 'His brief was to develop business in the Far East,' he told us. 'But no clients came in.' When asked why, he replied, 'Perhaps our criteria were too high.' He added that he would be happy to discuss in more detail Mark's involvement with the bank if he received permission. This was not forthcoming.

CFES executives may have been happy with Mark's absences but the Swiss authorities were not so satisfied. By mid-June 1992, when his work and residency permits were due for renewal, the Swiss Federal Department of Justice and Police took an active interest in his affairs. They were concerned that he had not worked or spent enough days in Switzerland. 'It is not enough to simply bring money into Switzerland,' said Jourg Kistler, special counsellor to the minister of the interior. 'You must work in the bureau of a Swiss company to justify a resident's permit. There are only a limited number and we are besieged by requests for them every day.'[95]

Thatcher had been granted a 'B Permit', a *'permis de séjour'*, allowing him to make Switzerland his 'permanent home base' for one year until 1 June 1992. Despite his late application for renewal, this was granted for another 12 months. It was an astonishingly lenient decision. Under Swiss law, residents have to spend most of the year in the country. As Thatcher lived and worked in Texas and travelled abroad constantly, it was self-evident he did not meet that criterion. 'Mr Thatcher knows that he has been given the benefit of the doubt over his first year in the country,' said Kistler in the summer of 1992. 'He has been told there will be a check over the coming 12 months on his movements to ascertain that Switzerland is really his true home.'[96] Kistler added that the law stipulated he should have moved his wife and children into his Lausanne apartment.

Mark managed to keep his residency permit by telling the authorities he 'had problems moving'.[97] But his Swiss base came under threat in late 1992, after recurrent media claims about alleged arms deals in the Middle East. His employer, Espirito Santo SA, was anxious about how the allegations might affect their worldwide

318

business. So in October 1992, he voluntarily gave three months' notice and on 31 December his contract was terminated. In March 1993, Mark Thatcher's Swiss excursion ended when he informed the local police that he was leaving the country. He flew back to Texas but he often returned to Switzerland.

ELEVEN

Out to Africa

My sympathy is with the struggling white community [in South Africa].

– Mark Thatcher[1]

I never thought that I would see my family name on the front page of the *Sunday Times* associated with fraud.

– Denis Thatcher[2]

By the spring of 1995, ominous black clouds were hovering over Mark Thatcher. At least five separate legal actions in the USA were lurking menacingly and his multimillion-pound fortune was threatened by Inland Revenue investigations both in the UK and US. Faced with financial ruin and even a potential jail sentence, many people would have taken refuge in the bosom of their family. But Thatcher responded by taking a four-day sporting holiday without his wife and children. In mid-March, he went skiing at an exclusive resort outside Vancouver, Canada, and then flew to the Doral Country Club in Florida to play golf. There, he booked into a £200-a-night double room and ran up a bill of £2,000 over four days. Golfing fees alone were nearly £800, with £500 spent on food. Back home in Dallas, his wife Diane said that she had 'no idea' when her husband was returning home.[3]

The gloomy clouds of litigation promised a storm of court hearings, investigations and unwelcome scrutiny. The trouble had started in early 1993, when the spectre of his recurrent tax problems returned to haunt him. Hugh Thurston, his personal banker and adviser based in Jersey, always believed Thatcher 'sailed close to the wind' on his tax affairs. This was confirmed by outside legal advice which argued that he was in constant danger of investigation by the Inland Revenue.

Thatcher ignored this advice and thought that he could out-manoeuvre the authorities. At one stage, he even told the taxman that his net worth and declared assets were only £600,000. This was greeted with almost universal derision and by the summer of 1993 the Revenue were again taking a close interest. Thatcher faced the frightening prospect of being compelled to declare all his income from the previous ten years if he was deemed to be a UK resident for tax purposes. And so in August 1993, Thurston hired the top City law firm of Simmons and Simmons to examine and advise on the tax implications of the wealth accrued by the former prime minister's son. Filed under 'Thurston' inside the law firm's office, the documents were labelled 'MT Tax Advice – M76209'. The inquiry focused on his offshore status and advised that their client should spend less time in the UK. Within two months, Thatcher had put his lavishly decorated Kensington house on the market (renting it out at £2,000 per week while waiting for a sale) and moved permanently back to Texas.

He thus avoided further investigation by the UK Inland Revenue but two years later in Dallas, Thatcher was facing a different kind of tax investigation: the prospect of a jury trial over claims by the US government that he had evaded the payment of taxes of nearly $3 million. This related to his past shareholding and directorship of Emergency Networks Inc., the private security firm that manufactured alarm installations. A tip-off by a senior executive to criminal investigators in the IRS had triggered an inquiry into claims that taxes for wages of its employees had not been paid to the government. In late 1993, the IRS had issued proceedings against six former directors and investors of the company, including Thatcher.

The following year, a proposal for mediation was rejected by the IRS and the case was set for trial in a federal court in Dallas in March 1996. There was no sign that it might be settled out of court. On the surface, Mark Thatcher appeared nonchalant and unconcerned about his legal predators. He liked to dismiss the opposing law firms as 'Messrs Peanuts, Bubblegum and Squeak'. But privately, according to his friends, he was racked with insecurity and concerned about how the embarrassing litigation could affect his mother. The prospect of being cross-examined in court about how he had made an enormous commission from the Al-Yamamah arms deal terrified Lady Thatcher and her devotees. 'It would be a great, great mistake for Mark to be in court in America. Absolutely crazy,' said an influential confidante of the former prime minister. Her disciples were anxious that the lawsuits could harm the Thatcher reputation, especially in the US where she was raising funds for her foundation and selling her memoirs.[4]

As a result, Margaret Thatcher implored her son to resolve the disputes. But it was not until early 1996, just before the trial was due to start, that the IRS action against him over Emergency Networks was settled. 'We have dismissed him from the lawsuit,' said Andrew Sobotka, head of the IRS investigation, 'but there are disclosure laws which prevent me from revealing details of the case.'[5] Thatcher's lawyer, Bert Flagg, claimed that his client incurred no penalties but was required to pay his own legal bill of $30,000. When asked why, if there was no liability, Thatcher was not pursuing the IRS for his costs, Flagg replied they were 'irrecoverable'.

While warding off the IRS, Mark Thatcher was also being pursued by his former business associate, Jay Laughlin, former president and founder of Ameristar Fuels, sellers of jet fuel. Thatcher was an investor in Ameristar via his Jersey company Diversified Capital. Laughlin had been ousted in a boardroom coup instigated by Thatcher's then business partner David Wallace in January 1994. After the failure of his first lawsuit against Thatcher and Wallace, Laughlin filed a second writ in October that year under the civil clauses of the Racketeering Influenced Corrupt Organisations (RICO) Act, which was originally introduced to fight organised crime. He claimed that the former prime minister's son used fraudulent methods to 'hijack' his company. In essence, Laughlin alleged that they falsified the firm's financial position in order to engineer a cash crisis and take it over. He demanded $14 million in damages. If convicted, Thatcher faced a potential jail sentence. Publicly, he was full of typical bravado. 'Five or six people who are businessmen in the States – household names – have been ringing me up and saying, "Don't worry about this,"' he declared.[6]

However, Thatcher had plenty to worry about. He strongly rejected the accusations, even denying that he was the owner of Ameristar and claiming that he was merely 'a management consultant'. But internal documents showed that he attended board meetings and gave daily instructions to staff on the provision of credit facilities. Former executives were queuing up to swear affidavits revealing 'serious malpractice'. They claimed that Thatcher was paid substantial fees and used company money for cars, extravagant bar bills ($5,000 in one night at the Ritz Carlton in the Mexican resort of Cancun), expensive clothes, lavish parties and worldwide travel. Former financial controller Gretchen Hyland disclosed that she had investigated the movement of millions of dollars out of the company and soon adopted an attitude of 'outright concern and suspicion'.[7] But then Ameristar was put into bankruptcy, leaving a trail of angry creditors, unpaid debts and impoverished employees. 'Thatcher and Wallace raped and pillaged the Ameristar companies, misappropriating bank collateral, making fraudulent payments to themselves and related parties,' said Laughlin.[8]

Six months later, in March 1995, Lady Thatcher was dragged into her son's legal quagmire when a former Ameristar fuel broker, Emmanuel d'Hoop, filed a lawsuit in Houston. D'Hoop claimed that he was sacked without warning and left penniless by Mark Thatcher from his £80,000-a-year job, despite his contract entitling him to compensation. 'That's it,' Thatcher apparently told him brusquely, with no hint of an apology. But it was the alleged financial involvement of the former prime minister that unnerved her inner circle. D'Hoop claimed that her son told him more than once that her finances were linked to Ameristar. 'She is indirectly involved in the company,' said Mark Thatcher. 'It's family money and this money is being used by Ameristar.' A father-of-five and unemployed, D'Hoop promptly wrote to Lady Thatcher in London and asked her to intervene and 'bring Mark to his senses'.[9] This lawsuit was later settled out of court.

Within a few days, Mark Thatcher was on a flight to London for a family summit and read the riot act by his parents. 'I never thought I would see my family name on the front page of the *Sunday Times* associated with fraud,' Denis told a friend. The next day, his son telephoned Laughlin and asked for a meeting. Surprised by his more conciliatory approach, the Texan agreed and over nine hours on 24 May 1995 they negotiated with their lawyers in a retired judge's chambers in Houston. It was an emotional meeting for Laughlin, who claimed Thatcher had stolen his company and accused him of being a thief and a liar. 'I honestly thought I might strangle him,' recalled the founder of Ameristar. But to his surprise, his former business partner was friendly and humble.

Within half an hour, Thatcher agreed to testify on oath against his business partner, David Wallace, and offered Laughlin a cheque for

$500,000. 'We are now convinced that Mark has been a victim in this affair, too,' said Laughlin. 'He says that he lost a large sum of money – $2 million. He may well have been part of the moves to take over the company, but that is business. However, he does not seem to have been part of any wrongdoing. I now believe what he says. I'm not saying he is a saint but if he's guilty, it is only by association. Mark will still have to give a deposition and will almost certainly be a star witness.'[10]

By 6.30 p.m., the former bitter rivals had agreed a formal deal: $500,000 and Thatcher would testify and provide a deposition against his former close friend and business ally, David Wallace, on condition that his name was dropped from the suit. 'His information indicts the hell out of Wallace,' said Laughlin gleefully. 'I believe it could put him in jail.'[11]

After the meeting, the two chatted casually. Thatcher admitted that he was depressed by his public image as a rude, untalented exploiter of his mother's good name. 'One of the things you could do is spend more time with your family,' remarked Laughlin. 'Don't travel so much.' This was greeted with a brooding silence.

Almost inevitably, Wallace responded by obtaining an injunction against Thatcher to block his out-of-court settlement with Laughlin. The court papers reveal the close nature of their relationship. Thatcher had control over Wallace, his business front man who had been made personally bankrupt before they met. Wallace insisted that he had no alternative but to file the lawsuit against his former friend because he had previously signed an agreement that no legal action could be settled 'without the prior consent of the other partner'. But within two weeks, the lawsuits were suddenly and mysteriously settled, and Thatcher and Wallace paid an estimated $1 million in damages to Laughlin.

That was not quite the end of the affair. Creditors of Ameristar had filed a $4 million lawsuit against Thatcher after the aviation fuel firm was placed into bankruptcy. For months, Thatcher ducked and dived the action, and lawyers for the creditors discovered that he possessed few assets in the USA – apart from his house in Dallas. Everything else was offshore. Eventually, a bankruptcy judge in Houston ordered that Thatcher must pay $180,000 in settlement to the liquidators acting for the creditors of Ameristar. One of the bankruptcy trustees, Barnet Skelton, said that he expected the payment to be made from a 'blind trust', making it 'impossible to know where it came from'.[12]

In fact, the money came from Lady Thatcher's private fortune.

Ever since her son's American commercial interests started to fall apart in a flurry of lawsuits from former business partners, trustees of one of his bankrupt companies and US tax authorities, the former prime minister had regularly bailed him out. Between 1993 and 1996, she paid a total of $3 million to settle the legal actions and costs, the last tranche being $1 million. 'The Texas business has finally gone away, she's sorted it out for him,' said a Thatcher family friend. 'Mumsie has bailed Mark out again,' another remarked.[13]

Former business associates who knew how much he made from the Al-Yamamah arms deal were surprised that Lady Thatcher needed to rescue him. 'Where has all the money gone?' one asked. Much of it disappeared in ill-judged investments like Emergency Networks and Ameristar.

But Mark Thatcher also lived an extravagant lifestyle: he always flew first class, stayed in the most luxurious hotels and spent a fortune on clothes and cars. He also gave nearly £1.5 million to his parents to help refurbish and renovate their house in Chester Square, Belgravia.

Beleaguered and embarrassed by his chaotic financial affairs, Mark Thatcher's swagger and braggadocio of the 1980s was no longer apparent. He was less sure of himself and developed a surprising capacity for self-parody. On the wall of his office in Dallas was a framed newspaper cartoon showing his parents moving into 10 Downing Street soon after the 1987 general election victory. A removal van is taking a large pool table into the house. 'That should keep Mark out of trouble,' his mother is depicted as saying.[14] But some friends say he relished his notoriety. At his home in Cape Town, the cartoons hung up outside his study depicted him as a chancer riding on mother's coat-tails. His favourite is a picture of Lady Thatcher descending from an airplane and greeting a host of wealthy Arabs. Beside her is a little boy wearing a suit and a smug expression. The caption reads: 'As far as business is concerned, Mark's keeping a low profile at the moment, but have you met my grandson?'[15]

As the lawsuits and tax investigations intensified, Thatcher decided to leave the USA and relaunch his career, away from regulators and litigious American businessmen. Closeted away in the Houston offices of his lawyers for much of 1995, he was frustrated, angry and drained. 'I am totally sick of the Texan crap,' he told a friend. 'I want a fresh start.' He cast his eyes across the Atlantic and settled on South Africa. There were several attractions: a weak rand gave him substantial purchasing power if he paid in sterling or dollars, a benevolent tax regime, a sports-mad culture, beautiful scenery, sunshine virtually all year round and, most appealing, the press were far less inquisitive. On her company website, Cheryl Taylor, a Cape Town estate agent, gushed, 'Around R8,000 [$1,128] a month will do for a married couple . . . What kind of lifestyle will this buy you? A villa with a pool, a car and a daily maid . . . South Africa is one of the few places in the world where you'll find First World comforts and infrastructure, and Third World prices on everything else – from food to diamonds to real estate . . . South Africa has problems but that's what makes for opportunity.'[16] Mark Thatcher was hooked.

It was a renewal of a lifelong love affair. As a callow, bumptious schoolboy in the 1960s, he was often packed off to the Cape in the summer holidays to clear up his acne. 'I always send Mark to South Africa to clear up his spots,' said his mother at the time.[17] Hence the nickname 'Scratcher' used by the coup leader Simon Mann in his infamous letter from Chikurubi Prison in Harare. After leaving Harrow in 1972, young Thatcher was dispatched back to South Africa, where he worked for stockbrokers Davis, Borkum and Hare, spending four months compiling reports on the motor industry.

During the early 1980s, Thatcher returned to Africa while struggling to make his name as a racing driver. He once devised, with almost military-style precision, an ambitious race from Southampton to Cape Town but it never came to fruition. This was at the peak of apartheid and his mother's refusal to support sanctions earned her heroic status and popularity amongst the minority white population (after leaving office she was awarded the Order of Good Hope, Grand Cross Class, the highest South African honour). Her son even appeared to back apartheid. 'My sympathy is with the struggling white community,' said Mark. In a later visit, in May 1989, as a guest of Arnold Jager, a businessman in Cape Town, his remarks were more measured. 'The country has changed enormously,' he told SABC TV after visiting the local Kango Caves and looking at some ostrich farming. 'I'm impressed with the changes that have taken place.'[18]

After the demise of his racing career, Thatcher saw South Africa as a business opportunity and adventure playground. His father, a passionate admirer of the country and vociferous opponent of the ban on overseas rugby tours during the apartheid era, had been a regular visitor since the 1950s. Indeed, in 1959, when Margaret Thatcher was selected as the parliamentary candidate for Finchley, Denis was boarding a plane in Johannesburg after a long visit. Five years later, he returned to South Africa when on 'the verge of complete nervous breakdown', according to his daughter Carol.[19] Suffering from depression, anxiety and overwork, Denis, then 49, embarked on the *Warwick Castle* cruiser ship and landed at Durban. He seemed to be in the midst of a midlife crisis and spent the next three months on an extended safari, touring the game reserves at Kruger, Wankie and Nairobi.

Soon after his African sabbatical, Denis Thatcher sold the family firm Atlas Preservatives to Castrol Oil, which made him a millionaire. But he retained his commercial interests in the region. In 1974, he became a director of Quinton Hazell Ltd, a motor components firm which owned a South African subsidiary called Quinton Hazell Superite Holdings and was part of the Burmah Oil group. In the mid-1980s, the company was repeatedly and strongly criticised by the EEC for paying 'starvation wages' to its black workers. An active board member, Denis visited South Africa in 1984 at the height of the controversy but, as ever, kept a diplomatic silence and remained a director until 1998.

Captivated by his father's fond memories, Mark Thatcher saw South Africa as a potential area in which to invest his new fortune, based on the Al-Yamamah deal. In the mid-1980s, the apartheid regime was a lucrative market for arms dealing. Its procurement agency, Armscor, was reported to have sold weapons to anyone who paid, notably Saddam Hussein during the Iraq–Iran war. The perennial conflicts in Angola and Mozambique provided ripe pickings for selling military hardware and Mark Thatcher could not resist. On 7 June 1988, he attended a drinks party at 10 Downing Street accompanied by George Brownlow, export manager of Sentrachem Ltd, a plastics firm based in Germiston, Transvaal. Another guest was Alison Porteus, a film-maker and friend of Carol Thatcher. She noticed how detached Brownlow and his South African sidekick were from the other guests, who included Jeffrey Archer and Cecil Parkinson. 'They stood out because they were on their own,' recalled Porteus. 'I went over to talk to them because I heard their South African accents. They were definitely both military and they told me they were Mark Thatcher's bodyguards. We had an argument about apartheid because they were defending it, saying it wasn't so bad for the blacks. They invited me to South Africa to film. We parted on reasonable terms.'

But Brownlow was more than just Thatcher's bodyguard. 'We were working together and were doing some interesting things,' he told us by telephone from Johannesburg. 'On the business front, it was plastics but there was another overall reason why we were together.' When asked about the nature of the business, he became more sheepish and replied, 'Political, maybe military, I don't know.' He then paused.

'You mean military equipment?'

'It may have been.'

Later in the conversation, Brownlow said, 'I want to check with Mark first about talking to you about the business I was doing with him.' We never heard from him again.

On 6 January 1990, Mark Thatcher arrived at the exclusive Mala Mala game reserve with his wife Diane and his recently acquired butler, Graham Henderson. The timing was not astute at such a politically sensitive point. His mother had recently declared that she would not set foot in the country until Nelson Mandela was released. But her son told friends that it was a private visit and 'a shopping trip for investing my loot'. Wearing dark glasses and trying to be discreet, he met Chris Stals, then governor of the State Reserve Bank, and Mike Myburgh, chief executive of South African Airlines. The Thatchers then moved to Cape Town, where they stayed in the presidential suite of the five-star Cape Sun Hotel for five nights. After that, they transferred to the Drakensberg Sun Hotel, a picturesque lodge overlooking a stunning mountain range in Natal.[20]

After apartheid's demise, Mark Thatcher returned to South Africa with his mother in May 1991, where she was courted and lauded by the white farmers who had regularly sent protea flowers – the national emblem – to her at 10 Downing Street. As he compared South Africa's sun-drenched spectacular scenery with the flat plains of Texas, and its relaxed financial climate with the litigious business culture of America, he considered a permanent move to South Africa. For a base, he looked at Constantia, the plush suburb of Cape Town where the rich and infamous retreat from the prying eyes and ears of the media. Anonymity and privacy is almost guaranteed, and it has proved an attractive bolthole for people like the Earl of Spencer, Sir Elton John and film star Michael Douglas. 'The chances of getting photographed naked on the beach are very slim,' said a local resident. 'There are no local paparazzi, no zoom lenses. For the most part the press here are fast asleep . . . They [celebrities] will mix with the same kind of people as themselves, people who want to keep the outside world at bay, too. Their secrets will remain secret in what is a very wealthy and closed community.'[21]

For Mark Thatcher, Constantia was ideal: a small, secluded pocket of South Africa that still embodies in essence the White Man's Dream, the promised land of wealth, health, traditional sports, fine wine and scenic beauty – where black people still work silently and gratefully to make the lives of white people more comfortable. It represents prodigious new money, ostentatiously displayed and crudely articulated, but with enough of the old benevolent *noblesse oblige* approach to black workers to appease white middle-class consciences. Life is undeniably better for Constantia's black domestics but their material lifestyle remains unaltered. As one observer described it: 'Villas, mansions and manor houses undulate and ooze all over this irrigated emerald landscape. The glories of the Atlantic Ocean sparkle on one side and on the other a sweep of vineyards unrolls like a bolt of new green corduroy to the chaos of wild hills behind it. It is Beverly Hills and the Rockies in one glance. The sun seems to shine permanently, gravel drives murmur with the comforting crunch of scuttling uniformed maids and from all sides there is just enough of a glint of a swimming pool, silver Mercedes and Rolex watch. The houses are huge. Ranch-style overlooks Mock-Tudor which backs on to Cape Dutch and nestles beside faux-Afro-neo-Provencal-Georgian. Constantia is the Irish stew of architecture – anything can be put into it with the certainty that it will improve the general effect.'[22]

Sheltered from the south-easterly gales which batter the rest of the Cape Peninsula, centuries-old oak trees and sycamores soar to the cloud-free sky. All the tracks found on the earliest maps have been preserved as bridle paths which wind across the valley undisturbed by any traffic. And the millionaires' mansions form a contour line of their own, with Table Mountain behind and spectacular bays in the distance. 'It is as though Beverly Hills has been transplanted to San Francisco,' said Ray Whittaker, foreign editor of the *Independent on Sunday*, who grew up in South Africa, after a visit in 2004.[23]

It was a Thatcherite dream and Mark was smitten. 'Just look at that sunset – the way it lights the underside of the clouds,' he grinned and nudged his friend Rodney Tyler while they were having drinks in a rented house in Bishops Court, Cape Town. 'Where else would you get a view like that?'[24]

In the autumn of 1995, Thatcher soon found his very own new Number 10, on Dawn Avenue, while surfing on the Internet in the offices of prominent local estate agent Pam Golding. He paid £570,000 for the imposing white-walled mansion, which has six bedrooms, four bathrooms and a cocktail bar set on two acres of land with an immaculate landscaped garden, a swimming pool and four garages. It looks out towards the majestic Table Mountain and from the back windows there are panoramic views of the Atlantic Ocean stretching for some 40 miles. He registered the house's ownership under Kosovo Investments (Pty) Ltd, a South African company, and immediately spent £20,000 on a new thatched roof.

Inside the 15,000 square-foot house, there is a snooker room, a cherry, beech and mahogany wine cellar and a gym overlooking the pool. The living areas are decorated with bamboo furniture and there is a 100-square-metre room called 'the Safari Lounge'. Many of the walls are covered by Thatcher's wildlife photographs and cartoons from British newspapers satirising his controversial past and relationship with his mother. But by far the most intriguing area is hidden away on the ground floor: a walk-in strong room with its walls reinforced with solid steel. The size of a small kitchen, this is the repository of the secret documents that catalogue his colourful business life.

Even before moving into his new home, Thatcher turned it into a high-security fortress. He persuaded Captain Kobus Stipp, the local police chief, to dispatch armed officers and carry out 24-hour surveillance at the property while it was being renovated. He secured the special protection after his security consultant, Mike Winton, told the police that Thatcher was 'feeling vulnerable' and was 'an assassination target for IRA terrorists'. Given the ceasefire in Northern Ireland was still in place at the time, this was unlikely. But Captain Stipp approved the request and said that 'there were specific reasons' which he declined to disclose.[25] After his family moved in, Thatcher again asked for round-the-clock protection. This time it was refused. Unperturbed, he hired local police reservists who withdrew firearms from Wynberg Police Station and patrolled the grounds and Dawn Avenue for £17.50 per hour. One guard was reported to have opened fire on a man who was fleeing after being disturbed trying to break into a neighbouring house. Nobody was injured.[26]

Inside the house, £20,000 was spent on installing state-of-the-art security equipment – bullet-proof curtains, intercoms, an intruder-detection device, closed-circuit TV, a sentry box for a gateman and powerful floodlights to illuminate the spacious grounds. On the outside, a new eight-foot wall was built, ringed by an electronic fence, and muscular guards and fearsome Alsations provided 24-hour protection. For his wife, Diane, two private security guards, armed with pump-action shotguns and high-powered .357 magnum pistols, were hired to escort her while Mark was in Johannesburg or travelling in Africa. The total bill for the renovation and security installations was an estimated £200,000.

While Cape Town undoubtedly has a crime problem, these were characteristically extreme measures. And when his mother came to visit, nothing was too much trouble. On one occasion, Thatcher asked the local authority to close down Dawn Avenue to ensure his mother's security. The request was refused but again he ignored officialdom and recruited off-duty policemen who used a police radio to coordinate Thatcher's private force. 'If you have the right radio and know the call signs and codes, you need only to put them on the air and the cavalry will descend in minutes,' said a police source. 'Also, you can listen in to all the police traffic.' Using the code 'Whiskey Whiskey 71', his officers turned the surrounding streets into a 'no-go' area. 'These men would stop anybody driving nearby and demand to know what they were doing,' said an indignant local resident. 'It's a public thoroughfare, for God's sake, but Thatcher thought he owned the place.'[27]

As Lady Thatcher became a frequent visitor, her son built a thatched gazebo cottage in the garden of his home for her use with its own vehicle entrance, state-of-the-art fireplace and wooden deck. Local residents objected, pointing out that planning laws prohibit second dwellings on plots of land. But Thatcher pressed ahead. Citing a loophole, he claimed that it was designated for 'staff accommodation' but such a cottage would have been rather grand for his £200-a-month domestic servants.[28]

When Lady Thatcher stayed at the house in the late 1990s, she behaved as if she was still prime minister. On her arrival, the fax machine began spewing out reams of paper – endless drafts of speeches, briefing memos and newspaper articles. 'Suddenly, she expected to be briefed on world events as if it was vital that she responded,' said an aide who travelled with her. 'She kept a punishing schedule and she looked exhausted. Mark and Denis tried to reduce her commitments without telling her but she felt compelled to accept all invitations. We had to drive hundreds of miles across country in South Africa so she could give this speech. It was crazy. I could see that she did not relish the journey but she kept saying that "Thatcherism must be kept alive".'

Mark Thatcher felt right at home in Constantia and his neighbours set the tone: a Belgian cheese baron; Wilbur Smith, the bestselling adventure novelist and South Africa's equivalent of Frederick

Forsyth; some Taiwanese and Hong Kong entrepreneurs; and an Italian billionaire who reputedly made his fortune from selling silk brassieres. It is an area where new money has flooded in but no one wanted to ask where it came from. As African dictators arrived with suitcases full of dollar bills, the old inhabitants watched with a mixture of delight at the surging value of their property and disdain at the brashness of the new residents.

Mark Thatcher's presence was greeted with a mixture of excitement because of his famous name and trepidation based on his reputation for dubious business deals and a rude manner. When he first arrived in November 1995, a special dinner party was thrown for him by Pam Golding, his estate agent, at a top local restaurant where he was introduced to 22 handpicked luminaries of Cape Town society. At first, Thatcher tried to make a good impression. He was polite, told a series of amusing anecdotes and, most shockingly, thanked the waiter and his hostess. But he then reverted to type. 'He started banging on about his contacts throughout the world and the millions he made in the Middle East,' said one guest, 'but when it came to a serious discussion about world affairs, international business or politics, he did not seem to have much to offer.'[29] But it was his bragging about avoiding tax because the bulk of his income was earned overseas that really alienated people. 'We were not impressed,' said another. 'What really left a sour taste was his boasting about living the grand life in Cape Town and not having to pay tax. It was a very silly thing to say in front of complete strangers who did have to pay their taxes.'[30]

Bored with social chit-chat and politics, Thatcher much preferred the company of like-minded men who could drink for hours and talk about big money, fast cars, golf, helicopters, risky business deals and dark deeds by mercenaries and Special Forces. There is no doubt that he had mellowed socially and made an effort to blend in with the locals. But when faced with a room full of conventional South Africans outside his immediate circle, the old arrogance rose to the surface. During one party, Thatcher's car was blocked in by another guest. Instead of quietly asking the person to move their car, he just stood at the door and bellowed loudly, 'Which idiot has parked their car in front of mine? Move it now.'

Even his friends were appalled by Thatcher's legendary bullying and intimidation of waiters who, of course, cannot answer back. 'Oi, arsehole,' was a favourite form of address. If the white wine was not chilled adequately or the food did not arrive within ten minutes, he would click his fingers and summon the waiter. 'Listen, moron,' he said while winking at his fellow diners. 'I have an agreement with your manager that all your blunders will be added up by the end of the evening and then deducted from your wages, so shape up.' Some of his friends chuckled, most were outraged.

Word of his abrasive manner soon spread through Cape Town society, although this was not why he was refused membership of the prestigious Royal Cape Golf Club. Like his father, Thatcher has always been an excellent golfer and played off an eight handicap. In March 1996, several members, notably Roger Hamilton-Brown, the former Warwickshire county cricketer and local property developer, proposed the former prime minister's son for membership. But during the heated debate, the club president said that Thatcher's past involvement in arms deals counted against him. 'It would be too controversial,' he told the committee. He added that the new government could take retaliatory action because Lady Thatcher had opposed sanctions against apartheid and once branded the ANC as terrorists. 'His membership will cause too much aggravation,' he concluded. The majority agreed and Mark Thatcher was the first person to be 'blackballed' for decades. 'Thatcher had a very high opinion of himself and a weird offhand manner,' said one supporter. 'But he did not deserve that treatment. It was entirely a political decision.'

Privately, Mark Thatcher was deeply disappointed and began spending more time in Johannesburg, where he bought an apartment and stayed for three nights a week. He joined the Rand Club, the influential private haven for businessmen, accountants, property developers and lawyers. Founded in 1887 by gold mine entrepreneurs, it was modelled on the Reform Club of Pall Mall with its Victorian-style interiors and boasts 2,000 members.

While Mark was delighted with his new life, his wife Diane was less enamoured. She was unhappy about moving so far from her friends and family and agonised for a long time over whether to join her husband. 'She's going on a trial period, and she's moving for God not for Mark,' said a friend.[31] She insisted on keeping their house in Highland Park, Dallas, in case it did not work out. That was also a smart move legally: when a couple divorces in Texas, the mother invariably wins custody of the children so long as she has her primary residence in the state. Despite the expensive and exhausting flight home (£3,300 for a Club Class ticket routed via Miami and taking a total of 21 hours), she often returned to Texas.

Diane admired the natural beauty of the Cape peninsula, but bridge parties, cricket, bowls clubs and colonial-style afternoon tea gatherings did not appeal to the homespun Texan girl. Her interests are working out at the gym, clothes shopping, attending Bible study groups and spending time with her children. An elegant, attractive and immaculately groomed blonde, Mrs Thatcher had little in common with Cape Town society. At dinner parties, her conversations were limited to the well-being of her children, religion and her gym. While pleasant and cordial, she shows little interest in anything outside her immediate family and friends. But Diane is conscious of social status and her famous name. Within days of the death of Sir Denis Thatcher on 26 June 2003, she commissioned new personal stationery with the inscribed 'Lady D. Thatcher' at the top of the page now that her husband was elevated to 'Sir Mark'. She also used 'Lady D. Thatcher' to book her airline tickets.

Diane and Mark Thatcher are very much the odd couple. Apart from their children and love of titles, they have little in common. Diane despises politics and disapproves of his business deals, while Mark despairs of her lack of interest in the outside world. They squabble frequently – usually about the most trivial domestic issues – and adopt a radically different approach to parenting: she is benevolent and nurturing, while he is strict and demanding. They demonstrate little affection, apart from the occasional nonchalant peck on the cheek. This was starkly illustrated on 5 January 1996, when Diane arrived in South Africa and joined her husband for their new life together. Instead of welcoming her with reassuring words and hugs and kisses after a gruelling 21-hour journey, Mark marched yards ahead silently as they left the arrivals hall at Cape Town airport, pushing his daughter's trolley stone-faced. They then moved into the Vineyard Hotel and promptly had a blazing row.[32]

The long-suffering Diane endures much in the marriage – Mark's long absences abroad, his temper tantrums, being in the spotlight of notoriety and unwelcome publicity. But the most painful source of tension was her husband's close friendships with other women. In Texas, Mark had often preferred to stay at a five-star hotel in Houston near his office at Ameristar Fuels rather than take the one-hour flight back to his home in Dallas. He reportedly became close to his secretary, a 32-year-old brunette called Debbie Milner. Star-struck by the Thatcher name, she became besotted with her gruff-mannered boss and, according to fellow employees, he responded by showering her with gifts including lingerie.[33] When Diane discovered his close friendship, she calmly asked Mark about it and accepted his explanation.

Diane responded in a similar fashion when speculation grew about Mark's close friendship with Jilly Susman, a charismatic blonde socialite who lived next door in Cape Town. While his wife was still in Texas, Mark and Mrs Susman, a 40-year-old wealthy divorcee, had dinner together on several occasions and attended the same parties. Four leading South African newspapers ran stories about their late-night dates. 'I found him amusing and charming. Nothing like his reputation,' said Mrs Susman, who was described as unconventional, strong-minded and unruly. A style magazine once photographed her, fully clothed, relaxing in a pond of water lilies. She could not have been more different from Diane.[34]

It was all very upsetting for the old-fashioned, deeply devout Christian girl. Her salvation – and some say the main reason they remain married – are her two children. When the Thatchers moved to South Africa in January 1996, their daughter Amanda, barely three years old, had no trouble uprooting. But their son Michael, then seven, found it more difficult. By all accounts, Michael Thatcher is a gifted, pleasant child, academically bright and talented on the sports field. In Texas, he loved baseball and soccer. But when he arrived in Cape Town, his father banned him from playing football. 'It's a game for oiks,' he told him. While proud of his son's sporting prowess at rugby and lacrosse, Mark Thatcher is characteristically over-critical – to the point where Michael refuses to play him at squash.[35]

Since 1996, the children, like their parents, have virtually commuted between their schools in Dallas and Cape Town. Inevitably, they adopted, almost certainly subconsciously, cross-national accents. In late 2002, when the children returned to Cape Town after several months at school in Dallas, Michael, then 13, spoke with a bizarre South African–American brogue, while Amanda then had a Texan twang. Their mother was tickled by their funny accents, knowing that they would soon fade away. But their Old Harrovian father was incensed. 'They must speak proper English,' he loudly insisted.[36] This amused their friends, who pointed out that Mark spoke like a 1940s cockney spiv most of the time, with quirky colloquialisms, except when his mother was present, of course.

While Diane was constantly homesick, Mark Thatcher felt comfortable in his adopted country. Apart from his marital problems, the press left him alone and he developed other interests, notably wildlife photography. But he still needed to make money. He had invested recklessly, and first-class travel and luxury hotels were fast reducing his vast fortune, so he needed to resume his commercial deals. But the South African government was uneasy about his track record: international arms deals, impending trial in the USA for alleged tax evasion over Emergency Networks and alleged past links to General Magnus Malan, the hated defence minister during the apartheid regime. In early 1996, the Ministry for Internal Safety and Security conducted an investigation into whether he was 'an undesirable citizen' but in April he was granted permanent residency status.

Within a year, Mark Thatcher was wheeling and dealing, and it was not long before he was in trouble. The controversy stemmed from his 25-year obsession with security and bodyguards. In April 1997, he began paying off-duty police officers to provide protection at his house. One senior reservist, Inspector Neville Whitney, was uncomfortable about receiving an £800 cheque from Thatcher after learning that he was lending money to non-commissioned police officers at Wynberg station. Whitney said that when the time came to repay a loan, he was asked to accompany another officer to Thatcher's home. 'He went into the guardhouse and came out soon afterwards with a white envelope stuffed with money as well as a cheque,' recalled Whitney, who said he was instructed to cash the cheque. Uneasy about the arrangement, he reported the transaction and an inquiry was launched into whether the payments and loans were illegal. As there was already a wider investigation into police corruption, detectives raided Thatcher's home in Cape Town. But the inquiry found no evidence of illegal activity.[37]

The former prime minister's son saw nothing wrong in setting up a money-lending scheme which targeted civil servants, court officials, servicemen and women, as well as police officers. He hired several police book-runners to run his new business of lending relatively small amounts of money but at high interest rates. It was almost as if he got a thrill out of commanding a group of police officers. This certainly appeared to be the case at the exclusive Steenberg golfing estate in Cape Town on 17 January 1998, when he addressed 15 senior police officers who were his 'runners'. As reported by David Jones, the *Daily Mail* correspondent in South Africa who broke several stories about Thatcher in the mid-1990s, the former prime minister's son seemed to think that he was a detective inspector in charge of the Flying Squad. He banged his fist on the wooden table and the officers instantly fell silent.

Addressing his troops in suitably clipped, military tones, the Old Harrovian began with a few words of praise. Barely ten months after the venture began, they had delivered high-interest loans to 900 hard-up clients, including several policemen. They had penetrated 26 police stations and forces bases – but now it was time for the really big push. 'We must send out much more money,' he urged his team. 'If we are successful, the size of our company will increase by a factor of ten by the end of 1998. Ambitious plans. Can we do it? Certainly not if we don't try!' As a sweetener, he offered everyone seated around the table, the opportunity of an expenses-paid trip to the 1999 rugby World Cup in Wales and a stay in one of London's finest hotels. 'It's just around the corner from my mother's house,' he chimed in, just in case anyone had forgotten his pedigree. And to rouse the locals with an evocative rallying cry, he declared, 'Our goal is to become the dominant force south of the Hottentot Hollands,' a range of mountains in the south-west Cape.[38]

Such bold words fell on receptive ears. Many Cape Town police officers were poorly paid – £250 per month – and lived in cramped state-owned apartments with a wife and children to support. Perpetually in debt, taking a second part-time job was not unusual. 'When Mark Thatcher said he wanted me to work for him, I was delighted,' recalled police officer George Matfield. 'At first, he was very friendly and generous. He gave me and the runners a book, *The Downing Street Years*, signed by his mother, and a bottle of 1981 Cuvee Bacard vintage champagne for my wife's birthday. But he could turn very quickly. One of the runners addressed him as "Mark" in one of the meetings and he shouted, "I'm not your friend. You call me Mr Thatcher or Boss."'[39]

The loans were small – never more than £600 – so they could circumvent South Africa's laws governing interest rates. Word spread among those who were not credit-worthy that Thatcher's agents could be tapped for easy money. But the interest rates were 20 per cent per month and so they fell further into deep debt. It was crude loan sharking, which was compounded by Thatcher's shambolic operation, according to Matfield. His 'receipts' were scribbled on bits of torn-out paper. 'I just used to go up to his [Thatcher's] house and he would give me cheques to cash at his bank,' said the police officer. 'If he was travelling, he left blank signed cheques. There was never a problem cashing one of his cheques, no matter how large, at his bank. Sometimes, he would just take cash from his drawer. There was no proper organisation. More than once he said in front of witnesses that he "owned" Wynberg police station.'[40]

As Thatcher demanded that more cash be 'pushed out' as fast as possible, the business veered out of control and into chaos. Virtually anyone who asked received a cash loan. As there was no scrutiny or vetting of potential borrowers, the majority of whom were low-paid workers, the inevitable happened: many could not repay the loans. When Thatcher found out, he went ballistic. He warned his police runners that he was recruiting his own debt-collecting team to bring people into line. 'If people won't pay us, then do what you must to get the money but don't assault the guys,' said Thatcher, as if he was running a shakedown operation in New Jersey, USA.

Some people who owed as little as £200 were harassed by Thatcher's henchmen. They then received threatening letters from lawyers representing Thatcher's company in Cape Town, which he called Matrix Churchill (ironically, the same name as the firm at the centre of the arms-to-Iraq scandal at the time). But many, including police officers, claim that they were never asked to sign for their cash advances and hotly disputed the sums demanded by Thatcher and his debt collectors.

All too predictably, the crude scheme ended in chaotic calamity and embarrassment. 'But, Mark, this is fucking loan sharking. What are you doing?' asked a concerned friend. And though Thatcher ignored the warnings, the Consumer Institute agreed with his friend. Its chief executive, Diane Terblanche, described his operation as 'common loan sharking' and raised the case with the government, which was already introducing new regulations governing the numerous small-loans businesses. To make matters worse, the Police Commissioner of Western Cape Province, Leon Wessels, ordered the anti-corruption unit to investigate Thatcher's activities.

While no legal action was taken over the debacle, it reinforced the image of the former prime minister's son as an inept spiv who would do almost anything to make money. In response to the criticism, Thatcher portrayed himself as the victim of fraud, because some of his police runners ran fake books with phantom borrowers. 'It was like opening a telephone book, choosing a name and filling in the loan forms,' said one.[41] There was substance to this claim, and Thatcher lost an estimated £200,000. But his main justification was less credible and almost risible: that his motives were charitable and altruistic. In an interview with David Jones of the *Daily Mail*, Thatcher said he saw himself as a white knight, championing the rights of impoverished policemen and helping them prosper in the new South Africa. And if he made a few rand, so be it. His intention, he said, was never to make money but to perform a form of social service, although he baulked at the phrase. 'I think the amazing thing is that the people who abused it [his generosity] were the guardians of the law in South Africa,' he reflected. 'That's the disappointment to me.'[42]

Thatcher denied that he was a street-level loan shark with a famous name. 'Are you blaming me for lending money to people?' he asked Jones. 'Are you saying that because they have got acute difficulties, I shouldn't deal with them? I'm not the one that elects to increase their debt, they are. What's wrong with that?' But the reality, according to the police officers involved, is that Thatcher placed them under intense pressure to lend more and more cash to desperate debt-ridden people in order to accumulate larger financial returns, which would, in his words, 'increase the size of the company by a factor of ten'. It was a commercial money-making Thatcherite enterprise.

While indulging in loan sharking, Thatcher also dabbled in more 'orthodox' business endeavours. He tried investing in a variety of ventures, from security devices to shopping trolleys. The scheme that attracted him most combined his two lifelong passions: cars and security. In December 1996, he bought the South African franchise for Eagle Eye, a satellite tracking system that claimed it could locate a vehicle to within a few metres. It was designed to help police and drivers trace stolen cars. 'In an emergency, Eagle Eye can guide police or breakdown services directly to your vehicle,' said the promotional brochure, 'and pinpoint accurate tracking to within one metre anywhere on Earth.'

The project was brought to Thatcher by his new business partner, Graham Lorimer, a New Zealander and former racing driver. In the autumn of 1996, they flew to Britain and met the businessman behind Eagle Eye, Harry Harvey, based in the Cheshire stockbroker belt. Colourful, charismatic and notorious, Harvey is the type of dubious salesman that attracts the former prime minister's son. A former painter and decorator and policeman, he ingratiated himself with the locals by being the Hunt Master for the Cheshire Farmer's Drag Hunt and became friends and business partners with William Shand-Kydd, a relative of Princess Diana.

But in 1981, Harvey was jailed for two years along with a fellow company director of his motor dealership. The pair were convicted at Manchester Crown Court for conspiring to burn down their own garage as part of an insurance swindle. A business associate of Harvey had entered the premises using his key and dowsed the place with petrol. Clearly, chemistry had not been his best subject at school, as he dropped some matches on the petrol and the office went up. When he frantically tried to escape from the showroom, he was involved in a serious road accident. He was then arrested, as he still had the keys to the premises in his possession when the police arrived. Harvey claims that the convictions were overturned on appeal in 1982.

Using four different names, Harvey is the archetypal plausible but dubious salesman, often on the edge of financial ruin and yet claiming to be buying Bentleys and Rolls-Royces. By August 1994, he had run up so many debts that he was declared officially bankrupt. Two years later, he still had ten county court judgements against his name for unsatisfied debts of at least £27,000 and left behind a trail of disgruntled former business partners. In October 1996 came the final ignominy, when Harvey was banned from being a company director in the UK for eight years. The High Court ban was imposed after a DTI investigation into an advertising firm which Harvey set up in the late 1980s and sold at a substantial profit.[43]

A mere month after the ban, Mark Thatcher was being welcomed by Harvey at his £1 million mansion at Mill Farm in the village of Mottram St Andrew near Macclesfield, Cheshire. At the outset, Harvey told him that he was a bankrupt but Thatcher casually brushed this aside. He loved the Eagle Eye project, which was devised by NASA for the US government. With its 24 orbiting satellites watching over vehicles and the ultrasonic sensors, it was exactly the type of hi-tech security gadget that excited the car fanatic. He immediately paid thousands of pounds for the rights to sell the product in South Africa.

However, when Eagle Eye arrived in South Africa it did not work. The system was plagued with technical problems and Thatcher could not develop it in a market already saturated with similar devices in a country where car-related crime was then rampant. Despite being under development at Manchester University, it was a dud and Thatcher withdrew. 'After further investigations into the technical capabilities of the system and further discussions with the company, we decided not to take up the option,' he acknowledged.[44]

Perhaps the most revealing feature of the Eagle Eye deal was that Thatcher knew in advance that his prospective business partner was an undischarged bankrupt. It is even possible that he knew about Harvey's troubled past. Unmoved, it was almost as if Thatcher revelled in and preferred dealing with disreputable characters rather than honest brokers. 'Mark does not believe that the normal business rules apply to him,' said a close friend. 'He has convinced himself that he is not vulnerable to scrutiny. But, because of his name and reckless behaviour, he is even more vulnerable than most.'

Increasingly, Thatcher's commercial activities resembled a hobby or recreation for this twitchy, middle-aged man with the short attention span who constantly needed a shot of adrenalin – whether it was from driving a racing car or rushing into a reckless business venture. After all, Mark Thatcher did not need to work. Financially, the Thatchers are far more wealthy than is assumed. His father Denis left a sizeable fortune and friends say that the combined family coffers are filled with at least £50 million. During Margaret's eleven-and-a-half-year tenure as premier, Denis Thatcher raised an estimated £2 million a year from pro-Conservative tycoons and friends to finance her lifestyle and to host private dinner parties and drinks receptions at 10 Downing Street. This was partly to ensure that such entertainment was not funded from the public purse but it also enabled the thrifty Margaret Thatcher to save funds for the future.

By the mid-1990s, the school fees of Mark Thatcher's two children were being paid for by the family trusts administered in Jersey and he also received a £250,000 annual allowance. The mortgages on the houses in Dallas and Cape Town were paid off. 'Why are you still working?' asked a close friend. 'I would get bored and I need the buzz of doing the deals,' he replied.

Negotiating a contract was now akin to playing a game of golf and Thatcher increasingly took on the persona of a Harrovian Arthur Daley with a peculiar line in self-deprecating humour. When Peter Mandelson met him in 2002 at a dinner party hosted by Tony O'Reilly, the wealthy owner of Independent Newspapers, in Constantia, he was shocked. 'Oi, you're Peter Mandelson,' said the former prime minister's son, striding towards the former cabinet minister. 'I've always wanted to meet you.' Startled by his manner, the New Labour Svengali barely listened to what he was saying. 'He was a combination of a 1940s spiv and a 1980s barrow boy, and spoke as if he was in a Marbella golf club,' recalled Mandelson. 'He reminds me of those rather amiable, entertaining twits that P.G. Wodehouse used to write about,' said a Cape Town hostess.

The P.G. Wodehouse analogy was remarkably perceptive and accurate. 'Come on, we're going to put our bums in the butter dish or our heads will be flushed down the loo,' said Thatcher while discussing a potential commission on a typically risky African scheme. There was a yawning gap between Mark Thatcher's view of himself and the reality which, especially in the early 1980s, was distinctly unpromising as he stumbled Mr Toad-like from one enthusiasm to another. He has always exhibited an airy confidence which is uncannily similar to Lupin Pooter, the fictional son of Charles and Carrie Pooter in the satirical novel *Diary of a Nobody*, written by George and Weedon Grossmith in 1892. Young Lupin was a great worry to his parents: he was always mixing with people richer than himself and seemed incapable of retaining steady employment in Mr Perkupp's office.

Lupin Pooter, like Thatcher, was a manic wheeler-dealer, had an unwavering belief in the quick buck, a love of speed, a taste for flashy formality and a conviction that if you look and act rich you will sooner or later accumulate big money. In both their stories, this tactic somehow worked. Like Lupin, Mark also showed a lofty disdain for the fact that many people hated him, cheerfully reminding anyone in earshot that his mother was also despised but had won three successive elections. And yet Lupin, who was the despair of his hard-working parents, was anxious to demonstrate his material success: 'Having been in the firm of Job Cleanands, Stock and Sharebrokers a few weeks, and *not* having paid particular attention to the interests of my superiors in the office, my Guv'nor, as a reward to me, allotted me £5 worth of shares in a really good thing. The result is, today that I have made £200.[45]

The uncanny resemblance between Lupin Pooter and Mark Thatcher even extends to their personal lives. *Diary of a Nobody* concludes with Lupin proudly announcing his engagement to Miss Lillie Posh, heiress to a hat fortune, while Mark married Diane Burgdorf, the daughter of a wealthy car dealer.

By 2000, Mark Thatcher, 47, was less arrogant but he still appeared to relish his reputation for associating with colourful businessmen. He was spending a lot of time with John Bredenkamp, a UK-based Zimbabwean businessman whose £700 million fortune was derived from sports management, tobacco trading and alleged arms dealing. Born in South Africa in 1940, he grew up in Zimbabwe, then known as Rhodesia. His early life was dominated by hardship and tragedy. When he was a teenager, his father, a tobacco farmer of modest means, killed his wife and then himself. Young Bredenkamp channelled his energy into sport. Obsessed with winning, he played rugby with relentless zeal and became captain of the Rhodesian national team.

But 'money became his God', according to a long-time friend.[46] As a young, tough tobacco and arms salesman, he was driven and intense, and, by his own admission, an alcoholic. It was not until 1982, aged 42, that he stopped drinking. In the 1980s, Bredenkamp made a fortune from selling weapons to both sides during the Iran–Iraq war. In one deal, according to his former salesman Mike Pelham, he made a £60 million commission by supplying air-defence guns manufactured by Oerlikon to Iran. 'I had a great deal to do with Mr Bredenkamp's bank accounts in Zurich,' Pelham told Channel 4's *Dispatches* programme, which also claimed that the Zimbabwean was operating with the tacit approval of the CIA and MI6.

A UN report in 2002 claimed that Bredenkamp made millions from illegally exploiting natural resources in the Democratic Republic of Congo. It disclosed a network trading in weapons and valuable minerals which helped fuel a conflict that has claimed nearly three million lives and been called Africa's 'First World War'. A Bredenkamp-controlled company, Aviation Consultancy Services, allegedly brokered sales of BAE equipment in Africa. The report also claimed that he provided £2 million of spare parts for Hawk jets to the Zimbabwean air force in breach of UN sanctions.[47]

Bredenkamp – who voluntarily cooperated with the UN over the report – angrily and vigorously rejected the allegations. He wrote to the UN Secretary-General Kofi Annan, protesting that much of the material was inaccurate and adding that he would contest vigorously his inclusion on any list of sanctions busters. 'I have certainly not contravened any sanctions,' he said.

While admitting that he violated UN sanctions against Rhodesia in 1972 when he bought aircraft for the white-run government led by Ian Smith during its brutal civil war, Bredenkamp denies that arms are the source of his wealth. 'I made all my money in tobacco,' he said.

Unpretentious, aggressive, domineering and secretive, Bredenkamp invested much of his wealth in property. He bought a sprawling £9 million Lutyens-style mansion in Sunningdale, Berkshire, with six reception rooms, five bedrooms and vast landscaped gardens with a long private drive. In London, he owns a house on Chester Square, Belgravia, close to Margaret Thatcher's home. Her son Mark was fascinated and fixated by the blunt, gruff Zimbabwean tycoon and his fortune. They played golf together and Thatcher enjoyed flying in his hero's Gulfstream private jet, where they discussed business schemes, although there is no evidence that any deals were closed.

The British government was horrified. Bredenkamp was banned

from travelling to the USA and cited by the UN as a sanctions buster and arms dealer. MI6, via intermediaries, told Mark Thatcher that he should avoid Bredenkamp. But the former prime minister's son ignored these official warnings. It was almost as if he enjoyed associating with such notorious characters. A close friend was very concerned. 'You've got to stay away from these barrow boys,' he implored. Thatcher paused and then half-smiled. 'But I'm a bit of a barrow boy, really,' he replied.

The sight of Mark Thatcher swimming in such murky waters was a familiar one to MI6 and British embassies in Africa and the Middle East. But in early 2001, he raised the stakes by introducing the former prime minister into his network of gun-runners, foreign intelligence agents and mercenaries. The occasion was a special dinner organised by Mark Thatcher in his mother's honour. But typically, the setting and guests were not well chosen.

The host for the evening was Jean-Yves Ollivier, a businessman and representative for Thomson-CSF, the French arms manufacturer, in Africa. A smooth-talking middleman, Ollivier has a long track record for cultivating connections with the French intelligence agencies DGSE and DRM in Africa. He has often been used to mediate between warring factions, notably in the Congo, while promoting French foreign interests. He boasts that he sees nothing wrong with using his political and intelligence contacts to secure business favours. His modus operandi is to negotiate peace in countries like Mozambique and the Congo and be rewarded with lucrative stakes in profitable hotels and telephone companies.[48]

In South Africa, Ollivier forged close links with the defence minister, General Magnus Malan, during the apartheid era and acted as a diplomatic trouble-shooter in the country's relations with France. 'I have business interests in the region,' he acknowledged, and by the late 1980s he had met Mark Thatcher. During his trips to South Africa in June 1989 and January 1990, Thatcher had at least two meetings with General Malan, which were facilitated by Ollivier.

As Malan was viewed as one of the most aggressive exponents of apartheid, Ollivier's effortless and unashamed move into the ANC's inner sanctum demonstrated his deft survival skills. His transition was so smooth that he was awarded the Order of Good Hope by President Mandela in 1995. But he remained a commercial operator and on 14 May 1996, his company Gestilac acquired a 5 per cent stake in Thomson-CSF Holdings (Southern Africa) Pty Ltd.

A flamboyant character with a camp manner, Ollivier loved South

Africa and in the mid-1990s bought General Malan's house in Bantry Bay, just outside Cape Town, with its stunning panoramic views of the ocean. It was here that Mark Thatcher invited a bizarre mix of car dealers, French military intelligence officers and oil traders. 'Only Mark could introduce Britain's second greatest-ever prime minister to a bunch of French spooks and dodgy businessmen,' said a guest who was present.

A more distinguished guest was Ann Grant, the newly appointed British High Commissioner in South Africa who had just arrived from the Foreign Office in London. Well informed and serious minded about Africa, she glanced nervously and quizzically at the other diners. When told by a guest that she was sharing a table with some of the most notorious rogues, mercenaries and spivs on the continent, she looked anxiously at her fellow guests around the table and went white as a sheet. She then joined Margaret Thatcher's table. On returning to her office at the High Commission, Grant wrote a report that warned that Thatcher was mixing in the wrong circles. She sent the document to the Foreign Office in London but no action was taken. 'I was briefed by the High Commissioner,' recalled a senior official. 'She was very, very worried about Mark Thatcher and his associates.'

It was, of course, such 'dodgy' associations with mercenaries that landed Thatcher in such trouble when he was arrested for his involvement in funding the coup operation in Equatorial Guinea (EG). After his court appearance on 25 August 2004, he returned to his house in Cape Town but was immensely frustrated and angry. The bail restrictions impaired his favourite pursuits: incessant travelling, racing cars, wheeling and dealing. Instead, he spent most of his time talking to his lawyers and his mother by telephone twice a week (although he claimed his phones were tapped). His main concern was avoiding extradition to EG, where suspects are habitually tortured and traitors shot, and he hired Desmond de Silva QC. Known as the 'Scarlet Pimpernel' for saving so many defendants from execution overseas, de Silva reassured Thatcher. 'South Africa cannot extradite him as it has laws preventing it from extraditing people wanted for political offences and treason is clearly a political offence,' said de Silva, who also represented Lord Brocket, jailed for two years for insurance fraud.[49]

Pacing the grounds of his house impatiently, Thatcher's lifelong persecution complex was never far from the surface and he kept returning to a comment from a friend, who told him, 'Mark, you were born guilty.' But, while he kept his emotions in check, his mood swung from despair to fury. 'Who will want to deal with me after this?' he moaned.

While her grim-faced husband stayed at home, Diane Thatcher was in a state of shock. Very upset and in emotional turmoil, the humiliating arrest was the final insult. She was moving permanently back to Texas with the children. She said goodbye to the minister at her local church, Rev. John Broom, and on 31 August, six days after the court hearing, landed at Dallas airport and was greeted emotionally by her 77-year-old mother, Lois Burgdorf. Her parents insisted that the marriage remained strong but it was only Diane's uncompromising religious convictions and devotion to her children that prevented a divorce.

It was another six weeks before Diane returned to Cape Town to see her husband. She flew via London and visited her mother-in-law at her Belgravia house, where they discussed Mark's plight for two hours before the pair were driven in Lady Thatcher's green Jaguar to the Ritz Hotel for lunch. The two women have a cool, almost formal, relationship. Apart from a fascination for clothes, they have little in common and, according to a family friend, Diane can barely stay in the same room when Margaret Thatcher embarks on an ill-tempered political lecture. Orchestrated by her media guru Lord Bell, the London visit was carefully leaked to the media and designed to show 'a united front'. The beleaguered women even briefly posed for pictures.

Back in Cape Town, Mark Thatcher was desperately trying to escape the dreaded extradition to EG, where he faced a potential death sentence. On 6 September 2004, the South African justice minister, Bridgette Mabandla, met a team of investigators and prosecutors from the brutal oil-rich state. They agreed that Thatcher should be questioned in open court over his role in the coup. The next day, he was formally subpoenaed by the South African government. After reading the 43 proposed questions drafted by EG prosecutors, Thatcher described the ruling as 'irrational', maintained his innocence and applied to have the subpoena overturned. He remained anxious that his responses could still lead to attempts by the EG government to extradite him. 'Any answers to the questions that I might give may well cause the authorities in EG to prosecute me and seek my extradition,' he stated in an affidavit. He also charged that South Africa had turned a blind eye to 'the flagrant denial of justice and violation of human rights that occur in Equatorial Guinea'.

On 25 October 2004, Thatcher, surrounded by television cameras, appeared in court for the first time since his arrest. His lawyer, Peter Hodes, argued that the South African government would be assisting EG in an unfair trial and effectively remove Thatcher's constitutional right to silence, which allowed him to avoid self-incrimination. 'What we are dealing with in EG is a military tribunal,' he said. But on 24 November, the High Court ruled that Thatcher's legal rights were not threatened and he must submit to questioning in South Africa. The judgement was a crushing blow, although it did reaffirm his right to silence.

Christmas was a frustrating and infuriating time for the son of the former prime minister. His wife Diane decided to stay in Dallas with the two children, a decision that appeared to sum up the state of their marriage. His mother flew out to Cape Town for the holiday but Mark's bail conditions prevented him from greeting her at the airport. On Christmas Day, he invited the right-wing British historian Andrew Roberts and his partner, the biographer Leonie Frieda, for drinks. On their way to the house, Frieda's 13-year-old son Jake put on a new T-shirt with 'I fancy your Mum' emblazoned across the front but fortunately he took it off before they arrived. 'At Chez Thatcher,' Frieda wrote in her diary column in the *Daily Telegraph*, 'the atmosphere was one of British-bulldog stoicism and pathos-laden cheer. Awaiting the extradition papers at any moment, wifeless, childless and to a large extent friendless, the world's most famous mummy's boy looked tanned and well. But on close examination his sad eyes belied the chipper, breezy chat. He may have alienated the public's affection in the past but the strongest feeling he evoked in me was compassion. Despite her torment, Lady Thatcher chatted good-humouredly to our children, even the youngest of whom seemed aware that he was standing next to a giant in a world of political pygmies.'[50]

Over the New Year break, Mark Thatcher contemplated the case with his friends and lawyers. Confidantes of his mother were concerned that a rigorous cross-examination in court would reveal the secrets of the Thatcher family finances and their source. Lady Thatcher consulted Lord Renwick, British ambassador to South Africa while she was prime minister, who counselled that the authorities would not budge. For Mark, the issue was more pragmatic: how to stay out of jail. The Scorpions were pursuing the case vigorously. His lawyers advised him to negotiate a plea bargain that would involve admitting to lesser charges and paying a fine but escaping prison. Desperate to return to his freewheeling life, Mark agreed.

For the South African prosecutors, a compromise was attractive, because their case was not legally watertight. Their chief witness, Crause Steyl, the pilot who dealt directly with all the coup plotters, could not prove conclusively that Thatcher knew the helicopter was for the coup operation. Despite being abandoned by his 'friends', Simon Mann, who was spending most of his time in jail reading the complete works of Shakespeare, refused to testify. And the anti-mercenary legislation was a relatively new statute which was yet to be tested in the courts. A very public failure to convict Thatcher in a long and expensive trial could irretrievably damage the law.

In the first few days of January 2005, the lawyers negotiated a plea bargain. Thatcher admitted that he had known Simon Mann for many years and that they met in November 2003 to discuss business ventures in West Africa. He also acknowledged the meetings and payments to Steyl for chartering the helicopter. According to the plea bargain, Thatcher then 'began to suspect that the helicopter might in fact be intended for use in mercenary activity'. Despite his misgivings, he invested the money and admitted: 'In fact, Mann and Steyl did intend to use the helicopter in mercenary activity.'

On 13 January 2005, a visibly tense and nervous Thatcher appeared in the High Court in Cape Town and pleaded guilty to 'wrongfully and unlawfully attempting to finance mercenary activity'. He was fined R3 million, given a four-year suspended jail sentence and ordered to cooperate with the ongoing police investigation. His composure only slipped when Judge Abe Motala said that he must pay the fine within seven days or he would be jailed for five years. He winced at this statement but overall it was a huge relief to Thatcher: he was allowed to walk free and travel at will. He now had a criminal conviction but told friends that it was 'a mere technical infringement'. But the mercenaries being held in Harare prison were furious. 'The families are bitter because one of the financiers walked out of court with a fine and a suspended sentence,' said their lawyer Alwyn Griebenow. They claimed that Thatcher escaped lightly and pointed out that he could have withdrawn his funding when, as he acknowledges, he suspected Mann was planning a coup and the helicopter was part of the plot.

Standing on the steps of the Cape Town High Court, Thatcher said, 'I am willing to pay any price to be reunited with my family and I am sure all of you who are husbands and wives would agree.' Two protesters jeered but the media scrum prevented him noticing a banner hanging from an office block declaring: 'Save Me, Mummy'. Later that afternoon, he flew to London by British Airways and immediately went to Belgravia to see his relieved mother, who paid the R3 million fine. 'See you later, guys,' he told reporters as he left for the airport on his way to England, appearing happy and jaunty. He was confident of selling his house in Constantia and returning to the United States on a permanent basis. But it was not that simple. He now had a criminal record and his application for a visa was being carefully scrutinised. The US embassy in London said that immigration law was more complicated than assumed and each case was dealt with on its individual merits.

The next day, Friday, 14 January 2005, Thatcher flew to Frankfurt to pick up a connecting flight to Dallas but found himself stranded because his passport and visa had expired. He had not noticed, he said, because the South African police had confiscated his passport during their investigation. Delayed in Frankfurt over the weekend, his lawyers negotiated with the US authorities for a new visa. But it was taking longer than expected and on the evening of Sunday, 17 January, he returned to London.

On 10 February 2005, Thatcher flew back to Cape Town and received some good news for a change: his house in Constantia had been sold for an estimated £1.5 million. It was a rare financial coup, because he only paid £200,000 for it ten years earlier. The sale, to the Sahara Group, a cricket sponsorship company, was the highest price ever for that area.

A week later, he was back in court to respond to the subpoena issued by the South African justice department at the request of the EG government. Appearing before Wynberg magistrate Helen Allman, Thatcher admitted meeting Simon Mann four times during the planning period of the coup. He also said that he knew all but two of the alleged conspirators, including Jeffrey Archer, but only on a social level. 'It was all guilt by association,' he said outside the court, dressed in his trademark blue blazer with a large colourful handkerchief in the breast pocket. 'It is patently clear that I had nothing to do with the financing of any coup in EG.'

That court appearance was uncomfortable but far less stressful for Thatcher, and in the afternoon, Friday, 18 February, he flew to London. The next day he was in Motcombs, the lively wine bar in Belgravia with an interesting clientele, drinking champagne with New Zealander car dealers and loudly pronouncing that South Africa was not the same country 'since the blacks took over'. Now living with his mother in nearby Chester Square, Mark waited for the verdict on his visa application. On 1 April 2004, it was refused, and he was effectively banned from travelling to the US. 'It was always a calculated risk when I plea bargained in South Africa,' he said in a statement. In fact, his criminal record was only one factor behind the ban. The real reason was that his past business misdeeds and controversial deals had returned to haunt him. 'If Thatcher had asked for a temporary or a multi-entry visa for brief holidays, he would have been fine,' said a US State Department source. 'But the arrogant idiot applied for permanent residency, which meant there was a full-blown inquiry and they turned up all the files on the IRS investigation, the arms deals from the 1980s and the lawsuits. That made it impossible, so that was the problem, not the conviction.'

Thatcher announced that he would be resettling 'somewhere in Europe', and the following week he was seen eagerly examining an estate agent's window in the tax haven of Monte Carlo. But by May 2005, he had not decided where to base himself permanently, with Switzerland being a favourite candidate. He was now living back with his mother in London, 26 years to the day that she became prime minister and when her son also moved into 10 Downing Street. From there, he traded off his name and became a multimillionaire. The bizarre story of the attempted coup in EG had resulted in Mark Thatcher being exiled for the third time. His secret past had finally caught up with him.

TWELVE

A True Thatcherite

The answer to the question 'Who disciplines the prime minister?' is that no one does.
– Lord Blake, Conservative Party historian[1]

On Monday, 12 October 1994, at a time when allegations about Mark Thatcher's commercial involvement in the Al-Yamamah arms deal resurfaced, the former prime minister was talking to one of her closest confidants. She was very distressed and upset.

'I'll just go down in history as Mark's mother,' she said.

'No, no, Margaret,' replied the friend, a former Conservative cabinet minister. 'Your place in history is secure, really.'

'No, they want to do me down,' Lady Thatcher said repeatedly. 'They want to do me down.' She added that the National Audit Office had examined the arms deal for three years but could not publish their report because prominent Saudi Arabians were involved. 'Publishing their names could lose us this huge order,' she said.

The former minister was so concerned about his mentor's state of mind that he decided she needed reassurance. So he asked for a special section to be inserted into the inaugural speech of Jeremy Hanley, the new Tory Party chairman, at the Tory Party conference in Bournemouth the following day. Sure enough, early in his address Hanley paid a distinctive tribute to her. Turning towards her he said, 'Mr Chairman, Margaret Thatcher's place in history is absolutely assured. She will be seen worldwide as one of the leading figures of the twentieth century, whoever writes the history books.'

Margaret Thatcher's place in history is, of course, very secure. On her tombstone, she will be remembered as one of the most remarkable and politically successful prime ministers of all time. Winning three successive general elections was no mean achievement. Historians will describe her as someone who broke with consensus politics and by sheer driving force and determination introduced waves of revolutionary legislation, notably privatisation and trade-union reform.

But her legacy will be stained and besmirched. For the Thatcher years will also be known as a period when the prime minister's name was used to enrich her own son, when 10 Downing Street effectively became a registered office for a family business called Mark Thatcher Enterprises Ltd, and when Thatcherism began at home. For the most enthusiastic exponents of Thatcherism were the Thatchers. Mark was just the most vigorous and fervent – if crude – disciple. Although he was not a political evangelist, he is a child of Margaret Thatcher's in every sense of the phrase. For the Thatcher family, money and material wealth are God. They worshipped at the temple of the almighty sterling (and often Swiss francs and US dollars).

The complex web of offshore accounts in Jersey and Guernsey, the Swiss-based trust companies and family trusts have made it almost impossible to evaluate Mark Thatcher's true wealth. Our sources close to Hugh Thurston indicate that at his peak in 1990 he was worth at least £40 million, but that has dwindled dramatically in recent years. Certainly Mark is keeping mum, so to speak. When questioned by David Jones of *Today* in 1994, he described himself as a 'pauper' compared to fellow Dallas millionaires like Ross Perot. But he admitted he was 'doing well' in British terms. 'It's all comparative,' he reflected.

The exact amount is to some extent inconsequential. What has become apparent is that material wealth is absolutely paramount in his life. 'Mark always wanted to be a tycoon and had a strong urge for recognition as a commercial force,' said a Hong Kong investment banker who dealt with him in the mid-1980s. 'But I would also say he was avaricious and craved the lifestyle of the rich and famous. He loved the glamour. I don't think Mark has ever made a secret of wanting to be very rich or admiring those who are – on an indiscriminate basis. Money is what lures him rather than quality. If you look at who he knows around the world, they are invariably self-made wealthy people or heirs or heiresses. There is very little breadth in his address book. If they have money, they are [in it]. There are not many out-of-work painters or authors, or even politicians. He is only interested in politicians who could be useful for business.'

Mark Thatcher would, according to an Arab businessman who dealt with him, 'do anything for money. Anything that was asked of him.' Even Margaret Thatcher's political admirers accept there is a strong mercenary streak and bounty hunter mentality running through the family. 'She was a money snob,' said one former senior Conservative grandee. 'She admired people who made a lot of money. I didn't mind that, but her weakness was that she didn't seem to mind how the money was made. Money talks as far as she was concerned.'

It was not so much what Margaret Thatcher occasionally did to help her son in his commercial endeavours. It was that she did nothing to prevent him from capitalising on her name and office. Officially, she professed ignorance of his activities. The standard line among her friends and admirers was: 'Well, yes, Mark may have done all those things and made all that money but I can assure you that Margaret knew nothing about it.' But that argument is undermined by the letter of introduction she wrote to Sheikh Zayed in 1980 and by her son's own admission: 'I discuss everything with my mother.'

At the heart of the 'What did she know and when did she know it?' issue lies Mark's relationship with his mother. From an early age, Mark, like most children, aimed to fulfil his parents' aspirations and expectations. But it was soon apparent he had neither the appetite nor the aptitude to achieve success at the level of his mother and father. 'Mark always wanted to be as big as them but could never quite make it on his own,' said Andrew Thomson, Margaret Thatcher's constituency agent in Finchley from 1982 until 1987.[2] During his mother's tenure as prime minister, his behaviour was that of a man who could not cope with the fact that both his parents were successful in their own right. He set himself targets that were far beyond him and so he became chronically insecure. As a result, he was reduced to exaggerating his own importance, boasting and telling harassed shopkeepers, 'But don't you know who I am?'[3] or ostentatiously pulling out his mobile telephone during dinner parties and speaking to his bodyguards.

Such arrogance, born of insecurity, was usually displayed more in public than in private. When he walked into a glass door by mistake at an architect's office, he wanted to sue the builders. When he leaned back in his chair and toppled over into the dessert trolley in a restaurant, he loudly announced that the management would have to pay his dry-cleaning bill.[4] 'I found that Mark's behaviour changed dramatically when he was with a group of people,' said Jim Paterson, who knew him in the mid-1980s. 'When I was on my own with him, he was a decent guy – good company and could be quite funny. But when he was in a public place, he could be very pompous and rude.'[5] Ironically, in later years he appeared to acknowledge this reputation. 'Hello, I'm charmless Mark' was an occasional opening gambit at social functions.[6]

In recent years, Mark has certainly calmed down and mellowed by his standards. He can be generous to friends in his private Thatcherite inner circle. After Jonathan Aitken, the disgraced former Tory cabinet minister and former boyfriend of his sister Carol, was released from jail, he was shocked to receive a phone call from Mark. 'Over lunch,' recalled Aitken, 'Mark poured out the milk of human kindness. Was I all right? Did I need money? Would I like to have a holiday in his guest house in South Africa?'[7]

The other consequence of his vulnerability was the constant need to promote and project himself by showing off his wealth (hence the valet). He would mix only with the rich, tycoons and celebrities, always with a swagger and an airy confidence. At parties, unless the guest is wealthy and famous, Mark is not interested. 'He is by far the rudest person I have ever met,' said a friend of his sister, Carol. 'He just acts so superior, as if he is so important and successful and you are a mere blip on the universe.' This contrasts with his actual business record, which by any objective standards was a failure.

Yet Mark Thatcher maintained a relentless desire to achieve and make his mother proud. His chosen route was to accumulate a huge pot of gold. Nothing wrong with that, many people would say. But his insecurity also bred impatience and he cut corners. He became so driven by the desire to make money that he became an exponent of the 'get rich quick' school of wealth-creation. He was indiscriminate about his business associates and the type of deal he was brokering. He wanted cash and he wanted it fast. The problem was that he had no business prowess or even, at first, any decent contacts. So when his mother became prime minister in 1979, he exploited the one saleable asset at his disposal – his name – and, as several of his former associates have testified, he was brilliant at it. It was almost as if Mark believed he was an unofficial appendage of the government. One lunch-time in June 1993, he walked into the drawing-room of his Kensington house and saw John Major speaking on television. 'God, he's useless,' he said. 'It wasn't like this when we were in power.'[8]

From Margaret Thatcher's perspective, her son could do no wrong. He was her adored child and she bristled with indignation whenever anyone criticised him. Even while she was prime minister she pampered and doted on him when he stayed with her in 10 Downing Street. When he sought attention, she hovered and fussed, indulging in what Mark called 'little spurts of mothering'. She would wash and iron his shirts, folding them into neat little squares and slipping them carefully into plastic bags for travelling. The inevitable result was that he became a spoilt young man with an inflated sense of his own importance which swelled grotesquely with his mother's fame, prestige and power. In public, however, Margaret Thatcher appeared to gloss over her maternal over-indulgence. 'You can't just tie young men and women to their mother's apron strings,' she said. 'You just can't. You can't take all the challenge out of life for young people. It wouldn't be right to do so.'[9]

Margaret Thatcher allowed her son to use her position in his business ventures for two reasons. First, she could not see anything wrong with it. He was merely being a Thatcherite. Second, she felt guilty and blamed herself for his inadequacies and flaws. 'My perspective is that she felt that when the twins were very young, she decided early to pursue a political career in the hope that it would not affect the kids,' said a former Tory official who worked closely with her in the early 1980s. 'Carol could handle it. But Mark's hang-ups were so bad that when his mother was away that only made him more insecure. After that, every time he screwed up – like his accountancy exams – she blamed herself. She reacted in exactly the same way when she was prime minister. She felt that if she had spent more time with him when he was younger, he would have turned out better.'

This resulted in Mark Thatcher being the prime minister's perpetual blind spot: even the most blinkered Thatcherites accept that basic truth. She could not see the implications of what was happening and would not hear any criticism of him. 'Margaret Thatcher's mind is very compartmentalised,' said a former long-serving senior Tory Central Office director. 'She would listen to advice and you could discuss anything with her, but you couldn't talk about Mark. It was just impossible. All of her friends or people on her political staff knew they could not broach the dreaded subject, because she saw it as a criticism of herself.' When Sir David Frost asked her on BBC TV in June 1995, whether her son used her name, she quickly interrupted:

'Now, I'm *not* going to discuss my children. We've just been saying that it's vital for them to keep their privacy.'

The result of Margaret Thatcher's indulgence was that her son grew up permanently sealed and isolated from responsibilities and accountability. This was exacerbated by her tendency to portray her son as a victim. 'She would talk of nothing else,' said a family friend. 'Drag the conversation away and after a minute or two she would go silent and get back on to the subject of "poor Mark".' As a result, he virtually had licence to do almost anything, knowing she would not admonish or correct him. 'In Margaret Thatcher's eyes, there is nothing for which Mark requires forgiveness,' said Andrew Thomson.[10]

That raises the crucial question of how much knowledge she had about Mark's business activities. She knew for four reasons.

First, her relationship with her son, by their own and everyone else's account, was and remains extraordinarily close. During the mid-1980s, he would telephone her every Sunday night regardless of where he was in the world. They discussed 'everything'.

Second, nobody disputes that Margaret Thatcher was the most meticulous and punctilious of prime ministers. Her attention to detail and her thorough reading of almost every document that crossed her desk were unsurpassed, and her capacity for knowledge was unrivalled. It is inconceivable that she did not know what her own son was doing.

Third, her most senior ministers had, at the very least, some knowledge of what was going on. This was partly because of their departmental responsibilities but also because they received informal verbal reports from senior Conservative MPs. For example, John Wakeham, chief whip from 1983 until 1987, provided at least one such report to her in 1984. It is possible that ministers did not inform Mrs Thatcher about her son's activities. If they did not, they should have done.

Fourth, and most crucially, she was informed by her own civil servants, ministers and security services. They could not fudge it. They were officially duty-bound to tell her. This occurred in 1984, at the height of the Oman contract controversy. A former minister was present in her room when a senior civil servant entered and presented to Margaret Thatcher a MI6 dossier, collated in Vienna, on her son's commercial activities. Normally she was fascinated by Intelligence reports, especially those from the Joint Intelligence Committee. But on this occasion, as the prime minister stared at the document, she was almost in tears. 'I don't want to read it,' she said, her voice quivering. 'I don't want to read it. I can't.'

Mark was not slow to take advantage of his mother's weakness. He knew how to exploit her self-imposed guilt and keep her under his psychological thumb. One of his favourite tactics while she was prime minister was to telephone 10 Downing Street at about 1.45 p.m. on a Tuesday or Thursday afternoon. This, of course, was at the precise moment when she was being briefed and preparing herself for prime minister's question time in parliament and was under the most extreme pressure. When Mark's telephone call was put through to her private secretary, he would naturally be told she was too busy to talk to him at that time. Her son would then tell the official that if she didn't come to the phone immediately he would never talk to her again. When this message was relayed, Margaret immediately came to the phone. Former aides at Number 10 recall that the prime minister could be charming and cooperative for five days in a row and then neurotic and short-tempered on the sixth day. They would then discover that her son was in the flat upstairs and had been 'winding her up'.

The remarkable inability or unwillingness of the usually hard-headed Margaret Thatcher to deal with her son and put him on the straight and narrow lies at the heart of the matter. Her defenders argue she was merely being a doting mum and it was a typical mother–son relationship. She spoiled him because he was weak and needed her. But she went much further than maternal fretting and fussing and it was the absence of action that is the crucial issue. 'My mother loved me too,' said a former cabinet minister now in the House of Lords, 'but she knew when I was being a bloody idiot – and she said so.'[11]

Denis Thatcher did not fare much better in dealing with Mark. His relationship with his son was cool and formal and did not warm over the years. Privately, Denis was deeply disappointed with Mark. 'I can spot a wrong 'un a mile off,' he would say. He would have liked his son to have earned and worked for his money – the old-fashioned way. 'Doing favours for Arabs is not a proper job,' he once remarked. And he often despaired of the press revelations about his son's commercial activities. 'I never thought I'd see my family name on the front page of the *Sunday Times* associated with fraud,' he said dejectedly on one occasion.[12]

In the early 1980s, Denis Thatcher was relatively relaxed about his son's business aspirations and accident-prone racing career, and used to joke about his finances. 'Again!' he shouted as Mark sidled up to him at a Number 10 cocktail party. 'I gave you £100 last night!'[13] But by the end of the decade, he was far more concerned. Denis was worried that the lack of visible or credible means of support for his son's wealth would damage his wife politically. He frequently warned her while she was prime minister that she was over-protective and uncritical of their son. 'I don't think Denis thought there was any evidence that Mark had done anything illegal but he was worried that it would undermine her,' said a former Thatcherite minister.[14]

Mark sensed his father's disapproval and so rarely discussed his business affairs. He also reacted petulantly to Denis's title. During the last week of her premiership in November 1990, his parents were having dinner late one night. 'What do you think about being a baronet?' she asked him. Denis was taken aback but delighted. He thought it would be particularly beneficial for his grandson Michael and accepted. 'That would be wonderful,' he replied. Mark was less pleased. When told about the honour by his father the next day in the upstairs flat in 10 Downing Street, Mark replied, 'I suppose that's what you wanted.' He promptly walked out of the room without a further word. It was a surprising response, given that he knew that he would inherit the title and become Sir Mark. According to Carol, the honour was created by Margaret partly so that Mark could inherit it because he had been 'hounded'.[15]

There are conflicting views on who was the real boss and chief executive in the Thatcher family. Some of Mark's friends say Denis always had the last word. Others are not so sure. One of them, Charlie Crichton-Stuart, former sponsorship consultant to Frank Williams Racing, recalls an incident which illustrates what he saw as the true balance of power.

In 1982, Crichton-Stuart was having lunch with Mark, when at 3.25 p.m. Mark suddenly said, 'Would you like to come up to the ranch?' The sponsorship consultant agreed and off they trooped to 10 Downing Street, where they met Denis in the top-floor flat. He was in a jovial mood. 'Would you like a drink?' he asked. Crichton-Stuart was not a drinker, as alcohol did not agree with him, but he could hardly refuse an invitation from the prime minister's husband in 10 Downing Street. So Denis went to the drinks cabinet, prepared two large gin and tonics and lit a cigarette. As he was handed the glass, Crichton-Stuart heard an unmistakable voice haranguing and abusing an official as she walked up the stairs. 'The poor man was getting a horrendous bollocking,' he recalled. 'I've never heard anything like it.'

Suddenly, Denis gulped his double gin and tonic down in one movement and quickly stubbed out his cigarette just as Margaret passed by the room. For Crichton-Stuart, sitting petrified with a large gin in one hand and a cigarette in the other, it was a real eye-opener as to who had the clout in the Thatcher clan. As another member of the family reflected: 'It was Margaret who wore the trousers.'

How much Denis knew about his son's business activities is also unclear. Certainly, they went on business trips together. But on private social occasions he professed ignorance. 'I don't know how Mark made his money,' he said in January 1994. 'I made enough but he's made a lot more.' He was no more forthcoming with the authors. Thanking us for our 'kind letter', he wrote: 'Some 20 odd years ago I made a rule for myself, namely, *never* to make speeches except at sports occasions, *never* to give interviews to the press or others, *never* to write anything for publication except for sport, and *never* to "go on the box". By and large my "rule" has maintained me in a low profile (awful word) as befits my small position in public life. In my advanced years I see no reason to depart from it' [his emphasis].[16]

As for Carol Thatcher, she has been perennially frustrated by her mother favouring her twin brother in every way. She always felt that she came second out of two. 'Oh, she just *adores* Mark,' is a common remark by Carol to her friends. She has always been anxious for Margaret's love and affection. On one occasion she confronted her mother. 'Why does Mark get away with everything?' she asked. 'Why is *everything* he does all right? Don't you know I have feelings, too?' The former prime minister replied, 'Because, darling, you and I are the strong ones.' In some ways, Carol suffers from being Margaret Thatcher's daughter whereas Mark exists by being his mother's son.[17] In stark contrast to Mark, Carol was largely left to fend for herself. She grew up with low self-esteem and was sent to a less-prestigious private school, despite being more intelligent than Mark (she obtained seven O Levels to his three). As a result, she became far less pretentious and status-conscious, and developed a self-deprecating personality as opposed to her brother's endless boasting and braggadocio.

The differences between the Thatcher twins have only accentuated the favouritism shown to Mark. Carol is single with no children while Mark has a wife and two children – for the time being at any rate. Carol dresses informally while Mark always wears a formal suit and tie. Mark is a multimillionaire 'businessman' living in a large mansion while Carol earns a modest living as a journalist and lives in a rented holiday flat in a ski resort since moving to Switzerland in the late '80s. For Margaret Thatcher – whose only personal interests and hobbies are money, family and clothes – these factors are very important. It has little to do with who is the stronger personality.

The tension has been exacerbated by the way Lady Thatcher has often responded as if her daughter were a struggling subsidiary company in Thatcher plc. In early 1993, when Carol appeared depressed about her life, the former prime minister responded by handing over thousands of pounds to pay for a large extension and decoration in her Fulham house.

The contrast between Carol and Mark is quite stark. He traded off his mother's name while she went to Australia to make her own living as a journalist. He lived in 10 Downing Street while she bought a house in Fulham. Professionally, she undoubtedly secured an advantage in gaining easy access to people and sources. But compared to Mark she did nothing to exploit her position as the prime minister's relative. Carol may have got some contacts but Mark obtained the contracts. In fact, Carol was very conscious of avoiding even publicity, let alone notoriety. 'In some ways he [Mark] has behaved appallingly,' she said in 1996. 'I tried to behave in a vaguely respectable fashion because Mark got such awful publicity. I didn't want everyone saying, "Mrs Thatcher must be awful – both her children are off the rails."'[18]

It is therefore not surprising that Carol and Mark have never been close. Virtually all they have in common is their fervent defence of their mother against criticism. It is not a warm relationship and several friends of Carol have told the authors of her intense dislike for her twin. 'I don't mind being described as Mrs Thatcher's daughter but I get stroppy with "Mark's sister",' she once said.[19]

Despite her frustration, Carol decided not to cooperate with this book. 'I'm afraid that I have to decline your invitation to be interviewed for your book on my brother,' she told us. 'I'm sure you'll appreciate that I got rather maxed out [weary] on the family interview scene during the 11 years my mother spent in Number 10.' In private and public, she professes not to know how her brother acquired his millions. 'The only thing I don't want to comment on is Mark's money,' she told *Today* for a series of interviews six months after she refused our offer. 'I don't know how he made it, so it's not up to me to say anything. Besides, he's kind enough not to comment on my lack of it.'[20] She was more forthright to a friend: 'Of course, he has made a lot of money but God knows how.'

A key reason why the former prime minister did not prevent Mark from amassing his fortune was that she never came to terms with either the notion or the danger of conflicts of interests. When asked whether she knew her son had a commercial interest in the Oman and Saudi Arabian contracts she negotiated, she refused to address the question. Instead, she denied there was any impropriety. Apart from evading the fundamental issue, she also missed the point. As Ronald Dworkin, professor of jurisprudence at Oxford University, pointed out: 'A conflict of interest is a *situation* [his emphasis], not any particular piece of wrongdoing. The difference is very important, because avoiding conflicts means avoiding relationships and connections that might raise questions of improper motives.'[21]

The cabinet rules governing ministers' financial interests are quite clear. They were first laid down by Sir Winston Churchill in 1952: 'It is a principle of public life that ministers must so order their affairs that no conflict arises or appears to arise between their private interests and their public duties.'[22]

Margaret Thatcher has never been able to reconcile that guideline with her own affairs. This was illustrated in 1986 when it was revealed that as a cabinet minister she had bought shares in her own name. In 1971, while education secretary, she purchased 348 shares for £2,142 in Broken Hill Pty, an Australian oil and steel conglomerate. After she joined the company's reinvestment scheme, her holding increased to 1,327 shares. Over the next 14 years, the stock, held in her own name, increased in value through rights and dividend issues to £4,470.[23] She retained the shares when she became prime minister in 1979, and they appeared in Broken Hill's company register as 'The Hon. Mrs M. Thatcher c/o Miss J. Robillard [her constituency secretary], 10 Downing Street, London SW1'.

It was not until 1985 that the prime minister transferred her holding and other shares to nominee discretionary accounts, to be controlled by a firm of investment fund managers.[24] Thus for six years Margaret Thatcher held a direct stake in a company that was quoted on the stock exchange. As prime minister and first lord of the Treasury, she could theoretically have had access to a great deal of sensitive economic and industrial information. It was a potential conflict of interests, because she kept the shares under her own name from 1979 until 1985.

When questioned in parliament, Thatcher denied she had breached the cabinet office rules. 'Under those conventions,' she said, 'there is nothing which requires me, on assuming office, to dispose of my shares or to transfer them into a trust or in the name of investment managers.'[25] But *Questions of Procedure* states: 'There may be less clear-cut cases where a minister would feel it appropriate to place his holding in the hands of trustees.'

For close relatives and spouses, the cabinet office document is clear-cut and pertinent: 'It is a well established and recognised rule that no minister or public servant should accept gifts, hospitality or services from anyone which would, or might appear to, place him or her under an obligation. The same principle applies if gifts, hospitality or services are offered to a member of their family.'[26]

Fortunately for Margaret Thatcher, she was the final judge and jury on the matter. It is, of course, the prime minister who is responsible for the conduct of ministers. 'The answer to the question "Who disciplines the prime minister?" is that no one does,' said Lord Blake, the historian of the Conservative Party. 'The other ministers, if in doubt, are enjoined to consult the prime minister. But the prime minister is on his or her own in this respect and not accountable, in that sense, to any particular person. But, of course, he or she is always in the last resort accountable to Parliament.'[27]

The argument that the prime minister is answerable to the Commons is flawed, because it simply does not work in practice. In the Oman case, Margaret Thatcher refused to make a statement to the House. She answered questions either by arguing it was a private issue or by saying that she was batting for the British company not her son. Lord Blake agreed with her: 'I think that the prime minister, in taking the line that in purely private matters she is not prepared to answer in public in Parliament, is only doing what any other prime minister would have done.'[28] This was also her response to the authors when we requested an interview. 'Lady Thatcher has a standard policy not to comment on her family,' said her office.

However, it was much more than a private or family matter. In the Oman situation, her son was being paid by a public company for which she was lobbying for a multimillion-pound contract. Over in Saudi Arabia, he received a commission fee for another public contract which she not only negotiated but also signed. The public interest issue was recognised by Howard Teicher, a former senior US National Security Council official, who saw documents on Mark Thatcher's financial involvement in the Al-Yamamah arms deal. 'I think it's totally inappropriate,' he said, 'for family members of elected officials to engage in commercial transactions involving governments where, even if the law permits such involvement, the appearance of impropriety is quite apparent and the family member is exploiting his family connection to the possible detriment of his own taxpayers . . . In a democratic society, this is the worst form of nepotism – to see a member of a political family clearly exploit the connection to carve out power and influence in order to make money.'[29]

The problem became exacerbated over the years because Mark Thatcher was never answerable or accountable for his actions. The only person, officially and personally, who was responsible was his mother, the prime minister. Yet she was often implicated herself, so she was judge and jury in her own cause.

Very early in her premiership, her son claimed he was aware of the dangers of trading off his name. 'It seems a pompous thing to say but I now have a responsibility to Mum in how I behave,' he commented in February 1980. 'I have to deliberate about everything I contemplate doing and think of the possible repercussions. There have been times when I've known I've been guilty, and got it straight in the back of the neck. My mother is pretty efficient at shooting you down – there is no doubt about that.'[30]

Clearly, that never happened. Mark was never able to succeed on his own merits, so he utilised his one asset – his name. And he never cared about what anyone thought. 'I am responsible to three people on this planet,' he said in 1984. 'One of them is my mother, the second is the Almighty and the third is me. My responsibility is to her as my mother, not as prime minister. To me, that is peripheral.'[31]

His defenders argue that Mark is merely a private businessman who has been attacked as a way of undermining his mother. This ignores the fact that some of his strongest assailants have been her most ardent and sycophantic supporters, notably *The Sun*, *Daily Mail* and *Daily Express*. Mark Thatcher may be a private businessman but he is also the only child of a post-Second World War British prime minister to have traded off his name. When Sir Alec (later Lord) Douglas-Home became prime minister in 1963 (after being foreign secretary for three years), his son David worked for Morgan Grenfell International in Abu Dhabi. Not once did he or Lord Home exploit their positions to make money for their family or the merchant bank. Other children of prime ministers have virtually been invisible. Few people even knew Harold Wilson had two sons. The Thatcher experience is unique.

'Margaret Thatcher's blind spot' has been a familiar phrase to describe her son. But it was much more than that. He was the one emotional and dangerous political chink in her otherwise impenetrable public armour. Some of her policies were unpopular and her critics attacked many of her decisions and actions. But, according to her closest confidants and even her husband, it was Mark who could have brought her down. 'He was a threat to the stability and very survival of the prime minister herself,' said one. 'The only consolation I had when I left 10 Downing Street was that I was not there when the government fell apart over Mark Thatcher,' said one former senior Downing Street official. 'There was a real possibility that the government would fall because of him. It was that serious.'

Since leaving 10 Downing Street, the unshakeable bond that binds Mark and Margaret Thatcher appears to have, if anything, tightened. Since the death of Denis in June 2003, and as her health has declined, they have grown closer. Friends say they now behave like an old married couple rather than mother and son. They bicker about domestic and administrative details and Mark is concerned about her health and drinking habits. During her visits to South Africa, he tried to reduce her alcohol intake because drinking makes her even more aggressive and abrasive. When Lady Thatcher asked for a drink at her son's home in Cape Town, Mark would pour half the whisky away and fill the rest of the glass with water when she was not looking. On one occasion, he was not too happy when a friend promptly replaced the water with more whisky.

However, there is an intrinsic connection between them. Friends say they can communicate without speaking. After all, Margaret and Mark Thatcher have a lot in common. They have the same brittle, aggressive, impatient temperament. They are both money-orientated, materialistic and obsessed by clothes. In his house in Cape Town, Mark had at least 100 suits and dozens of shoes in his bedroom and walk-in closet. 'You are the Imelda Marcos of Constantia and you dress like a Cosa Nostra [Mafioso],' remarked an amused visitor from Italy. 'Oh, come off it, darling,' replied Mark in his mock-cockney accent. Equally, his mother has long been mesmerised by jewellery and spends hours on her appearance and trying on different outfits.

Since 2001, Lady Thatcher has suffered from a series of small strokes. She looks drawn, is increasingly frail and suffers from a loss of short-term memory. She often appears confused and becomes repetitive, asking the same questions over and over again and not absorbing other people's comments. When she could not remember old friends, she turned on Denis in her frustration.

As long as she had a script, she remained a consummate professional and could still turn in a word-perfect delivery. But when there was no prepared statement, she was alarmingly unpredictable or merely repeated lines she had used a thousand times before (or even just a minute earlier). Like Ronald Reagan while he was president, Lady Thatcher needed Denis or an aide to whisper the right word in her ear or nudge her at the appropriate moment. As a result, on 22 March 2003, it was announced that she would stop all public speaking following medical advice. Like Harold Wilson in his later years, Lady Thatcher was a forlorn figure. It was noticeable that during a rare interview with ITN during the 2005 general election campaign, she was reserved, reticent and withdrawn.

However, in lucid moments, the former prime minister can still deliver a robust riposte to anyone who dares to describe an event during her premiership years, particularly if she is fortified by a glass of her favourite whisky. 'No, no, no, no, no, that's not what happened,' she responds and delivers a sharp rebuke.

Even without her memory loss, Lady Thatcher's assessment of her Downing Street years and subsequent years was selective and self-delusional when it came to her son's business deals and African adventures. For her, Mark could do no wrong. Sigmund Freud once famously observed: 'The young man who is his mother's unquestioned favourite develops a triumphant sense of self-esteem and, with that, the strength for success in later life'. Few mother–son combinations illustrate Freud's tenet so well as Mark and Margaret Thatcher. But the 'enterprise culture' in which he acquired his mysterious fortune was also the world his mother created. The values that his actions represent – even his involvement in the attempted coup in Equatorial Guinea – are the same values that she promoted and gave birth to. Like mother, like son, Mark was the last true Thatcherite.

Notes and References

Preface
1. Peter Carter-Ruck and Partners was also used by Mark Thatcher to pass on payments for one of his business deals. In May 1993, Thatcher commissioned a company called Saladin Holdings Ltd, a security and arms-dealing firm, to do some work on a commercial project in the Middle East and the USA.

   The funds were paid to Saladin Holdings by Carter-Ruck & Partners. For one contract, £10,000 was paid to two security consultants. This sum included £5,000 for one to travel to the Middle East between 13 and 17 May 1993, and £5,000 for the other to visit the USA. Their fees were £600 per day plus £250 subsistence and VAT.

   Mark Thatcher hired Saladin on the recommendation of David Hart, the controversial right-wing property speculator. Hart, an adviser to Margaret Thatcher while she was prime minister, is best known for helping to finance the working miners during the 1984–5 strike. He knew Saladin through his friendship with Major David Walker, the company's chairman. It was Hart who telephoned Alasdair Pepper to say that Mark Thatcher needed the client account number and bank details for payment purposes.

   When asked about his relationship with his heroine's son, Hart replied, 'He's a friend of mine. Decent chap. I see him occasionally when he's in town. We've shot a couple of times together.' But when questioned about introducing Saladin to Thatcher, he denied it: 'It's untrue. It never happened.'

   Saladin Holdings Ltd (SHL) 'provides management, marketing and technical services to clients,' according to its accounts. It has two wholly owned subsidiary companies. On 15 May 1987, SHL bought 100 per cent of Saladin Security Ltd – 'a company active in the security field'. On 23 May 1988, SHL acquired 100 per cent of Saladin Trading Ltd – 'a UK company specialising in buying and selling military equipment,' according to its latest accounts. On 1 October 1993, Sir Archie Hamilton, a former Conservative MP, became a director of Saladin Holdings Ltd. Sir Archie was a junior minister for defence procurement, 1986–7; parliamentary private secretary to Margaret Thatcher 1987–8; and minister for the armed forces, 1988–93. From 1978 until 1979 his political aide was David Hart.

   David Walker, chairman of SHL, is also a director and shareholder of Saladin

Security Ltd and Saladin Trading Ltd. A former Conservative councillor and SAS major, Walker was hired by Oliver North in the early 1980s to implement 'certain special operations' in Nicaragua to support the Contras against the Sandinista government.

Chapter One

1. Memo written by Simon Mann, 12 January 2004.
2. *Vanity Fair*, January 2005.
3. *The Guardian*, 19 May 2004.
4. *Daily Mail*, 7 October 2004.
5. *The Money Programme*, BBC2, 17 November 2004.
6. *The Guardian*, 26 August 2004.
7. *CBS News*, 18 September 2003.
8. *Africa Confidential*, 29 June 2004 and 8 March 2004.
9. BBC News24.com, 26 April 2004.
10. Onda Cero, Spanish radio station. Quoted on BBC *News24.com*, 29 April 2004.
11. *Sunday Times*, 29 August 2004.
12. *Sunday Telegraph*, 29 August 2004.
13. *Vanity Fair*, January 2005.
14. *Sunday Times*, 5 December 2004.
15. Margaret Crick, *Mary Archer: For Richer, For Poorer* (Simon and Schuster, London, 2005), pp. 191–2.
16. *Africa Confidential*, 8 March 2004.
17. *The Guardian*, 28 August 2004.
18. *Daily Telegraph*, 28 August 2004.
19. *The Money Programme*, BBC2, 17 November 2004.
20. *Sunday Telegraph*, 2004.
21. BBC News24.com, 29 April 2004.
22. *Africa Confidential*, 10 September 2004.
23. *Sunday Telegraph*, 19 June 2005.
24. *Vanity Fair*, January 2005.
25. *The Times*, 26 August 2004.
26. *Vanity Fair*, January 2005.

Chapter Two

1. Andrew Thomson, *Margaret Thatcher: The Woman Within* (W.H. Allen, London, 1989), p. 118.
2. *Financial Mail on Sunday*, 22 January 1995.
3. *Sunday Times*, 21 November 2004.
4. *Jersey Evening Post*, 29 August 1973.
5. *Ibid.*
6. *Ibid.*
7. *Sunday Times*, 14 September 2003.
8. *Financial Times*, 16 November 2002.
9. Nigel Lawson, *The View from Number 11* (Bantam, London, 1992), p.178.
10. *Institutional Investor*, June 1993.
11. *Ibid.*
12. London *Evening Standard*, 2 October 1987.

13. *Financial Times*, 31 October 1994.
14. *Sunday Times*, 14 September 2003.
15. *Sunday Times*, 12 September 2004.
16. Hugo Young, *One of Us* (Macmillan, London, 1989), p. 4.
17. *Sunday Express*, 20 July 1975.
18. Christopher Ogden, *Maggie* (Simon & Schuster, New York, 1990), p. 24.
19. Penny Junor, *Margaret Thatcher: Wife, Mother, Politician* (Sidgwick & Jackson, London, 1983), p. 3.
20. Young, *One of Us*, p . 22.
21. Junor, *Margaret Thatcher*, p. 12.
22. Ogden, *Maggie*, pp. 40–1.
23. Junor, *Margaret Thatcher*, p. 40.
24. Hugo Young and Anne Sloman, *The Thatcher Phenomenon* (BBC Publications, London, 1986), p. 17.
25. Ogden, *Maggie*, p. 46.
26. Junor, *Margaret Thatcher*, p. 26.
27. *Ibid.*
28. Interview with *The Times*, 5 October 1970.
29. Diana Farr, *Five At Ten*, (Andre Deutsch, London, 1985), p. 173.
30. Farr, *Five at Ten*, p. 173.
31. *Ibid.*, p. 176.
32. *Ibid.*, p. 174.
33. *Ibid.*, p. 175.
34. *Ibid.*, p. 178.
35. *Ibid.*, p. 178.
36. *Ibid.*, p. 180.
37. Margaret Thatcher, *The Downing Street Years* (HarperCollins, London, 1993), p. 22.
38. Farr, *Five at Ten*, p. 180. See also *Sunday Times*, 3 December 1995.
39. Nicholas Wapshott and George Brock, *Margaret Thatcher* (Macdonald & Co., London, 1983), p. 57.
40. *The Observer*, 29 May 1983.
41. *Independent on Sunday*, 25 November 1990.
42. Farr, *Five at Ten*, p. 177.
43. Interview with *The Times*, 5 October 1970.
44. Interview with authors.
45. Ogden, *Maggie*, p. 60.
46. George Gardiner, *Margaret Thatcher: From Childhood To Leadership* (William Kimber, London, 1975), p. 46.
47. *Ibid.*, p. 47.
48. Wapshott and Brock, *Margaret Thatcher*, p. 56.
49. Ogden, *Maggie*, p. 70.
50. Junor, *Margaret Thatcher*, p. 35.
51. *Ibid.*, p. 34.
52. Gardiner, *Margaret Thatcher*, p. 51.
53. *Sunday Graphic*, February 1952. Quoted in Young, *One of Us*, p. 36.
54. Ogden, *Maggie*, p. 70.
55. Carol Thatcher, *Below the Parapet: The Biography of Denis Thatcher* (HarperCollins, London, 1996), p. 69.

56. Ogden, *Maggie*, p. 70.

57. *Daily Mirror*, 13 March 1981.

58. Farr, *Five at Ten*, p. 189.

59. Ogden, *Maggie*, p. 71.

60. Wapshott and Brock, *Margaret Thatcher*, p. 60.

61. Gardiner, *Margaret Thatcher*, p. 51.

62. Ogden, *Maggie*, p. 71.

63. Gardiner, *Margaret Thatcher*, p. 52.

64. Junor, *Margaret Thatcher*, p. 40.

65. Gardiner, *Margaret Thatcher*, p. 54.

66. Junor, *Margaret Thatcher*, p. 41.

67. Interview with *The Times*, 5 October 1970.

68. *Spectator*, 7 May 1988.

69. *London Evening News*, 10 October 1959.

70. *Sunday Times*, 24 November 1974.

71. Patricia Murray, *Margaret Thatcher* (W.H. Allen, London, 1980), p. 59.

72. Interview with Carol Thatcher, *Today*, 16 November 1993.

73. Junor, *Margaret Thatcher*, p. 49.

74. *Today*, 26 October 1993.

75. Interview with authors.

76. *Daily Mail*, 10 October 1961.

77. *Sunday Telegraph*, 24 November 1974; *The Sun*, 8 February 1982.

78. *The Sun*, 8 February 1982.

79. Junor, *Margaret Thatcher*, p. 49.

80. *Ibid.*

81. Interview with authors.

82. *Punch*, 14 March 1984.

83. Murray, *Margaret Thatcher*, p. 63.

84. Interview with Carol Thatcher, *Today*, 16 November 1993.

85. Farr, *Five at Ten*, p. 194.

86. Interview with authors.

87. Brenda Maddox, *Maggie* (Hodder and Stoughton, London, 2003), p. 63–4.

88. Junor, *Margaret Thatcher*, p. 64.

89. Interview with authors.

90. Jeremy Paxman, *Friends in High Places* (Michael Joseph, London, 1990), p. 167.

91. Michael Cockerell, *Dear Bill* (profile of William Deedes), BBC2, 9 January 1994.

92. *The Downing Street Years*, BBC1, 20 October 1993.

93. Interview with authors.

94. *Harpers and Queen*, April 1991.

95. Murray, *Margaret Thatcher*, p. 59.

96. *Daily Telegraph*, 24 November 1994.

97. Junor, *Margaret Thatcher*, p. 64.

98. Interview with authors.

99. Murray, *Margaret Thatcher*, p. 60.

100. Interview with authors.

101. Interview with authors.

102. *Tatler*, April 1991.

103. Interview with *The Times*, 5 October 1970.

104. Interview with authors.
105. Interview with authors.
106. *Old Harrovian*, 20 March 1971.
107. *Sunday Times*, 12 February 1984.
108. Interview with authors.
109. *Daily Express*, 28 October 1969.
110. Letter to authors.
111. Interview with *Woman's Own*, 2 February 1980.
112. Interview with authors.

Chapter Three
1. Quoted in Farr, *Five at Ten*, p. 205.
2. *The Times*, 5 October 1970.
3. Interview with authors.
4. Interview with authors.
5. *Woman's Own*, 2 February 1980.
6. *Ibid.*
7. *Daily Express*, 13 February 1975.
8. *Daily Express*, 21 February 1975.
9. Interview with authors.
10. *Daily Express*, 11 April 1995.
11. *Daily Express*, 25 July 1975.
12. Murray, *Margaret Thatcher*, p. 63.
13. *Ibid.*, p. 64.
14. *London Evening News*, 30 April 1975.
15. *Daily Express*, 18 May 1977.
16. *Sunday Telegraph*, 19 July 1981.
17. Interview with authors.
18. Interview with Hong Kong *Tatler*, December 1991.
19. Interview with authors.
20. Junor, *Margaret Thatcher*, p. 114.
21. *Accountants Weekly*, 18 June 1979.
22. *Ibid.*
23. *Daily Express*, 24 March 1975.
24. Interview with authors.
25. Interview with authors.
26. *The Guardian*, 14 February 1980; *Daily Express*, 15 February 1980.
27. *Daily Mail*, 15 July 1988.
28. *Nationwide*, BBC1, 28 February 1980.
29. *Daily Mail*, 15 July 1988.
30. *Woman's Own*, 2 February 1980.
31. Interview with authors.
32. *Sunday Mirror*, 16 February 1975; *Daily Express*, 25 July 1975.
33. *The Times*, 18 October 1994.
34. *Woman's Own*, 2 February 1980.
35. *Tatler*, December 1994.
36. Interview with authors.
37. *Woman's Own*, 3 May 1986.

38. *Daily Express*, 13 October 1978.
39. *Daily Mail*, 15 October 1978.
40. *News of the World*, 15 February 1987.
41. London *Evening Standard*, 23 April 1979.
42. *London Evening News*, 24 April 1979.
43. *Ibid.*
44. *Woman's Own*, 2 February 1980.
45. *Ibid.*
46. Ronald Millar, *A View from the Wings* (Weidenfeld & Nicolson, London, 1993), pp. 267–9; Farr, *Five at Ten*, p. 200.
47. *Woman's Own*, 2 February 1980.
48. *Ibid.*
49. *Ibid.*
50. Accounts of Monteagle Marketing Ltd, 1979–80.
51. *Washington Post*, 2 July 1979.
52. Accounts of Monteagle Marketing Ltd, 1979–80.
53. *Woman's Own*, 2 February 1980.
54. *Washington Post*, 16 February 1987.
55. *Sunday Times*, 4 March 1984.
56. *Ibid.*
57. *Woman's Own*, 2 February 1980.
58. *Daily Mail*, 14 February 1980.

Chapter Four
1. Thatcher, *Below the Parapet*, p. 187.
2. *London Evening News*, 7 June 1979.
3. *Daily Mail*, 18 September 1979.
4. *Woman's Own*, 2 February 1980.
5. *Daily Telegraph*, 1 October 1979.
6. Interview with authors.
7. *Daily Mail*, 13 February 1980.
8. London *Evening Standard*, 13 February 1980.
9. Interview with authors.
10. *Daily Telegraph*, 13 February 1980.
11. *Daily Mail*, 13 February 1980.
12. *London Evening News*, 13 February 1980.
13. *Daily Mail*, 13 February 1980.
14. London *Evening Standard*, 13 February 1980.
15. *Sunday Times*, 17 February 1980.
16. *Daily Telegraph* and *The Times*, 29 February 1980.
17. *Daily Mail*, 13 February 1980.
18. *Daily Express*, 14 February 1980.
19. Press Association, 18 February 1980.
20. *The Sun*, 6 March 1981.
21. *Daily Mail*, 14 February 1980.
22. *Daily Express* and *Daily Telegraph*, 15 February 1980.
23. *Daily Telegraph*, 16 February 1980.
24. *Daily Mail*, 16 February 1980.

25. *News of the World*, 17 February 1980.
26. *Western Mail*, 29 February 1980.
27. *Daily Express*, 14 February 1980.
28. *Daily Mail*, 16 February 1980.
29. *Daily Telegraph*, 13 February 1980.
30. *Ibid.*, 29 February 1980.
31. *Nationwide*, BBC1, 28 February 1980.
32. *Ibid.*
33. *Daily Mail*, 29 February 1980.
34. *The Sun*, 6 March 1981.
35. Interview with authors.
36. *Daily Mail*, 22 April 1980.
37. *Autosport*, 26 June 1980.
38. *Daily Mail*, 16 June 1980.
39. *Daily Express*, 29 May 1980.
40. Interview with authors.
41. Interview with authors.
42. *Daily Mail*, 28 April 1980.
43. *Sunday Telegraph*, 2 August 1981.
44. *Daily Mail*, 22 April 1980.
45. *Daily Express*, 12 August 1980.
46. Interview with authors.
47. New Zealand Press Association, 25 September 1980.
48. *Sydney Morning Herald*, 1 October 1980.
49. *Daily Express*, 16 February 1981.
50. Peter Taylor, *Smoke Ring: Tobacco, Money and multinational Politics* (Sphere, London, 1984), p. 145.
51. *Daily Mail*, 6 August 1981.
52. *Woman's Own*, 2 February 1980.
53. *Sunday Telegraph*, 19 July 1981.
54. *The Times*, 14 May 1981.
55. *New York Times*, 12 October 1980.
56. London *Evening Standard*, 29 June 1981.
57. *Daily Mail*, 1 July 1981.
58. *Daily Express*, 6 October 1981.
59. *Sunday Express*, 9 August 1981; *Sunday Telegraph*, 19 July 1981.
60. *Daily Express*, 11 March 1981.
61. *Sunday Express*, 22 August 1982; *Options* magazine, November 1982.
62. *Daily Express*, 11 January 1982.
63. *Daily Telegraph*, 8 March 1982.
64. *The Times*, 16 January 1982.
65. Thatcher, *Below the Parapet*, p. 183
66. Junor, *Margaret Thatcher*, p. 156.
67. Thatcher, *Below the Parapet*, p. 183.
68. *The Times*, 15 January 1982.
69. *Ibid.*
70. *Daily Express*, 13 January 1982.
71. Thatcher, *Below the Parapet*, p. 183.

72. *Daily Telegraph*, 14 January 1982.
73. *Daily Mail*, 14 January 1982.
74. *Ibid.*
75. Junor, *Margaret Thatcher*, p. 157.
76. Thatcher, *Below the Parapet*, p. 184.
77. *Daily Telegraph*, 8 March 1982.
78. Press Association, 15 January 1982.
79. *Daily Express*, 15 January 1982.
80. Thatcher, *Below the Parapet*, p. 184,
81. *The Times*, 16 January 1982.
82. *Ibid.*
83. *Daily Mail*, 16 January 1982.
84. *The Times*, 16 January 1982.
85. Press Association, 16 January 1982.
86. *Daily Mail*, 16 January 1982.
87. *Daily Express*, 16 January 1982.
88. *Daily Telegraph*, 25 January 1982.
89. *Daily Telegraph*, 18 February 1982.
90. *Daily Mail*, 26 January 1982.
91. *Ibid.*
92. *News of the World*, 24 January 1982.
93. Carol Thatcher, interview with *Sunday Express*, 22 August 1982.
94. Interview with authors.
95. Interview with authors.
96. *Daily Express*, 5 March 1982.
97. *Honey* magazine, April 1982.
98. *Private Eye*, 10 February 1984.
99. Donald C. Bauder, *Captain Money and the Golden Girl: A $200 Million Fantasy of Love, Power and Greed* (Harvest and HBJ Books, San Diego, 1986), p. 122.
100. *Ibid.*
101. *Daily Express*, 5 November 1982.
102. *Ibid*, 28 March 1988.

Chapter Five
1. Interview with *The Lady* magazine, August 1996.
2. Interview with authors.
3. House of Commons, *Hansard*, 15 March 1984, col. 17.
4. *Economist* Special Report, 11 August 1979.
5. *Ibid.*
6. *The Observer* archives.
7. 'Business In Oman', *World in Action*, Granada TV, 23 July 1984.
8. *Ibid.*
9. Export Intelligence Service Notice, No. 404.
10. *The Observer*, 26 February 1984.
11. House of Commons, *Hansard*, 13 February 1984, col. 23.
12. *The Times*, 20 April 1981.
13. *The Times*, 21 April 1981.
14. *The Observer*, 22 January 1984.

15. *Ibid.*
16. Thatcher, *The Downing Street Years*, p. 163.
17. *Sunday Times*, 31 May 1981.
18. Interview with authors.
19. *The Times*, 25 April 1981.
20. Trade minister during interview with authors.
21. *The Observer*, 15 January 1984.
22. Thatcher, *The Downing Street Years*, p. 163.
23. *Panorama*, BBC1, 9 April 1984.
24. 'Business in Oman', *World in Action*, 23 July 1984.
25. Douglas Hurd, *Memoirs* (Little Brown, London, 2004), p. 306.
26. *The Observer* archives.
27. Letter to *The Observer*, 18 January 1984.
28. *Weekend World*, LWT, 15 January 1984.
29. *Financial Times*, 17 March 1982.
30. *Daily Mail*, 9 March 1984.
31. *Ibid.*
32. *The Observer*, 5 February 1984.
33. *8 Days* magazine, 18 August 1979.
34. *Reading Evening Post*, 22 March 1979.
35. *Daily Express*, 18 October 1994.
36. Letter from Richard Helms, president of Safeer International Consulting Group, to Orin Atkins, chairman and CEO of Ashland Oil Inc.
37. *The Observer*, 5 February 1984.
38. 'Business in Oman', *World in Action*, 23 July 1984.
39. Interview with authors.
40. *The Observer*, 5 February 1984; 'How Mrs Thatcher Swung University Contract', special report, *The Times*, 18 November 1981.
41. *Sunday People*, 1 April 1984.
42. *Sunday Times*, 4 March 1984.
43. *The Observer*, 18 March 1984.
44. Letter to the authors, 11 February 1994.
45. Thomson, *Margaret Thatcher*, p. 115.
46. *Ibid.*
47. Tom Bower, *Tiny Rowland: A Rebel Tycoon* (Heinemann, London, 1993), p. 447.
48. Alan Clark, *Diaries* (Weidenfeld & Nicolson, London, 1993), p. 70.
49. Thomson, *Margaret Thatcher*, p. 115
50. *Panorama*, BBC1, 9 April 1984.
51. House of Commons, *Hansard*, 5 April 1984, col. 122.
52. *Panorama*, BBC1, 9 April 1984.
53. Letter from Margaret Thatcher to Peter Shore, 11 April 1984.
54. House of Commons, *Hansard*, 17 January 1984, col. 159.
55. *Ibid*, 18 January 1984, col. 242.
56. *Ibid.*, col. 243.
57. *Ibid.*, 24 January 1984, col. 326.
58. *Ibid.*, 2 February 1984, col. 268.
59. *Sunday Times*, 12 February 1984.
60. *Mail on Sunday*, 1 April 1984.

61. *Harpers and Queen*, April 1991.
62. *Sunday Times*, 26 January 1992.
63. *Event* magazine, 16 October 1983.
64. *Daily Mirror*, 30 January 1986.
65. *Mail on Sunday*, 1 April 1984.

Chapter Six
1. *Woman's Own*, 31 October 1987.
2. *Mail on Sunday*, 1 April 1984.
3. *Sunday Telegraph*, 8 June 1980.
4. *Mail on Sunday*, 1 April 1984.
5. Interview with authors; *Mail on Sunday*, 16 November 1986.
6. *Daily Express*, 26 March 1984.
7. *Mail on Sunday*, 1 April 1984.
8. Correction in *New York Times*, 28 March 1984.
9. *Mail on Sunday*, 1 April 1984.
10. *Daily Mirror*, 5 January 1984.
11. *Ibid.*, 13 March 1984.
12. *Mail on Sunday*, 25 March 1984.
13. *Ibid.*, 1 April 1984.
14. *Daily Mail*, 12 September 1983.
15. Interview with authors.
16. *Ibid.*
17. *Ibid.*
18. *People Weekly* magazine, 12 March 1984.
19. *News of the World*, 13 May 1984.
20. *Harpers and Queen*, April 1991.
21. *News of the World*, 13 May 1984.
22. *Daily Mail*, 9 January 1984.
23. *News of the World*, 13 May 1984.
24. *Daily Mail*, 20 February 1984.
25. *News of the World*, 13 May 1984.
26. *Daily Mail*, 14 May 1984.
27. *The Sun*, 22 July 1984.
28. *Ibid.*
29. *Sunday Times*, 26 January 1992.
30. *Mail on Sunday*, 1 April 1984.
31. *Daily Mail*, 11 January 1984.
32. *Daily Express*, 30 March 1989.
33. *Ibid.*
34. *New York Times*, 27 April 1986.
35. *The Times*, 13 February 1989.
36. *Vanity Fair*, June 1991.
37. *Dallas Morning News*, 11 August 1984.
38. Twentieth Anniversary of Harvard and Radcliffe Alumni Report, 1991. Quoted in *Dallas Morning News*, 11 August 1984.
39. *Harpers and Queen*, April 1991.
40. *Tatler*, April 1991.

41. Hong Kong *Tatler*, December 1991.
42. *Dallas Morning News*, 20 April 1994.
43. *Dallas Times Herald*, 14 November 1986.
44. *Daily Star*, 11 April 1985.
45. Interview with *Ultra* magazine, Dallas, March 1990.
46. *The Sun*, 11 April 1985.
47. *Daily Star*, 11 April 1985.
48. *Daily Express* and *The Sun*, 7 March 1988.
49. *Daily Telegraph*, 13 November 1986.
50. *Ibid.*, 14 November 1986.
51. *Daily Telegraph*, 14 November 1986.
52. *The Times*, 14 November 1986.
53. *Daily Mail*, 14 November 1986.
54. *Daily Express*, 3 October 1994.
55. *Daily Mail*, 12 February 1987.
56. *Mail on Sunday*, 15 February 1987.
57. Interview with authors.
58. *Sunday People*, 8 February 1987.
59. House of Commons, *Hansard*, 9 March 1987, col. 31.
60. *The Sun*, 14 February 1987.
61. *Daily Mail*, 14 February 1987.
62. *The Times*, 16 February 1987.
63. *Daily Mail*, 16 February 1987.
64. *Daily Express*, 16 February 1987.
65. *Daily Star*, 24 February 1987.
66. *Today*, 29 March 1994.
67. *Ibid.*
68. *Ibid.*
69. *Ultra*, March 1990.
70. *Daily Star*, 12 February 1987.
71. *Today*, 29 March 1994.
72. London *Evening Standard*, 3 March 1989.
73. *Daily Express*, 30 March 1989.
74. *Daily Mail*, 4 March 1989.
75. *Ultra*, March 1990.
76. *The Sun*, 9 June 1994.
77. *Daily Express*, 12 and 13 October 1994.
78. *Sunday Express*, 30 October 1994.
79. *Ibid.*
80. Hong Kong *Tatler*, December 1991.
81. *Daily Express*, 13 October 1994.
82. *The Sun*, 9 June 1994.
83. *Financial Times*, 31 October 1994.
84. *Tatler*, April 1991.
85. *Sunday Times*, 26 January 1992.
86. *The Observer*, 22 November 1987.
87. Deposition of David Wallace, Laughlin v. Wallace, 14 April 1994, p. 46.
88. *Ibid.*, p. 49.

89. *Ibid.*, p. 66.

90. *The Observer*, 22 November 1987.

91. *The Guardian*, 4 December 1987.

92. *Ibid.*, 21 November 1987.

93. *The Observer*, 22 November 1987.

94. Ogden, *Maggie*, p. 79.

95. *Daily Express*, 19 October 1987.

96. *Ibid.*

97. London *Evening Standard*, 15 October 1987.

98. *Dallas Morning Herald*, 3 November 1987.

99. *Ibid.*

100. Thatcher, *The Downing Street Years*, p. 700.

101. *Dallas Morning Herald*, 11 April 1989.

102. *Financial Times*, 31 October 1994.

103. *Ibid.*

104. Wallace deposition, p. 26.

105. *Financial Times*, 31 October 1994.

106. *Dallas Morning News*, 17 October 1994.

107. *Sunday Times*, 2 April 1995.

108. US Internal Revenue Service Counter-Claim, 23 December 1992.

109. Wallace deposition, p. 64.

110. *The Independent*, 17 October 1994.

111. *Financial Times*, 31 October 1994.

112. *Vanity Fair*, June 1991.

113. *The Sun*, 3 June 1990.

Chapter Seven

1. *Mail on Sunday*, 16 April 1995

2. *Mail on Sunday*, 3 January 1993.

3. London *Evening Standard*, 28 September 1981.

4. *Today*, 9 April 1988.

5. *The Times*, 21 February 1980.

6. John Junor, *Memoirs: Listening for a Midnight Tram* (Chapman, London, 1990), p. 259.

7. *Woman's Own*, 7 April 1984.

8. *Sunday Express*, 23 January 1983.

9. *Daily Telegraph*, 29 March 1982.

10. *Daily Mail*, 8 April 1982.

11. Interview with authors.

12. Interview with close and long-standing friend of Mark Thatcher; *Daily Star*, 10 December 1988.

13. Letter from William Whitelaw, then home secretary, to Douglas Hoyle, then Labour MP for Warrington. Quoted in *Sunday People*, 19 September 1982.

14. *Daily Mirror*, 5 October 1982.

15. House of Commons, Hansard, 18 October 1982, col. 8.

16. *Daily Mirror*, 5 October 1982.

17. House of Commons, Hansard, 18 and 19 October 1982, cols 8 and 90.

18. *Daily Mail*, 31 January 1993.

19. ANS news agency copy, 26 May 1983.
20. *Ibid.*, 7 June 1983.
21. *Today*, 9 April 1982.
22. *The Times*, 21 June 1984.
23. House of Commons, *Hansard*, 30 January 1984, col. 131.
24. Interview with authors.
25. *Ibid.*
26. Evidence to 'Exports to Iraq', an inquiry by the House of Commons Select Committee on Trade and Industry, 5 February 1992, p. 338; DTI report into the affairs of Astra Holdings plc.
27. Interview with authors.
28. *Ibid.*
29. *Ibid.*
30. *Ibid.*
31. Frank Greve, *Philadelphia Inquirer*, 25 April 1987.
32. Interview with authors.
33. *Mail on Sunday*, 29 January 1984.
34. Interview with authors.
35. *Ibid.*
36. John Campbell, *The Iron Lady* (Jonathan Cape, London, 2000), page 342.
37. *Ibid.*, p. 343
38. The source for this exchange was Adel Jubeir, an aide to Prince Bandar. Quoted in *GQ* magazine, February 1993
39. *Philadelphia Inquirer* and *Miami Herald*, 10 November 1991.
40. *New Yorker*, 9 June 1986.
41. *Financial Times*, 8 June 1991.
42. Union Bank of Switzerland, Phillips & Drew analysts report, UK Equities, May 1992.
43. *Ibid.*
44. *GQ*, February 1993.
45. *The Guardian*, 23 November 1991.
46. *GQ*, February 1993.
47. *Sunday Times*, 12 February 1984.
48. *Ibid.*
49. *GQ*, November 1992.
50. *Ibid.*
51. *Ibid.*
52. Register of Members Interests, 13 January 1992, HMSO 170.
53. *Business Age* magazine, June 1994.
54. *GQ*, November 1992.
55. *Daily Mail*, 12 December 1990.
56. *Daily Telegraph*, 26 September 1994 .
57. 'The First Thatcherite', *Dispatches*, Box Productions for Channel 4, 25 November 1992; *New York* magazine, 1 February 1993.
58. 'The First Thatcherite', *Dispatches*, 25 November 1992.
59. *The Observer*, 1 February 1998.
60. *Business Age*, June 1994.
61. *GQ*, November 1992.

62. *Ibid.*
63. *Sunday Times*, 9 October 1994.
64. *The Guardian*, 13 May 1992.
65. *GQ*, November 1992.
66. *Mail on Sunday*, 13 October 1987.
67. *Daily Mail*, 17 December 1990.
68. *Jane's Defence Weekly* magazine, 10 June 1989.
69. *Tatler*, August 1990.
70. *Financial Times*, 26 November 1991.
71. Union Bank of Switzerland, Phillips & Drew Report, UK Equities, May 1992.
72. *GQ*, February 1993.
73. Thatcher, *The Downing Street Years*, p. 626.
74. *Sunday Times*, 9 October 1994.
75. *The First Thatcherite*, Channel 4, 25 November 1992.
76. *Ibid.*
77. *Ibid.*
78. *Ibid.*
79. *Ibid.*
80. *Sunday Times*, 27 February 2000.
81. *Today*, 10 October 1994.
82. *Financial Times*, 31 October 1994.
83. *The Observer*, 19 March 1989.
84. Interview with authors.
85. *The Independent*, 11 October 1994.
86. Interview with authors.
87. *Ibid.*
88. *Ibid.*
89. *Tracking Down Maggie*, Lafayette Productions for *True Lives*, Channel 4, 19 May 1994.

Chapter Eight
1. *Sunday Times*, 21 April 1991.
2. Hong Kong *Tatler*, December 1991.
3. *Hong Kong Standard*, 14 August 1981.
4. London *Evening Standard*, 23 September 1982.
5. Company accounts of Ulferts Services, 1981–82.
6. Press statement by Monteagle Marketing Ltd, 24 March 1984.
7. *Ming Pao Weekly*, 10 December 1983.
8. *Hong Kong Standard*, 16 March 1984.
9. *Ibid.*
10. *Ibid.*
11. *Ibid.*
12. *Ibid.*
13. Press statement by Monteagle Marketing Ltd, 24 March 1984.
14. *Insight* magazine, Hong Kong, December 1982.
15. Interview with Ho-Pak Hong.
16. *Hong Kong Standard*, 18 March 1984.
17. *The Observer*, 29 January 1984.

18. Interview with authors.
19. *South China Morning Post*, 25 November 1980–14 June 1981.
20. *Ibid.*, 4 January 1986–7 July 1986.
21. *Ming Pao Weekly*, 10 December 1983.
22. *Sunday Times*, 12 February 1984.
23. *Ming Pao Weekly*, 10 December 1983.
24. *Mail on Sunday*, 4 December 1983.
25. Gower Report. Quoted in *The Observer*, 11 March 1984.
26. *The Observer*, 11 March 1984.
27. Press statement by Monteagle Marketing Ltd, 24 March 1984.
28. Interview with authors.
29. *South China Morning Post*, 31 May 1994.
30. *Eastern Express*, 13 December 1994.
31. *South China Morning Post*, 6 August 1994.
32. *Sunday Times*, 12 February 1984.
33. *New Statesman*, 16 February 1984; *Daily Mirror*, 17 February 1984.
34. *Ming Pao Weekly*, 10 December 1983.
35. *South China Morning Post*, 26 November 1983.
36. *Ming Pao Weekly*, 10 December 1983.
37. Hong Kong *Tatler*, December 1991.
38. *The Guardian*, 23 November 1991.
39. Interview with authors.
40. *Vanity Fair*, June 1991.
41. House of Commons, *Hansard*, 5 May 1993, col. 145.
42. *New Straits Times*, Malaysia, 28 September 1988.
43. *Jane's Defence Weekly*, 25 March 1989.
44. *New Straits Times*, Malaysia, 2 September 1990.
45. *The Guardian*, 16 February 1994.
46. *Sunday Times*, 25 February 1994.
47. *Ibid.*, 6 March 1994.
48. *The Guardian*, 3 March 1994.
49. *Sunday Times*, 6 March 1994.
50. *Ibid.*, 25 February 1994.
51. *The Times*, 12 May 1992.
52. Interview with authors.
53. Letter to authors, 9 May 1994.
54. Memorandum of conviction from West London Magistrates' Court, 24 June 1989; *News of the World*, 30 July 1989.
55. Official record of Sri Lankan parliament, 18 June 1993.
56. Interview with authors.
57. *Daily Mirror*, 16 December 1982.
58. *Newslanka*, 18 September 1993.
59. *Silverarrow*, September 1993.

Chapter Nine

1. Thatcher, *The Downing Street Years*, p. 525.
2. *Ibid.*, p. 526.

3. *Ibid.*, p. 524.
4. *The Independent*, 9 June 1993.
5. *Ibid.*
6. *Today*, 28 March 1994.
7. *Mail on Sunday*, 14 August 1994.
8. *Today*, 30 March 1994.
9. *The Guardian*, 12 February 1994.
10. *Today*, 30 March 1994.
11. *Ibid.*
12. Legal petition by John J. Laughlin lodged in Harris County Court, Texas, Laughlin v. David G. Wallace, 28 January 1994, p. 5.
13. *Ibid.*
14. *Today*, 28 March 1994.
15. *Houston Chronicle*, 25 June 1994.
16. Laughlin petition, p. 22.
17. *Ibid.*, p. 7.
18. *Ibid*, p. 10.
19. *Houston Chronicle*, 25 June 1994.
20. *Ibid.*
21. *Today*, 15 August 1994.
22. *Ibid.*
23. *Ibid.*
24. *Sunday Times* magazine, 21 July 1996.
25. *Ibid.*
26. *Mail on Sunday*, 23 October 1994.
27. *Sunday Times* magazine, 21 July 1996.
28. Clark, *Diaries*, p. 187.
29. Interview with authors.
30. *Daily Mail*, 15 November 1989.
31. *Today*, 28 March 1994.
32. *The Observer*, 15 December 1991.
33. *Today*, 28 March 1994.
34. *Today*, 27 October 1990.

Chapter Ten

1. Epigraph to Thomson, *Margaret Thatcher*.
2. Kenneth Baker, *The Turbulent Years* (Faber and Faber, London, 1993), p. 153.
3. Carol Thatcher, page 264.
4. *The Downing Street Years*, BBC1, 7 October 1993.
5. Carol Thatcher, page 267.
6. *The Independent*, 24 November 1990.
7. The 'Taffy Mafia' was generally considered to be Michael Heseltine, who stood against Margaret Thatcher, Geoffrey (now Lord) Howe, whose resignation speech inspired Heseltine's candidature, and Tristan Garel-Jones, the former Foreign Office minister, who hosted a party at his house between the first and second ballots to discuss what should happen next in the Tory leadership challenge.
8. *Sunday Times*, 1 September 1991.

9. *Ibid.*, 16 December 1990.
10. *Ibid.*
11. *The Guardian*, 2 October 1993.
12. *Sunday Times*, 11 June 1995.
13. *Vanity Fair*, June 1991.
14. *The Guardian*, 26 April 1991.
15. 'Selling Thatcher', *World in Action*, Granada TV, 11 November 1991.
16. *The Times*, 13 March 1991.
17. London *Evening Standard*, 24 September 1991.
18. *Vanity Fair*, June 1991.
19. *Dallas Morning News*, 12 March 1991.
20. *Vanity Fair*, June 1991.
21. *Daily Mail*, 17 June 1991.
22. *Sunday Telegraph*, 23 June 1991.
23. *The Observer*, 11 August 1991.
24. *The Independent*, 3 September 1991.
25. *Hong Kong Standard*, 13 September 1991.
26. *Ibid.*, 18 March 1991.
27. *Mail on Sunday*, 6 September 1992.
28. *Ibid.*
29. *Ibid.*
30. *Ibid.*
31. *Independent on Sunday*, 22 December 1992.
32. *Financial Times*, 29 June 1991.
33. *Ibid.*
34. *Sunday Times*, 11 April 1993.
35. *Ibid.*, 19 July 1992.
36. 'The Fag Lady', *World in Action*, Granada TV, 11 July 1994.
37. *Ibid.*
38. *Sunday Times*, 19 July 1992
39. Woodrow Wyatt, *Journals*, Volume 3, 19 July 1992, (Macmillan, London, 2000), page 75.
40. 'The Fag Lady', *World in Action*, 11 July 1994.
41. London *Evening Standard*, 11 November 1992.
42. *The Times*, 20 July 1992.
43. ASH-UK press briefing, autumn 1992.
44. 'Selling Thatcher', *World in Action*, 11 November 1991.
45. *Ibid.*
46. *Vanity Fair*, June 1991.
47. Wyatt, *Journals*, p. 483.
48. Alan Clark, *Diaries*, pp. 284–385.
49. *Ibid.*, p. 386.
50. *Vanity Fair*, June 1991.
51. George Greenfield, *A Smattering of Monsters* (Little Brown, London, 1995), p. 35.
52. London *Evening Standard*, 9 February 1995.
53. Roy Greenslade, *Maxwell's Fall* (Simon & Schuster, London, 1992), p. 358.
54. 'Selling Thatcher', *World in Action*, 11 November 1991.
55. *Vanity Fair*, June 1991.

56. *Sunday Times*, 26 January 1992.
57. *The Times*, 18 February 1994.
58. John Beasant and Christopher Ling, *Sultan in Arabia* (Mainstream Publishing, Edinburgh, 2004), p. 120.
59. *Ibid.*
60. Rachel Ehrenfeld, *Evil Money* (SPI International, New York, 1994), p. 159.
61. *Sunday Times*, 13 November 1994.
62. Peter Truell and Larry Gurwin, *BCCI: The Inside Story of the World's Most Corrupt Financial Empire* (Bloomsbury, London, 1992), p. 87.
63. *The Guardian*, 3 May 1994.
64. *Vanity Fair*, June 1991.
65. *New Yorker*, 6 September 1993.
66. *Ibid.*
67. *Ibid.*
68. Interview with authors.
69. *Today*, 6 June 1992.
70. *Vanity Fair*, June 1991.
71. *Ibid.*
72. *Sunday Times*, 21 April 1991.
73. *The Observer*, 25 June 1991. Confirmed by former officials of Lady Thatcher's private office.
74. *Sunday Times*, 21 April 1991.
75. *Vanity Fair*, June 1991.
76. Woodrow Wyatt, *Journals*, Volume 3 (Macmillan, London, 2000), pp. 420–1.
77. *Vanity Fair*, June 1991.
78. Channel 4 News, 28 June 1991.
79. Press release by Charities Aid Foundation, 24 November 1991.
80. *Sunday Telegraph*, 24 November 1991.
81. *Sunday Mirror*, 4 October 1992.
82. *Ibid.*
83. *Ibid.*
84. *The Guardian*, 22 November 1991.
85. *Business Age*, September 1993.
86. Deposition by David G. Wallace, in Laughlin *v.* Wallace, 14 April 1994, p. 13.
87. *The Guardian*, 11 October 1995.
88. London *Evening Standard*, 21 November 1994.
89. *Mail on Sunday*, 13 November 1994.
90. *Daily Mirror*, 10 November 1987.
91. Woodrow Wyatt, *Journals*, Volume 2 (Macmillan, London, 1999), p. 82.
92. *Institutional Investor*, international edition, September 1991.
93. *Ibid.*
94. *Today*, 27 February 1992.
95. *Ibid.*
96. *Daily Express*, 27 August 1992.
97. *Mail on Sunday*, 27 December 1992.

Chapter Eleven
1. Mark Thatcher, remark to Gary Smith, international oil trader, 4 December 1987.
2. Denis Thatcher quoted in Thatcher, *Below the Parapet*, p. 284
3. *Mail on Sunday*, 19 March 1995.
4. *The Observer*, 9 July 1995.
5. *Sunday Times*, 8 December 1996.
6. *Today*, 10 October 1994.
7. *Sunday Times*, 2 April 1995.
8. *Daily Telegraph*, 8 April 1995.
9. *Today*, 21 March 1995.
10. *Mail on Sunday*, 4 June 1995.
11. *Ibid.*
12. *Sunday Times*, 8 December 1996.
13. *Ibid.*
14. *Sunday Times*, 2 April 1995.
15. *Vanity Fair*, January 2005.
16. Quoted in *The Guardian*, 2 September 2004.
17. *Today* (Weekend Section), 28 October 1995.
18. South African Broadcasting Corporation, 16 May 1989.
19. Thatcher, *Below the Parapet*, pp. 91–2.
20. *Today*, 23 January 1990.
21. *Sunday Times* (Style), 4 February 1996.
22. *The Times* Magazine, 9 December 1995.
23. *Independent on Sunday*, 26 November 2004.
24. *Mail on Sunday* (You Magazine), 7 April 1996.
25. *Sunday Times*, 12 August 1997.
26. *Ibid.*
27. *Ibid.*
28. *Mail on Sunday*, 28 January 2001.
29. *Daily Telegraph*, 26 August 2004.
30. *Independent on Sunday*, 26 November 2004.
31. *Today* (Weekend Section), 28 October 1995.
32. *Mail on Sunday*, 7 January 1996.
33. *Daily Mail*, 15 January 1996.
34. *Ibid.*
35. *Daily Mail*, 4 September 2004.
36. *Ibid.*
37. *Sunday Times*, 12 August 1997.
38. *Daily Mail*, 8 August 1998.
39. *Ibid.*
40. *Ibid.*
41. *Mail on Sunday*, 16 August 1998.
42. *Daily Mail*, 8 August 1998.
43. *Sunday Times*, 8 February 1998.
44. *Ibid.*
45. This comparison was first noticed by Henry Porter, *The Guardian*, 2 October 1993, and by Francis Wheen, *The Guardian*, 31 May 1995.
46. *Golfweb Magazine*, 27 October 2002.

47. *The Observer*, 27 October 2002.
48. *Mail and Guardian* (South Africa), 14 June 2002 and *Africa Confidential*, 13 October 2000.
49. *Sunday Telegraph*, 12 September 2004.
50. *Daily Telegraph*, 8 January 2005.

Chapter Twelve
1. *Today*, 15 August 1994.
2. Thomson, *Margaret Thatcher*, p. 116.
3. Farr, *Five at Ten*, p. 205.
4. *Tatler*, December 1994.
5. Interview with authors.
6. *Tatler*, December 1994.
7. *Sunday Telegraph*, 16 January 2005.
8. *Harpers and Queen*, April 1991.
9. *Ultra*, March 1990.
10. Thomson, *Margaret Thatcher*, p. 118.
11. *Sunday Times*, 21 April 1991.
12. Thatcher, *Below the Parapet*, p. 284.
13. Charles Moore, the official authorised biographer of Margaret Thatcher, *Daily Telegraph*, 26 August 2004.
14. *Daily Mail*, 10 April 1995.
15. Ogden, *Maggie*, p. 80.
16. Letter to the authors, 16 March 1993.
17. Ogden, *Maggie*, p. 80.
18. *The Lady*, September 1996.
19. *Today*, 15 November 1993.
20. *Ibid.*
21. *The Observer*, 26 February 1984.
22. House of Commons, *Hansard*, 25 March 1986, col. 781.
23. *Mail on Sunday*, 23 March 1986.
24. House of Commons, *Hansard*, 25 March 1986, col. 781.
25. *Questions of Procedure*, p. 2.
26. *A Week In Politics*, 23 March 1984.
27. *Ibid.*
28. *A Week in Politics*, Brook Productions for Channel 4, 23 March 1984.
29. 'The First Thatcherite', *Dispatches*, 25 November 1992.
30. Interview with *Woman's Own*, 2 February 1980.
31. *Sunday Times*, 12 February 1984.

Bibliography

Baker, Kenneth, *The Turbulent Years* (Faber and Faber, London, 1993)

Bauder, Donald C., *Captain Money and the Golden Girl: A $200 Million Harvest Fantasy of Love, Power and Greed* (Harvest and HBJ Books, San Diego, 1986)

Beasant, John, (with Ling, Christopher and Cummins, Ian) *Oman: The True-Life Drama and Intrigue of an Arab State* (Mainstream, Edinburgh, 2003)

Beasant, John and Ling, Christopher, *Sultan in Arabia: A Private Life* (Mainstream, Edinburgh, 2004)

Bower, Tom, *Tiny Rowland: A Rebel Tycoon* (Heinemann, London, 1993)

Campbell, John, *Margaret Thatcher, vol. I: The Grocer's Daughter* (Jonathan Cape, London, 2000)

– *Margaret Thatcher, vol. II: The Iron Lady* (Jonathan Cape, London, 2003)

Clark, Alan, *Diaries* (Weidenfeld & Nicolson, London, 1993)

Crick, Margaret, *Mary Archer: For Richer, For Poorer* (Simon and Schuster, London, 2005)

Ehrenfeld, Rachel, *Evil Money* (SPI International, New York, 1994)

Farr, Diana, *Five at Ten* (Andre Deutsch, London, 1985)

Gardiner, George, *Margaret Thatcher: From Childhood to Leadership* (William Kimber, London, 1975)

Greenslade, Roy, *Maxwell's Downfall* (Simon & Schuster, London, 1992)

Hollingsworth, Mark, *The Ultimate Spin Doctor: The Life and Fast Times of Tim Bell* (Hodder and Stoughton, London, 1997)

–– *Saudi Babylon: Torture, Corruption and Cover-Up Inside the House of Saud* (Mainstream, Edinburgh, 2005)

Hurd, Douglas, *Memoirs*, (Little Brown, London, 2004)

Junor, John, *Memoirs: Listening for a Midnight Tram* (Chapman, London, 1990)

Junor, Penny, *Margaret Thatcher: Wife, Mother, Politician* (Sidwick & Jackson, London, 1983)

Lawson, Nigel, *The View from Number 11* (Bantam, London, 1992)

Maddox, Brenda, *Maggie: The First Lady* (Hodder and Stoughton, London, 2003)

Millar, Ronald, *A View from the Wings: West End, West Coast, Westminster* (Weidenfeld & Nicolson, London, 1993)

Murray, Patricia, *Margaret Thatcher* (W.H. Allen, London, 1980)

Ogden, Christopher, *Maggie: An Intimate Portrait of a Woman in Power* (Simon & Schuster, New York,1990)

Paxman, Jeremy, *Friends in High Places: Who Runs Britain* (Michael Joseph, London,1990)

Ranelagh, John, *Thatcher's People: An Insider's Account of the Politics, the Power, and the Personalities* (HarperCollins, London, 1991)

Spicer, Tim, *An Unorthodox Soldier* (Mainstream, Edinburgh, 1998)

Taylor, Peter, *Smoke Ring: Tobacco, Money and multinational Politics* (Sphere, London, 1984)

Thatcher, Carol, *Below the Parapet: The Biography of Denis Thatcher* (HarperCollins, London, 1996)

Thatcher, Margaret, *The Downing Street Years* (HarperCollins, London, 1993)

–– *The Path to Power* (HarperCollins, London, 1995)

Thomson, Andrew, *Margaret Thatcher: The Woman Within* (W.H. Allen, London, 1989)

Truell, Peter, and Gurwin, Larry, *BCCI: The Inside Story of the World's Most Corrupt Financial Empire* (Bloomsbury, London, 1992)

Wapshott, Nicholas, and Brock, George, *Margaret Thatcher* (Macdonald, London, 1983)

Wyatt, Woodrow, *The Journals of Woodrow Wyatt*, 3 volumes (Macmillan, London, 1998, 1999, 2000)

Young, Hugo, *One of Us* (Macmillan, London, 1989)

Young, Hugo, and Sloman, Anne, *The Thatcher Phenomenon* (BBC Publications, London, 1986)

Index

MT = Mark Thatcher
MgT = Margaret Thatcher